Hermeneutics at the Crossroads

Indiana Series in the Philosophy of Religion
Merold Westphal, general editor

Hermeneutics at the Crossroads

Edited by
Kevin J. Vanhoozer,
James K. A. Smith, and
Bruce Ellis Benson

INDIANA UNIVERSITY PRESS
Bloomington and Indianapolis

This book is a publication of

Indiana University Press
601 North Morton Street
Bloomington, IN 47404-3797 USA

http://iupress.indiana.edu

Telephone orders 800-842-6796
Fax orders 812-855-7931
Orders by e-mail iuporder@indiana.edu

The paper used in this publication meets the minimum requirements of American National Standard for Information Sciences—Permanence of Paper for Printed Library Materials, ANSI Z39.48-1984.

Manufactured in the United States of America

Library of Congress Cataloging-in-Publication Data

Hermeneutics at the crossroads / edited by Kevin J. Vanhoozer, James K. A. Smith, and Bruce Ellis Benson.
p. cm. — (Indiana series in the philosophy of religion)
Includes index.
ISBN 0-253-34746-7 (cloth : alk. paper) — ISBN 0-253-21849-7 (pbk. : alk. paper) 1. Hermeneutics—Congresses. I. Vanhoozer, Kevin J. II. Smith, James K. A., date III. Benson, Bruce Ellis, date IV. Title. V. Series.
BD241.H368 2006
121'.686—dc22 2005031637

1 2 3 4 5 11 10 09 08 07 06

Contents

PREFACE
Kevin J. Vanhoozer / vii
ACKNOWLEDGMENTS / xi

Introduction
Bruce Ellis Benson, James K. A. Smith, and Kevin J. Vanhoozer / xiii

Part 1. Philosophical Hermeneutics Revisited: Miracles, Resuscitation, Questions

1. Discourse on Matter: Hermeneutics and the "Miracle" of Understanding
Kevin J. Vanhoozer / 3

2. Resuscitating the Author
Nicholas Wolterstorff / 35

3. Gadamer's Hermeneutics and the Question of Relativism
Eduardo J. Echeverria / 51

4. "The Knowledge That One Does Not Know": Gadamer, Levertov, and the Hermeneutics of the Question
Christina Bieber Lake / 82

Part 2. Derrida and Deconstruction: Haunted Hermeneutics and Incarnational Iterability

5. Hauntological Hermeneutics and the Interpretation of Christian Faith: On Being Dead Equal before God
John D. Caputo / 95

6. Limited Inc/arnation: Revisiting the Searle/Derrida Debate in Christian Context
James K. A. Smith / 112

Part 3. Literature's Contribution to Christian Understanding: Pointing, Witnessing, Exchanging

7. Meeting at the Modern Crossroads: Fiction, History, and Christian Understanding
Roger Lundin / 133

8. The Hermeneutics of Deliverance: *Robinson Crusoe* and the Problem of Witnessing
Brian McCrea / 150

9. John Calvin's Notion of "Exchange" and the Usefulness of Literature
Michael VanderWeele / 164

Part 4. The Ethics of Interpretation: Improvisation, Participation, Authority

10. The Improvisation of Hermeneutics: Jazz Lessons for Interpreters
Bruce Ellis Benson / 193

11. Ethical Hermeneutics and the Theater: Shakespeare's *Merchant of Venice*
Ben Faber / 211

12. (Revelation, Interpretation) Authority: Kierkegaard's *Book on Adler*
Norman Lillegard / 225

CONTRIBUTORS / 241
INDEX / 243

PREFACE

In the summer of 2002 fourteen pilgrims from across North America met at Calvin College for an unusual five-week academic retreat. The occasion: a seminar on the topic "Hermeneutics at the Crossroads: The Disciplines of Text Interpretation." The following collection of essays had its genesis in that seminar, which I directed under the auspices of the Calvin College Seminars in Christian Scholarship program. My primary task was to select the participants and the readings, and to facilitate an interdisciplinary conversation. I selected the fourteen from a pool of some forty-five applicants representing a number of academic disciplines, including the natural sciences. The academic departments eventually represented in the seminar included philosophy, English, French, and biblical studies. Each person had a tale to tell about why hermeneutics mattered to him or to her and what problems came to the fore in one's respective discipline.

Thanks to the generous support of the Fieldstead Corporation, we were able to invite guest speakers to come and spend a day with our group, read a paper, and field questions. One of Fieldstead's explicit goals is to present a distinctly Christian point of view on a given topic, in our case, hermeneutics: the discipline, and disciplines, of text interpretation. Another goal was to engage points of view that were contrary to or critical of Christian perspectives. To that second end, I invited two philosophers who I was sure would fit the bill. Given our topic—hermeneutics—I wanted to hear challenges from both continental postmodern philosophy and Anglo-American post-analytic philosophy. Accordingly, I invited John D. Caputo, arguably Jacques Derrida's most capable North American spokesman, and Richard Rorty, the most prolific of the "neo-pragmatists" in America, who are calling for an "end" to philosophy and to the typical Western preoccupation with questions of meaning, knowledge, and truth. Two other witnesses were also invited as guest speakers: Roger Lundin and Susan Felch, who interacted with the thought of Gadamer and Mikhail Bakhtin, respectively.

A seminar, it has been said, is a species of coordinated action. Our group was especially privileged to be coordinated by Felch, then the director of the Calvin College Seminars in Christian Scholarship, and by her very capable team—Kara Van Drie and Alysha Chadderdon—who deserve a special thanks. There was also an order to our syllabus. As a way of providing some context and background for this collection of studies, here, in brief narrative fashion, is a summary of what we did during our summer vacation.

In the first week, we let the history of biblical interpretation throw out some of the fundamental problems, such as the role of authorial intention. In the second week, we focused on contemporary continental philosophy and the "universalizing" of the hermeneutic problem by relating it to the nature of human being. We looked at the dialogue between Gadamer and Derrida, and enjoyed hearing from Caputo as our first visitor. In week three, we studied the work of Paul Ricoeur, a continental philosopher who interacts with Anglo-American philosophy and literary criticism, develops a comprehensive interpretation theory, and, for good measure, brings it to bear on the Bible. We also had our second guest lecturer, Roger Lundin. Our focus in week four turned from authors and texts to readers and interpretative communities. Our guest that week was a philosopher who has done as much as anyone else to construe philosophy as a local and practical community enterprise: Richard Rorty. The subject of our fifth and final week was Christian perspectives on hermeneutics, along with two hermeneutic handmaidens: speech act theory and Bakhtin's dialogism. Susan Felch took time off administrating and was kind enough to introduce us to Bakhtin.

A follow-up public conference, still entitled "Hermeneutics at the Crossroads," was held at Calvin College in May 2003. Early drafts of the papers in the present volume were there delivered, digested, and debated. We were particularly pleased to welcome Roger Lundin and John Caputo back, and to have a new presentation by Nicholas Wolterstorff, who had also been at Calvin in the summer of 2002, though otherwise engaged.

To be understood is to be blessed. The summer saw its share of blessings, yet it was not without its share of pain as well. For understanding others is hard work, even when the "others" in question are one's academic colleagues and brothers and sisters in Christ. The facilities and personnel at Calvin College are wonderful, yet Grand Rapids is not heaven. Ours was not always the ideal speech situation. To paraphrase a piece of urban graffiti wisdom: misunderstanding happens. Our seminar was no exception. We had to work hard to fathom what was being said by inhabitants of different disciplines. And often, the tensions and misapprehensions occurred not between English and philosophy, but between the philosophers, some of whom enjoyed our "continental" breakfast readings (e.g., Gadamer, Ricoeur, Derrida) more than others.

While hermeneutics may be the art and science of understanding, it should be obvious that it is hardly an exact science! Understanding, whether of one's parents, the book of Ezekiel, a painting by Paul Klee, or a sonata by Scriabin, is often hard work. Interdisciplinary understanding is even more difficult. The fact is that we often come to the table to discuss texts—novels, poems, the book of nature—with entrenched positions. Interpretative disagreements over entrenched positions can easily escalate into trench warfare. The search for understanding is not only hard work, then, but also virtuous endeavor. Understanding requires patience, carefulness, attentiveness, humility—not always the first qualities that come to mind in describing academics. Understanding may be, in the final analysis, a spiritual exercise. In this respect, the summer seminar was less a vacation than a vigorous workout.

What follows is the fruit of our pilgrim labors as we sought to walk the "Calvinbury" trail. The harvest is interdisciplinary and multifaceted. There are philosophical engagements with the leading hermeneutical theorists as well as literary applications of these same theorists to specific texts. Together, they comprise a show-and-tell of the state of the contemporary hermeneutic art (and inexact science). I offer my own contribution to the volume—"Discourse on Matter: Hermeneutics and the 'Miracle' of Understanding"—as a tribute to the members and guest speakers of our summer seminar. Though it was written in the quiet of my individual closet, it is nevertheless suffused with the grateful afterglow of our midsummer's conversations.

Kevin J. Vanhoozer

ACKNOWLEDGMENTS

Kevin Vanhoozer's essay (chapter 1) previously appeared in slightly different form in the *International Journal of Systematic Theology* and is here reprinted with the permission of Blackwell Publishers. Some of the material in chapter 7 reproduces elements of "The Truth beyond Method: Fiction and the Limits of Experience" as it appears in Roger Lundin, *From Nature to Experience*, and is included here with the permission of Rowman & Littlefield Publishers. Finally, we like to thank Jeff Witt for his work on the index.

INTRODUCTION

Bruce Ellis Benson,
James K. A. Smith, and Kevin J. Vanhoozer

That hermeneutics is indeed at many crossroads is well demonstrated by this volume. Yet these chapters also make clear that understanding the other—across the road—certainly does happen, in many ways.

What are those crossroads? There is, first, the intersection of disciplines, which often have different ways of interpreting. Second, we are at a critical point in history where we are poised uneasily between premodernity, modernity, and postmodernity. A third intersection is that of cultural-linguistic traditions. There is the German school, arguably most strongly represented by Hans-Georg Gadamer (and his Heideggerian roots). Of course, the longstanding Gadamer/Habermas debate shows that, even in Germany, there is nothing like a hermeneutical consensus. In France, both Paul Ricoeur and Jacques Derrida come immediately to mind. But they, too, represent widely differing views. And then there is the Anglo-American tradition, in which J. L. Austin's speech act theory (adopted and adapted by John Searle) has played a pivotal role. Finally, Christian interpreters find themselves at the ultimate crossroad, the "road of the cross." For Christians, hermeneutics has a theological dimension—and perhaps even a theological *foundation*. For a tradition that confesses that "in the beginning was the Word" confesses not only the originality and ubiquity of hermeneutics, but perhaps also a sense of transcendence that gives birth to interpretation.

This collection of studies represents a sustained attempt to grapple with these many crossroads in contemporary hermeneutics, traversing intersections between different disciplines, genres, languages, and religious commitments. We have organized the book into four parts: the opening section includes four engagements with key themes in philosophical hermeneutics, particularly in dialogue with its most notable master, Hans-Georg Gadamer. But even here we'll find disciplinary crossings as Gadamer is approached not only from philosophy, but also along paths originating in theology and poetry. In part two we include two essays that engage the "radicalization" of hermeneutics in the work of Derrida and deconstruction. The third part of the book comprises three chapters that operate at the crossroads of philosophical hermeneutics, literature, and the arts. In these essays, instead of a top-down "application" of hermeneutics to literature, the authors explore the unique theories of interpretation that emerge *from* literature. Finally, part four explores questions at the intersection of interpretation and ethics, raising important questions about justice, charity, and authority in hermeneutics. Each of these parts contributes to an overall account of hermeneutics, like love, as a "many-splendored thing," which, in the end, is a kind of relational charity—a way of encountering and responding to the Other.

Kevin J. Vanhoozer's opening chapter, "Discourse on Matter: Hermeneutics and the 'Miracle' of Understanding," launches both the topic and the tenor of the volume by situating his discourse at the intersection of many of these crossroads. While his earlier work in hermeneutics focused primarily on a normative account of hermeneutics, here he offers a descriptive treatment that depends more on Gadamer than Ricoeur (on whom he has written extensively). As the lone full-time theologian in the seminar, he makes a special effort to bring the discussion to a theological level. But his paper also crosses the disciplinary crossroads, opening with a quote from a novel by Wendell Berry and then moving to discussions of Philip and the Ethiopian eunuch in Acts 8, René Decartes's *Meditations*, and Karl Barth's *Römerbrief*. With the questions that these examples raise in mind, Vanhoozer then provides an explication and critique of Gadamer. Along the way, he makes reference to Ricoeur and provides a critique of Wolterstorff. Although Vanhoozer affirms much of Gadamer's hermeneutics, he criticizes Gadamer's use of the incarnation in a purely "notional" (rather than truly "operational") way. His charge is "that Gadamer has not plundered the Egyptians but robbed Peter (or, in this case, John) to pay Plato."

In "Resuscitating the Author," Nicholas Wolterstorff puts forth the view that interpretation is an act of "engagement with a person that is mediated by the artifact." Since we are engaging with other people in interpreting texts, there is an important ethical dimension to interpretation. Although writing from the perspective of speech act theory, Wolterstorff here provides his most sustained interaction with Gadamer to date. Not surprisingly, he criticizes Gadamer and others who in effect hold to what Wolterstorff labels "hermeneutic orthodoxy": that interpretation is about understanding the sense of the text. Given that texts can have multiple meanings, Wolterstorff insists that proper interpretation must focus on the text as the illocutionary act of the author. Wolterstorff compliments Vanhoozer for being very close to being right, but ultimately mistaken in assuming that illocutionary acts are equivalent to "communicative acts." Although Wolterstorff's essay is not explicitly theological in nature, one can read it as a supplement to his *Divine Discourse*.

Gadamer is likewise the subject of Eduardo J. Echeverria's chapter, "Gadamer's Hermeneutics and the Question of Relativism." Although many have criticized Gadamer's theory of hermeneutics as being inherently relativistic, Echeverria wants to defend Gadamer against that charge. After explaining why Gadamer is sometimes interpreted as a relativist, he turns to a defense of Gadamer as a "realist." In effect, Echeverria stands at the crossroad of Gadamer interpretation, for he acknowledges that his defense of Gadamer differs sharply from that of Jean Grondin (not to mention other well-known Gadamerians). For Grondin, Gadamer in effect escapes the very dualism of absolutism and relativism by going beyond metaphysics. But Echeverria argues that Grondin's defense is itself problematic, for it fails to recognize that truth claims ultimately imply a correspondence to something outside of them.

Christina Bieber Lake's essay "'The Knowledge That One Does Not Know': Gadamer, Levertov, and the Hermeneutics of the Question" is situated at the crossroads of literary, theological, and philosophical interpretation. She considers the role of the question in Gadamer's hermeneutics by turning to the book of Job and the poetry of Denise Levertov. Not only is the book of Job filled with questions, but it also ends with God questioning Job. She develops the notion of the question in Gadamer by way of the intrinsic alterity of experience, the openness that a genuine question presupposes, and the resulting understanding that brings about a communion. Precisely those characteristics can be found in Levertov's poem "Primary Wonder" (as well as many of her other poems). We become wise, notes Bieber Lake, when we are willing to listen to the other. And that is possible only if the question is truly "open."

Equally inspired by Derrida and Søren Kierkegaard, John D. Caputo's "Hauntological Hermeneutics and the Interpretation of Christian Faith: On Being Dead Equal before God" is a meditation on death, on conversing with the dead, and on being dead equal. Here the crossroad is that of the cemetery, a crossroad between life and death. Caputo follows Kierkegaard's injunction in *Works of Love* to "go out to the dead" to see that we are equal before God. Caputo's "quasi-Derridean hauntological hermeneutics" reminds us that God, death, and eternity can be thought in terms of the "secret." They are all things to which no one has "secret" access. But that very lack of access makes us chase the secret all the more. Caputo argues that Christianity finds itself in the *différance* framed by the Messiah's first arrival and the Messiah's *à venir.* Following Derrida, though, Caputo sees the "messianic" as constantly haunting any concrete "messianisms" that claim to have the secret. Thus, Caputo's Messiah is "a kind of Jewish gadfly" that stands at the crossroads of all concrete messianisms.

In "Limited Inc/arnation: Revisiting the Searle/Derrida Debate in Christian Context," James K. A. Smith works at a number of crossroads. Insisting that taking the Bible as God's word means that one take authorial intention seriously, Smith shows that Christian scholars who criticize Derrida as having no concern for authorial intent do so on the basis of Searle's misreading of Derrida. Smith takes both Vanhoozer and Wolterstorff to task for having bought into what he terms the "received" Derrida (as mediated by American English departments). Although Smith does not want to "defend" Derrida because he is a "Derridean," he does want to defend Derrida's account of language because he sees it as phenomenologically correct. Smith argues that Searle in effect sets up a false dichotomy, in which we must choose between Derrida's iterability (the idea that texts can "mean" without the presence of the author) and authorial intention. But Searle misses the point of Derrida's iterability, which is not that authors' intentions cannot be communicated at all but that there are limits to communicability. Although misunderstanding can take place when texts are displaced from their contexts, understanding can likewise take place within a proper context and proper community. The result is that, while communication is inherently risky, it is still possible.

Roger Lundin's chapter "Meeting at the Modern Crossroads: Fiction, History, and Christian Understanding" is situated at the crossroad between William Faulker's *Absalom! Absalom!* and Gadamer's *Truth and Method*. Here we find yet another way of reading Gadamer. Lundin argues that Faulkner complicates the hermeneutical problem in this text by "placing the crucial activity of the novel in the nineteenth century and its narration in the twentieth." But, as Lundin reminds us, Gotthold Ephraim Lessing and Kierkegaard had also recognized this problem of action as historical and interpretation as present. With Lessing, overcoming historical distance becomes an acute problem. Lundin argues that Faulkner provides a middle way between the ideas that interpretation is either a return to the past or simply a reflection of the present. From there, Lundin turns to parallels between Faulkner and Gadamer. Just as Faulkner's character Shreve McCannon says, "let me play for a while now," so play becomes key to understanding for Gadamer because play is necessary for a genuine conversation. Yet, although Gadamer and Faulkner present us with an idea of understanding that points us in the right direction, Lundin claims that neither is fully Christian in his respective conception of interpretation.

Brian McCrea begins his essay by pointing out that his own particular context (the University of Florida) provides a special challenge for him as a Christian interpreter. He proposes "witnessing" as a way of walking the crossroad between the religious and the secular. "The Hermeneutics of Deliverance: *Robinson Crusoe* and the Problem of Witnessing" is an attempt to understand what witnessing entails by way of Daniel Defoe's *Robinson Crusoe*. McCrea focuses on the difficulties that Crusoe has in narrating his own experience and on how his journals have marked discrepancies with the text *Robinson Crusoe*. Defoe explains these discrepancies by way of the historical distance between the journal (which Crusoe only begins to write sometime after he is shipwrecked) and the events themselves. McCrea connects this difficulty of narrative to Ricoeur's point that the Gospels are themselves witnesses to past events and so there is a historical difference that separates them from the events they narrate. But McCrea concludes not only that this distance is inevitable in bearing witness but also that judging the "truth" of that witness involves looking to the lives of the witness bearers who, we might say, are a book to be read.

"John Calvin's Notion of 'Exchange' and the Usefulness of Literature," Michael VanderWeele's contribution, stands at the crossroads of literature, theology, and economics. VanderWeele opens his essay by pointing out that literary studies tend to emphasize either the free individual or else domination by political and economic entities. As an antidote to these two alternatives, VanderWeele suggests a more communal way of reading inspired by John Calvin. As examples of the individualistic way of reading, VanderWeele points us back to Friedrich Schiller, the English Romantics, and New Critics such as Cleanth Brooks (though the ultimate figure is that of Hamlet). He reads Martha Woodmansee as representing the opposite pole. While he sees Woodmansee as helpful in liberating us from the view of literature as liberating the individual, he likewise sees her focus on the political and economic as too amorphous. VanderWeele looks to Calvin for an economic notion of exchange that promotes true neighborliness. Calvin often couches doctrine in explicitly economic terms and uses the metaphor of "exchange and barter" for proper communal relations. VanderWeele then turns to Augustine's *Confessions* for an example, first of a "false economy" and then of "true economy," one characterized by seeking, knocking, and opening. Finally, VanderWeele proposes a rhetorical aesthetic that results in a "double exchange."

Bruce Ellis Benson's chapter "The Improvisation of Hermeneutics: Jazz Lessons for Interpreters" turns in an explicitly ethical direction. His concern is how a "hermeneutical justice" can be achieved in which an author's intentions, texts, the tradition that surrounds those texts, and interpreters can all be given their due. For him, jazz improvisation provides a promising model. Defining improvisation as a kind of adaptation, he sees jazz improvisations, musical scores, and even written texts as improvisatory "all the way down." Benson points out that improvisation first requires becoming part of a practice or tradition (whether jazz or Old Testament interpretation) and then learning how to elaborate on a structure in order to bring out what it "has to say." While Benson recognizes that there are important differences between jazz improvisation and other types of interpretation, he contends that, even if we wish to be "faithful" to an author's intentions, interpretation can never be simply repetition. In the end, Benson suggests that we think of interpretation as situated between the two poles to which Derrida refers: a doubling commentary, on the one hand, and a reading that "opens" the text, on the other.

"Ethical Hermeneutics and the Theater: Shakespeare's *Merchant of Venice*" carries on this ethical theme, moving from music to the theater. Ben Faber begins by pointing out that current interpretations and staging of Shakespeare tend in the anti-essentialist or anti-illusionist direction that "shatters the aesthetic completeness of the play." As a way to counter such interpretations, Faber suggests an ethical hermeneutics grounded in Gadamer and Ricoeur. From Gadamer, he takes the notion of art as presenting truth to a spectator who is also a participant in that art. From Ricoeur (who builds on Gadamer), he takes the mediation of hermeneutical distance and the connection of subject and object (as well as actor and spectator). Applying these notions to theater, Faber points out that a script must be brought to life, for "the stage is about embodiment and actual presence." Faber uses the character Shylock as an example. In his (in)famous demand for a literal pound of flesh, we (in this age and with the background of the Holocaust) see and hear this "other" demanding justice. Even if Shakespeare could not see Shylock as *l'autre*, we do. Faber, then, shows how a play that predates modernity can have a very different meaning for us in postmodernity.

Norman Lillegard continues the ethical theme, though his concern is that of authority. In "(Revelation, Interpretation) Authority: Kierkegaard's *Book on Adler*," he echoes Kierkegaard's lament that respect for authority has been replaced by insubordination. For Kierkegaard, authority is based upon revelation, and one feels the demands of that authority when one is contemporaneous with the other. In the *Book on Adler* Kierkegaard is concerned with God's speaking to us and the authority such speech entails. Kierkegaard thinks that authority is very much dependent upon a particular person. Lillegard ties this view to Wolterstorff's distinction between speaking and revelation and, in so doing, criticizes Ricoeur for locating the meaning in the text. The problem with Ricoeur's view, according to Lillegard, is that there can be no real sense of contemporaneity, and thus no authority. Contra Ricoeur, Lillegard argues that interpretation is a conversation. Even in Paul's writing, it is God who is speaking. And it is precisely because it is God speaking that the speech carries authority.

Each of these essays, from different paths and byways, points to an ultimate crossroads: the charged intersection between God and humanity in general, and divine and human authorship in particular. By engaging the many crossroads of hermeneutics and interpretation "in Christian perspective," this collection considers the micro-intersections of disciplines against the macro-intersection that is the Incarnation, where divinity and flesh meet. A number of the studies suggest that the road to the Cross—which is not properly understood until one takes the road to Emmaus—has important implications not only for the "special" hermeneutics of biblical interpretation, but also for broader, "general" accounts of language and interpretation. But even on the way to (and from) the Cross we encounter a number of hermeneutical crossroads: difficulties in understanding and communication, frustrating relationship and communion. The net effect of this, however, should not be despair over understanding but rather humility and thanksgiving: humility because each of our disciplines is on the hither-side of this final crossroads and lacks any final authority to determine the "right way"; thanksgiving because we rejoice in ad hoc and local events of understanding even though exhaustive understanding—and any single unified hermeneutical theory—ultimately eludes us. Which is simply to say that we have many miles to go before we sleep; conversation along the way—and the miracle of understanding—is a gift to be enjoyed en route.

PART 1

Philosophical Hermeneutics Revisited: Miracles, Resuscitation, Questions

1

Discourse on Matter

Hermeneutics and the "Miracle" of Understanding

Kevin J. Vanhoozer

The hermeneutical task is to discern the 'matter' of the text.[1]
—*(Ricoeur)*

The task of hermeneutics is to clarify this miracle of understanding, which is not a mysterious communion of souls, but sharing in a common meaning.[2]
—*(Gadamer)*

The unspiritual man does not receive the gifts of the Spirit of God, for they are folly to him, and he is not able to understand them because they are spiritually discerned.
—*(1 Cor 2:14)*

Introduction: The Hermeneutic Crossroads and the Road to Gaza

Wendell Berry inserts the following "Notice" on a page of its own, just between the acknowledgments and the table of contents of his novel *Jayber Crow:*

> Persons attempting to find a "text" in this book will be prosecuted; persons attempting to find a "subtext" in it will be banished; persons attempting to explain, interpret, explicate, analyze, deconstruct, or otherwise "understand" it will be exiled to a desert island in the company only of other explainers. BY ORDER OF THE AUTHOR.[3]

It is a dark day indeed when authors have to issue a prophetic blast against the monstrous regiment of interpreters. What author in his or her right mind would not wish readers to "understand" one's books! But is "understanding" only a bastard product of the latest interpretative technologies and hermeneutic mills, what Umberto Eco calls "overinterpretation" and what Kierkegaard views as procrastination—an attempt to busy oneself with the text in any number of ways that enable one to avoid responding to its real address and subject matter? Answering that query is the purpose of the present essay. What already appears clear, however, is that in the current hermeneutical climate it is open season on the concept of the author. And virtually no one thinks the author's order can stave off the conflict of interpretations.

Descriptive and Normative Theories of Interpretation

I have spent a disproportionate amount of time elsewhere trying to establish and protect the rights of authors.[4] While I am not yet ready to recant (I view my earlier work much as did Barth his—"Well roared, lion"), I now see the need to supplement my normative account with a more descriptive treatment of what actually happens in understanding. And that means grappling with Gadamer, whose magnum opus, *Truth and Method,* is still the most comprehensive and influential description of the event of understanding.

To distinguish descriptive from normative approaches to interpretation is to recognize two more trajectories that bump into one another in the hermeneutic crossroads. Normative theories tend to give rules, methodological procedures, and criteria for "correct" (e.g., non-arbitrary) interpretation. Of the proposed norms, perhaps the most familiar is the charge to discover what the author intended to communicate. Descriptive accounts, by contrast, treat understanding as a mode of being, as something that happens to interpreters "above our wanting and *doing*" (*TM*, p. xxviii). A rough generalization: normative accounts tend to be epistemological; descriptive accounts tend to be ontological.[5]

Active and Passive Understanding

In describing the event of understanding, my major concern will be to gain clarity as to *who is doing what to whom.* Is understanding a type of active mastery or a passive happening? Is it something the interpreting subject *does,* or is understanding *done to* the interpreter by the subject matter? Will the real subject please stand up? Both Gadamer and Ricoeur contend that the active agent as it were in the event of understanding is the "matter of the text": the *Sache.* The matter is the master, one might say, to whom author and interpreter alike must bow the knee. Yet *mastery* may not be the best metaphor with which to describe the relation of the *Sache* to the interpreting subject. Gadamer's preferred term is *miracle.*

Understanding how the *Sache* makes itself understood is my quarry, in search of which I shall take a somewhat circuitous path—elliptical, to be exact, in the geometric sense only, I hope! The two focal points are "discourse" and "understanding." By discourse, I mean "what someone says/writes to someone about something."[6] By understanding, I mean "getting it," where the "it" is the discourse, especially the subject matter or "aboutness" of discourse. My concern, then, is the "turn to the *Sache*" in contemporary hermeneutics and the subsequent fate of authorial discourse: *to what extent is the event of understanding intelligible without recourse to the notion of authorial discourse?*

Scripture indirectly describes the conditions for and event of understanding, at least with regard to the biblical text, in the story of Philip and the Ethiopian eunuch in Acts 8. "Do you understand what you are reading?" Philip asks. The Ethiopian, puzzling over the book of Isaiah, replies, "How can I, unless someone guides me?" and then inquires: "About whom, pray, does the prophet say this, about himself or someone else?" (Acts 8:34). Clearly, the matter of the text, the *Sache* of Isaiah, eludes him: about what, about whom, is Isaiah speaking? Though the author is not available to consult, understanding eventually dawns. What happened? Who, or what, is the catalyst or agent of the Ethiopian's understanding? Philip, obviously. But what does Philip stand for: the teaching authority of the church? a mystical experience? scholarship? The answer, I believe, is "Tradition," yet tradition needs to be described, and not in terms of philosophical hermeneutics only.[7]

Philosophical and Theological Hermeneutics

The road to Gaza with Philip and the Ethiopian thus brings us to yet another hermeneutic crossroad, though whether it is indeed an intersection or a fork in the road is an open question. I refer to the distinction between general and special hermeneutics, between the way we understand texts in general and the way we understand the Bible in particular. The distinction between general and special hermeneutics is not unrelated to the distinction between the respective subject matters of philosophy and theology: anthropology and God.

There is nevertheless good reason to question whether there really are two separate roads toward understanding, one for the Bible and one for all other texts. If Gadamer is right and understanding is a mode of being (so Heidegger), then philosophical hermeneutics becomes a virtual theory of existence, a full-scale anthropology that describes the human condition (finitude) and is thus applicable whether one is reading Isaiah, the I Ching, or Ibsen. If hermeneutics and the event of understanding are ultimately matters of ontology (e.g., human being; self-understanding), then reading the Bible becomes only a regional instance of a universal or general phenomenon. The question thus becomes whether theology has anything to contribute to the description of textual understanding—and, for that matter, ontology itself—or whether it has been frozen out of the discussion. If the secret of hermeneutics is anthropology (and philosophical anthropology at that), then do Christian categories (e.g., sin and grace) have no substantive role to play in describing the event of understanding?

The present discourse on the matter of understanding has three parts: (1) I begin with a case study of two texts—Descartes's *Discourse on Method* and Barth's *Romans*—in order to introduce the two key terms (viz., "discourse" and "*Sache*") and the two approaches to understanding (viz., philosophy and theology). Barth's commentary is particularly relevant in its explicit privileging of the *Sache* of the text over the psyche of its author and in its invoking its own way of describing the miracle of understanding. Indeed, Barth's attempt prompted Gadamer to call *Romans* a "hermeneutical manifesto" (*TM*, p. 509), even though the term "hermeneutics" does not even appear in any of the editions of Barth's *Römerbrief*. (2) The second part examines Gadamer's description of what he calls the "miracle" of understanding and asks how Gadamer might handle the "*Sache*" of Descartes's and Barth's discourses respectively, which leads to (3) a critique (and Christian counterproposal) of the way Gadamer appropriates theological categories for his philosophical hermeneutics.[8] I conclude with some reflections on understanding as "enlightenment." The goal is to make a distinctly Christian contribution to the broader conversation taking place at the hermeneutical crossroads concerning the understanding of discourse and the discourse on understanding.

Two Types of Discourse on Matter: Philosophy and Theology

We begin with two seminal texts, one in philosophy and the other in theology. Each is a discourse on understanding, of the world and of the Word of God respectively. While both texts treat understanding, the one suggests that understanding is something subjects do by following method, the other that understanding is something that happens to subjects for whom the Bible becomes the Word of God.

Descartes's Discourse on Method

Descartes's *Discourse on Method*, published in 1637, is one of the seminal texts of modern philosophy. It both treats the subject of understanding and confronts the interpreter with the problem of how to understand it. Descartes's text is philosophical discourse: "A philosophical text is generally an attempt to communicate the thoughts of an author on a given subject (or subjects) of philosophical concern."[9] What is Descartes's *Discourse on Method* about? It is a discourse on method, to be sure, but it also discusses God and the nature of human beings. Most centrally, it sets out a procedure for discovering truth. Descartes challenges the Aristotelian view of scientific knowledge as deduction from first principles and argues for a new model of scientific knowledge based on scientific experiment and mathematics. Descartes's is literally a discourse on matter—the objects of nature—and how to come to know them. It is a "discourse" instead of a "treatise" because, in his own words, "I did not plan to explain my whole method, but merely to say something about it."[10]

The authorial voice in *Discourse on Method* is, at least on the surface, mild-mannered. Descartes explicitly denies that he is offering a normative account that everyone else must follow in order to claim to be rational: "my plan here is not to teach the method that everyone must follow in order to guide their own reason, but merely to explain how I have tried to guide my own" (*DM*, p. 7). His initial assumption is that everyone has an equal measure of *le bon sens.* The diversity of human points of view "does not result from the fact that some people are more reasonable than others, but simply from the fact that we guide our thoughts along different paths and do not think about the same things" (*DM*, p. 5), in large part because of differences in education.

Descartes notes that he too was nourished by books since he was a child. He even anticipates something of Gadamer's dialogical hermeneutics: "the reading of all good books is like a conversation with the most eminent people of past centuries, who were the authors. . . . [I]t is even a studied conversation in which they reveal to us only the best of their thoughts" (*DM*, p. 8). Those who know him as the father of modern philosophy may find it surprising that Descartes had a broad tolerance of cultural diversity: "It is helpful to know something about the customs of different peoples in order to make a more sensible judgment about our own, and not to think that everything that is different from our ways is ridiculous and irrational" (*DM*, p. 8). However, as a result of his travels and conversations with many sorts of people, Descartes says he ultimately learned "not to believe anything too firmly about which I had been convinced by example and custom alone" (*DM*, p. 11).

Discourse on Method is an impassioned plea for a new kind of hypothetico-deductive scientific reasoning, for thinking on the basis of reason alone. Descartes begins his philosophical reformation with himself: "My objective was never anything more than an attempt to reform my own thoughts and to build on a foundation that was entirely my own" (*DM*, pp. 13–14). Accordingly, he resolves to follow the four rules that make up the heart of his famous methodological proposal, the most important being the first: "never to accept anything as true if I did not know clearly that it was so; that is, carefully to avoid prejudice and jumping to conclusions, and to include nothing in my judgments apart from whatever appeared so clearly and distinctly to my mind that I had no opportunity to cast doubt on it" (*DM*, p. 16).

As is well known, the truth that grounds all other truths in Descartes's system of knowledge is the truth of his own existence. "I knew from this fact [that he could not doubt the fact that he existed because he was thinking] that I was a substance, the whole essence or nature of which was to think and which, in order to exist, has no need of any place and does not depend on anything material" (*DM*, p. 25). Descartes states his criterion for truth in no uncertain terms: "those things that we conceive very clearly and distinctly are all true" (*DM*, p. 25). Descartes responds to Socrates' philosophical injunction ("Know thyself") by attempting to know his own mind. As part four of the *Discourse* clearly shows, however, Descartes is able to trust the deliverances of his mind only on the assumption that God would not have designed it to mislead us.

Two points in particular deserved to be noted given the purposes of the present essay: first, for Descartes, *understanding is something that subjects do.* That is the whole point of presenting a method: methods establish the steps to take in order to succeed at a given task, in this case, discovering truth. Second, the central issue in trying to make sense of Descartes's *Discourse* is the problem of knowing what he means in his first rule by accepting only those ideas that appear "so clearly and distinctly to my mind." This second point complicates the first: to what extent is the knowing subject the active agent of the appearance of clear and distinct ideas and to what extent is she the passive recipient?[11] Does clarity appear or is clarity achieved?

I have quoted from *Discourse on Method* at length in order to provide a backdrop for the task at hand: namely, describing what it is to understand Descartes's discourse, to determine what it is about, to discern its *Sache*.[12] How would Gadamer describe the event of understanding Descartes's *Discourse*? This query is more subtle than it first appears. For as we shall see, Gadamer (and Ricoeur) relate understanding primarily to the *matter* of the text, not to the intentions of the author.

Descartes's *Discourse* is best known today for its argument on behalf of securing foundations of knowledge. This is how Gadamer seems to read it too: Descartes's point, he says, is to subject authority and communal traditions to the individual's right use of reason (see *TM*, pp. 277–79). Others, however, argue that it is a distortion to see Descartes's interests as primarily epistemological. Read in historical context, Descartes was not suffering from what Rorty terms the "Cartesian anxiety" ("How can I know anything for certain?"); rather, he was preoccupied with showing "how the world of physics, the mathematically describable world, could be reliably mapped out independently of the often vague and misleading deliverances of our sensory organs."[13] I am less interested in entering into the conflict of interpretations over Descartes, and much less in defending what has come to be known as Cartesianism, than I am with pressing home the question of what it means to understand Descartes's *Discourse*. Again: how might Gadamer describe what happens when we understand *Discourse on Method*?

Barth's Epistle to the Romans

THE SUPERIORITY OF *SACHE:* WHAT PAUL'S EPISTLE TO THE ROMANS IS ABOUT

Karl Barth turned to the book of Romans in the hope of hearing the Word of God and in the hope of finding a new starting point, and principle, for theology. Instead of interpreting the Bible as an expression of human religious experience, as was typical of theological liberalism, Barth turned to Scripture not so much to discover God but to be discovered by God. Whereas "religion" concerns humanity's search for God, the message of Christianity was, for Barth, that God "found the way to us."[14] God is not an "object" of human reflection but an active *subject*. Theology's task therefore is not to formulate human thoughts about God but to explicate God's thoughts about us.[15] The challenge for Barth was to affirm the reality and activity of God while at the same time forestalling its becoming an object of human historical or rational investigation. If God is God, he must remain free to make himself known.

Barth's *Römerbrief* has been likened to a bombshell dropped into the playground of the theologians. It was equally explosive in the laboratory of the hermeneuticians.[16] In a draft to the preface of the first edition, Barth wrote that his *Romans* was "an attempt to read the Bible differently. . . . [I]n what way different? I wish to answer: more in accordance with its subject matter, content, and substance, focusing with more attention and love upon the meaning of the Bible itself."[17] Historical critics, he says, are not critical enough; they do not penetrate as far as the text's distinctive and unique subject matter. They do not perceive "what there is" or "what stands" in the Bible. The meaning of the words in the biblical text can be determined only in relation to the *Sache* of which they speak. To read for the human author's intention fails to do justice to the freedom of God's Word speaking in Scripture. Schleiermacher, in suggesting that the Bible was an expression of human experience, got the subject matter exactly the wrong way round. Barth's aim, in his own words, was to bring the reader "face to face with the subject-matter of the Scriptures."[18]

The subject matter of Scripture is not merely history, a system of morality, or religious piety but the *God of the gospel:* the message of what God was and is doing in Jesus Christ for the sake of a fallen world.[19] This is a crucial point, for it is the driving assumption and material insight behind Barth's biblical hermeneutics. The subject matter of theology is not merely historical but eschatological: the "world of the text" (Ricoeur) is the "world of God."[20] The Bible is about the breaking-in of *God's world* (the "kingdom of God"; "real history") into the world order ("so-called history") in order to judge the world and renew it. However, though God enters the world he continues to remain God; he is in the world but not of it. By the very nature of the case, then, *this* subject matter is not under human control. God's self-revelation is not a matter of "clear and distinct ideas," but of God-in-communicative-action. "Real history"—the time and space of God's making himself known—is beyond the reach of the historian. The *Sache* of the Bible is not an object at our disposal. Interpreters are not merely "spectators" of God's Word but, in God's grace, participants who may be caught up into the subject matter (viz., the fellowship-creating triune economy).

THE MIRACLE OF UNDERSTANDING: HOW IT COMES ABOUT

Barth argues that the criterion for every science is the adequacy of a discipline to its particular subject matter. Theology's subject matter is God in loving, free, communicative, and self-communicating action. The *Sache* or subject matter of Scripture, likewise, is itself an active subject, unlike every other type of object of scientific study. It is this subject matter, and not some method, that is ultimately normative for theology and for biblical interpretation.

Barth believes that God makes himself known preeminently in Jesus Christ, but also in Scripture, the human witness to the Word. The *Sache* of Scripture reveals itself both by appropriating creaturely media (the human words of Scripture, the humanity of Christ) as its objective content and by enabling the *reception* of that content, the subjective side of revelation. Neither creaturely media nor creaturely ears have an innate capacity to bear or to hear God's Word. In conventional terms: for Barth, both inspiration and illumination are necessary ingredients in divine revelation and hence the event of understanding Scripture. That human words can convey the Word of God is a divine possibility, not a human possibility. The revelation is never identical with its medium for, if it were, then God would be a worldly object, not God at all.

The hermeneutical challenge remains: how do humans come to understand *this* subject matter? Barth's reply: God not only gives the grace to think appropriately about him, he also "gives himself as the subject matter of this thinking."[21] In short: the *Sache,* or matter of discourse, *reveals* itself, makes itself known. Understanding results not from some natural or semantic connection between sense and referent (a given), but from the act of divine revelation (a gift). For Barth, revelation is not the transmission of information about God, but God's own self-giving: "God is who He is in the act of His revelation."[22] Moreover, revelation happens only when God in his freedom decides to make himself known: "Because God is free . . . any attempt to bind or contain Him or any attempt to force Him to conform to any method or hermeneutic came down not simply to a matter of inadequacy, but to a matter of reduction and distortion."[23] Hence for Barth, "the being of God is the fundamental hermeneutical problem, not the problem of human understanding."[24]

It is in and through human words that God's gospel Word may nevertheless be heard. The apostle Paul and the other human authors of Scripture are witnesses not to their own experience, nor even to past events, but to the living God, who is no inert matter but the speaking subject of biblical discourse. That the human words of Scripture indicate the Word of God is nothing less than miraculous: "The word, which enters human ears and is uttered by human lips, is the Word of God—only when the miracle takes place" (*Rom,* p. 366). But what precisely is the nature of this miracle? There is no suggestion in Barth that the *sense* of the biblical words changes when God decides to reveal himself through them. The *Sache* does not mysteriously change the words on the page or what is said. What, then, actually happens? Just this: the miracle is that God, the active subject, "commandeers" the language of Scripture so that it discloses Jesus Christ. Just as the humanity of Jesus is taken up into the divine service to reveal God, so God can take up human words to reveal himself in and as Jesus Christ. Thus God used and continues to use the words of the Bible to bear witness to the evangelical *Sache:* the history of Jesus Christ.

The ability to participate in the Bible's subject matter does not figure in the repertoire of human possibilities. It demands more than reading for the human author's intended message, more even than believing the author's message: "No amount of empathy or congeniality can substitute for the inward illumination of the Holy Spirit."[25] The gap between what is written (the sense) and what is written about (reference) is closed, from above, by the Holy Spirit. It is the Spirit who brings about in the interpreter the correspondence between scriptural sense and Christological referent by redirecting his or her cognitive apparatus.

The Word of God creates, as it were, its own hearer: "When God's Word is heard and proclaimed, something takes place that for all our hermeneutical skill cannot be brought about by hermeneutical skill" (*CD* I/1, p. 148). Understanding God's Word is a matter of the *Sache* of Scripture actively disclosing itself and redirecting the interpreter's thoughts. Understanding God's Word is not something humans can do, for the event of understanding depends upon God's making himself known (and felt); but the presence and activity of God is never the secure possession of the human subject. Understanding, in the case of Scripture, is for Barth a matter not of the interpreter grasping the Bible but of the Bible—its *Sache*, to be precise—grasping the interpreter in a free and loving embrace. The biblical interpreter is less the active agent than the grateful patient of the event of understanding.

THE ROLE OF AUTHORIAL DISCOURSE: TOWARD A SPECIAL (I.E., THEOLOGICAL) GENERAL HERMENEUTICS

Perhaps the most persistent criticism of Barth's *Romans* is that its turn to the *Sache* comes at the expense of the historical Paul. Some critics went so far as to speak of the "violence" Barth had done to Paul.[26] The charge is that Barth moves to the revelatory referent too fast, bypassing the historical sense of Scripture in his haste to come face to face with the revelatory *Sache*.

Barth responds to this charge in his celebrated preface to the second edition of *Romans*. Barth here explains how his attempt to recover the *Sache* can also be construed in terms of understanding *Paul*. The goal of the exegete is to paraphrase Paul's thoughts so as to make them contemporaneous. One does this by becoming so familiar with the text that, to cite what is perhaps Barth's most controversial claim, "the document seems hardly to exist as a document; till I have almost forgotten that I am not its author; till I know the author so well that I allow him to speak in my name and am even able to speak in his name myself" (*Rom*, p. 8). Barth describes this exegetical approach as a form of *Nachdenken*, which is not a "thinking after" in Schleiermacher's sense of recreating the author's creative process but a "thinking with": "To understand an author means *to stand with him*, to take each of his words in earnest, . . . to participate with him in the subject matter."[27]

To participate with the author in the subject matter is to look in the direction where the author's words point. To stand with the author is to treat the author not as a source, much less an object, but as a signpost. The alternative to thinking with the author is to think about the author, to examine the author's historical, cultural, psychological, and such contexts in order to learn more about the author's world. Barth is less interested in the origin of Paul's religion, however, than in the import of what Paul actually says. The primary task of the interpreter is not to interpret the author's world but the author's *words*, and to do so in light of the subject matter to which the words bear witness.

Barth nevertheless acknowledges the legitimacy of the concern of general hermeneutics to avoid arbitrary or subjective interpretations, interpretations that Barth views as "the sickness of an insolent and arbitrary reading in" (*CD* I/2, p. 470). Interpretation must be principled. On the other hand, Barth was convinced that the general hermeneutics practiced by the commentators of his day failed to do justice to the unique subject matter of Scripture. Barth's solution to this dilemma—to use or not to use general hermeneutics in biblical interpretation—comes as something of a surprise. Instead of making biblical hermeneutics a mere subset of general hermeneutics, and instead of simply dismissing general hermeneutics, Barth instead moves in the other direction, from the particular to the general: "It is from the word of man in the Bible that we must learn what has to be learned concerning the word of man in general" (*CD* I/2, p. 466). Barth begins from the *actuality* of what happens in Christian understanding in particular, not from the possibilities for the condition of understanding in general, and moves toward general hermeneutics. Instead of reading the Bible "like any other book," he proposes to read every other book as he does the Bible: "my 'Biblicist' method—which means in the end no more than 'consider well'—is applicable to the study of Lao-Tse and Goethe" (*Rom*, p. 12).

Barth is not saying that the texts of Jane Austen or John Steinbeck contain the Word of God. He is simply saying that one should strive to honor the subject matter of every text, to which the author's discourse bears witness, and not be content with philological analysis or any other kind of criticism that stops short of expositing and engaging with the *Sache*: "Is it not the case that whatever is said to us by men obviously wants . . . to make itself said and heard? It wants in this way to become to us a subject-matter. . . . In order to be understood by us, it wants not to be mastered by us but to lay hold of us" (*CD* I/2, p. 471). The difference between the Bible and all other texts is that in the Bible's case, its subject matter is a sovereign Subject, the living and active Word of God. No other matter speaks for itself as does God in his self-revelation: "God's revelation . . . not only wants but *can* make itself said and heard" (*CD* I/2, p. 471).

To what extent is Barth's hermeneutic oriented to authorial discourse? Everything depends on what it means to "understand Paul better than he understood himself." Barth rejects the hermeneutics of "empathy" that aims to recover the inner life of the author, as in the case of Schleiermacher. It is too easy, Barth thought, to impute all sorts of motives and intentions to Paul on the assumption that he was fundamentally like us. Nor is Barth interested in claiming that he knows the author better because he is able to reconstruct the author's historical situation. Both empathetic and reconstructive approaches mistakenly interpret the author apart from the point of *Sache* of his or her discourse.[28] In contrast, Barth posits, on the basis of the revelation of the *wholly other*, a certain degree of authorial *otherness*, especially as this concerns the author's knowledge of a particular subject matter.

Understanding an author means attending patiently and faithfully to what the author has said, attending until one can see just what an author "intended," that is, until one can see that to which the author directed his or her thoughts.[29] Understanding an author means following the direction that his words point, just as John the Baptist's finger points in Barth's beloved Grünewald altarpiece. In sum: understanding an author involves the interpreter's insight into the *Sache*, the truth content of the author's discourse.

Understanding thus calls for faithful attention, even love, on the interpreter's part toward an author. However, Barth has an "emergency clause" that allows him under certain circumstances to opt out of the relationship: "so long as it is not proven otherwise that he does not deserve this trust."[30] An author shows himself to be unworthy of our trust when he is an unreliable or incompetent witness, and only in this case could we say that we understand the author better than he does himself. In the case of the apostle Paul, Barth defers to Paul's commissioned witness; we have no other access to the *Sache* of the biblical text than its author. Such is not the case with other texts.

The final word, however, belongs to "standing with." Barth learns by reading Scripture that understanding in general means taking authorial words in earnest and in trust. The interpreter, of the Bible or any other text, is first and foremost a servant of word, one who attends it in the hope that it will disclose its "spirit," its *Sache*: "For the sake of better general hermeneutics it must therefore dare to be this special hermeneutics" (*CD* I/2, p. 472).

Discourse on Understanding: Philosophical Hermeneutics

No figure looms larger in discussion of contemporary philosophical hermeneutics than Hans-Georg Gadamer. Gadamer's theory is well known and too vast to rehearse here. Suffice it to say that he and Ricoeur have spearheaded the turn away from the author to the *matter* of the text, reorienting hermeneutics away from epistemology (viz., interpreting to know the author's mind) toward ontology (viz., interpreting for self-understanding). Understanding for Gadamer does not come about by following some method for correct interpretation but through a disclosure of truth that bears a resemblance to how we experience art or the playing of a game. The title of Gadamer's *Truth and Method* was originally to have been *Verstehen und Geschehen — Understanding and Happening*. He changed the title, but the bulk of the book is still devoted to describing the "happening"—the experience, the event—of understanding. I can here only highlight certain problems that Descartes's and Barth's texts each pose for Gadamer's hermeneutics and for his project of clarifying the "miracle" of understanding.

Understanding as Agreement: To Fuse or Not to Fuse with Cartesian Horizons

For Gadamer, understanding happens when we participate not in the *Sache* itself, but in a conversation about the *Sache*. Understanding is a matter of agreement with another about a specific subject matter: "Understanding is first of all agreement" (*TM*, p. 180). To interpret is to enter into a dialogue with the text, a dialogue prompted by the question that addresses the interpreter and to which the text was an answer. This dialogue, which is interpretation, has as its aim not the discovery of what was in the author's mind but rather a genuine engagement with the *Sache*. To understand is to be seized by the truth of the matter.[31] Is there a truth that discloses itself in Descartes's *Discourse* or through the conversation to which the text has given rise? The question needs to be asked, for as one critic points out: "We can have an experience of disclosure that leads us not to truth but to untruth."[32]

On the one hand, Gadamer acknowledges the importance of an openness to the other and to having one's own position challenged and transformed. To be open is to acknowledge the possible superiority of one's conversation partner: "This is the essence, the soul of my hermeneutics: To understand someone else is to see the justice, the truth, of their position. And this is what transforms us."[33] On the other hand, it is not quite clear just what the locus of this otherness is. Is the "other" the historical author Descartes, the *Sache* of his discourse, or something else altogether?

Gadamer is clear that whatever speaks to and challenges us through the text is not the authorial voice: "Not just occasionally but always, the meaning of a text goes beyond its author" (*TM*, p. 296). Gadamer's variation on the idea that we understand an author better than the author understands himself is that we are sometimes able to see what the author says in light of a truth the author did not have. It is possible, therefore, for the interpreter to have insights into the *Sache* that the historical author did not have or could not have had. Perhaps this is how he would respond to Descartes. However, Gadamer adds that these insights into the "real intention" or import of an author's ideas are "intentions he [the author] would have shared if his thinking had been clear enough" (*TM*, p. 195). The author, in other words, would agree with the interpreter, conceding that the interpreter had a better insight into the *Sache* under discussion. One wonders how the conversation between Descartes and Gadamer would actually proceed. In a sense, this is a moot point for Gadamer, who directs dialogue partners not to focus on one another but instead to focus on what is being spoken about (*TM*, p. 367).[34]

The question to be asked at this point is whether Gadamer's notion of tradition-as-dialogue is not in fact too monological. *Can* Descartes's discourse really be heard? If so, what are we hearing? If not, what kind of conversation with his discourse are we having?[35] Here is one commentator's terse statement of the fundamental problem: "The notion of tradition functions monolithically in such a way as to diminish alterity."[36]

A "Middle" Runs through It: On Conversations and Criteria of Truth

Discourse, spoken or written, involves someone saying something to someone about something. How does Gadamer account for the event of understanding: who is doing what to whom? Gadamer's concern is with "what happens to us over and above our willing and doing" (*TM*, p. xxviii). He reverses the received picture—authors are communicating through texts to readers—ascribing the role of communicative agent not to the author but to the *Sache*. It is the *Sache* that "comes" to language as interpreters dialogue about the text's meaning and significance.[37] As the translators of *Truth and Method* put it: "What makes 'coming to an understanding' possible is language, which provides the *Mitte*, the 'medium' or 'middle ground,' the 'place' where understanding, as we say, 'takes place'" (*TM*, p. xvii).

Philippe Eberhard argues that the "medial" character of the hermeneutic event is the key to understanding Gadamer.[38] Understanding is a "middle voice" phenomenon, neither wholly active nor wholly passive: "In the middle voice, as opposed to the active, the subject is within the action which happens to him or her *and* of which he or she is subject."[39] The interpreter is neither simply active nor simply passive but caught up in a larger process; understanding is both "happening" and "doing." The main thrust of thinking in terms of the middle voice, however, is to shift the emphasis away from agency toward the notion of *location.* The interpreter is in the *middle,* in the midst of a conversation, in language. At the same time, the interpreter is not simply tossed to and fro by the currents of the conversation but can contribute to the conversation as well. The event of understanding happens *and* I am its subject.

Nevertheless, the outcome of the conversation can be neither calculated nor controlled, for engaging in dialogue involves more than following technical procedures. In Gadamer's words: "it is generally more correct to say that we fall into conversation" (*TM,* p. 383). Interpreters are no more in control of conversations than players are of a game; as Gadamer says, "the play plays."[40] "The connection between play and truth as disclosure is a subordination to an entity greater than oneself."[41] Similarly, in genuine dialogue "something emerges that is contained in neither of the partners" (*TM,* p. 462). And the same is true of the experience of understanding as well: "Understanding is to be thought of less as a subjective act than as participating in an event of tradition" (*TM,* p. 290).

Gadamer's central insight is that language is not a tool to manipulate, a means by which communication takes place, but the *medium* in which the *Sache* makes itself known: "language is the game in and of which we all partake."[42] Language speaks us yet we still speak. Understanding "happens" when the thing itself—the *Sache*—comes-to-language: "The point is that *res,* the *Sache,* is itself the process that carries the subject."[43] Note that the celebrated "fusion of horizons" that takes place in understanding "is actually the achievement of language" (*TM,* p. 378). The miracle, one could say, is a word-event. Gadamer is not making the Rorty-esque point that language creates reality, but rather that the real "shows itself" (or comes to light) in (as?) language: "One seeks the correct word, that is, the word that truly belongs to the thing [*Sache*], so that thereby the thing itself comes into language" (*TM,* p. 417).

"A true word is not the object of clear thinking but the clearing of thinking speaking itself out."[44] With this thought we are as far as possible from what Descartes wants to say about understanding. Joel Weinsheimer puts it like this: "Being presents itself in the light of words which reflect it as it truly is, just as beauty is revealed in what makes it beautiful."[45] In sum, Gadamer describes the event of understanding as the self-presentation in language of the *Sache* to the interpreting subject.[46] Eberhard insists that the interpreting subject is not merely a passive recipient: "It is important to note what kind of miracle understanding is; it is a miracle that happens only with the participation of the subject."[47] What does the interpreter do? This is perhaps the key question. Eberhard's answer: "to understand is to open oneself to something that speaks to us (*sprechen*) so as to *cor-*

respond to it (*entsprechen*)."[48] To say "I understand," then, is like saying "I'm getting married"; the subject is neither merely active nor merely passive but medially involved in a more encompassing process, namely, the process of the *Sache*'s coming to language.

Conversation happens. Indeed. But so, alas, does misunderstanding. There is a positive charge to Gadamer's hermeneutics, a fundamental tendency to trust the direction of the conversation, but not to the point where he simply abandons the attempt to distinguish proper from improper understanding, legitimate from illegitimate prejudices.[49] Some commentators believe that tradition—the whole history of the conversation—governs a text's interpretation. Against this, Gadamer appears still to be able to appeal to the text as over against the conversation about it: "The harmony of all the details with the whole is the criterion of correct understanding" (*TM*, p. 291).[50] Other commentators, by contrast, reject the idea that Gadamer had a truth criterion for understanding.[51]

Gadamer's approach to criteriology and the legitimation of prejudices resembles Heidegger's, whom Gadamer cites in this connection (see *TM*, p. 267). Both encourage the interpreter to focus on "the things themselves," the *Sache* of the text. We experience the truth of the matter when the conversation discloses a perspective of the thing itself, that is, when the conversation is *enlightening* (*einleuchtend*). True understanding is a consequence of the *Sache*'s "shining forth." Gadamer attributes the power to enlighten to language itself: it is "the light of the word" (*TM*, p. 483). We shall return to the theme of enlightening below. Enough has been said already to indicate that the interpreting subject is caught up in a process that transcends his or her individual agency.

Gadamer's Hermeneutical Escape Clause: Preaching versus Interpreting

While Barth attempts to derive lessons for general hermeneutics from biblical interpretation, Gadamer moves in the opposite direction, proposing to exempt Scripture from his hermeneutic theory. Whereas Barth had an "emergency clause" that allowed him under certain circumstances to opt out of interpreting for authorial discourse, Gadamer has a kind of "escape clause" that makes of biblical interpretation an exception to his general hermeneutics.

Before we examine the escape clause, a word must be said about Gadamer's use of theological themes. Unlike Barth, who roots his reflections within divine actuality (e.g., the self-revelation of the *Sache*), Gadamer uses theological ideas in a strictly notional way. For example, he invokes Christology for the sake of articulating the relation between word and thought, thus prompting one commentator to say that "[t]he spoken word reveals thinking to us because speaking and thinking are *homoousios*."[52] Yet Gadamer does not ground this claim in the historical reality of the Incarnation but appeals to it as an analogy only.

Back to the "escape clause." Given Gadamer's appeal to Christological analogies for the sake of his general hermeneutics, it comes as something of a surprise to learn that the Christian kerygma falls outside the hermeneutical circle. Gadamer describes the "big difference" between legal and theological hermeneutics in the following terms: "Unlike a legal verdict, preaching is not a creative supplement to the text it is interpreting. Hence the gospel acquires no new content in being preached that could be compared with the power of the judge's verdict to supplement the law" (*TM*, p. 330). Neither the conversation about nor the application of biblical texts seems to affect them in return. The Word of God stands outside interpretation. At least in the case of the Bible, then, there is a meaning *in* the text.

This is not to say that Gadamer attends to authorial discourse in Scripture either. On the contrary, what comes to language in the Gospels is not "someone's speech" but "an expression of religious faith elicited by the Holy Spirit."[53] The Bible is the Word of God that the church has heard in its communal tradition and, as such, takes precedence over its interpretation. Unlike other texts, then, Scripture does not have its being in constant reinterpretation.

Eberhard contends that Gadamer abandons his theory about the *Sache* coming to language when it comes to Scripture. Understanding Scripture is ultimately a matter of faith and hence pure passivity; it is a matter of receiving Scripture as a sign, not of understanding a *Sache*: "The *kerygma* is so incomprehensible that to envision it one must be converted to it by an act of God."[54] Eberhard complains that faith in Gadamer's hands loses its character as a hermeneutic experience. Ironically, the one text that is exempt from what Gadamer says elsewhere about the miracle of understanding is the Bible itself! Whether or not Eberhard is right that Gadamer makes a hermeneutical exception of the Bible, though an interesting sidelight, must not detract from the primary point at hand, namely, the extent to which the interpreting subject is active or passive in the miracle of understanding.

Paul Ricoeur: The Strange Case of the Disappearing Discourse

Paul Ricoeur could not be accused of making an exception of the Bible to his theory of interpretation. Yet, like Gadamer, Ricoeur appeals to theological terms in order to describe the event of textual understanding and, like Barth, Ricoeur sees a certain approximation between what happens when we read Scripture and when we read poetic texts in general. The most important of these terms is *revelation*. Understanding is a matter of grasping not the author's intention, but the "world" (Ricoeur's preferred term to *Sache*) projected or manifested or revealed by the text. Ricoeur is clear that there is a difference between the authorial referent and the textual referent: "Understanding has less than ever to do with the author and his situation. It seeks to grasp the world-propositions opened up by the reference of the text. To understand a text is to follow its movement from sense to reference: from what it says, to what it talks about."[55]

According to Ricoeur, the main characteristic of discourse is its being "said by someone to someone else about something" (*IT*, p. 30). He further distinguishes "what is said" or the sense of discourse and "that about which something is said" or the reference of discourse (*HHS*, p. 167). To the extent that understanding has "less than ever to do with the author," however, it is far from clear *whose* discourse one is interpreting, or even how one knows what a given text is about. The intended meaning of the text is not the presumed intention of the author, "but rather what the text means for whoever complies with its injunction" (*HHS*, p. 161). The text places the reader "in" its meaning, in its *sens* (to use the French term), in the same direction. Note that Ricoeur here relocates Husserl's idea that intention is "directedness" and makes the text, not the author, the director, as it were. Still, it is far from clear how readers know what direction to follow if the one sense can lead to many possible referents.[56] While Ricoeur's motives are laudable—he wants us to hear something in texts beyond the "desert of criticism"—and while it is clear that he believes texts disclose truth, it is not clear how he discerns *what* truths are being disclosed, or how.

Who in Ricoeur's scheme is the active agent of understanding? The reader appropriates, to be sure, but appropriation for Ricoeur is as much a matter of "letting-oneself-be-grasped" as it is of grasping. Moreover, what the reader appropriates is "the power of disclosing a world that constitutes the reference of the text" (*IT*, p. 92). Readers appropriate, but the text discloses; what is made one's own is paradoxically *given* to the subject.[57] Hence appropriation for Ricoeur is less "taking possession" than dispossessing, or even, at the limit, "being possessed." Ricoeur calls the link between disclosure and appropriation "the cornerstone of a hermeneutic which would claim both to overcome the shortcomings of historicism and to remain faithful to the original intention of Schleiermacher's hermeneutics" (*IT*, p. 93). Ricoeur too is able to speak of understanding an author better than he could understand himself, then, but for Ricoeur this means "to display the power of disclosure implied in his own discourse beyond the limited horizon of his own existential situation" (*IT*, p. 93).

The *Sache*—the world of the text—exercises a kind of sovereignty over the interpreting subject, disclosing new modes of being and hence giving to the subject a new capacity to know himself (*IT*, p. 94). Ricoeur uses the term "second naiveté" to refer to the general hermeneutical idea that we receive self-understanding from texts rather than from the autonomous ego. It is a second Copernican revolution that dethrones the Cartesian ego from its self-founding pedestal. "To understand is not to project oneself into the text but to expose oneself to it. . . . [I]t is the *matter of the text* which gives the reader his dimension of subjectivity" (*HHS*, p. 94, emphasis mine). Though Ricoeur does not employ the term, I think it is fair to say that here too, with the notion of a self-presenting *Sache* or self-manifesting matter, the event of understanding is a *miracle*.

Faith Seeking Understanding: From the Road to Gaza to the Road from the Cross

Miracle or not, understanding does in fact happen (though not nearly enough!). The Ethiopian in Acts 8 eventually understands what he is reading. He understands the divine as well as the human authorial discourse, led as he is by Philip and the Holy Spirit to see what Isaiah's text is really about. And his understanding is evidenced in his action; he gets baptized.[58]

This is not the place to develop a full-orbed theological hermeneutics. I will therefore limit myself to adding a distinctly *theological* description to (and commentary on) what the philosophers (viz., Gadamer and Ricoeur) have said concerning discourse and the "miracle" of understanding. Whatever differences emerge between philosophical and theological descriptions of the event of understanding are no doubt symptomatic of the broader way in which philosophy and theology relate. As we have seen, both Gadamer and Ricoeur make generous use of theological concepts in their philosophical hermeneutics. But how do they conceive the relation of philosophy and theology?

The following typology is not intended to be comprehensive, merely representative of certain ways in which philosophers discourse with or about theological categories. Neither Ricoeur nor Gadamer fits into the extreme position, which is to *eliminate* all trace of theological categories. Nor are they so disrespectful of the integrity of theology that they go to the opposite extreme and *assimilate* these categories for their own purposes. On the contrary, Ricoeur and Gadamer seek to *appropriate* or *approximate* theological categories to clarify or illustrate something philosophical.[59] My concern, however, is that even these more moderate strategies end up treating theological categories as merely *notional*. The notions of "God" or "revelation" or "miracle" are invoked, but they do not do any real conceptual work.[60] It is a weakness of philosophical hermeneutics that, in its search for self-understanding, it cannot fully acknowledge Calvin's dictum that "there is no self-knowledge without knowledge of God." I therefore propose in the present section not merely to approximate, much less to correlate, theology with philosophy, but rather to *activate* theological categories, to make them *operational* rather than merely notional.[61]

Credo: An Interpreter's Confession

I begin with a hermeneutical confession, an acknowledgement of what I think I know about authors, texts, and meaning. It is not a manifesto because I am declaring, not showing, what I believe, though hopefully the present essay does practice what it preaches toward the authors mentioned herein.

I believe, with Gadamer and Ricoeur, that hermeneutics is ultimately a matter of discerning the discourse—what someone says to someone about something—in the text as work. To be sure, there are a number of subsidiary aims interpreters can have: to reconstruct the history of a text's composition; to determine how a text functioned in the life of its original audience; to discover something about a particular language (e.g., Greek) at the time of the text's composition; to describe the text's employment of rhetorical strategies; to study the material—social, economic, gender—conditions of a text's production; to expose the distorting influence of the ideologies behind, and in, the text; to uncover the author's motives for producing the text; to learn more about a subject matter by joining a text-generated conversation; to learn more about oneself in light of the mode of being displayed in the text; to imagine what a text would have meant had I been its author. However, if the ultimate aim is discerning the discourse in the work, one has to discern what the author said and did with regard to a particular subject matter. For "*someone's* saying something" is as intrinsic and essential an element of discourse as is "about something."

At this point a few clarifications may perhaps be in order. They should be fairly noncontroversial, at least to those who agree, as Ricoeur and Gadamer seem to, that the task of hermeneutics is to discern the discourse in the text. To begin with: the text is a work of discourse. Specifically, the text is a verbal work by which or in which various persons have made or discovered the attempt to say something about something. As such, the text is the site for a work of meaning. Meaning, furthermore, exists only for persons. Strictly speaking, inanimate physical objects (such as tables, trees, and texts) cannot mean (unless of course, they are made—or in the case of the heavens, created by God to declare his glory—to mean). To mean is something persons do. Words in a language system have dictionary definitions, but these are only indications of the meanings these terms typically have for persons in society.

A text is an instance of discourse because someone has put the language system into motion in order to say something to someone about something. "Putting the language system into motion" means using the conventional meanings associated with a language at a particular time and place. Of course, meaning can be imputed to a text by persons other than the historical agent responsible for first producing the physical object.[62] Some distinguish the creator of the text as an object and "the author of the text as an utterance—the person who first ascribes meaning to the relevant physical object."[63] Certain strong "applications" of the text are such that a later interpreter may be the first to ascribe a certain meaning to the text. In such cases, we might say that the interpreter becomes the author *of that meaning*, for the interpreter becomes the "someone" who "says something about something," and because what is said goes beyond the discourse of the historical author (what the historical author could have meant). The key question for interpretation thus becomes: *whose discourse, and whose understanding counts, and why?*

Obviously, we cannot say how a text will be received or applied in the future. In this sense, its understanding is indeterminate.[64] But there is no reason why we cannot discern how the epistle to the Romans, for example, has been understood by persons in the past, including its author. Again, the key question for interpretation is *whose* discourse/understanding counts: are we more interested in what Paul is saying to his readers about the gospel or in what Barth is saying. Whose discourse—whose saying something about something—are we after? Those who doubt that the author's discourse can be recovered must explain how, if we cannot access *that* past meaning, we are able to say how texts have been understood in the past by others. I believe that we can to some extent recover both, and that it is important to acknowledge which task we are undertaking at any given time. Whenever one lodges a claim with regard to the meaning of the text, one must specify: meaning *for whom?* Texts have neither meanings nor intentions apart from being considered *someone's*. In short: discourse is always *someone's* performance.[65]

I believe in authorial discourse, then, and in the possibility of understanding it with relative adequacy.[66] I have argued for this at length elsewhere.[67] To interpret a text obliges us to try to discover what authors were doing in tending to their words/texts in just this way/these ways. Is it possible, however, that part of what authors are doing in tending to their words is "intending" (in the technical sense of directing their consciousness toward) certain matters of which they had only a partial grasp? There is good reason to think that such was precisely the case with the Isaianic text the Ethiopian was reading. The author of Isaiah was directing his attention to the (for him) incomplete and therefore vague notion of the Suffering Servant. In a real sense, then, the author of Isaiah "intended" more than that of which he was explicitly aware. The *Sache* to which Isaiah was ultimately referring in his so-called Servant Songs turns out to be the Son of God incarnate in Jesus Christ.

Surely this example can be presented as evidence in Gadamer's defense? For here is a case where the human author *says* more than he can *know*. In fact, I do not think this example proves Gadamer's rule. It is instead a case of what Wolterstorff calls double agency discourse, in which the divine discourse is discerned in the light of the canonical context taken as a whole. While a theologian might be able to make sense of this notion, a philosopher would be ill-advised to take the Ethiopian's Gaza road experience as paradigmatic for the event of understanding.

While we're on the subject of authorial discourse, let me here take a moment—two paragraphs to be exact—to address Wolterstorff's concern with an earlier statement of my position. First, the concession: my earlier work suffers from certain conceptual imprecisions. For example, a text is not itself a communicative act but a medium of illocutionary acts. Second, the rebuttal: Wolterstorff is troubled by language of "authorial intention," and he draws a sharp contrast between trying to get at the author's intention and trying to get at what the author said. As one who reads to recover what the author has said and done (viz., the illocutionary acts), I feel that I have gotten a bad rap (as Wolterstorff thinks Schleiermacher did at the hands of Gadamer, and for much the same reason!). I am not interested in recreating the inner life of the author or in reconstructing the author's motives but in giving a description, as thick as it is correct, of the author's *Akt des Redens* (speech act, discourse).

In the course of criticizing Ricoeur, Wolterstorff considers what is involved in interpreting nonliteral discourse. He notes: "what leads us to infer that the sentence is being used non-literally is not facts about how it functions in its linguistic context . . . but rather our knowledge that the speaker wouldn't have wanted to say what he would have to be reckoned as saying if he had been speaking literally."[68] Is not "wanted to say" very closely tied to "intended to say"? Indeed, for my own part it is too close for comfort! I worked hard at distinguishing my use of the concept "intention," drawn from recent work in the philosophy of action, from the psychological sense of the term ("planned to"). Like Wolterstorff, I practice authorial discourse interpretation; I am interested in discovering what an author said/did in tending to his or her words in just this way. And, while I am happy to abandon the term "intention" and speak simply of authorial discourse, I find that the term is virtually unavoidable in certain circumstances. In assessing degrees of liability for criminal action in a court of law, for instance, the agent's intention (which should not simply be equated with premeditation) is everything. And, with regard to interpretation, how else can we understand whether or not a text is, say, ironic if not by some kind of an appeal, however nuanced, to the author's intended meaning, where "intended" means not "planned" but something like "directed one's energies and attention toward"? But these are minor disagreements, I think, and should not be allowed to overshadow the substantial agreement between us. We are both in search of the right words, as Gadamer might say, and no doubt we would find them over an extended conversation (accompanied by the appropriate libations, of course!).

The Mystification of Secular Hermeneutical Reason: A Critique

From the standpoint of authorial discourse interpretation, Gadamer's account of the miracle of understanding remains something of a mystery. Just how the *Sache* comes to language in the process of conversation is positively mystifying, not least because of the merely notional role that his appeal to theological hermeneutics plays in his argument. On the one hand, Gadamer makes an exception of the Christian kerygma to his hermeneutics; on the other, he appeals to the Christian doctrine of the Incarnation at a crucial point in his account of the "ontological shift of hermeneutics guided by language," to use the words that make up the title of the third and final part of *Truth and Method.*

To return to Gadamer's central insight: understanding is not a methodical activity of the subject, but something that the *Sache* does and that the interpreting subject "suffers." The miracle is undergirded by an ontology: "Being that can be understood is language" (*TM*, p. 474). The interpreting subject is neither the active agent of understanding nor simply a passive recipient but rather "in the middle" of an all-encompassing process in which one nevertheless participates, as in a game. But in what kind of process do interpreters find themselves caught up? According to Gadamer, it is a thoroughly *verbal* process, namely, a conversation (*TM*, p. 384). The miracle of understanding, the self-presentation of the *Sache,* happens in and through and *as* conversation: "a conversation has a spirit of its own . . . the language in which it is conducted bears its own truth within it . . . [and] allows something to 'emerge' which henceforth exists" (*TM*, p. 383). As we have seen, what ultimately matters to Gadamer in a conversation is understanding the *Sache,* not one's conversation partner (*TM*, pp. 394–95). Furthermore, conversation is not simply something that we do; it is something that we *are.* The task of ontology is thus to describe the conversation that we are.

Understanding is a being-spoken-to, a happening that is not the result of the interpreting subject's doing, but a happening *in* language (the middle or medium in which the process of understanding takes place) (*TM*, p. 389). Language is not the object but the medium of thought. It is just here, in his account of the ontology of language, that Gadamer invokes an analogy with the Incarnation. However, instead of relating it to the theme of embodiment, Gadamer employs the idea of Incarnation to address the relationship between human speech and thought. To be precise: the mystery of the unity of God the Father and God the Son "is reflected in the phenomenon of language" (*TM*, p. 419). The point in both cases is that the act of becoming—God into man; thought into speech—is *not* the kind "in which something turns into something else" (*TM*, p. 420). Eberhard's paraphrase is apt: "The spoken word reveals thinking to us because speaking and thinking are *homoousios*."[69]

It turns out that the "miracle" of understanding is precisely the miracle of an "inner word" becoming an "external word" while all the while remaining itself. Language is the self-presentation of the *Sache*: "It has its being in its revealing" (*TM*, p. 421). Gadamer acknowledges that to explain the coming of being to language with the aid of Nicene theology is to risk being accused of explaining the unintelligible by the unintelligible (*TM*, p. 421). Accordingly, he presents an ontology of the "inner word" itself: "it is the subject matter thought through to the end" (*TM*, p. 422). But he explains this process in turn by appealing to the "emanation" that (according to him) characterizes the process of the Son from the Father. The process of words emanating from thought is like the flowing forth from a fountain: "Thus the process and emergence of thought is not a process of change (*motus*), not a transition from potentiality into action, but an emergence *ut actus ex actu*" (*TM*, p. 424).[70]

Gadamer's concern throughout his exposition is to stress that language is not the tool but the medium of thought. It must be kept in mind that Gadamer is developing a view of language in ontological, not epistemological, terms. This comes to the fore as well when he says that the thoughts seeking expression in words refer "not to the mind but to the thing" (*TM*, p. 426). It is not the man but the matter, as it were, that is striving to speak.

What comes into language, therefore, is different from the spoken word (*parole*) itself. The matter of discourse that understanding seeks is *not discourse*—what someone says about something in a particular language—but its *Sache*, or truth content. A word is a word "only because of what comes into language in it. Its own physical being exists only in order to disappear into what is said" (*TM*, p. 475). Despite Gadamer's appeal to the Incarnation, the notion that the *Sache* swallows up words conjures up a rather unorthodox picture in which the "inner word" overwhelms the historical particularities of discourse. The actual text assumed by the *Sache* is not the locus of the miracle, as was Christ's flesh. Rather, the miracle concerns the self-presentation of the *Sache* through the veil of textual flesh to those caught up in the contemporary conversation about it.[71] Note, too, that Gadamer distinguishes the truth of revelation or the *Sache* itself from the truth of statements about it: "The fact that the verbum is spoken differently in different languages . . . means only that it cannot reveal itself through the human tongue in its true being" (*TM*, p. 420).[72]

Despite his emphasis on historical horizons, therefore, Gadamer ultimately directs understanding to what we might call *incorporeal discourse*: the self-presentation of the "inner word" or *Sache*. What authors are actually doing with language (e.g., their illocutionary acts) fades away into insignificance in the light of the being that comes to language. What happens in conversation is not our action on the *Sache* but the *Sache*'s action on us ("Tun der Sache selbst"). The "corporeal" discourse—the actual experience of conversation—is simply the means to the end of the being of language.[73]

Our first concern, then, is that Gadamer's exposition of the miracle of understanding privileges an incorporeal *Sache* to the detriment of corporeal discourse: what someone situated in a particular language says about something. The larger concern, however, is that Gadamer has not plundered the Egyptians but robbed Peter (or in this case, John) to pay Plato. For though Gadamer describes the event of understanding in terms that are formally very similar—indeed, almost identical—to those of Barth, they differ *materially* from Barth's view in radical (or should I say "secular") fashion.[74] Hence it is far from clear how a *Sache*—an anhypostatic matter that is clearly not a knowing, acting, willing *subject*—can actually make itself known in language.

It is sheer mystification to say that the process itself—whether it be "history," "mind," or "language"—*does* something to bring about understanding if the theological concepts to which one appeals in analogy have only notional force. Neither "history" nor "language" nor "play" nor "conversation" is a subject, and it is difficult to see how an impersonal process could have the ability to disclose truth. The persuasiveness of Gadamer's account would thus seem to depend on the extent to which the analogy is not simply notional but operational. The *Sache* itself does *not* literally speak or show itself to us, *except* when the subject is the sovereign speaking God (so Barth).

Martin Buber may be right to claim that "What Christianity gave the world is hermeneutics" but philosophical hermeneutics, alas, has not always returned the compliment. What we have in Gadamer's account of the "miracle" of understanding is, in the final analysis, secular reason expounding upon a secular transcendence. There is ample evidence in both Gadamer and Ricoeur that they try to "correlate" or "approximate" Christian doctrines by purely secular means. Recently, however, the very notion of secularity—the belief in purportedly objective accounts of human life untainted by faith perspectives—has been questioned, deconstructed even.[75] Yet Gadamer's account is "secular" because it employs theological categories in a merely notional fashion and, as we have seen, because it distorts orthodox doctrine in the process. As Gianni Vattimo states: "We are led to the hypothesis that hermeneutics itself, as a philosophy with certain ontological commitments, is the fruit of secularization as the renewal, pursuit, 'application' and interpretation of the substance of the Christian revelation, and preeminently the dogma of the incarnation of God."[76]

The Miracle of Understanding: An Immodest Proposal

Gadamer's description of the miracle of understanding ultimately suggests a process of—why not say it?—*grace*. The *Sache* presents—*gives*—itself in language through the (verbal) process of conversation. The miracle of understanding implies not only the Gadamerian "being which is understood is language" but the Pauline "by grace you have been given understanding through language." As we have seen, Gadamer insists that it is the *Sache* that initiates the process that catches up the interlocutors and bears them along, over and above their own willing and doing. I therefore submit that Gadamer's description illumines only if the theological concepts to which he appeals are not merely notional but operative. In short: Gadamer's description of the hermeneutical condition ultimately fails *unless* it employs Christian categories and makes them not simply illustrative but operational.

Ironically, Gadamer's description seems most appropriate as a description of how the *Sache* of the Bible makes itself known, even though Gadamer himself makes something of an exception of the Christian kerygma. What if Barth were right about the paradigmatic nature of biblical interpretation? What if we were to dare to promote this special hermeneutic for the sake of a better general hermeneutic? I am not suggesting that every book must be read exactly as we do the Scriptures; I am rather suggesting that we take theological categories seriously (e.g., operationally) even for the project of general hermeneutics. Why? Because, as Gadamer rightly insists (against Descartes and his ilk), hermeneutics is a matter not merely of methods but of ontology, which is to say, *anthropology*.

Amending Barth, then, we might say that for the sake of better general ontology it must therefore dare to be this special (e.g., Christian) ontology, that for the sake of better anthropology it must therefore dare to be a theological anthropology. My proposal, as radical as it is unapologetic, is that we *employ specifically Christian categories not only notionally but operationally for the sake of a description of the miracle of understanding and of the being whose being consists in understanding.*[77] I am assuming not that ontology is one thing for Christians and another for non-Christians, but that human being is inadequately described if we neglect the resources of Christian faith, and in particular, the creation-fall-redemption-consummation narrative framework of Scripture. If in Christ all things are indeed made new, this fact should have some kind of ontological significance.

How can those who consistently repress the truth in unrighteousness (Rom 1:18) ever engage in conversations in which they let themselves be told something, especially when that something is threatening to their whole way of life (e.g., prideful self-love)? In order for understanding to "happen," interpreters must exhibit certain virtues (e.g., openness, humility, attention). To the extent that these virtues are fruits of the Spirit, or at the very least evidences of common grace, a hermeneutics will be able to get beyond "thin" descriptions of the event of understanding only by employing distinctly theological categories (e.g., sin, sanctification). Barth is therefore right to wonder whether we can ever take the *willingness to understand* for granted: "Not even myths or persons like Goethe for instance can be understood without this initial willingness, that is, without something such as *the school of the Holy Spirit*."[78] Whereas Gadamer speaks of effective historical consciousness, a Christian account may well want to explore the category of effective *pneumatic* consciousness.

To be sure, the Spirit's ministry of the Word of God is unique and distinct. Yet to the extent that the interpretative virtues (e.g., humility, openness) are spiritual virtues, it may be that the Spirit performs a ministry of "word" and *Sache* as well. And this brings us back to the question of the agent of understanding. Given Christian ontological categories, how might one describe the miracle of understanding? Augustine employed Christological concepts operationally in his *De Magistro* to claim that understanding dawns not from an "inner word" but from an "inner teacher," namely, Jesus Christ. This was Augustine's solution to the paradox of which came first: a knowledge of the sign or a knowledge of the reality to which the sign refers. According to Augustine, the reality to which a sign refers is known through consulting the inner teacher, through whom all things were made.

Eberhard's own response to the question concerning the agency of understanding is to liken Gadamer's process of understanding to the mediality of faith. Whereas Gadamer views understanding as something that happens to us "over and above our willing and doing," Eberhard recalls Paul's comment in Philippians 2:13 that "God is at work in you, both to will and to work for his good pleasure." Christian faith does not only seek understanding; it *mediates* it: "Faith as an object of our knowledge and faith as a gift from God are exclusive alternatives only as long as one keeps thinking in terms of subject and object instead of subject and verb."[79] Faith, then, is not something one merely does or merely has but a *Sache* the subject gets involved in but never controls: "Interpreting faith as a *Sache* allows one to understand it as something we do while it happens to us."[80] One's (ontological) location in the process is the key: "Hermeneutics says that we are in conversation; from a Christian perspective we are in Christ."[81]

This is not to say that the miracle of understanding is reduced to one's mystical union with Christ. No, a robust doctrine of Incarnation demands that we reject the notion of disembodied discourse and give due attention and respect to *corporeal* discourse: what someone in a particular time and place and language says to someone about something. While I agree with Barth and Gadamer that understanding is not to be identified with (or reduced to) coming to know the conditions behind authorial discourse—the reasons why an author said what he said—the question remains whether we can understand textual discourse without also understanding *what the author said/did* with respect to the matter of the text. No *Sache*, except the living Logos, is self-presenting; on the contrary, what we understand in discourse is someone's *witness* to the *Sache*.

Finally, it is doubtful whether the event of understanding is best described as a "fusion of horizons." Love is always for another—that is, an *other*—and this demands what Bakhtin calls "outsidedness."[82] Barth dismisses as Romantic the notion that love means "losing oneself in another." What kind of loving unity is signaled by Gadamer's phrase "the fusion of horizons"? Is it the love that makes two into one or a love that remains dialogical, a *plural* unity?[83] Interestingly enough, just before he turns to discuss the doctrine of Scripture in the *Church Dogmatics*, Barth says that love has to do with receiving a witness. Understanding requires love: not just interest in a person *in abstracto* but interest in and patient attention to what that person is saying.[84] We can read not just for the information transmitting—the truth claim of the *Sache*—but for what the author is *doing* with the *Sache*, and for the author's perspective on the *Sache*. It is one thing to understand discourse—what *someone* says about something—and quite another to understand what that discourse is *about*. The two tasks are intimately related, but they should not be confused.

My immodest proposal thus consists in the recommendation that we replace the sub-Christian, secular ontology presupposed by philosophical hermeneutics with a distinctly Christian ontology of understanding—one that would make Augustinian and Trinitarian categories not merely notional but operational. I do not claim to have done that here, only to have called for it, and perhaps to have given some indication of its promise. On the other hand, to the extent that Gadamer uses theological ideas in a notional manner only, they fail to do real explanatory work, and in the end we are left contemplating not a miracle of understanding, but an obscure *myth* . . .

Conclusion: Enlightened Understanding— An Impossible Possibility?

"As ministers we ought to speak of God. We are human, however, and so cannot speak of God. We ought therefore to recognize both our obligation and our inability and by that very recognition give God the glory."[85] This was Barth's manifesto for dialectical theology, his statement of the "impossible possibility" of doing theology. Philosophical hermeneutics sets forth a similar tension: "As interpreters we ought to understand (grasp the *Sache*). We are situated humans, however, and so cannot understand. We ought therefore to recognize both our obligation and our inability and . . ." And *what*? At this point the theorists of interpretation disagree.

Why do the hermeneuticians rage? Perhaps it is because debates about what understanding is are inextricably tied up with our anthropologies and self-understandings. The ultimate anthropological question amounts to just this: are human beings *answerable* and, if so, to whom? John Webster rightly comments that "the very activity of interpretation is itself an episode in the struggle between faith and repudiation of God."[86] Discourse is demanding. Too many words demand things of us that we would prefer not to give: attention, energy, obedience, love. Yet no amount of hermeneutical sophistication or deconstructive deferral can lessen the urgent and persistent interrogatives and imperatives that confront us in biblical discourse: who do you say that he is? Repent and believe!

Understanding—of texts, family members, situations, God—is a wonderful thing but all too rare an experience. Given the law of supply and demand, understanding—like wisdom—is greatly to be prized. Yet some people evidently do understand one another, and the Scriptures too—the latter evidenced by so many joining the company of the baptized. Is the miracle of understanding thus an impossible possibility? No more so than the event of salvation! In both cases, there seems to be a kind of "grace" involved, one moreover that involves both faith (being caught up in, an active surrendering to) and works (an active participation in) the "matter" at hand. The purpose of this essay has been to assess the adequacy of Gadamer's description of what happens in the event of understanding. Everything depends on how one describes the nature of and the conditions for one's participation in the *Sache*.

All parties to the conversation agree that the miracle of understanding involves a kind of enlightenment. The question is: what *kind* of enlightenment?

For Descartes, and for many in the modern West, reason is an instrument for "seeing" in the mind's eye, a kind of intellectual scope (e.g., micro-, tele-, peri-) that brings things into focus through the power of its operation. Reason is moreover a scope that contains the source of its own light, a beacon that shines on those things toward which the mind directs its attention. Given enough light, the mind is able to form "clear and distinct" notions of what is there. Understanding is on this view a by-product of the active subject's agency on the matter.

By contrast, enlightening is for Gadamer not something that subjects do so much as something that is done to them. When being appears in language, human consciousness is not the active agency but the clearing space into which the *Sache* shines as it presents itself in language. Call it hermeneutical fideism: an enlightening conversation, like art, needs no justification: "The experience of the enlightening perspective requires no further justification; it is enlightening. To ask what one should believe is to presume that what was experienced was not enlightening."[87] "Enlightenment" for Gadamer is not a matter of perceiving a correspondence between one's idea and a state of affairs as it was for Descartes. There is no comparing something linguistic with something nonlinguistic because the *Sache* appears in, and *as*, language, not as something extralinguistic. The human subject is a (purely?) passive recipient of enlightenment: "This event is primarily an act of the thing itself and not a judgment of consciousness."[88] Contra Descartes, it is the *matter* that enlightens the subject.

What Gadamer says makes perfect sense for Barth, but only perhaps with regard to the matter of Scripture. For the *Sache* of the Bible is not a subject matter but an active and sovereign subject: Jesus Christ, the living logos, the "true light that enlightens every man" (Jn 1:9). Of course, one cannot read every other book like the Bible; for no other book has the self-communicating presence and action of God as its *Sache* as does Scripture. According to John Webster, Scripture is clear because "God is light" and the one whose splendor radiates out from the witness of the prophets and apostles. The Holy Spirit sanctifies the human words of Scripture and employs human discourse to publish the gospel.[89] Uniquely in the case of Scripture, then, the *Sache* does in fact shine of its own accord; the *res* is resplendent. Christ presents himself.

And what of other, non-biblical texts? Whence comes enlightenment for understanding them? Do interpreters more resemble active Cartesian subjects or passive Gadamerian recipients? Is there a place for a theological description of the general hermeneutic event? Most definitely, for hermeneutics after Gadamer has become ontology, and Christians have something distinctive to say about the human condition—including human noetic functions such as understanding—in light of creation, the fall, and redemption. No description of the human hermeneutical condition is complete if it mentions only finitude and not fallenness besides. Significantly enough, there is a special theological category to account for why those who lack Christian faith may nevertheless understand: common grace.[90] Because Christians are *simul justus et peccator*, they too need the Spirit's sanctifying work in their lives in order better to cultivate the interpretative virtues such as openness and humility. Nonetheless, those who lack faith will find it harder to understand those things that come closest to challenging their denials, both theoretical and practical, of God and the gospel.

Does the miracle of understanding depend on nothing more than the sanctification of the interpreter? Can we go further? Yes. We can follow Augustine and make the Christological categories to which philosophical hermeneutics ascribes *fully* operational. For Augustine, the analogy between physical and mental light not only illustrates but explains how the mind comes to know things: Christ is the light in, by, and through whom all intelligible things are illumined. Illumination is the operative term. Yet it need not imply that human subjects are merely passive recipients. Augustine suggests that the human mind *participates* in the divine light. Moreover, he writes that illumination "plays a role in believing, knowing, remembering, imagining, sensing, and, in fact, every area of knowledge."[91] It is Christ, according to Augustine, who shines in all that's meaningful.

"I am illumined" and "I understand" are thus middle-voiced terms. The miracle of understanding is not that the interpreter is either simply active or simply passive before the object of understanding, but rather that the interpreter is located in an all-encompassing process (or rather *person*?) in which he or she is nevertheless active. Described in terms of Christian categories, this process is nothing less than conformity to Christ. The Christian interpreter is not simply in a conversation; he or she is "in Christ." Is understanding an impossible possibility? Certainly not! "I can do all things *in* him who strengthens me" (Phil 4:13).

NOTES

1. Paul Ricoeur, *Hermeneutics and the Human Sciences*, trans. and ed. John B. Thompson (Cambridge: Cambridge University Press, 1981), p. 111. Hereafter abbreviated *HHS* in the text.

2. Hans-Georg Gadamer, *Truth and Method*, 2nd rev. ed., trans. Joel Weinsheimer and Donald G. Marshall (New York: Continuum, 2002), p. 292. Hereafter abbreviated *TM* in the text.

3. Wendell Berry, *Jayber Crow* (Washington, DC: Counterpoint, 2000).

4. See especially my *Is There a Meaning in This Text? The Bible, the Reader, and the Morality of Literary Knowledge* (Grand Rapids: Zondervan, 1998).

5. For more on the distinction between normative and descriptive approaches, see William Irwin, *Intentionalist Interpretation: A Philosophical Explanation and Defense* (Westport, CT: Greenwood Press, 1999), ch. 1.

6. Gadamer too acknowledges that discourse is a matter of someone saying something to someone else about something (see his *Philosophical Hermeneutics*, trans. David E. Linge

[Berkeley: University of California, 1976], p. 101), but, as we shall see, he gives inordinate pride of place to the latter element: "about something."

7. I deal with the nature of Philip's "help" at greater length in *The Drama of Doctrine: A Canonical-Linguistic Approach to Theology* (Louisville: Westminster John Knox, 2005), ch. 4.

8. My interrogation of Gadamer is limited to this one point. With regard to his critique of the Enlightenment prejudice against prejudice, his rehabilitation of authority, and his recovery of *phronesis*, I am largely in agreement.

9. Irwin, *Intentionalist Interpretation*, p. 114.

10. René Descartes, *Discourse on Method and Related Writings*, trans. Desmond M. Clarke (London and New York: Penguin, 1999), p. 58. Henceforth abbreviated *DM* in the text.

11. There is some debate in the secondary literature as to whether we *will* to believe clear and distinct ideas. For a brief, though somewhat dated, introduction to this question, see Bernard Williams, "Descartes," in *The Encyclopedia of Philosophy*, ed. Paul Edwards, vol. 2 (New York: Macmillan, 1967), pp. 344–54.

12. The author of *Discourse* at one point addresses contemporary interpreters: "I want to plead here with future generations never to believe something if they are told that it originated with me, when I have not published it myself" (*DM*, 49). I suspect that Descartes would strongly resist identifying the meaning of his text with the tradition of its interpretation.

13. James Cargile, "Descartes, René," in *The Oxford Companion to Philosophy*, ed. Ted Honderich (Oxford: Oxford University Press, 1995), p. 189.

14. Karl Barth, "The Strange New World within the Bible," in *The Word of God and the Word of Man* (Gloucester, MA: Peter Smith, 1978), p. 43.

15. Bruce McCormack comments that Barth's task was to try to think "from a standpoint lying in God Himself" (*Karl Barth's Critically Realistic Dialectical Theology: Its Genesis and Development 1909–1936* [Oxford: Clarendon, 1995], p. 129).

16. Richard E. Burnett claims that Barth's text "challenged the most influential tradition of the nineteenth and twentieth centuries, the hermeneutical tradition of Schleiermacher and Dilthey" (*Karl Barth's Theological Exegesis* [Tübingen: Mohr Siebeck, 2001], p. 49). Barth was as revolutionary to the hermeneutical tradition of his day as Descartes was to the scientific tradition of his.

17. First preface to 1922 ed., cited in Burnett, *Barth's Theological Exegesis*, p. 277 (emphasis mine).

18. Barth, *The Epistle to the Romans*, trans. Edwyn C. Hoskyns (London: Oxford University Press, 1968), p. x. Hereafter abbreviated *Rom* in the text. Similarly, Brevard Childs aims to have his Biblical Theology move "from a description of the biblical witness to the object toward which these witnesses point, that is, to their subject matter, substance, or *res*" (Childs, *A Biblical Theology of the Old and New Testaments* [Minneapolis: Fortress, 1993], p. 80).

19. McCormack comments that "The theme of the Bible is a *dialectical relation*; the relation of a holy God to a fallen creature and the crisis which results from such an encounter" (*Barth's Critically Realistic Dialectical Theology*, p. 271).

20. Barth, "Strange New World within the Bible," p. 33.

21. See Christoph Schwöbel, "Theology," in *The Cambridge Companion to Karl Barth*, ed. John B. Webster (Cambridge: Cambridge University Press, 2000), p. 29.

22. Karl Barth, *Church Dogmatics* II/1 (Edinburgh: T and T Clark, 1956–75), p. 257. Hereafter abbreviated *CD* in the text.

23. Burnett, *Barth's Theological Exegesis*, p. 49.

24. Ibid.

25. Ibid., p. 259.

26. See Burnett, *Barth's Theological Exegesis*, p. 17. Other scholars conclude that Barth's commentary said more about Barth than it did about Paul.

27. Barth, Preface Draft II, cited in Burnett, *Barth's Theological Exegesis*, p. 284.

28. Or, in Schleiermacher's terms, the assumption "that each person contains a minimum of everyone else," cited in Burnett, *Barth's Theological Exegesis*, p. 154.

29. See Burnett, *Barth's Theological Exegesis*, p. 197, n. 287, on whether Barth was ambivalent to the concept of authorial intention. For more on the notion of "attending" the text, see my *Is There a Meaning in This Text?* pp. 247, 262.

30. Barth, Preface Draft IA, cited in Burnett, *Barth's Theological Exegesis*, p. 281.

31. Apparently Gadamer had such an experience upon reading Aristotle in Heidegger's class: the text "asserted itself and captivated us before we can come to ourselves and be in a position to test the claim to meaning that it makes" (*TM*, p. 490).

32. Irwin, *Intentionalist Interpretation*, p. 82.

33. Gadamer, *Hans-Georg Gadamer on Education, Poetry, and History*, ed. Dieter Misgeld and Graeme Nicholson (Albany: SUNY, 1992), p. 152.

34. Robert Bernasconi comments that philosophers tend to discount dialogue unless it is "about something" ("'You Don't Know What I'm Talking About': Alterity and the Hermeneutic Ideal," in *The Specter of Relativism: Truth, Dialogue, and Phronesis in Philosophical Hermeneutics*, ed. Lawrence K. Schmidt (Evanston: Northwestern University Press, 1995), p. 190.

35. Interestingly enough, according to Gadamer it is only when one finds oneself unable to take what an author says as true that we have recourse to authorial intentions!

36. Bernasconi, "Alterity and the Hermeneutical Ideal," p. 184.

37. Gadamer comments that even the questioning that generates a conversation is "more a passion than an action" (*TM*, 366).

38. Philippe Eberhard, *The Middle Voice in Gadamer's Hermeneutics* (Tübingen: Mohr Siebeck, 2004).

39. Ibid., p. 2.

40. See *TM*, 104–10, especially p. 105, where Gadamer mentions the "medial" sense.

41. Irwin, *Intentionalist Interpretation*, p. 80.

42. Eberhard, *Middle Voice*, p. 98.

43. Ibid., p. 82.

44. Ibid., p. 105.

45. Joel C. Weinsheimer, *Gadamer's Hermeneutics: A Reading of Truth and Method* (New Haven: Yale University Press, 1985), p. 257.

46. Because languages are perspectival, there is no one language that speaks the whole truth. It would therefore be more accurate to say that the *Sache* presents a perspective of itself and of its truth in language.

47. Eberhard, *Middle Voice*, p. 112.

48. Ibid., p. 111.

49. Note that metaphysics for Gadamer is "philosophizing in the hope of finding the right word" (Eberhard, *Middle Voice*, p. 120). Just which criteria Gadamer employs is the

subject of continuing dispute. See Lawrence K. Schmidt, "Uncovering Hermeneutic Truth," in *The Specter of Relativism*, pp. 72–83.

50. Irwin points out by way of criticism, however, that this criterion fails to rule out multiple, mutually contradictory interpretations of the whole (*Intentionalist Interpretation*, pp. 96–97).

51. So Jean Grondin, *Hermenutische Warheit? Zum Wahrheitsbegriff Hans-Georg Gadamers* (Königstein: Athenäum, 1982).

52. Eberhard, *Middle Voice*, p. 182.

53. Gadamer, "Herméneutique et théologie," *Revue des sciences religieuses* 51:4 (1977): 389; my translation.

54. Eberhard, *Middle Voice*, p. 202.

55. Ricoeur, *Interpretation Theory: Discourse and the Surplus of Meaning* (Fort Worth: Texas Christian University Press, 1976), pp. 87–88. Abbreviated henceforth as *IT* in the text.

56. Cf. Nicholas Wolterstorff's critique in *Divine Discourse* (Cambridge: Cambridge University Press, 1995), ch. 8, especially the section "What happened to discourse in Ricoeur?" pp. 148–52. Note that these critical questions do not lessen my appreciation for what Ricoeur has to say about the importance of form and literary genre.

57. Ricoeur comments: "The link between disclosure and appropriation is, to my mind, the cornerstone of a hermeneutic" (*IT*, p. 93).

58. "To get baptized" (at least as an adult) is a quintessential middle-voice action in which the subject gets caught up in a broader process (viz., incorporation into Christ) while nevertheless remaining active (viz., confessing faith).

59. Yet another strategy is to *procrastinate*, that is, to defer action or opinion with regard to theology. This does not eliminate theology in theory, but it tends to do so in practice.

60. How can one ever know whether or not an author's use of a concept is "purely notional"? This is a fair question, especially as concerns matters of personal faith. With regard to internal evidence, there is a point in Gadamer's argument where he simply admits that "the theological question as such can be of no further help to us" (*TM*, p. 421). There is also some evidence that toward the end of his life Gadamer was interested in the conversation between the world religions as an avenue to transcendence. The question remains, however, whether he was working with a secular or a distinctly Christian conception of transcendence. As Ricoeur observes: "One must choose between the 'encipherment' of all things, and the Christian Incarnation" ("The Relation of Jasper's Philosophy to Religion," in *The Philosophy of Karl Jaspers*, ed. P. A. Schlipp [New York: Tudor, 1957], p. 624). See further on Gadamer's own relation to Christian faith, Eberhard, *Middle Voice*, pp. 177 ff. and Jens Zimmerman, *Recovering Theological Hermeneutics: An Incarnational-Trinitarian Theory of Interpretation* (Grand Rapids: Baker Academic, 2004), ch. 5.

61. I am grateful to Mark Bowald for alerting me to the importance of this distinction.

62. Alexander Nehamas makes a similar distinction. The "writer" is the historical person who is the efficient cause of the text's production; the "author" is whoever "meant" a particular meaning. For Nehamas, the author should always be seen as a plausible historical variant of the writer. Hence a text cannot mean what its writer could not historically have meant. See "Writer, Text, Work, Author," in *Literature and the Question of Philosophy*, ed. Anthony J. Cascardi (Baltimore: Johns Hopkins University Press, 1987), pp. 265–91.

63. Mark Bevir, "What Is a Text? A Pragmatic Theory," *International Philosophical Quarterly* 42 (2002): 503. Obviously, in many cases, the author of a text is also its creator.

64. To borrow an analogy from the philosophy of science, we could say that interpretations (theories about what a text means) are always "underdetermined" by the textual data.

65. This is true also of what Wolterstorff calls "performance interpretation," though he restricts this term to the attempt by persons other than the author to say what a text means.

66. I don't see the need to go so far and claim that there is perfect adequation between meaning as an "ideal object" and the reader's interpretation of it. I see meaning not as an ideal object but as an actual act, a communicative act. We understand texts more or less the way we understand human agents in general—which is to say, neither perfectly nor exhaustively but with relative adequacy for everyday purposes. In this respect, my credo resembles Bruce Benson's in "'Now I would not have you ignorant': Derrida, Gadamer, Hirsch and Husserl on Authors' Intentions," in *Evangelicals and Scripture: Tradition, Authority and Hermeneutics*, ed. Vincent Bacote, Laura C. Miguélez, and Dennis L. Okholm (Downers Grove, IL: InterVarsity Press, 2004), pp. 173–91, esp. p. 173.

67. See *Is There a Meaning in This Text?* and *First Theology: God, Scripture, and Hermeneutics* (Downers Grove, IL: InterVarsity Press, 2002), ch. 6.

68. Wolterstorff, *Divine Discourse*, p. 151.

69. Eberhard, *Middle Voice*, p. 182; cf. Gadamer: "The inner mental word is just as consubstantial with thought as if God the Son with God the Father" (*TM*, p. 421).

70. Gadamer acknowledges significant differences between the formation of human and divine thoughts, but these are inconsequential for the purposes of the present analysis.

71. Of which Christological heresy is Gadamer's position the hermeneutical equivalent? "Docetism" (Gk. *dokeo* = "to appear") is the heresy that claims that the Son only "appeared" to take on flesh. Does the *Sache* only "appear" to take on text? Perhaps the better comparison would be to that form of Monophysitism associated with the extreme Alexandrian view in the early church called "Apollinarianism." This position so emphasizes the one divine nature of Jesus Christ that the Logos virtually takes the place of the human mind of Jesus. The position is heretical because it ultimately calls the true humanity of Jesus into question. Gadamer's focus on the *Sache*, or "inner" word, may similarly impugn the integrity of the "external" word of authorial discourse.

72. At this point the analogy with Christology would appear to break down; for Hebrews 1:3 says that Jesus is "the exact representation" of God's being.

73. Though beyond the scope of the present chapter, a comparison with Bakhtin's conception of discourse could prove illuminating. Bakhtin too invoked Christological categories, though he drew more from Chalcedon than Nicea. For a preliminary treatment of this question, see Alexander Mihailovic, *Corporeal Words: Bakhtin's Theology of Discourse* (Evanston: Northwestern University Press, 1997).

74. Burnett agrees, observing that Gadamer, though he admires Barth's emphasis on *Sache*, "does not understand the basis of Barth's *sachlicher* approach (viz., 'the sovereign freedom of the subject matter' at issue)" (*Barth's Theological Exegesis*, p. 203, n. 307).

75. Its critique of secular reason is one of the main contributions of Radical Orthodoxy, according to James K. A. Smith, *Introducing Radical Orthodoxy* (Grand Rapids: Baker Academic, 2004), ch. 2.

76. Gianni Vattimo, *Beyond Interpretation: The Meaning of Hermeneutics for Philosophy* (Stanford University Press, 1997), p. 52.

77. See John Webster's fine theological description of biblical interpretation in *Word and Church*, pp. 47–86. One need not reduce the Bible to other types of literature to suggest that Christian dogmatics may have something distinctive to contribute to a description of reading in general. That, at least, is the suggestion I am pursuing here.

78. Barth, "Rudolf Bultmann: An Attempt to Understand Him" as translated and cited in Burnett, *Barth's Theological Exegesis*, p. 60. Burnett comments: "From the beginning,

he believed that the way we come to understand not only the Bible but the words people address to one another was by the Holy Spirit" (62).

79. Eberhard, *Middle Voice*, p. 209.

80. Ibid., p. 212.

81. Ibid., p. 217.

82. See Gary Saul Morson and Caryl Emerson, *Mikhail Bakhtin: Creation of a Prosaics* (Stanford: Stanford University Press, 1990), pp. 53–54.

83. There is some evidence that Gadamer himself would resist equating a "fusion" of horizons with an "assimilation" of horizons. In a late essay, he speaks of the "other" who "breaks into my ego-centeredness and gives me something to understand" (Gadamer, "Reflections on My Philosophical Journey," in *The Philosophy of Hans-Georg Gadamer*, ed. Lewis Edwin Hahn [Chicago: Open Court, 1997], p. 46).

84. See CD I/2 465. Note that interpreters can "love" even those authors with whom they ultimately disagree in the sense that they try to interpret those authors as *charitably* as possible.

85. Barth, *Word of God and the Word of Man*, p. 186.

86. Webster, from "On the Clarity of Scripture."

87. Lawrence K. Schmidt, "Uncovering Hermeneutic Truth," in *Specter of Relativism*, p. 79.

88. Ibid., p. 82.

89. See John B. Webster, *Holy Scripture: A Dogmatic Sketch* (Cambridge: Cambridge University Press, 2003), ch. 2.

90. See Richard J. Mouw, *He Shines in All That's Fair: Culture and Common Grace* (Grand Rapids: Eerdmans, 2001).

91. Ronald H. Nash, "Illumination, Divine," in *Augustine through the Ages: An Encyclopedia*, ed. Allan D. Fitzgerald (Grand Rapids: Eerdmans, 1999), p. 438. See also Nash, *The Light of the Mind: St. Augustine's Theory of Knowledge* (Lexington: University Press of Kentucky, 1969).

2

Resuscitating the Author

Nicholas Wolterstorff

After word was spread abroad that the title I had proposed for my talk that became this paper was "Resurrecting the Author," several correspondents pointed out to me that this title had already been used by Kevin Vanhoozer for a chapter in his book *Is There a Meaning in This Text?* I had forgotten that. What was in my mind when choosing the title were the title and last clause of Roland Barthes's well-known essay "The Death of the Author." The last clause goes like this: "we know that to give writing its future, it is necessary to overthrow the myth: the birth of the reader must be at the cost of the death of the Author." But since I believe that those who first hit on a good title should be allowed to exult in it and not have it treated as common property, my proposed title is not my actual title. My actual title is, "Resuscitating the Author." It's a better title, since the author never really was dead; all he ever needed was resuscitation!

Correspondents have not merely remarked on the non-originality of the title I had proposed for this paper; several also expressed their hopes for what would be in the paper. Some expressed the hope that the proposed title indicated that I would be interacting with the contents of Vanhoozer's chapter 5; others expressed the hope that I would be doing something overtly theological; yet others expressed the hope that I would be laying out my case for authorial discourse interpretation as forcefully as possible and with as little distraction from other issues as possible; others hoped that I would be engaging Gadamer, since I said nothing at all about him in my *Divine Discourse*; others again hoped that I would be engaging Jorge Gracia's recent book, *How Can We Know What God Means,* since they regarded that as the principal competitor on the contemporary scene to my theory of divine discourse. I have no basis for inferring that any of my readers have *high* hopes for this paper; but that all together you have *many* hopes, of that I have been left in no doubt.

I could not possibly satisfy all those hopes without being so shallow as to satisfy none of them. Since I have committed myself to reviewing Gracia's book for *The Philosophical Quarterly*, I will say nothing about that here. I will, however, engage both Gadamer and Vanhoozer in the course of setting forth, once again, my argument for authorial discourse interpretation. To my great regret, I cannot in this paper explore the implications for theology of my account of divine discourse.

An orthodoxy of twentieth-century theory of interpretation, both continental and Anglo-American, has been that interpretation is an action or set of actions performed upon an artifact, the paradigmatic species of such an artifact being a text. My view is that interpretation at bottom is not things done to an artifact but engagement with a person, albeit a mode of engagement *mediated* by the artifact; if the artifact in question is a text, it's a mode of engagement with the authorizer of the text, be it author or editor. Orthodoxy's talk is all about *texts*, not about authors; it holds that it is just the text we are dealing with when we take *Proslogion* in hand and interpret. I hold that we are engaging Anselm.

If it is a person one is engaging, then it will be appropriate to consider whether one is engaging the person justly or unjustly, rightly or wrongly, with charity or not, in an honoring or dishonoring way. But if one is acting only upon an artifact, then moral considerations will enter the picture only when one considers the consequences, for oneself or others, of what one did to the artifact. Admittedly it would be possible to hold that texts have rights; such rights, however, would not be *moral* rights.

I must be more precise about the claim I am making. Our word "interpretation" covers a variety of distinct, albeit related, activities; though Freudian interpretation is very different from the sort of thing the New Critics did when they interpreted texts, both are properly called "interpretation." It follows that it is a mistake to ask what is *the* goal and *the* nature of interpretation; it all depends on the sort of interpretation one has in mind. My own judgment is that one of the most serious flaws of the so-called hermeneutic tradition is its essentialism on this point; the question running through Gadamer's *Truth and Method* is, what is *the* nature and *the* goal of interpretation? Derrida perpetuates this essentialism; his discussion of interpretation is as essentialist as are his discussions of many other topics—for example, of *the* gift. And Vanhoozer is like the others on this point; he offers an account of what he calls "*the* goal of understanding."[1]

My claim will be that, among all the different activities that have fair claim to being called interpretation, most of the time all of us practice one, that it is basic to almost all other kinds of interpretation, and that this kind of interpretation, rather than consisting at bottom of things done to an artifact, consists of an engagement with a person, which is mediated by the artifact.

The orthodoxy in question arose as a reaction to the view that the interpretation of texts is at bottom an engagement with the person who authored the text; in that way, my view is a recovery of what preceded the formation of orthodoxy. But I join with orthodoxy in rejecting what the pre-orthodox said it was that we try to discover and understand when we interpret; that is to say, I hold that our mode of engagement with the author, when we interpret, is different from what the pre-orthodox thought it was. They held that its goal is to get at the authorizer's intention; I hold that its goal is to get at what the authorizer said. Those two, I argue, are not to be identified with each other.

The story that Gadamer tells of hermeneutics prior to his own work follows Dilthey's story in its chronicle, though not in its evaluations; whereas Dilthey praises the developments whose story he tells, Gadamer regards them as a profound error. Schleiermacher is the hero in the story, or the culprit—take your pick. Founding father of "Romantic hermeneutics," as Gadamer calls it, perhaps even of hermeneutics as such, Schleiermacher held that the main goal of text interpretation is to understand that part of the author's mental life of which the text is an "expression." Or so, at least, Dilthey and Gadamer interpret Schleiermacher. Since any part of an author's mental life can be fully understood only by placing that part in the context of the author's mental life as a whole, the goal expands to understanding the author. In Gadamer's words, "what is to be understood is . . . not only the exact words and their objective meaning, but also the individuality of the speaker or author."[2] The text, says Gadamer, is regarded by Schleiermacher "as a unique manifestation of the author's life" (*TM*, p. 191); accordingly, "what is to be understood . . . is not a shared thought about some subject matter, but individual thought that by its very nature is a free construct and the free expression of an individual human being" (*TM*, p. 188).

Among the implications Gadamer draws from this view of interpretation that he attributes to Schleiermacher are the following. Interpretation thus understood can be viewed as reversing the direction of the author's production; the aim of interpretation is to arrive at a "re-creation of the creative act," a "reproduction of the original production" (*TM*, p. 187), a "reconstruction of a construction" (*TM*, p. 189). And secondly, to view interpretation as aimed at recovering "what the author meant and expressed" (*TM*, p. 192) is tacitly to treat the text as an aesthetic artifact. In Gadamer's words, regarding "understanding in this way . . . means that the structure of thought we are trying to understand as an utterance or as a text is not to be understood in terms of its subject matter, but as an aesthetic construct, as a work of art or 'artistic thought'" (*TM*, p. 187). Texts are construed as "purely expressive phenomena" (*TM*, p. 196), and "the discourse of the individual" that generated the text as "a free creative activity" (*TM*, p. 196).

I think this is a serious misinterpretation of Schleiermacher. Schleiermacher says that the central goal of interpretation is to get at what he calls the "*Akt des Redens*" of the author; such an act is in no way to be identified with the conscious life of the author. Schleiermacher has gotten a bad rap. But on this occasion I will have to forgo speaking up on his behalf, since for the purpose of understanding the origins of twentieth-century orthodoxy, what's important is what thinkers such as Dilthey and Gadamer *interpreted* Schleiermacher as saying, not what he actually said. And though it was not Schleiermacher's view that the central goal of interpretation is to get at the author's intentions, that definitely was the view of other theorists.

What is it, according to the hermeneutic orthodoxy of the latter half of the twentieth century, that the interpreter should aim at? Here we encounter a parting of the ways among the orthodox. Deconstructionists such as Derrida offer a different answer to this question from their orthodox predecessors. They retain the orthodox position that interpretation deals with texts rather than persons; indeed, they tend to be even more ferocious on this point than their predecessors; but they have a different view as to what should be done with texts.

The pre-deconstructionist orthodoxy held that the goal of interpretation is the identification and grasping of something—the discovery and understanding of something. Specifically, the goal of interpretation, said Monroe Beardsley, the premier theorist of the so-called New Critics—I. A. Richards, William Empson, Cleanth Brooks, Rene Wellek, William Wimsatt, and others—is to discover and understand *the meaning*, or *the sense*, of the text; those in the hermeneutic tradition were of the same view. *Textual-sense interpretation*, as I call it, has been the orthodoxy of pre-deconstructionist twentieth-century interpretation theory.

In my *Divine Discourse* I focused on how Ricoeur developed the theory; on this occasion, let me look at how Gadamer developed it. There is a good deal more to Gadamer's account of interpretation than his claims as to what it is that the interpreter should try to identify and understand. Indeed, Gadamer's claims on this score are simply ignored by most commentators, partly because this part of his theory is not very well articulated, and partly because, so I guess, this is not what most charms most of Gadamer's readers. Nevertheless, it is an essential component of his account as a whole.

Return to one of the passages I quoted from Gadamer in which he is both describing and implicitly criticizing Schleiermacher's theory of interpretation, as he understands it: "What is to be understood . . . is not a shared thought about some subject matter, but individual thought that by its very nature is a free construct and the free expression of an individual being" (*TM*, p. 188). An implication here is that interpretation, if rightly practiced, will aim to discover and understand "a shared thought about some subject matter." The same point is made more forthrightly in this passage: "whenever an attempt is made to understand something . . . there is reference to the truth that lies hidden in the text and must be brought to light. What is to be understood is, in fact, not a thought considered as part of another's life, but as a truth" (*TM*, p. 185).

To get Gadamer right, a qualification must immediately be added. When interpretation is going well, we move beyond identifying and grasping "the content of what is said" to appropriate that content into our own pursuit of truth.[3] As it were, we read and interpret the text as "an inner dialogue of [our own] soul seeking understanding." But sometimes we find ourselves "disturbed" in this attempt at appropriation. Then we pause and consider the possibility that what was said was poorly expressed, or merely "the opinion of another," and so forth—though even then "one attempts to reach a substantive agreement—not just sympathetic understanding of the other person—and this in such a way that again one proceeds via the subject matter."

But sometimes one continues to be frustrated in "all these movements comprising the art of conversation—argument, question and answer, objection and refutation, which are undertaken in regard to a text as an inner dialogue of the soul seeking understanding." Only then, as a last resort, "does the effort of understanding become aware of the individuality of the Thou and take account of his *uniqueness.*" Only then do we give up on "the endeavor to understand the content of what is said"; only then do we bring the author into the picture and ask what might have led him to say such a thing, "how did he come to such an opinion"—assuming that what's said is clear enough to be an opinion. This "kind of question reveals an alienness that is clearly of a quite different kind and ultimately signifies a renunciation of shared meaning." In short, the goal of interpretation that Gadamer thinks Schleiermacher regards as normal is regarded by Gadamer as a fall-back goal; if normal interpretation is frustrated, then one falls back on becoming "aware of the individuality of the Thou and [taking] account of his *uniqueness.*"

Back, then, to interpretation when it goes well. What does Gadamer have in mind in speaking of "the meant" of the text, "the truth that lies hidden in the text," "the content of what is said," the "shared thought about some subject matter"? It is only a good deal later, in the section entitled "Language as the medium of hermeneutic experience," that he becomes explicit. "What is stated in the text," he says there, "must be detached from all contingent factors and grasped in its full ideality, in which alone it has validity" (*TM*, p. 394). More elaborately:

> [The] capacity for being written down is based on the fact that speech itself shares in the pure ideality of the meaning that communicates itself in it. In writing, the meaning of what is spoken exists purely for itself, completely detached from all emotional elements of expression and communication. A text is not to be understood as an expression of life but with respect to what it says. Writing is the abstract ideality of language. Hence the meaning of something written is only what was actually deposited in the written record. This indicates that "repetition" cannot be meant here in its strict sense. It does not mean referring back to the original source where something is said or written. The understanding of something written is not a repetition of something past but the sharing of a present meaning. (392)

Gadamer is here appropriating Frege's concept of a *Gedanke,* a *thought,* a concept that played a central role in Frege's anti-psychologism, that was later appropriated by Husserl for a variety of uses, and was then passed on to Gadamer, to Ricoeur, and to a large number of other writers. A *Gedanke,* for Frege, was not a *thinking* but *a thing thought,* not a mental state or event but an entity that can be repeatedly thought, by both the same person and others, repeatedly asserted, repeatedly expressed in language, and so forth. In the tradition of analytic philosophy it is what has customarily been called a *proposition.* It's an abstract entity, or as those in the continental tradition, echoing Plato, have preferred to call it, an "ideal" entity. Gadamer observes that when a person several times over thinks or asserts the same *Gedanke*, the *Gedanke* itself is not, strictly speaking, repeated; rather, the person repeatedly thinks or asserts the *Gedanke*; a *Gedanke* is not the ontological sort of thing that could be repeated. That which one understands, when one understands a text, is not "a repetition of something past" but "a present meaning" shared between author and interpreter. It is, if you will, an *ever*-present meaning.

Another point in the passage just quoted should be noted. Speech "shares in the pure ideality of the meaning," says Gadamer. The point he is making here was first developed by C. S. Peirce with his distinction between a word *qua* type and a word *qua* token. A word *qua* type is an abstract or ideal entity in the same way that a *Gedanke* is an ideal entity; by contrast, a word *qua* token is a concrete perishable entity—bits of ink on a page, sounds in the air. Gadamer claims that a condition of the fact that words can be written down is that they are ideal; and conversely, that "writing is the abstract ideality of language." The emphasis here must fall on the word "abstract." A text is abstracted from, detached "from all emotional elements of expression and communication"; it "exists purely for itself."

It is on account of its abstract ideality that a text is properly to be understood not "as an expression of life" but "with respect to what it says," that is, with respect to the *Gedanken* expressed. "In writing, language gains its true ideality" (*TM*, p. 391).[4] "What is fixed in writing has detached itself from the contingency of its origin and its author and made itself free for new relationships" (*TM*, p. 395). Accordingly, understanding a written text "does not mean primarily to reason one's way back into the past, but to have a present involvement in what is said. It is not really a relationship between persons, between the reader and the author (who is perhaps quite unknown), but about sharing in what the text shares with us. The meaning of what is said is . . . quite independent of whether the traditionary text gives us a picture of the author" (*TM*, pp. 391–92).

I have quoted Gadamer as saying that "the understanding of something written is . . . the sharing of a present meaning," a "sharing in what the text shares with us," and that "the meaning of something written is only what was actually deposited in the written record." Let me elaborate just a bit Gadamer's thought at this point. Suppose that what the text means at a certain point is that Napoleon overreached with his march into Russia; this is the meaning that, to quote Gadamer, was "deposited in the written record." Then when I adequately and correctly interpret the text, what I identify and grasp *as the meaning of the text* is that Napoleon overreached with his march into Russia. What I grasp is identical with what the text means. In the most literal sense, I share in what the text shares with me—again to use Gadamer's language. The achievement of such a sharing is, for Gadamer, the essence of successful interpretation.

The point is highlighted in an illuminating way by Ricoeur—though to get to the highlighting we have to take note of the way in which Ricoeur expands on Gadamer's account while nonetheless agreeing fully on the ontology of meaning. In fact, whereas Gadamer says nothing in *Truth and Method* about the ancestry of his ontology of meaning, Ricoeur explicitly traces it through Husserl to Frege. For "Frege and Husserl," says Ricoeur, "a 'meaning' . . . is not an idea that somebody has in mind. It is not a psychic content, but an ideal object which can be identified and reidentified by different individuals at different times as being one and the same. By ideality they meant that the meaning of a proposition is neither a physical nor a psychic entity." A meaning is an "omnitemporal" entity.[5]

Ricoeur expands on Gadamer's account by means of his appropriation of speech act theory. Following Austin, Ricoeur distinguishes between locutionary and illocutionary acts; and then, within the illocutionary act, he distinguishes between the propositional content of the act and the taking up of an illocutionary stance toward that content. That done, he then shapes his subsequent discussion in terms of what he calls "the dialectic" of event and meaning. Whereas the taking up of an illocutionary stance toward some propositional content is a perishing event, the propositional content itself is eternal; it is a Fregean *Gedanke.* And the meaning of the sentence—this is perhaps Ricoeur's most important move—the meaning of the sentence used to perform the illocutionary act is identical with the propositional content of the act. The meaning of the sentence "Napoleon overreached with his march into Russia" is that Napoleon overreached with his march into Russia. Accordingly, when I, by inscribing that sentence, assert that Napoleon overreached with his march into Russia, the propositional content of my illocutionary act is identical with the meaning of the sentence I used. The propositional content of my illocutionary act is, to use Gadamer's language, "deposited in the written record."

For Ricoeur, as for Gadamer, the central goal of interpretation is to identify and grasp the meanings of the sentences of the text. But since the meaning of a sentence is identical with the propositional content of the illocutionary act that the inscription of the sentence was used to perform, we can just as well say that the goal of interpretation is to identify and grasp the propositional content of the illocutionary act. To grasp the one is to grasp the other. Suppose that the sentence in the text before me is "Napoleon overreached with his march into Russia." Now abbreviate the meaning of this sentence as *P.* Then P is the meaning of the sentence, P is the propositional content of the illocutionary act, and P is that which I, the interpreter, grasp. This is as elegant as philosophical theories ever get. There is yet more elegance. Ricoeur holds that by perception, consciousness, and the like, one may be aware that something is so-and-so. Abbreviate that which I am aware of on some occasion as P, and suppose that I assert P with a sentence that means P, and that you interpret the sentence adequately and correctly. Then P is what I was aware of, P is what the sentence I used meant, P is the illocutionary content of my assertion, and P is what you grasp upon interpreting my sentence. This is elegance to the nth degree.

But why do I say that Ricoeur is a proponent of textual-sense interpretation, rather than saying that he is a proponent of propositional content interpretation, since the sense of the text and the propositional content of its initiating illocutionary act are identical? Because Ricoeur holds that, when interpreting texts at a distance from their originating events, what we have available to us is not the originating illocutionary act but only the text and its meaning.

I led into this discussion of Ricoeur with the comment that Ricoeur *highlights* the way in which, on Gadamer's account, *Gedanken* function in interpretation; but thus far I have focused exclusively on the way in which Ricoeur expands on Gadamer's account. So on to the highlighting. An obvious question to ask of Ricoeur is, what happened to the stance component of the originating illocutionary act? All the emphasis has been on the propositional content of the act. What role, if any, is played in interpretation by the author's taking up of an illocutionary stance toward the propositional content? When we interpret are we not interested, for example, in whether we are dealing with fiction or biography? Yet grasping the meanings of the sentences, and thus the propositional content of the originating illocutionary acts, will not tell us anything one way or the other on this score, since the very same sentences occur in fiction and biography.

Even Ricoeur's most devoted followers will have to concede that what he says on this matter is vague and indecisive. The fact of his vagueness and indecisiveness is less important than the reason for it, however. Ricoeur concedes that sometimes it is important to determine the character of the originating illocutionary stance; and he notes that texts do, fairly often, carry what he calls "marks" of those stances. But the relation of those marks to those stances is very different from the relation of the sentences to the propositional content. The meaning of the sentence *just is* the propositional content of the originating illocutionary act; they are identical. By contrast, the taking up of an illocutionary stance toward that propositional content is a perishing event. The meanings of the marks of that event, if indeed we can properly think of the marks as having meanings, are not identical with the event; rather, the marks are *evidence* of the originating event. If I draw the right inferences from the mark, then I come to believe, say, that the originating stance was an act of asserting. That which I thus come to believe, namely, that the originating stance was an act of asserting, is indeed a Fregean *Gedanke*; but the act itself was not that. One simply cannot get an act of asserting in mind in the way in which one can get an asserted *Gedanke* in mind.

Now return to a sentence quoted earlier from Gadamer: Understanding a written text "does not mean primarily to reason one's way back into the past, but to have a present involvement in what is said." If we are to know the illocutionary stance component of the originating event, we must reason our way back into the past; by contrast, to come to know the propositional content is to grasp what is present here and now. For Ricoeur, as for Gadamer, *Gedanken* are at the heart of what makes interpretation a unique activity. Assembling evidence as to the originating act is no different, in its structure, from what natural scientists do; interpreting texts for their meaning is different in its very nature.

Gadamer's account of the role of *Gedanken* in interpretation is elegant; Ricoeur's is yet more elegant. One wishes that theories so elegant were true. Specifically, one wishes that the textual-sense theory of interpretation were an accurate account of the sort of interpretation that most of us do most of the time. Sad to say, it is not.

The reason it's not is that there is no such thing as *the* sense of a text. I do not contest the ontology of sense that those in the New Critical and hermeneutic traditions have employed to articulate their theory of textual-sense interpretation. Thus Derrida's objection to the textual-sense theory of interpretation is not mine. Derrida rejects the Fregean ontology; I accept it. Right now I see that there is a computer before me. My seeing that there is a computer before me evokes in me the belief that there is a computer before me. My belief that there is a computer before me leads me to tell you that there is a computer before me. Upon interpreting what I said, you also believe that there is a computer before me. The natural interpretation of these phenomena is that what I see is identical with what I believe and is identical with what I assert and is identical with what you grasp when you interpret what I said and is identical with what you come to believe on the basis of my asserting it. One can indeed acknowledge this identity without buying into everything in Frege's ontology of meaning. But those who hold that there is no identity here at all, as for example Derrida, owe us an alternative account; the burden of proof is on them. I know of no place in Derrida's writings in which he even attempts to bear that burden—no place in which he even attempts to construct an alternative, equally plausible, account of these phenomena; nothing that he says, so far as I know, would give Frege and Husserl even a nano-second's pause. Yes, it's true, their account presupposes presence. So what? And while I am acting the role of provocateur, let me add one further provocation: my belief that there is a computer before me and my assertion that there is a computer before me are true if and only if it is the case that there is a computer before me—true if and only if it is a fact that there is a computer before me. The burden of proof is on those who deny the correspondence account of truth. As for myself, I do not believe that that burden has been borne.

Nonetheless, I hold that there is no such thing as *the* sense of a text. To explain why not, I must now introduce a correction in my exposition of the textual-sense account of interpretation. So as not to make my exposition too complicated all at once, I have thus far spoken of the meaning of a sentence in the language. But every textual-sense theorist insists, and rightly so, that that is much too simplistic. Many sentences in a language mean a number of different things. And not only do many of them mean a number of different things, but one can also use a sentence in any one of its meanings to say many different things; one can use it loosely, hyperbolically, metaphorically, sarcastically, and the like. In all such cases, the propositional content of one's illocutionary act will not be identical with any of the meanings that the sentence has in the language—that is to say, with any of its strict and literal meanings.

How do textual-sense theorists propose coping with these facts? They all propose coping with them in the same way—the only way, so far as I can see, that both is available to them and holds out any promise whatsoever. The goal of the interpreter is not to discover the meaning of the sentences of the text in the language; she already knows that. Her goal is to discover the meaning that the sentence has *in its occurrence in this particular position in this text.* Call that the *sense* of the sentence. And the thesis of the textual-sense theorist is that the sense of a sentence in its occurrence in a particular position in a text is a function of its meaning in the language plus what the sentence must mean if the text as a whole is to have a unified sense. To forestall misunderstanding, the textual-sense theorist immediately adds that texts will always incorporate ambiguities, some of these constituting merits rather than demerits in the text. Monroe Beardsley offers a nice formulation of the central point when he says that "texts acquire determinate meaning through the interactions of their words without the intervention of an authorial will. When possible meanings are transformed into an actual meaning, this transformation is generated by the possibilities (the Leibnizian *com*possibilities) themselves."[6]

The reason I hold that there is no such thing as *the* sense of the text is that the features of texts that, according to this proposal, determine a fixed sense for a text do not in fact do so. My argument rests on cases.

Imagine a novel in which there is a sentence that we would all naturally interpret as sarcasm. "Nice job!" says one of the speakers sarcastically, meaning the opposite. Why do we interpret this sentence sarcastically? Because, so it is said, only if the sentence, in its position within the text as a whole, is construed as having that meaning, that sense, can there be a unified meaning for the text as a whole; only thus can there be what Beardsley called a "compossible" meaning for the totality of the text's sentences.

I have two objections. I am dubious that the concept of *unified meaning of a text* is sufficiently clear to support the weight that textual-sense interpretation rests on it. But let that pass. My first objection is: why assume that the meanings of texts are always unified, in any natural sense of "unified," when it seems obvious that many are not?

Though the point that texts often if not always lack unity has been made ad nauseam by deconstructionists, it was in fact a staple in the trade of biblical interpreters long before deconstructionism turned up. Likewise Werner Jaeger argued that the text of Aristotle's *Metaphysics* is not unified, and Norman Kemp-Smith, that the text of Kant's first critique is not unified. Admittedly these interpreters argued for something more; they argued that the biblical, Aristotelian, and Kantian texts that we have are not "true" texts, but were stitched together out of texts that were true texts, the sign of their being composites of true texts, rather than themselves true texts, being that they lack the unity necessary for a true text. On that way of using the word "text," *being unified* is analytic of something's being a (true) text. It is in arguing that texts which are definitely not composites are also often full of *aporia* that deconstructionists have gone beyond what was already commonly assumed. I agree.

But secondly, consider those texts, if any, that are unified (whatever "unified" might mean here). Why assume that the meaning of the rest of the text of the novel that we imagined determines that the sense of "Nice job!" is sarcastic? Why not instead assume that the meaning of the rest of the text falls in line with the literal meaning of "Nice job!"? It may well be that if we resolve to take the literal meaning of "Nice job!" as a determining center of our interpretation, proceeding from there to interpret the rest of the text so as to make it harmonious with that meaning, we will wind up with a bizarre meaning for the text as a whole. So what? Why rule out bizarre meanings? Perhaps there is a sentence in the text that says that it is not bizarre. Why interpret that sentence literally?

Or consider some sentence in a text that we all naturally interpret as metaphorical—for example, John Donne's famous line, "No man is an island." Why not take the sense of this sentence as its literal meaning in the English language? How does the requirement of compossibility force a metaphorical meaning? It will be said that the literal meaning of this sentence in the language would be a jarring intrusion into the flow of the thought of the text, and so obviously true as to have no point. Maybe so. But sometimes there are jarring inexplicable intrusions into a flow of thought. Or if it is unity that we insist on, then why not do our best to interpret the rest of the text so that this is no longer a jarring truistic intrusion? Who knows what interesting possibilities might be forthcoming?

Jorge Borges, in his well-known story "Pierre Menard, Author of Don Quixote," makes my point more elaborately, and in a wonderfully quirky way. Pierre Menard is an obscure French writer of the early twentieth century who undertook to write *Don Quixote—the Don Quixote.* "It is unnecessary," says Borges's narrator, "to add that his aim was never to produce a mechanical transcription of the original; he did not propose to copy it." That is to say, Menard's aim was not simply to copy out the sentences, thus to have a copy of the novel in longhand. Rather, his "admirable ambition was to produces pages which would coincide—word for word and line for line—with those of Miguel de Cervantes," but to do so as "Pierre Menard and to arrive at [the sentences of] *Don Quixote* through the experiences of Pierre Menard." Menard's strategy, in his own words, was

> governed by two polar laws. The first permits me to attempt variants of a formal and psychological nature; the second obliges me to sacrifice them to the "original" text and irrefutably to rationalize this annihilation. . . . To these artificial obstacles one must add another congenital one. To compose *Don Quixote* at the beginning of the seventeenth century was a reasonable, necessary, and perhaps inevitable undertaking; at the beginning of the twentieth century it is almost impossible. It is not in vain that three hundred years have passed, charged with the most complex happenings—among them, to mention only one, that same *Don Quixote.*

The narrator nicely describes the differences of meaning between one of the passages from the *Don Quixote* of Cervantes and the same passage from the *Don Quixote* of Pierre Menard:

> The text of Cervantes and that of Menard are verbally identical, but the second is almost infinitely richer. (More ambiguous, his detractors will say; but ambiguity is a richness.) It is a revelation to compare the *Don Quixote* of Menard with that of Cervantes. The latter, for instance, wrote ". . . truth, whose mother is history, who is the rival of time, depository of deeds, witness of the past, ex-

> ample and lesson to the present and warning to the future." Written in the seventeenth century, written by the "ingenious layman" Cervantes, this enumeration is a mere rhetorical eulogy of history. Menard, on the other hand, writes: ". . . truth, whose mother is history, who is the rival of time, depository of deeds, witness of the past, example and lesson to the present, and warning to the future." History, *mother* of truth; the idea is astounding. Menard, a contemporary of William James, does not define history as an investigation of reality, but as its origin. Historical truth, for him, is not what took place; it is what we think took place. The final clauses—*example and lesson to the present, and warning to the future*—are shamelessly pragmatic.

The final page of the story wonderfully generalizes the point:

> Menard (perhaps without wishing to) has enriched, by means of a new technique, the hesitant and rudimentary art of reading: the technique is one of deliberate anachronism and erroneous attributions. This technique with its infinite applications, urges us to run through the *Odyssey* as if it were written after the *Aeneid*, and to read *Le jardin du Centaure* by Madam Henri Bachelier as if it were by Madam Henri Bachelier. This technique would fill the dullest books with adventure. Would not the attributing of *The Imitation of Christ* to Louis Ferdinand Celine or James Joyce be a sufficient renovation of its tenuous spiritual counsels?

In my *Divine Discourse* I called the sort of interpretation that Borges here fantasizes, *performance interpretation*: one imagines what some French writer of the early twentieth century might have meant had he produced the text of *Don Quixote*, what James Joyce might have meant had he produced the text of *Imitatio Christi*, what some writer of Kantian persuasion might have meant had he produced the text of the Prologue of John's Gospel, and so forth.[7] If we insist on leaving authors out of the picture, and taking the text in itself as the object of interpretation, then I think textual-sense interpretation cannot but give way to performance interpretation; there is no way to stop the slide.

Deconstructionist interpretation is performance interpretation. Listen to Roland Barthes, in the essay I mentioned: "Once the Author is removed, the claim to decipher a text becomes quite futile. To give a text an Author is to impose a limit on the text, to furnish it with a final signified, to close the writing." The truth is rather that "everything is to be *disentangled*, nothing *deciphered*; the structure can be followed, 'run' (like the thread of a stocking) at every point and at every level, but there is nothing beneath: the space of writing is to be ranged over, not pierced. . . . [L]iterature (it would be better from now on to say *writing*), by refusing to assign a 'secret', an ultimate meaning, to the text (and to the world as text) liberates what may be called an anti-theological activity, an activity that is truly revolutionary since to refuse to fix meaning is, in the end, to refuse God and his hypostases—reason, science, law" (147).

My contention is that none of us practices performance interpretation most of the time. Unlike textual-sense interpretation, there is nothing incoherent about such interpretation, either in its theory or in practice. Probably everybody employs such interpretation now and then; some seem to employ it rather often. But nobody employs it most of the time. Nobody employs it when they read the newspaper, read and sign legal contracts, read science, history, or autobiography, read instructions for the repair of appliances, read invitations to parties, read advice from the managers of one's retirement funds, read overdue notices from the library, read parking tickets, read summons to jury duty. And most of us most of the time do not want what we ourselves have said or written subjected to performance interpretation. Not even those who have written most rapturously in praise of performance interpretation want that praise itself to be subject to performance interpretation! Derrida, after mentioning a certain view of history that had been attributed to him, says that "it is difficult for me to see how a concept of history as the 'history of meaning' can be attributed to me."[8] And speaking of a theme present in his thought from the very beginning, he says, "This fanaticism or monotony might be startling, but I cannot seriously be made to say the opposite."[9]

The mode of interpretation that most of us practice most of the time is that which Derrida is calling for on the part of those who interpret *his* writings. I call it *authorial discourse interpretation.* In authorial discourse interpretation one seeks to identify and grasp the illocutionary acts that the authorizer of the text performed by inscribing, or in some other way authorizing, the words that one is interpreting. The reason none of us gives a literal interpretation to Donne's sentence "No man is an island" is that all the evidence available to us—the text, what we know about the language, what we know about Donne or can reasonably presume to be true of him, and so on—points to the conclusion that he did not, by inscribing this sentence, assert—speaking literally now—that nobody is an island. He said something else. We want to know what that something else is.

But if it is true that most of us most of the time practice authorial discourse interpretation, why have textual sense and performance interpretation been so popular among theorists? Why the twentieth century orthodoxy? Roland Barthes, in the essay to which I have already referred, "The Death of the Author," suggests that authorial-intention interpretation was the reflection in culture of capitalism's contradictory tendency to elevate the importance of the individual while at the same time placing the individual in servitude: the reader is in thrall to the author. Perhaps, then, the rise of textual sense interpretation, and even more, of performance interpretation, should be seen as the reflection in culture of capitalism's *tendenz* toward commodification. The text becomes a mere commodity.

There is much that begs to be said about authorial discourse interpretation. But since I have had my say on that at some length in *Divine Discourse*, let me instead close by engaging what Kevin Vanhoozer says in chapter 5 of his book *Is There a Meaning in This Text?*—the chapter titled "Resurrecting the Author."

To his great credit, Vanhoozer has broken with orthodoxy in his theory of interpretation; his theory is heterodox. In fact he comes close, very close, to being a proponent of authorial discourse interpretation. But he's not quite there yet. (I dare say he would return the compliment and say that I am close, very close, to his theory; but not quite there.)

Vanhoozer places what he calls "communicative acts" at the center of his theory. I think that is a mistake on his part—not a terribly serious mistake, but a mistake. It seems clear to me that not all illocutionary acts performed by the inscription of some text either achieve, or aim to achieve, communication; diaries meant for the eyes of the diarist alone are examples of exceptions. Yet those texts can be interpreted. Hence I think we must focus our theory of interpretation on illocutionary acts, whether or not they are, in fact or by intent, communicative acts.

Second, Vanhoozer often recommends that we consider texts as complex communicative acts; for example, on page 219 of his text he says that "[t]he basic unity of literary interpretation is . . . the text considered as a complex communicative act." Now it may be that the right interpretation of this comment, and others like it, carries the implication that the sentence is being used loosely rather than strictly. But if it is being used strictly, then it seems to me that what is being said is not true; texts are not and could not be acts. Though Vanhoozer and I share the view that texts and illocutionary acts are intimately related, they are not identical. They belong to fundamentally different ontological categories.

My principal disagreement with Vanhoozer's discussion, however, is over what he says about intention. He argues that the authorizer's illocutionary act—or communicative act—just is the authorizer's intention, in one standard use of the word "intention." Thus he holds that the goal of interpretation is to identify and grasp the authorizer's intentions. For example, on page 222 he says that "[i]ntention is still the ground, goal, and guide of textual interpretation, but it is an affair not of consciousness, but of communicative action." This seems to me not correct; one can perform an illocutionary action without in any way whatsoever intending to perform that action. This happens both in complicated ways and in straightforward and familiar ways. It will be sufficient to cite two examples of the straightforward and familiar ways. Sometimes we say things absent-mindedly. We really did say it, but we didn't intend to say it. We were, as it were, on autopilot, not paying attention to what we were saying. When it is pointed out to us what we said, we quickly correct ourselves. And sometimes we say things that we had no intention of saying because the words we used had a different meaning from what we thought they had. Though this happens when one is speaking one's native language, it probably happens more often when one is speaking a language that one is just learning. "Do you realize what you just said?" says the shocked or bemused native speaker to us.

The interplay between intentions and the performance of illocutionary acts is complex. But even without engaging in a detailed and lengthy analysis, this much can be said: it's not true that a condition of performing illocutionary action A is that one intend to perform A, nor that one perform A intentionally.[10]

These observations lead me to attach an explanatory qualification to my main thesis, however. Sometimes, when it is clear to us that what the author said is not what he intended to say, our interest is more in what he intended to say than in what he did say. Even to get to that point, however, we must have discerned what he did say.

My account of interpretation has important ethical implications. If the interpretation that most of us perform most of the time consists of engaging a person rather than just doing something to an artifact, then the issue arises of whether we have engaged that person justly, charitably, honorably, and the like. Those who have been my students will recall my chastising some of them for how they were treating Anselm, Plato, or whoever, with their interpretations. "Would you have said what you just said if Augustine were sitting right across from you?" they have heard me exclaim.

Likewise, my contention that God discourses with us has important implications for theology. The most important, of course, is just the resuscitation of God as one who discourses with us. Even Hans Frei, struggle as he did to undo the eclipse of biblical narrative, never managed to break free of the assumption that, when interpreting the biblical narratives, all we are doing is acting on an artifact—not engaging God. So far as I can see it never occurred to him to break free of this assumption, so strong was the grip on him of textual sense interpretation as employed by his New Critical friends at Yale. But beyond that, theology as a whole comes out looking different when the determining center of one's theological reflections is not God's ontological attributes but God's illocutionary acts of assuring, commanding, promising, asserting, and the like. One cannot just add to traditional onto-theology the claim that God discourses and keep everything else the same. The addition is disruptive.

I regret that I do not have the time on this occasion to explore either these ethical or these theological implications. I am currently working on a manuscript that I am calling, for the time being, *Justice: Divine and Human.* In the manuscript I develop in considerable detail the implications, for the nature of God, of God's commanding and promising.

So as they say: read my book. When it exists!

NOTES

1. Kevin J. Vanhoozer, *Is There a Meaning in This Text? The Bible, the Reader, and the Morality of Literary Knowledge* (Grand Rapids: Zondervan, 1998), p. 218 and passim.

2. Hans-Georg Gadamer, *Wahrheit und Methode*; English translation: *Truth and Method*, 2nd rev. ed., trans. Joel Weinsheimer and Donald G. Marshall (New York: Continuum, 2003), p. 186. Further references to this text will be cited parenthetically in the text as *TM*.

3. The quoted passages in this paragraph and the next are all from *TM*, pp. 180–81.

4. Cf. the following passage: "The detachability of language from speaking derives from the fact that it can be written. In the form of writing, all tradition is contemporaneous with each present time. Moreover, it involves a unique co-existence of past and present, insofar as present consciousness has the possibility of a free access to everything handed

down in writing. . . . A written tradition is not a fragment of a past world, but has already raised itself beyond this into the sphere of the meaning that it expresses. The ideality of the word is what raises everything linguistic beyond the finitude and transience that characterize other remnants of past experience" (p. 390).

5. Paul Ricoeur, *Interpretation Theory: Discourse and the Surplus of Meaning* (Fort Worth, TX: Texas Christian University Press, 1976), pp. 90, 93.

6. Monroe Beardsley, *The Possibility of Criticism* (Detroit: Wayne State University Press, 1970), p. 30.

7. This last seems to me the best way of construing that curious passage titled "The Personified Idea of the Good Principle," at the beginning of section one of Book Two of Kant's *Religion within the Limits of Reason Alone.*

8. Jacques Derrida, *Positions,* trans. and annot. by Alan Bass (Chicago : University of Chicago Press, 1981), p. 50.

9. Ibid., p. 54.

10. Thus I also disagree with the following statement by Vanhoozer: "the author's intention is what makes his or her words count as one kind of action rather than another." In chapter 5 of my *Divine Discourse* I have given what I called a *normative* account of what it is for a locutionary action to count as an illocutionary action—and in general, a normative account of what it is for one action to count as another. (I do not think that words can count as actions.)

3

Gadamer's Hermeneutics and the Question of Relativism

Eduardo J. Echeverria

The specter of relativism raises its head in the following passage from part 2 of Hans-Georg Gadamer's master work, *Truth and Method*, where he claims that human reason is situated in, and limited to, particular historical circumstances:

> Does being situated within traditions really mean being subject to prejudices and limited in one's freedom? Is not, rather, all human existence, even the freest, limited and qualified in various ways? If this is true, the idea of an absolute reason is not a possibility for historical humanity. Reason exists for us only in concrete, historical terms—i.e., it is not its own master but remains constantly dependent on the given circumstances in which it operates. This is true not only in the sense in which Kant, under the influence of the skeptical critique of Hume, limited the claims of rationalism to the a priori element in the knowledge of nature; it is still truer of historical consciousness and the possibility of historical knowledge.[1]

What is absolute reason? Gadamer does not say, but I think we can suppose—at least I will do so in this essay—that it refers to the aspiration of human reason to some kind of finding universal validity, of reaching absolute truth. This is how Thomas Nagel understands the idea of reason, whose essential feature is, he says, generality, universality, or objectivity: "Whoever appeals to reason purports to discover a source of authority within himself that is not merely personal, or societal, but universal—and that should also persuade others who are willing to listen to it."[2] Gadamer rejects a notion of human reason that can transcend history, aspiring to reach the truth in an absolute sense.

Roger Trigg, for one, is quick to point out with obvious reference to views such as Gadamer's that "repudiating a reason that can transcend history will only mean that we are trapped in our own historical period. We will share its assumptions and have no basis for questioning them."[3] Aidan Nichols, O.P., for another, underscores the point that "Human finitude, the socio-cultural 'embeddedness' of human judgements and the fact that all exercise of human reason has its context, rule out any establishing of universal norms or standards which could reflect the universal structures of being."[4] With this conclusion, he adds, "the issue of truth itself is irremediably entangled. Classical and modern notions of truth [in a realist sense] are deconstructed in the belief that truth—if the word still be used—is dependent on social norms and cultural warrants."[5]

But does Gadamer's repudiation of absolute reason have these relativistic implications? Robert Sokolowski does not think so: "It is regrettable that hermeneutics is often taken as a license for relativism, a use that Gadamer would certainly dispute."[6] Elsewhere Sokolowski says, "Gadamer's hermeneutic theory has often been misinterpreted as a kind of forerunner of deconstruction, a less Nietzschean version of the kind of thinking represented by Jacques Derrida. Because Gadamer stresses the involvement of the subject in the achievement of truth, his work is sometimes taken as a simple subjectivism or relativism."[7] Is Sokolowski right about Gadamer being misinterpreted?

Suppose we take *simple* relativism to be the idea that the same belief can be true for one person but not true for everyone. This idea is not about two people disagreeing with each other: what one believes to be true, the other believes to be false. Instead, simple relativism is "a belief that beliefs are true for those who hold them. They are not true for everyone, let alone objectively or absolutely true."[8] So for simple relativism, not only is belief person-relative, but truth is as well. Now, E. D. Hirsch argues that Gadamer's hermeneutics is a version of simple relativism.[9] Is he right about Gadamer, or is his hermeneutics a more *sophisticated* relativism? By sophisticated relativism I mean a view in which epistemic justification and truth receive different treatment: justification is relative to historical context, but truth is not. Michael Polanyi and Jeffrey Stout have defended versions of sophisticated relativism in *Personal Knowledge* (1958) and *Ethics after Babel* (1988), respectively. In their views, truth as a reality is distinguishable from what one is justified in holding to be true. That is, whether we are justified in believing something to be true is a relative matter, but truth itself is not.

Now, I contend that Gadamer's hermeneutics is best understood as a version of sophisticated relativism. In other words, his hermeneutics may be understood as an attempt to hold together a concept of truth with our historicity, with the former being irreducible to the latter, which is the epistemic context of justification and its embedded historical standards or warrants. In my view, distinguishing between justification and truth in Gadamer's hermeneutics helps us, on the one hand, to answer the question why Gadamer is often interpreted as a relativist. On the other hand, it also helps us to understand why philosophers such as Sokolowski and others deny that Gadamer is a relativist about truth.

My article is organized in the following way. I begin by defining relativism and its antithesis, realism. Then, by stating Hirsch's critique, I consider briefly why Gadamer is often interpreted as a relativist. I follow this by taking up Jean Grondin's defense of Gadamer's hermeneutics against the charge of relativism. My own defense of Gadamer follows, which contrasts sharply with that of Grondin by arguing that Gadamer is a kind of realist about reality and truth.[10] This is not to say that Gadamer develops a substantive conception of realism in *Truth and Method*. Rather, it is to say only that there are elements in Gadamer's hermeneutics that counteract his sliding from finitude and historicity to relativism about reality and truth. Pared down for my purpose here, I will highlight five aspects of Gadamer's hermeneutics that can be interpreted only as some of the necessary ingredients in a version of realism. These aspects are: (1) the realism of the truth-seeker; (2) an epistemological fallibilism, not to be equated with relativism; (3) an anti-Cartesian and anti-Kantian orientation against a subject-object dualism; (4) the Fregean and Husserlian ontology of the sense of the text; and (5) the thesis that relativism is self-refuting.

Relativism and Realism

John Henry Newman and Edmund Husserl in the nineteenth and twentieth centuries, respectively, and more recently Roger Trigg, Allen Wood, and Thomas Nagel define relativism as the view that beliefs are true for those who hold them, which implies that there is no such thing as objectively or absolutely true beliefs. All truth is then relative to the person who believes it.[11] As Husserl succinctly put it in 1900, "For each man that is true which seems to *him* true, one thing to one man and the opposite to another, if that is how he sees it."[12]

Critics of relativism argue that relativism is not only self-refuting, that is, necessarily false; they also argue that relativism leads to rejecting the distinction between the nature of the world and one's beliefs, between what is the case and what one believes to be the case: the consequence of rejecting this distinction is, according to Roger Trigg, "that reality drops out in favour of understandings of reality."[13] This in turn leads the relativist also to reject the distinction between correct and incorrect beliefs, and true and false beliefs, about reality.[14] For without true beliefs there are no false beliefs. The upshot of lacking any distinction between truth and falsity, between what is and is not so, is that *anything goes*. Trigg summarizes this criticism as follows: "The path to nihilism, where nothing seems to matter and no view is preferable to any other, beckons. There seems little point in believing anything if I can believe anything with impunity, without any idea of being constrained by the real world."[15]

The failure to recognize that justification and truth require different treatment is a corollary of denying the fundamental distinction between the way the world is and what we believe about it. The distinction between justification and truth reflects an intuition commonly shared by adherents of the Common Western Metaphysics (borrowing a phrase from Peter van Inwagen), namely, that a proposition's (*p*) being true (or false) in no way depends upon someone's being justified, or rational, in believing that *p*, nor upon someone's having reasons for believing that *p*; indeed, it does not depend upon someone's believing that *p*, because if *p* is true, it would be true even if no one believed it. Thus, according to the realist, objective truth exists. That is, a belief is true if and only if objective reality is the way the belief says it is; otherwise, the belief is false. Van Inwagen explains the two components of this metaphysical thesis we may also call *objectivism:* "First, our beliefs and our assertions are either true or false; each of our beliefs and assertions represents the World as being a certain way, and the belief or assertion is true if the World is that way, and false if the World is not that way. . . . The second component of the thesis . . . is this: the World exists and has the features it does in large part independently of our beliefs and our assertions." "The truth or falsity of our beliefs and assertions," van Inwagen adds, "is therefore 'objective' in the sense that truth and falsity are conferred on those beliefs and assertions by their objects, by the things they are *about.*"[16]

Having distinguished relativism from its antithesis, the objectivism or realism of the Common Western Metaphysics, I want briefly to distinguish several kinds of relativism.[17] I stated above that absolute reason is the idea of reason in which human reason is understood to be aspiring to some kind of universal validity, of reaching absolute truth. Let's call this idea epistemological absolutism. Now, absolutism and relativism are, in general, considered to be polar opposites. In holding, for example, a proposition to be absolutely true, the absolutist intends to assert that the proposition is not only true for him who believes it, but also equally true for the one who rejects it; indeed, true for everyone else.[18] Furthermore, epistemological absolutism is generally a corollary of objectivism, which is the metaphysical doctrine that "true . . . judgments describe a subject matter that is independent of the thoughts and feelings of finite sentient beings, and hence a subject matter that would exist even if no one believed in it or had certain feelings or attitudes towards it."[19] Moreover, an epistemological absolutist invariably holds to an objective notion of rationality.[20] He makes the epistemological claim that "at least some . . . judgments can be supported by evidence that any knowledgeable and rational individual would have to support."[21] That is, he holds the view that it is not possible to reject some propositions "without transgressing epistemological standards concerning reasoning, evidence, and rationality."[22]

By contrast, an epistemological relativist, given his commitment to fallibilism, rejects the epistemological claims of the absolutist, namely, the idea of reason reaching absolute truth as well as an objective notion of rationality, but not necessarily the distinction between truth and error. Truth, as a "transcendent," "regulative," "normative" ideal, and epistemological relativism are apparently compatible because an epistemological relativist is a relativist about rationality, not about truth itself. Unlike the epistemological absolutist, he holds instead to a permissive notion of rationality where one is justified in believing or warranted in asserting a belief according to one's intellectual standards, available reasons and evidence, in short, one's present epistemic circumstances. In these circumstances, we can, and generally do, make situation- and person-specific truth claims. But because of the fallible nature of those claims we can never attain a "wholly unconditioned truth." Rather, "the idea of [truth] is a driving force behind our critical-reflective practices."[23] How then does the epistemological relativist understand the practice of making truth claims in light of the fallibility of our epistemic condition? Thomas McCarthy gives us a glimpse of what such an understanding would look like:

> To grant that there is no final and conclusive theory of reality of which we are capable is not at all to abandon the distinction between truth and error. We make this distinction in relation to "the available means of cognition". The claim that a belief is true must stand the test of experience and practice *in the present.* Knowing that we are fallible, that what stands the test today may well fail to do so in the next century, does not prevent us, or even exempt us, from making and defending the claims to truth here and now. Consider the following: A claims that S is p. B disputes his claim. They resort to "experience and practice", the "available means of cognition", to settle the matter. This shows that S is indeed p. A was right. But B points out that there is no absolute warrantee of truth. Experience and practice are historically variable. If the past is any guide, the means of cognition available in the next century will be different from those presently available. Therefore B concludes, A should withdraw his claim to truth. I think it is clear that this conclusion does not follow. A's claim stands unless and until it is actually defeated.[24]

And when A's truth claim is actually defeated, according to McCarthy, what that claim loses is its justification: "That is, the belief, which we now know to be untrue, was warranted, justified, rationally acceptable in previous circumstances—but not ideally."[25]

Against this background we now turn to E. D. Hirsch, who has charged Gadamer with being a historical relativist, indeed, a "subjectivist," or worse, a "cognitive atheist," espousing a version of the "naïve, entrapped sort of Kantianism" as well as "skepticism regarding historical knowledge."[26] What do these charges mean? Is there any truth in them? Is there any basis in Gadamer's hermeneutics for them?

May Gadamer Plausibly Be Interpreted as a Relativist?

Briefly, we may answer yes to the question posed in the title of this section. Three principal features of Gadamer's hermeneutics stand out, opening him up to the charge of relativism. First, Gadamer rejects a "homogeneous human nature" (*TM*, p. 290; *WM*, p. 274), which essentially abides through the changes of history, as an adequate basis for historical understanding. That is, he distances himself from Vico's axiom, later embraced by Dilthey, that "we understand historically because we are ourselves historical beings" (*TM*, p. 230; *WM*, p. 217). Thus, the homogeneity of subject and object, of knower and known, according to Gadamer, does not make historical knowledge possible. "Rather," Gadamer says, "positing homogeneity as its condition conceals the real epistemological problem of history" (*TM*, p. 222; *WM*, p. 209). The real problem is, according to Gadamer, that the relativity of historical consciousness—which is a corollary of the idea that human nature is not basically unchanging, but rather is the changing product of historical context—endangers the fundamental claim to objective knowledge (*TM*, p. 231; *WM*, p. 217).

Second, rationality is historical, situational, and relative to varying epistemic circumstances. "Reason exists for us only in concrete, historical terms—i.e., it is not its own master but remains constantly dependent on the given circumstances in which it operates." It is situated in, and limited to, particular historical contexts. This makes "absolute reason" impossible, says Gadamer. The concept of absolute reason is apparently associated, if I understand Gadamer correctly, with the position I earlier called epistemological absolutism, and its corollary, an objective notion of rationality. This rejection, too, raises the question for Gadamer's critics such as Hirsch whether there is such a thing as a correct interpretation of a text.

Third, Gadamer apparently rejects the fundamental distinction between meaning and significance, that is, the meaning of a text, which does not change, and the significance of that meaning for us today, which does change. Says Gadamer:

> Every age has to understand a transmitted text in its own way, for the text belongs to the whole tradition whose content interests the age and in which it seeks to understand itself. The real meaning (*wirkliche Sinn*) of a text, as it speaks to the interpreter, does not depend on the contingencies of the author and his original audience. It certainly is not identical with them, for it is always co-determined also by the historical situation of the interpreter and hence by the totality of the objective course of history. . . . Not just occasionally but always, the meaning of a text goes beyond its author. That is why understanding is not merely a reproductive but always a productive activity as well. . . . It is enough to say that we understand in a *different way, if we understand at all.* (*TM*, pp. 296–97; *WM*, p. 280)

Is Gadamer suggesting here that there are as many possible legitimate readings of a text as there are contexts within and from which it can be read? Indeed, that is precisely what he seems to suggest: "It is part of the historical finitude of our being that we are aware that others after us will understand in a different way. And yet it is equally indubitable that it remains the same work whose fullness of meaning is realized in the changing process of understanding, just as it is the same history whose meaning is constantly in the process of being defined" (*TM*, pp. 373, 355). Again, he says, "all reading is application, so that a person reading a text is himself part of the meaning he apprehends. He belongs to the text that he is reading. The line of meaning that the text manifests to him as he reads it always and necessarily breaks off in an open indeterminacy" (*TM*, p. 340; *WM*, p. 323). In light of these claims, the blurring of the basic distinction between meaning and significance seems to follow, and this presents Gadamer with the threat of "hermeneutical anarchy," to borrow a phrase from Aidan Nichols, rendering unattainable, apparently, any notion of a correct interpretation, of a stable and recoverable textual content.

Hirsch then claims that Gadamer espouses the quasi-Kantian epistemological theory called *perspectivism.* Alleging that this theory holds interpretation to vary with the standpoint of the interpreter, Hirsch argues that it is, at its core, a form of skepticism.[27] This implication follows, he argues, not only from Gadamer's hermeneutical principle of the historicity of understanding but also from his doctrine of prejudice and pre-understanding. The former binds the interpreter to his own historical context, making it impossible for him to transcend (as Hirsch says) "the distorting perspective of his own historicity."[28] The latter reinforces the interpreter's inability to break out of his own perspective, hermeneutic situation, or horizon of interpretation, even if he wants to. The upshot of Gadamer's hermeneutic theory is, according to Hirsch, not only, first, a skepticism regarding the possibility of correct interpretation but also, second, the fallacious claim that the past is inscrutable.[29] This is a corollary, Hirsch adds, of the "historicist dogma that we cannot recognize past meanings," because "the past is ontologically alien to the present."[30] Says Hirsch, "Implicitly it rejects the possibility of an interpretation that is independent of the interpreter's own values and preconceptions; ultimately it repudiates correctness of interpretation as a possible goal." Hirsch adds, "Since all interpretations are perspective-ridden, disparate interpretations can be equally correct, or what is the same thing, equally incorrect. But in that case what is left as an acceptable critical standard?"[31] Hirsch summarizes his criticism of the hermeneutical position that Gadamer and others allegedly represent in the following passage:

> The main intellectual (and emotional) sanction for dogmatic skepticism in present-day literary theory is its assumption that all "knowledge" is relative. This cognitive atheism, as I call it, is based mainly on the idea that everybody sees literature from his own "angle of vision," and responds emotionally to literature through his own system of values and associations. Individualized in this way, cognitive atheism is straightforward subjectivism. But other closely related forms in literary theory and practice are cultural relativism, historical relativism, and methodological relativism. All exhibit the same structure; all of them make truth and reality relative to a spiritual perspective.[32]

For our purposes here, we have given a sufficient sketch of Hirsch's objection to Gadamer's philosophical hermeneutics. I turn now to sketch one possible defense of Gadamer against the charge of relativism.

Jean Grondin on Gadamer and Relativism

Jean Grondin defends Gadamer against the charge of relativism by claiming that it makes sense only against the background of a traditional conception of absolute truth. Says Grondin, "[R]elativism is hardly more than a conceptual bugaboo constructed by those who possess a foundational conception of what truth or interpretation should be."[33] What is Grondin's point here?

He rejects, first, the characterization of hermeneutics as a version of simple relativism because it abandons the concept of absolute truth. Relativism is, according to Grondin, the view that two incompatible beliefs are equally good—that "anything goes." But hermeneutics is not relativistic. "For there are always *reasons*, be they contextual or pragmatic, that urge us to choose in favor of one opinion rather than another," according to Grondin. "These reasons," he adds, "are less algorithmic than many rationalists imagine," and that is precisely what troubles those who call us relativists. Grondin argues, second, that "[o]nly one who claims an absolutist standard can speak of relativism. There is relativism only with respect to an absolute truth." Furthermore, Grondin claims that there is good reason to abandon a notion of absolute truth. The claim that human reason can reach absolute truth is irreconcilable with the experience of human finitude. Put differently, there exists, according to Grondin, an incompatibility between human fallibility and humans' claims to reaching absolute truth.

Now, Grondin claims that the charge of relativism makes sense only if we assume an epistemological absolutism, an objective notion of rationality, and its corollary, objectivism, which is the metaphysical doctrine about truth, namely, that a belief is true if and only if objective reality is the way the belief says it is; otherwise, it is false. Where does this leave Grondin's attempt to refute the charge that hermeneutics is not relativistic? Given the contextual nature of reasons, doesn't this charge reappear? That is, if reasoning is situated in, and limited to, particular historical contexts, and its embedded standards of rationality, then what are reasons for me, are, for you, not only not necessarily good reasons, but also possibly not reasons at all. Are there reasons that either party to a dispute can appeal to independently of, and so genuinely in support of, his own beliefs? If not, how can we meaningfully distinguish between truth and error, according to Grondin?

Significantly, Grondin does make room for some kind of objectivity within hermeneutics after abandoning epistemological absolutism, an objective conception of rationality, and objectivism. A concept of objectivity is needed, he says, in order to account for the knowledge that we already possess, that is, "knowledge that can be considered objective without claiming to be absolute."[34] If I understand Grondin correctly, he thinks hermeneutics still needs a notion of objectivity for exercising the critical function of showing that "some claims to knowledge and interpretations are *more reliable than others*" (italics added). For example, "We recognize that alchemy and chemistry, astrology and astronomy are *not on the same level*," Grondin adds, "and that a democratically elected government has a *more legitimate mandate* than a tyranny, and so on" (italics added).[35] But what is the basis of that reliability? Are these claims—distinguishing truth and error in science, politics, and the like—more reliable than others because they grasp truth about reality? If not, is that because Grondin makes the questionable move of separating reality from knowledge? Surely, it is one thing to abandon an absolute viewpoint—that is, claims to unconditional truth—because there seems to be no absolute guarantee of truth—at least according to Grondin and other fallibilists. It is, however, an entirely different matter to abandon the "distinction between the metaphysical status of what we believe in and our own ability to give a justification for the belief."[36] We may wonder, rightly, what to make of a notion of objective knowledge, such as Grondin's, that doesn't make truth claims about reality, that is, that does not have a conception about the nature of things. What then is the link between reality and our knowledge of it? Without the distinction between the way the world is and what we believe about it, even if we all happen to agree about legitimate and illegitimate forms of science and government, we have not successfully dodged the charge of relativism, because the process of justification is detached from the real world. Contextualizing the objectivity of belief in a normative context of reasons doesn't answer the question whether the belief is true or false. As Trigg rightly says, "Objectivity is a matter of being connected with the nature of things. . . . Only what is real can be a genuine source of truth."[37] Intellectual standards for evaluating claims have no essential connection with truth or falsity without the existence of objective truth.[38]

Now suppose we preserve the connection between knowledge and reality, and draw the distinction between what I am justified in believing to be true and truth itself; it is one thing for an individual to be justified in holding a belief and something else entirely for the belief to be true. As Allen Wood puts it, "If you and I hold mutually incompatible beliefs, then what at least one of us believes must be false; but it could still be true that my belief is justified on the evidence which I have and your belief is justified on the evidence you have."[39] It is precisely this distinction between justification and truth that Grondin fails to acknowledge and that leaves him vulnerable to the charge of relativism.[40] In other words, the problem with Grondin's position is not his denial that reasons favoring one opinion rather than another are rationally compelling for everyone. This point is logically independent of any metaphysical conception of reality and truth, that is, of what is really the case. In my view, rather, Grondin's problem is that he "runs together the reasoning by which we arrive at our beliefs with what our beliefs purport to be about."[41] That is, he fails to distinguish between the epistemological foundation of our knowledge and the metaphysical foundations on which our knowledge has to be anchored. Given the need to make this distinction, I affirm then with the realist that there is an objective reality independent of our knowledge, existing as a metaphysical foundation of our knowledge. So in deliberating about what is objectively rational to believe true, we may judge that a person's belief is justified for him, that is, given his epistemic context, he is justified in holding his belief, even though the belief is false, and even though it turns out that there are no objectively good reasons for the truth of his beliefs.

Grondin also objects to any talk about a metaphysical conception of reality and absolute truth as being difficult to reconcile with the experience of human finitude, that is, fallibility, because we might be mistaken in what we believe. Fallibilism is, however, distinct from skepticism. As Roger Trigg reminds us, "We can be mistaken in what we think, but it does not follow that we can never be right. The idea that the human mind is incapable of grasping the nature of any reality is a form of scepticism, which undermines both religious and all other forms of belief."[42] Let's distinguish then relativism from fallibilism and ask why fallibilism is inconsistent with holding beliefs about what is absolutely true. Grondin evidently thinks so, but this is a confusion between epistemological *infallibilism* and the metaphysical status of what we believe, between the epistemic status of what we believe and its truth status.[43]

With this clarification behind us, I would reply to Grondin as follows. I may firmly believe what I might conceivably doubt, and hold to be true what might conceivably be false (paraphrasing Michael Polanyi). When I assert that *p*, I am taking the risk that I will have to retract my assertion at some future time if it is shown to be false. If I knew now which ones were false, of course, I would cease believing them. Yet, when I assert that *p* I commit myself to holding that I am in fact not now mistaken in asserting that *p*. For to believe that *p* is no different from believing that *p* to be true. Beliefs aim at truth, and if truth is unattainable, it must logically be impossible to continue believing. Indeed, to have a belief is to be intellectually committed to the truth of some belief. Further, I am also committed to holding that people who disagree with beliefs I hold true are themselves holding false beliefs. This is not a denial of fallibilism. It is simply a matter of consistency when I conclude that my beliefs are true, and, by implication, that those who disagree with me hold false beliefs.[44]

But is believing that *p* the same as believing that *p* is absolutely true? Well, if "absolutely" true means that it is true not only for those who believe it but also equally true for those who reject it, thinking it false, then there is no difference between believing that *p* and believing that *p* is absolutely true. As Allen Wood correctly states:

> If relativists say that this isn't what they mean when they assert a proposition or say they believe it, then they are apparently using the terms 'assert' and 'believe' in a new and mysterious sense, which they apparently can't explain. Until they do explain the meanings these words have for them, we can't be sure what (if anything) they are really saying when their mouths make noises that sound (to us) like *assertions* of relativism. Understanding their words in the usual sense, if you try to assert or believe that there is no (absolute) truth, it has to follow that you can't believe anything at all (not even relativism), and so nothing can be true even *for you* (not even relativism). Relativism is self-refuting simply because it has no way of using or making sense of the expression 'true for me' without relying implicitly on the notion '(absolutely) true', the very notion relativism wants to reject.[45]

Against this background, let me turn straight to Gadamer, briefly highlighting five themes in his philosophical hermeneutics that bring out dimensions of his realism.

Five Dimensions of Gadamer's Realism

Realism of the Truth-Seeker[46]

First, Gadamer affirms what I shall call the *realism of the truth-seeker.* Truth is the indispensable presupposition of all thought and language, especially in the dialectical reasoning characteristic of conversations engaged in pursuing and attaining knowledge of truth. The pursuit of truth should be understood as the search for an answer to some sort of real question. The question provides a context within inquiry as an activity of thinking that is genuinely open to seeking truth regarding what one does not know, and this activity of questioning always includes both negative and positive answers to that question. Gadamer refers here to medieval dialectics and to the inherent connection it posits between attaining knowledge and dialectic, that is, between question and answer. Says Gadamer, "[I]t is the essence of knowledge not only to judge something correctly but, at the same time and for the same reason, to exclude what is wrong. Deciding the question is the path to knowledge." "What decides a question," adds Gadamer, "is the preponderance of reasons for the one and against the other possibility. But this is still not full knowledge." This last sentence suggests that what one does know he does not know exhaustively. But that is not inconsistent with saying, as Gadamer does, that we really know truth about many things. "The thing itself (*die Sache selbst*) is known only when the counterinstances are dissolved, only when the counterarguments are seen to be incorrect" (*TM*, p. 364; *WM*, pp. 345–47). The openness of conversation, then, characteristic of dialectical reasoning in the pursuit and discovery of truth does not mean that all beliefs are uncertain and that no belief is justified, according to Gadamer. It means only that interpretation, indeed human knowing, is fallible because of man's finitude.[47] Most important, the following passage makes clear that the aim of such reasoning is truth:

> Here again it is not simply a matter of leaving the subject undecided. Someone who wants to know something cannot just leave it a matter of mere opinion, which is to say that he cannot hold himself aloof from the opinions that are in question. The speaker is put to the question until the truth of what is under discussion finally emerges. . . . What emerges in its truth is the logos, which is neither mine nor yours. (*TM*, p. 368; *WM*, p. 350)

What kind of truth is Gadamer alluding to here in the concluding sentence of this quote? I'll return to this question below.

The realism of the truth-seeker is especially evident in interpreting texts. An author produces a text in order to communicate something; thus interpretation, like the genuine conversation between two people, is a process of coming to understand "the truth of what is said" (*TM*, p. 297; *WM*, p. 280). Given that the text is an act of communication, the interpreter approaches it "prepared for it to tell him something" (*TM*, p. 269; *WM*, p. 256). As Gadamer puts it, "The authentic intention of understanding . . . is this: in reading a text, in wishing to understand it, what we always expect is that it will *inform* us of something." That is, as interpreters we approach the text presupposing that "it really transmits to us the *truth*."[48] In other words, the type of text interpretation Gadamer describes as the aim of understanding is one chiefly concerned with "try[ing] to understand how what he [the author] is saying could be right" (*TM*, p. 292; *WM*, p. 276). Interpretation of this sort is not about understanding the text as a mere cultural historical document expressive of a worldview. Rather, Gadamer consistently describes the aim of interpretation as the concern with the text's "claim to truth" (*TM*, p. 297; *WM*, p. 280). Now, the general hermeneutical question Gadamer poses is this: How does the interpreter arrive at some understanding, a justified interpretation, of what is being communicated, which is "the truth of what he [the author] is saying" (*TM*, p. 385; *WM*, p. 363)? The brief answer to this question here has to be: not by the exclusion characteristic of interpretations that purport to be presuppositionless, which after all is impossible, but rather by being self-consciously aware of one's presuppositions "so that the text can present itself in all its otherness and thus assert its own truth against" them (*TM*, p. 269; *WM*, p. 256; cf. *TM*, p. 299; *WM*, p. 282).

Regarding interpretations whose concern is understanding the text's claim to truth, Gadamer says, "the main issue in all understanding concerns the meaningful relationship that exists between the statements of the text and our understanding of the reality under discussion."[49] According to Gadamer, understanding the text's statements requires that the interpreter go "behind what is said." Gadamer takes every statement to be an answer to a question that forms part of the original situation in which the author produced the text. "Every assertion has its horizon of meaning in that it originates in a question situation."[50] Indeed, Gadamer affirms the primacy of the question over against the assertion. He writes: "No assertion is possible that cannot be understood as an answer to a question, and assertions can only be understood in this way."[51] This is the logic of question and answer that Gadamer calls "the most original hermeneutical phenomenon."[52] Furthermore, says Gadamer, "If we go back *behind* what is said, then we inevitably ask questions *beyond* what is said. We understand the sense of the text only by acquiring the horizon of the question—a horizon that, as such, necessarily includes other possible answers" (*TM*, p. 370; *WM*, p. 352). Put differently, interpretation requires going behind what is said, the statements of the text, to the unsaid, which is everything that is not said, the motivational background, the original historical context, presuppositions, and the like, in order to understand what is said (*TM*, pp. 468–69; *WM*, pp. 444–45). Most important, in the course of interpretation there is a reversal of the relation of question and answer, according to Gadamer—the text puts a question to the interpreter: "The voice that speaks to us from the past—whether text, work, or trace—itself poses a question and places our suppositions into the open. In order to answer the questions put to us, we the interrogated must ourselves begin to ask questions" (*TM*, p. 374; *WM*, pp. 355–56).

Although Gadamer's point about understanding the text's statements by going behind them to the original hermeneutical situation, that is, the horizon of the unsaid, is a correct emphasis,[53] it seems to me that this is not where understanding *begins*. Understanding begins from what was said, and thus from the statements. This is always the case, but especially when the interpreter is interested in understanding the author's assertions—his truth claims. As Wolfhart Pannenberg puts it, "The implicit, unspoken horizon of meaning is accessible to the understanding only on the basis of the assertion and not without it."[54] Furthermore, although I agree that understanding the question to which the text is an answer is also a correct emphasis by Gadamer, there is good reason to reject his ascription of primacy to the question over against the assertion. Questions are not bearers of truth-value, but assertions are—they are sentences that express propositions, and the latter are truth-bearing statements. Moreover, a proposition is true if and only if what it asserts is the case; that is, if and only if objective reality is as the proposition says it is; otherwise, it is false. Gadamer agrees that propositions are bearers of truth-value.[55] Yet, he suggests that propositions are *not* the *primary* bearers of truth-value. Rather, Gadamer insists that the concept of "assertion," and hence of propositional truth, "is antithetical to the nature of hermeneutical experience and the linguistic nature of human experience of the world." He rejects "subordinating language to the 'assertion'" (*TM*, p. 468; *WM*, p. 444). He therefore seems to devalue assertions in coming to understand what the author of the text said.

On the one hand, Gadamer is attentive to various speech acts such as asking questions, issuing commands, expressing wishes, making requests, communicating, proclaiming, making promises, and so forth. He does not abstract the speech act of making assertions and concentrate on it to the exclusion of all the many other different things that can be done with language. According to speech act theory, speech acts have three dimensions describing different things we do with sentences: one, the illocutionary act, which is what I am doing when I am saying something (e.g., questioning, promising, requesting, and the like); two, the locutionary act, which is the sentence that is uttered (e.g., saying "I do" in response to the question, "Do you take this woman to be your wife?"); and three, the perlocutionary act, which is the effect produced by the act (e.g., conviction, understanding, an impression, confusion, and the like). Speech act theory also distinguishes two aspects of the illocutionary act: the force of the utterance and its propositional content. In addition, and at this point Gadamer would depart from speech act theory, this theory holds that various speech acts such as making promises, asking questions, and issuing commands have meaning, but that we cannot speak of them as being true or false because they do not express propositions. Assertions, by contrast, have truth-value because they express propositions, being the sorts of things that are true or false, or truth-bearing statements.[56]

On the other hand, Gadamer rejects the focus on "assertions" as an abstraction from the background of what is unsaid. Thus, he concludes, "In the assertion, the horizon of meaning of what actually wants to be said is concealed with methodical exactitude; what remains is the 'pure' sense of the assertions. . . . But meaning thus reduced to what is stated is always distorted meaning" (*TM*, p. 469; *WM*, p. 444). But this follows only if we neglect to recognize the horizon of the unsaid in the interpretation of what is asserted by the author. Earlier I agreed with Pannenberg that the unspoken horizon of meaning, the presuppositions that form the background of the original assertion, "is accessible to the understanding only on the basis of the assertion and not without it." I now want to agree with a second point that Pannenberg makes:

> The interpreter can only become clearly conscious of the unity of that background of meaning [with what has been said] made accessible by assertions, if

> this unity, for its part, also becomes the content of assertions. Gadamer's correct insight, that every spoken word has an infinite, unspoken background of meaning, does not therefore demolish the significance of the assertion for the spoken word and for an understanding of it, because that background of meaning can only be grasped on the basis of the assertion, and it will then—in the course of interpretation—be itself turned into something that is asserted.[57]

Gadamer's criticism of the "pure assertion" as an abstraction and thus as a distortion of meaning pertains only to a handling of assertions that overlooks their unspoken horizon of meaning, or the diversity of things that we do with language, as speech act theory has persuasively shown. Thus, not only is there no need to devalue assertions, as Gadamer suggests, in order to appreciate the essential importance of the horizon of the unsaid, but also assertions are absolutely necessary in order to reach an understanding among ourselves. Why? Because assertions express truth-claims about objective reality, namely, the objective world to which our beliefs direct themselves but which is independent of those beliefs: a shared world that is both knowable and independent. Indeed, Gadamer himself takes this to be the case. In conclusion of this first point and in preparation for the next, let me quote Gadamer on this matter. He writes:

> The peculiar objectivity [*Sachlichkeit*] of language is a consequence of its relationship to the world. What enters into language are states of affairs [*Sachverhalte*], i.e., an objective content [*Sache*] that is related in such and such ways [*sich so und so verhalt*]. Therein is acknowledged the independent existence of the other, which presupposes that it has its own measure of the distance between the objective content and what is being said about it. That something can be lifted out as a state of affairs in itself and be made into the content of an *assertion* that others also understand, depends upon this distance. (*TM*, p. 445; *WM*, p. 421)

Fallibilism

Second, Gadamer is a *fallibilist.* Earlier we defined fallibilism as the view that we might be mistaken about the beliefs that we hold to be true. Gadamer links his own account of our fallibility to an ongoing integrative dynamic generally operative in the human experience of life in which experiences encountered either confirm or refute our perspectives, resulting in the expansion of our horizon or vision of things. For Gadamer, experience is historical, hermeneutical (that is, rooted in tradition), and dialectical. Briefly, on its dialectical character, Gadamer holds that some experiences confirm the presuppositions we originally bring to those experiences, and others, which Gadamer following Hegel calls the negative aspect of experience, act as a corrective to what we had taken for granted. The negation by means of which this experience achieves this correction is a "determinate negation," involving a dialectical experience, that has a "curiously productive meaning," according to Gadamer. "It is not simply that we see through a deception and hence make a correction, but we acquire a comprehensive knowledge" (*TM*, p. 353; *WM*, p. 336). In other words, in our achieving this correction, which overturns an existing perspective, not only does the thing we experience assert itself more truly, so that we know it better now, but also this knowledge preserves the truth about what we had taken for granted in our perspective.

Significantly, comprehensive knowledge is not definitive knowledge. "'Being experienced' does not consist in the fact that someone already knows everything and knows better than anyone else," according to Gadamer. Rather, he adds, "The experienced person proves to be, on the contrary, someone who is radically undogmatic; who, because of the many experiences he has had and the knowledge he has drawn from them, is particularly well equipped to have new experiences and to learn from them. The dialectic of experience has its proper fulfillment not in definitive knowledge but in the openness to experience that is made possible by experience itself" (*TM*, p. 355; *WM*, p. 338). By denying man definitive knowledge, Gadamer means that human beings can never say the last word about something that is rich in meaning; there is always more to say; there is not too little but too much to be known. "Interpretation is always on the way," says Gadamer.[58] But not having exhaustive knowledge of something is not the same as not having any knowledge at all. Gadamer's fallibilism is *not* skepticism where all beliefs are uncertain and no belief is justified: "The claim . . . of interpretation . . . we always presume to be no more than an approximation: only an attempt, plausible and fruitful, but clearly never definitive."[59]

Experience in general is, says Gadamer, also historical—"Genuine experience is experience of one's own historicity" (*TM*, p. 357; *WM*, p. 340), meaning thereby that we belong to, or are situated in, traditions. In this connection, I cannot fail to note Gadamer's effort to rehabilitate the authority of tradition and, by implication, his rejection of the modernist thesis that an unconditional antithesis exists between tradition and critical reason. For Gadamer, I may be justified in holding a belief to be true on the word of another, his testimony or say-so, because of who says it—he is a well-informed person, for example, the teacher, the superior, the expert, who is in a privileged position to know that something is the case. As Gadamer says, "he has a wider view of things, or is better informed." "Thus," he adds, "acknowledging authority is always connected with the idea that what the authority says is not irrational and arbitrary but can, in principle, be discovered to be true. . . . The prejudices they implant are legitimized by the person who presents them. But in this way they become prejudices not just in favor of a person but a content, since they effect the same disposition to believe something that can be brought about in other ways—e.g., by good reasons" (*TM*, p. 280; *WM*, p. 264). By implication, tradition is an authoritative "source of truth," says Gadamer, indeed a source of "justified prejudices productive of knowledge" (*TM*, p. 279; *WM*, p. 263). Gadamer resists drawing the conclusion that is implied by opposing critical reason to tradition, as if the validity of tradition "does not require any reasons but conditions us without our questioning it." Indeed, Gadamer rejects "the automatic dominance of tradition, of its persisting unaffected by doubt and criticism. Rather a particular critical attitude again addresses itself to the truth of tradition and seeks to renew it" (*TM*, p. 281; *WM*, p. 265). But since critical reason isn't presuppositionless, being situated in, and limited to, particular historical context, we come now to the nub of the epistemological problem for Gadamer: "What is the ground of the legitimacy of prejudices? What distinguishes legitimate prejudices from the countless others which it is the undeniable task of critical reason to overcome?" (*TM*, p. 277; *WM*, p. 261).

Overcoming the Epistemological Problem

Three, Gadamer rejects the "turn to the subject" characteristic of modernism. In particular, the epistemology of modernity isolates man from the rest of the world. Man is taken to be an enclosed consciousness over against the world, as it were. In addition, this epistemology has a representational picture of the mind in which the ideas in the mind of the isolated thinking subject are the direct object of our conscious awareness, for instance, representations of remembered past events and perceived external objects. These ideas serve as the basis for inferring what the real world of the past and perceptual objects must be like. In short, the historical past and the perceptual world are not directly given to us, they are only inferences, and in this way we can indirectly know these external objects. A long-standing criticism of this representative theory of perception is that it leaves the knower in the egocentric predicament: he is unable to know whether his ideas have any relationship at all to reality, because he cannot transcend the veil of ideas. By contrast, Gadamer affirms that the world is directly *given* to us; indeed, that history is directly *given* to us. For him, there is no question of an isolated subject without world, without history, which would have to find its way out of the isolated consciousness; for example, both historical subject and historical object *belong* originally to each other.

Now, against the background of Gadamer's rejection of this epistemology of modernity we can understand why he regards classical metaphysics to have a real superiority, as he says, in answering the question, "How can we explain that mind and language are fit to grasp the reality of things as they really are?" Gadamer writes:

> The superiority of classical metaphysics seems to me to lie in the fact that from the outset it transcends the dualism of subjectivity and will, on the one hand, and object and being-in-itself, on the other, by conceiving their preexistent correspondence with each other. To be sure, classical metaphysics' concept of truth—the conformity of knowledge with the object—rests on a theological correspondence. For it is in their creatureliness that the soul and the object are united. Just as the soul is created to encounter beings, so the thing is created true, that is, capable of being known. An enigma that is insoluble for the finite mind is thus resolved in the infinite mind of the Creator. The essence and actuality of the creation consists in being such a harmony of soul and thing.[60]

It is the "truth of this correspondence" that is behind Gadamer's notion of "belonging": the idea that subject and object belong together. To be sure, Gadamer rejects the theological grounding of this correspondence. He writes: "The concept of belonging is no longer regarded as the teleological relation of the mind to the ontological structure of what exists, as this relation is conceived in metaphysics" (*TM*, p. 461; *WM*, p. 437). "The task of metaphysics continues," Gadamer adds, "though certainly as a task that cannot again be solved as metaphysics, that is, by going back to an infinite intellect. Hence we must ask: Is there a grounding of this correspondence that does not venture to affirm the infinity of the divine mind and yet is able to do justice to the infinite correspondence of soul and being? I contend that there is."[61] The truth of this correspondence is manifest at one level in that man's being is grounded in tradition. Gadamer explains in agreement with Heidegger:

> 'Belonging' is a condition of the original meaning of historical interest not because the choice of theme and inquiry is subject to extrascientific, subjective motivations (then belonging would be no more than a special case of emotional dependence, of the same type as sympathy), but because belonging to traditions belongs just as originally and essentially to the historical finitude of Dasein as does its projectedness toward future possibilities of itself. Heidegger was right to insist that what he called 'thrownness' belongs together with projection. (*TM*, p. 262; *WM*, p. 248)

That is, according to Gadamer, we are always and already historical beings who are, originally and essentially, rooted in traditions. This rootedness in historical life is a given rather than a matter of choice, because even before we engage in critical reflection we belong to tradition. Elsewhere Gadamer elaborates on our belonging to tradition:

> Research in the human sciences cannot regard itself as in an absolute antithesis to the way in which we, as historical beings, relate to the past. At any rate, our usual relationship to the past is not characterized by distancing and freeing ourselves from tradition. Rather we are always situated within traditions, and this is no objectifying process—i.e., we do not conceive of what tradition says as something other, something alien. It is always part of us, a model or exemplar, a kind of cognizance that our later historical judgment would hardly regard as a kind of knowledge but as the most ingenuous affinity with tradition. (*TM*, p. 282; *WM*, p. 266)

The notion that we belong to tradition is behind Gadamer's rejection of what he calls the "prejudice of the Enlightenment." "The fundamental prejudice of the Enlightenment is," adds Gadamer, "the prejudice against prejudice itself, which denies tradition its power" (*TM*, p. 270; *WM*, p. 255). Reflection is granted a "false power."[62] Gadamer's hermeneutics is a post-critical philosophy. "I cannot accept the assertion that reason and authority are abstract antitheses, as the emancipatory Enlightenment did."[63] That is, he rejects the Cartesian apotheosis of reason, which systematically and methodically elevates human reason to the final judge and guarantor of all truth. "Reason exists for us only in concrete, historical terms—i.e., it is not its own master but remains constantly dependent on the given circumstances in which it operates" (*TM*, p. 276; *WM*, p. 260). Yet, for Gadamer critical reason does have a subsidiary role to play in the free acceptance or acknowledgment of the authority of tradition because "true authority is neither blind nor slavish." "[A]uthority is rooted in insight as a hermeneutical process." "A person who comes of age need not—but he also from insight can—take possession of what he has obediently followed. Tradition is no proof and validation of something, in any case not where validation is demanded by reflection. But the point is this: where does reflection demand it? Everywhere? I would object to such an answer on the grounds of the finitude of human existence and the essential particularity of reflection."[64]

In other words, that all of us belong to traditions so much so that man's exercise of critical reason cannot extricate itself from them and hence that his reflections, however critical, are essentially particular is as true for interpretation as for any other activity. Says Gadamer, "belonging to a tradition is a condition of hermeneutics" (*TM*, p. 291; *WM*, p. 275). Indeed, the presuppositions that govern our interpretation of a text proceed from the tradition and bind us to it. "Thus the meaning of 'belonging'—i.e., the element of tradition in our historical-hermeneutical activity is fulfilled in the commonality of fundamental, enabling prejudices." "Hermeneutics must start from the position that a person seeking to understand something has a bond to the subject matter that comes into language through the traditionary text and has, or acquires, a connection with the tradition from which the text speaks." Significantly, hermeneutical reflection must exercise critical self-reflection because "hermeneutical consciousness is aware that its bond to this subject matter does not consist in some self-evident, unquestioned unanimity" (*TM*, p. 295; *WM*, p. 279). In short, tradition-bound interpretations of the text may be wrong.

This conclusion raises "the question of critique in hermeneutics, namely how to distinguish the true prejudices, by which *we understand*, from the *false* ones, by which *we misunderstand*" (*TM*, p. 299; WM, p. 282). Given the importance of this question, one would have anticipated Gadamer devoting much attention to it. Surprisingly, he doesn't; instead he gives a very brief, and unsatisfactory, answer to the epistemological question regarding the criterion. He says that temporal distance has a certain hermeneutical productivity in distinguishing between true and false presuppositions. Gadamer explains: "Only by virtue of . . . 'temporal distance' can the specifically *critical* task of hermeneutics be resolved, that is, of knowing how to distinguish between blind prejudices and those which illuminate, between false prejudices and true prejudices."[65] But is temporal distance a necessary condition for discerning true prejudices for interpreting a text? What about when historical distance is lacking? Gadamer tells us that we "cannot separate in advance the productive prejudices that enable understanding from the prejudices that hinder it and lead to misunderstandings" (*TM*, p. 295; *WM*, p. 279). But given the necessary condition of historical distance, how do we correctly interpret contemporary works of art, written works of philosophy, theology, literature, and the like? Gadamer doesn't say. And is historical distance a sufficient condition for discerning true prejudices? As Jean Grondin and others have written: "Tradition can obviously play a very negative role in the transmission of meaning by prescribing a systematically distorted interpretation of a written work or even of a historical event."[66] Thus the epistemic criterion of temporal or historical distance is much too general. Gadamer leaves us with the disconcertingly open question about the epistemological criteria for distinguishing true and false prejudices and, by implication, correct or incorrect interpretations. I will return to this crucial point below.

Gadamer's basic presupposition about the position of the human mind in the world, of the subject-object relation, is not only anti-Cartesian in orientation but also anti-Kantian. I agree with Brice Wachterhauser, who writes, "Gadamer is anti-Kantian inasmuch as he thinks we can know reality in itself, not the Kantian *Ding-an-sich*, which is always behind our representations, but the Hegelian reality in itself which is not forever behind the appearances but given to us *in* and *with* the appearances." I also agree with his suggestion that closely examining the way Gadamer uses concepts such as "being-in-itself" (*Ansichsein*), "the world" (*Welt*), and "thing-in-itself" (*Ding an sich*) would show that he is referring to "reality," that is, "the real world as it *presents itself finitely* through the lens of linguistically mediated dialogue."[67] Gadamer has a conception of the world that safeguards both its *knowability* and its *independence* beyond our beliefs, as I argued above.

For Gadamer, interpretation is pervasive in human life. Yet, he rejects the idea that human beings are in principle locked up into their separate interpretive worldviews. That is, Gadamer rejects what Nicholas Wolterstorff calls "interpretation-universalism," according to which *everything* is interpretation, and the corollary of which is metaphysical antirealism. Gadamer's view of interpretation is best described as (to use another Wolterstorff term) "perspectival particularism," which is the view that we interpret the world, text, or event from a particular perspective.[68] Gadamer's hermeneutics nowhere suggests, as interpretation-universalism does, that there is nothing behind our interpretations of the world, text, or events except more interpretations, and so on. Thus, Gadamer is a realist about human knowing, because he does not reject the presupposition that there is an objective reality there to be known and the corresponding possibility that finite human beings can know reality itself, the way things are. Still, given his perspectival particularism, his epistemology is, I dare say, best understood as a version of *perspectival realism.* The following three passages make that abundantly clear.

> [T]he verbal world, in which we live, is not a barrier that prevents knowledge of being-in-itself, but fundamentally embraces everything in which our insight can be enlarged and deepened.

No one doubts that the world can exist without man and perhaps will do so. This is part of the meaning in which every human, linguistically constituted view of the world lives. In every worldview the existence of the world-in-itself is intended. It is the whole to which linguistically schematized experience refers. The multiplicity of these worldviews does not involve any relativization of the "world." Rather what the world is is not different from the views in which it presents itself.

Seen phenomenologically, the "thing-in-itself" is, as Husserl has shown, nothing but the continuity with which the various perceptual perspectives on objects shade into one another. . . . In the same way as with perception we can speak of the "linguistic shadings" that the world undergoes in different language-worlds. But there remains a characteristic difference: every "shading" of the object of perception is exclusively distinct from every other, and each helps co-constitute the "thing-in-itself" as the continuum of these nuances—whereas, in the case of the shadings of verbal worldviews, each one potentially contains every other one within it—i.e., each worldview can be extended into every other. It can understand and comprehend, from within itself, the "view" of the world presented in another language. (*TM*, p. 447; *WM*, pp. 423–24)

Ontology of the Text

Four, Gadamer assumes an ontology of the sense of the text that he inherited from Frege via Husserl. Nicholas Wolterstorff has recently stated the clearest account of this ontology and its bearing on the hermeneutic tradition, especially Gadamer. He explains:

> Suppose we assume that the right way to analyze belief and judgment is into a content, on the one hand, and the *stance* of belief or the *action* of judgment, on the other hand. The content of the belief that 2+3=5, is *that* 2+3=5, and the content of the judgment that today is warm and sunny, is *that today is warm and sunny*. Let us further suppose that the content of beliefs and judgments are *entities* of some sort, so that believing something consists of taking up the stance of belief toward that entity which one believes, and judging something consists of performing the action of judging on that entity which one judges to be true. Frege called such entities *Gedanken*, that is, *thoughts*. . . . *Gedanken* are not states of mind. He argues that whereas you and I can believe and assert the same *Gedanke*, we cannot share the same state of mind. Obviously *Gedanken* are also not physical entities. And neither, so Frege argued, are they to be identified with sentences, for the reason that two distinct sentences may express one and the same *Gedanke*. *Gendanken* have to be abstract entities—or as the hermeneutic tradition preferred to call them, *ideal* entities. What distinguishes them from such other abstract entities as properties is that they can be believed and asserted, and that they are all either true or false.[69]

Indeed, Gadamer calls the ontological status of the sense of the text an "ideal" entity. On this point, we find Gadamer saying, "What is stated in the text must be detached from all contingent factors and grasped in its full ideality, in which alone it has validity" (*TM*, p. 394; *WM*, p. 372). He explains himself more fully in the following, often overlooked, passage that Wolterstorff brings to our attention.

> [The] capacity for being written down is based on the fact that speech itself shares in the pure ideality of the meaning that communicates itself in it. In writing, the meaning of what is spoken exists purely for itself, completely detached from all emotional elements of expression and communication. A text is not to be understood as an expression of life but with respect to what it says. Writing is the abstract ideality of language. Hence the meaning of something written is

> fundamentally identifiable and repeatable. What is identical in the repetition is only what was actually deposited in the written record. This indicates that 'repetition' cannot be meant here in its strict sense. It does not mean referring back to the original source where something is said or written. The understanding of something written is not a repetition of something past but the sharing of a present meaning. (*TM*, p. 392; *WM*, p. 370)

The Fregean-Husserlian ontology of textual meaning then affirms the objectivity of meaning in general and is thus anti-historicist. I join Wolterstorff in agreeing "with Frege and Husserl that the right analysis of judgment is that, in judgment, there is something that one judges to be true that's to be distinguished from both that particular act and the sentence one uses to make the judgment."[70] Propositions are the sorts of things that can be believed or asserted, being the sorts of things that are either true or false. What then does this mean for text interpretation?

Earlier I argued that Gadamer's solution—that is, historical or temporal distance—to the epistemological question of distinguishing true and false prejudices in interpreting texts is unsatisfactory. Temporal distance is neither a necessary nor a sufficient condition for discerning true prejudices. To quote Grondin again on this point: "Temporal distance *can sometimes* serve us with a *clue* when the time comes to detect the most authoritative ways of interpretation. It is, however, only a clue, nothing more."[71] Still, let us distinguish the epistemological problem of the criterion—historical or temporal distance—from the ontology of textual meaning that informs Gadamer's hermeneutics. Wolterstorff is right that Gadamer affirms the objectivity of textual meaning, ontologically speaking. This is evident from Gadamer's repeated reference to the text's truth-claim (*TM*, pp. 269, 297, 299; *WM*, pp. 256, 280, 282), to the truth of what is said by the author of the text (*TM*, pp. 297, 385; *WM*, pp. 280, 363), and the like.

Still, this conclusion brings us back to my earlier claim that Gadamer devalues assertions and, by implication, propositional truth. In short, he devalues the truth-stating function of language and hence, by implication, the assumption of an independent, shared world about which our beliefs make assertions. Rather, Gadamer ascribes primacy to the question rather than the assertion, and the corresponding proposition it expresses, so much so that being open to the text's truth-claim means, according to Gadamer, to be *questioned* by what is said: "That a historical text is made the object of interpretation means that it puts a question to the interpreter. Thus interpretation always involves a relation to the question that is asked of the interpreter" (*TM*, pp. 369–70; *WM*, pp. 351–52). Notwithstanding then the importance I understand Gadamer to ascribe to the objectivity of textual meaning, displacing assertions and propositional truth from a position of prominence in the process of interpreting texts has, I believe, serious consequences for Gadamer's hermeneutics. That is, "[w]ithout assertion," as Pannenberg rightly sees, "without the objectification that always occurs in the assertion, men cannot come to an understanding among themselves about something." "Without assertions," he adds, "there is no language."[72] In other words, the truth-stating function of language is to communicate a belief about what is the case, and hence making assertions presupposes a shared world independent of the one making it; otherwise, the very possibility of language is undermined. I think Pannenberg is right about this point, and I noted earlier that Gadamer himself says the same: "That something can be lifted out as a state of affairs in itself and made into the content of an *assertion* which others also understand, depends upon this distance [between the intended objective content] and what is being said about it" (*TM*, p. 445; *WM*, p. 421; italics mine). Pannenberg more than anyone else has, to my knowledge, seen the import of this point about the assertion, which is the truth-stating function of language:

> The priority of the assertion for hermeneutics is further confirmed by Gadamer's finding that understanding always means "coming to an understanding with reference to an objective content" (*TM*, p. 383; *WM*, p. 361). "Carrying on a conversation means to place oneself under the guidance of the objective content toward which the conversants are directed." The objectivity of language that is expressed in the form of the assertion thus constitutes the meaning of the conversation, too. A conversation has to do with bringing the objective content into language, i.e., putting it into the form of an assertion. When people come to an understanding on the objective content, they also understand each other. . . . Although, as we saw, interpretation has a different structure from a conversation, it also has to do with bringing out of the assertions of the text themselves the essential content (including the unspoken horizon of meaning which accompanies it) that they intended, and putting this into the form of assertion.[73]

Yet, Gadamer doesn't follow through on this point in his understanding of interpretation. And his failure to do so has, chiefly, two implications for his view of hermeneutics. First, Gadamer runs together different meanings of meaning, especially the distinction between meaning and significance; second, this conflation results in his inability to distinguish between interpreting what is meant or implied in what the author has said, on the one hand, and deciding about the validity and relevance of those meanings from the standpoint of the interpreter, on the other.[74] That is, the difference here is, for example, the difference between understanding what Gadamer has said or implied about hermeneutics in *Truth and Method* and asking whether what Gadamer says in this magisterial book is true.

Briefly, as to the first point: that a work, say, the Holy Scriptures, has great significance or value for me is different from the life-changing effects that this work has had in my life and the lives of countless others throughout history. Furthermore, meaning as significance and effect is also different from the meaning the Holy Scriptures represent or indicate as a sign of God's covenantal fellowship with His Church. This latter meaning of meaning is also different from the purpose for which the Word of God was written, namely "so that the man of God may be thoroughly equipped for every good work" (2 Tim 3:17). And this sense of meaning is again different from the cultural historical meaning of the Holy Scriptures as a foundational document for understanding the worldview of Western civilization. Lastly, we have another sense of meaning, namely the meaning that is sought in what Wolterstorff has called *authorial-discourse* interpretation, namely that "interpretation aimed at discerning what the speaker or writer said—that is to say, which illocutionary act he . . . performed."[75] The meaning of meaning is manifested here in, say, the author performing the illocutionary act of asserting that the Holy Scriptures are the Word of God.[76]

All these senses of meaning are different from the objective meaning of Holy Scriptures. The latter doesn't change because of its significance for me or its effect in my life. Of course its significance for me may change without the objective meaning of the Holy Scriptures changing. The difference here is clear so much so that I am baffled that Gadamer overlooks it by claiming that "a person reading a text is himself part of the meaning he apprehends. He belongs to the text that he is reading" (*TM*, p. 341; *WM*, p. 323). Of course this claim is even more baffling if we consider the many people who read, say, Holy Scriptures. Does the meaning of the text then change from reader to reader given their different hermeneutical situations? To be sure, if one has in mind here the significance, value, or relevance the text has for me, then of course that may change from reader to reader, but certainly *what the author said* does not vary in that respect. In the same vein, Gadamer says that the "real meaning of a text . . . is always co-determined by the historical situation of the interpreter and hence by the totality of the objective course of history" (*TM*, p. 296; *WM*, p. 280). Here too Gadamer seems to overlook the sense of meaning used when speaking of the effect that a text may have for readers. Without readers the text cannot have a history of effects, so that in this sense the effectual meaning of the text is dependent on the interpreter and, indeed, the course of effective history. But it seems to me that meaning in the sense of significance or effect is ontologically irrelevant. Denying this is, as far as I can see, inconsistent with Gadamer's affirmation of objective textual meaning.

As to the second implication, I must be exceedingly brief. *Pace* Gadamer, I see no reason for blocking the move to distinguish between interpreting what is meant or implied in what the author has said, on the one hand, and deciding about the validity and relevance of those meanings from the standpoint of the interpreter, on the other. Surely it makes good sense—common sense, one might say—to distinguish between "the subjectivity of the interpreter and the objectivity of the meaning to be understood" (*TM*, p. 311; *WM*, p. 294). Gadamer supports making a distinction like this in expressing his agreement with Heidegger: "All correct interpretation must be on guard against arbitrary fancies and the limitations imposed by imperceptible habits of thought, and it must direct its gaze 'on the things themselves'" (*TM*, pp. 266–67; *WM*, p. 251). In other words, "[A] person trying to understand a text is prepared for it to tell him something. That is why a hermeneutically trained consciousness must be, from the start, sensitive to the text's alterity." "But this kind of sensitivity involves neither 'neutrality' with respect to content nor the extinction of one's self," adds Gadamer. I agree. Furthermore, hermeneutical sensitivity is not merely about "acknowledging the past in its otherness," Gadamer rightly notes. It is rather about acknowledging the text's claim to validity "in such a way that it has something to say to me. This . . . calls for a fundamental sort of openness . . . to the truth claim encountered in it" (*TM*, p. 361; *WM*, p. 344). In sum, concludes Gadamer, "the important thing is to be aware of one's own bias, so that the text can present itself in all its otherness and thus assert its own truth against one's own [presuppositions]" (*TM*, p. 269; *WM*, p. 256). In this connection, surely we can appreciate the value of distinguishing between the cognitive and normative aims in interpreting texts. These are different but legitimate activities or goals in interpreting texts. For it is one thing to ask what the authors of Holy Scripture said about adultery, homosexuality, divorce, premarital sex, and the like; it is another thing to decide the validity and relevance of what they said.

Relativism and Its Flaws

In this final section, I want to come back briefly to the question of relativism. Gadamer himself tells us that relativism is self-refuting. "That the thesis of . . . relativism refutes itself to the extent that it claims to be true is an irrefutable argument" (*TM*, p. 344; *WM*, p. 327). What is the argument? Gadamer doesn't say, but I think we can state it as follows. The judgment of relativity cannot be applied to the judgment of relativity itself without self-contradiction. For the belief that truth is relative means that there is no such thing as objective truth. This implies that the belief in relativism is not true for everyone, that is, objectively or absolutely true. But in making the claim that truth is relative I am making a claim about the nature of truth. In that case the statement all truth is relative would be false, if true.[77] Unlike Hilary Putnam, who describes himself as "fascinated by the *different* ways in which relativism is incoherent or self-contradictory," and who also thinks that "each of the refutations of relativism teaches us something important about knowledge,"[78] Gadamer thinks that irrefutable arguments against relativism achieve nothing, tell us nothing. Indeed, Gadamer forthrightly expresses his view that "the formalism of such reflective argument is of specious philosophical legitimacy" (*TM*, p. 344; *WM*, p. 327). These arguments "are too slick" is the colloquial way Roger Trigg describes the response of some, and I would include Gadamer here, to their conclusion that relativism is "flagrantly self-contradictory."[79] As Gadamer also says echoing Heidegger: "all these victorious arguments have something of the attempt to bowl one over." "In making use of them one is proved right," adds Gadamer, "and yet they do not express any superior insight of value. . . . The reflective argument that proves successful here rebounds against the arguer, for it renders the truth value of reflection suspect. It is not the reality of . . . truth-dissolving relativism but the truth claim of all formal argument that is affected" (*TM*, p. 344; *WM*, p. 327).

Elsewhere Gadamer seems to back away from acknowledging the validity of the charge that relativism, or what he, along with others, has called *historicism*, is self-refuting. He writes in a paragraph worth quoting in full:

> [H]istorical thought itself has historical conditions of growth. This is true both of naïve historicism—i.e., of the development of a historical sense in the study of traditions—and of its refined form, which takes account of the existence of the knowing subject in his historicity. Although this is unquestionably correct, so is the conclusion that the *historical phenomenon of historicism*, just as it has had its hour, could also one day come to an end. This is quite certain, not be-

> cause historicism would otherwise "contradict itself," but because it takes itself seriously. Thus we cannot argue that a historicism that maintains the historical conditionedness of all knowledge "for all eternity" is basically self-contradictory. This kind of self-contradiction is a special problem. Here also we must ask whether the two propositions—"all knowledge is historically conditioned" and "this piece of knowledge is true unconditionally"—are on the same level, so that they could contradict each other. For the thesis is not that this proposition *will always be considered true*, any more than that it has *always been so considered*. Rather, historicism that takes itself seriously will allow for the fact that one day its thesis *will no longer be considered true*—i.e., that people will think "unhistorically." And yet not because asserting that all knowledge is conditioned is meaningless and "logically" contradictory. ("Hermeneutics and Historicism," *TM*, p. 534; *WM*, p. 505; italics mine)

If I understand Gadamer correctly, he seeks to meet the standard charge against historicism (aka relativism) by claiming that statements such as "all knowledge is historically conditioned" differ in logical type from statements such as "the statement 'all knowledge is historically conditioned' is true unconditionally." Gadamer doesn't actually say what the difference is between these two types of statements. Yet, I think we can surmise that he takes the former statement to be an example of historical thinking, an empirical generalization about human history, namely the "historical phenomenon of historicism," while the latter is a metaphysical assertion.[80] The question naturally arises whether historicism is an empirical generalization about human history. For example, consider Gadamer's claim that "absolute reason is not a possibility for historical humanity"—that is, his thesis that human reason is situated in, and limited to, particular historical circumstances. Surely this is a philosophical claim and not merely an example of historical thinking. Is the mere insistence that people change their minds about the propositions they consider true sufficient to justify historicism? As Emil Fackenheim asks, "Why should it be assumed that the historical changes to which man is subject affect him so profoundly as to make tomorrow's philosophical truth unpredictable today?"[81] Yet this is precisely what Gadamer suggests in the following passage, where we also find him again backtracking from the validity of the charge that historicism is self-refuting. He writes:

> Even if, *as people who know about history*, we are fundamentally aware that all human thought about the world is historically conditioned, and thus are aware that our own thought is conditioned too, we still have not assumed an unconditional standpoint. In particular it is no objection to affirming that we are thus fundamentally conditioned to say that this affirmation is intended to be absolutely and unconditionally true, and therefore cannot be applied to itself without contradiction. The consciousness of being conditioned does not supersede our conditionedness. (*TM*, p. 448; *WM*, p. 424; italics mine)

What exactly is Gadamer saying here? Why can we affirm that all human thought is historically conditioned without objection? Because the statement that we are historically conditioned is, I take Gadamer to be suggesting, a matter of historical knowledge, an empirical generalization about history, rather than a metaphysical assertion. But the historical knowledge that man is historically conditioned will not bear the weight of Gadamer's philosophical assertions about the historicity of the knowing subject, that reason must always be rooted in context, which he elevates to the status of a first principle in his hermeneutics. That relativism is self-refuting can, therefore, not be met by distinguishing types of statements, as Gadamer suggests. This conclusion brings us back to one final question: What insight is expressed by the reflective argument against relativism?

Pace Gadamer, Roger Trigg is correct in claiming that such an argument teaches us something important about language. Briefly, several presuppositions become evident to us once the truth-stating function of language is used to assert a belief in relativism to other people. These presuppositions must undermine the claim of relativism. One, communication with other people is impossible if relativism is true, because then truth claims cannot be made through language. Indeed, "The mere act of asserting the truth of relativism to other people is self-destructive." Two, relativism also makes communication with other people impossible, says Trigg, because "it loses any conception of a world beyond our beliefs." "The very existence of language, and the fact that it has been taught and learnt," Trigg adds, "suggest a shared world independent of the language." Three, "[W]hen language is no longer understood as being about a stable, shared world, all distinctions break down."[82] In this connection, it is significant to note that this concept of the real world must suppose that "To be this and not that constitutes the determinacy of all beings," as Gadamer correctly says (*TM*, p. 445; *WM*, p. 421). This conception of the world supposes the classical first principle of the law of contradiction. Consider Aristotle's three formulations of this principle: (1) "It is impossible to affirm and deny the same thing of the same subject simultaneously and in the same sense." (2) "It is impossible for a proposition and its contradictory to be simultaneously true." (3) "It is impossible for a thing to be and not to be at the same time and in the same respect." Ralph McInerny correctly notes that "neither (1) nor (2) will have any bite independently of (3)." He adds, "It is not the real that conforms to the logical but logic which reflects the real."[83] Against this background, we can understand why the reflective argument against relativism presupposes Aristotle's well-trusted definition of truth: "To say of what is that it is not, or of what is not that it is, is false, while to say of what is that it is, and of what is not that it is not, is true."[84] Surely then the refutation of relativism teaches us something important about truth.

NOTES

1. Hans-Georg Gadamer, *Wahrheit und Methode*, 3, erweiterte Auflage (Tubingen: J. C. B. Mohr, 1972), p. 260. English translation: *Truth and Method*, 2nd rev. ed., trans. Joel Weinsheimer and Donald G. Marshall (New York: Continuum, 1994), p. 276. Further references to these texts will be cited parenthetically in the text, citing the original German as *WM* and the English translation as *TM*.

2. Thomas Nagel, *The Last Word* (New York: Oxford University Press, 1997), pp. 4–5.

3. Roger Trigg, *Philosophy Matters: An Introduction to Philosophy* (Oxford: Blackwell, 2002), p. 9.

4. Aidan Nichols, O.P., "Relaunching Christian Philosophy," in *Christendom Awake: On Re-energizing the Church in Culture* (Grand Rapids, MI: Eerdmans, 1999), pp. 55–56.

5. Ibid., p. 56.

6. Robert Sokolowski, *Introduction to Phenomenology* (Cambridge: Cambridge University Press, 2000), p. 224.

7. Robert Sokolowski, "Gadamer's Theory of Hermeneutics," in *The Philosophy of Hans-Georg Gadamer*, ed. Lewis Edwin Hahn (Chicago: Open Court, 1997), p. 228.

8. Trigg, *Philosophy Matters*, p. 59.

9. E. D. Hirsch Jr. is one of the first American scholars to make this charge against Gadamer, in his *Validity in Interpretation* (New Haven: Yale University Press, 1967), appendix 2, "Gadamer's Theory of Interpretation," pp. 245–64. Hirsch's article on Gadamer was originally published March 1965 in the *Review of Metaphysics*. See also Hirsch, *The Aims of Interpretation* (Chicago: University of Chicago Press, 1976), especially ch. 2.

10. On Gadamer's realism, see two very well argued essays by Brice R. Wachterhauser, "Gadamer's Realism: The 'Belongingness' of Word and Reality," in *Hermeneutics and Truth*, ed. Brice R. Wachterhauser (Evanston, IL: Northwestern University Press, 1994), pp. 148–71, and "Getting it Right: Relativism, Realism and Truth," in *The Cambridge Companion to Gadamer*, ed. Robert J. Dostal (Cambridge: Cambridge University Press, 2002), pp. 52–78. I have profited from reading both these superb essays.

11. John Henry Newman, "Nature and Grace," *Discourses Addressed to Mixed Congregations* (Longmans, Green, 1849). Discourse VIII, p. 147, describes relativism this way: "[T]here is no such thing as a true religion or a false; that is true to each, which each sincerely believes to be true; and what is true to one, is not true to his neighbor." Edmund Husserl, *Logical Investigations*, vol. 1, trans. J. N. Findlay (London: Routledge & Kegan Paul, 1990), p. 138: "One of [relativism's] original forms is caught in the Protagorean formula: 'Man is the measure of all things', provided this last is interpreted as saying 'The individual man is the measure of all truth.' For each man that is true which seems to *him* true, one thing to one man and the opposite to another, if that is how he sees it. We can therefore also opt for the formula 'All truth (and knowledge) is relative—relative to the contingently judging subject.'" In a similar vein, Roger Trigg writes, "[A] belief in relativism is a belief that beliefs are true for those who hold them. They are not true for everyone, let alone objectively or absolutely true . . . truth is a consequence of belief for relativism, and is restricted to those who hold the belief" (*Philosophy Matters*, pp. 59–60). See also Allen Wood's (to my knowledge) unpublished paper, "Relativism," and Thomas Nagel, *The Last Word* (New York: Oxford University Press, 1997). I have especially profited from Trigg's and Nagel's critique of relativism. See Hugo A. Meynell, *Postmodernism and the New Enlightenment* (Washington, DC: Catholic University of America Press, 1999).

12. Husserl, *Logical Investigations*, p. 138.

13. Trigg, *Rationality and Religion: Does Faith Need Reason?* (Oxford: Blackwell, 1998), p. 35.

14. This too is John Paul II's analysis in his 1998 encyclical *Fides et Ratio:* there are those who in their "one-sided concern to investigate human subjectivity" seem "to have forgotten that men and women are always called to direct their steps toward a truth which transcends them. . . . It has happened therefore that reason, rather than voicing the human orientation toward truth, has wilted under the weight of so much knowledge and little by little has lost the capacity to lift its gaze to the heights, not daring to rise to the truth of be-

ing. Abandoning the investigation of being, modern philosophical research has concentrated instead upon human knowing. Rather than make use of the human capacity to know the truth, modern philosophy has preferred to accentuate the ways in which this capacity is limited and conditioned. This has given rise to different forms of agnosticism and relativism which have led philosophical research to lose its way in the shifting sands of widespread skepticism" (no. 5).

15. Trigg, *Philosophy Matters*, p. 61.

16. Peter van Inwagen, *Metaphysics* (San Francisco: Westview Press, 1993), p. 56.

17. I am adapting here the analysis of Robert L. Arrington on "the kinds of philosophical stances, epistemological and otherwise, usually associated with relativism" (*Rationalism, Realism, and Relativism* [Ithaca: Cornell University Press, 1989], pp. 192–99).

18. On whether or not the word "absolute" in "absolute truth" adds anything to a proposition being true *simpliciter*, see Rene van Woudenberg's insightful analysis in his (to my knowledge) unpublished paper, "Kinds of Truth? An Analysis of the Notions 'Relative Truth,' 'Absolute Truth,' and the Like."

19. Arrington, *Rationalism, Realism, and Relativism*, p. 193.

20. On objective rationality, see Del Kiernan-Lewis, *Learning to Philosophize* (Belmont, CA: Wadsworth Publishing, 2000), pp. 72–76.

21. Arrington, *Rationalism, Realism, and Relativism*, p. 193.

22. Ibid., p. 195.

23. Thomas McCarthy, "Contra Relativism: A Thought-Experiment," in *Relativism: Interpretation and Confrontation*, ed. Michael Krausz (Notre Dame, IN: University of Notre Dame Press, 1989), p. 260.

24. Ibid., p. 259.

25. Ibid., p. 260.

26. Hirsch, *The Aims of Interpretation*, pp. 36, 9, and *Validity in Interpretation*, p. 247, respectively.

27. Hirsch argues that perspectivism is a "total vulgarization of the great Kantian insight . . . that man's experience is preaccommodated to his categories of experience." "[T]he implied relativism in [perspectivism] is a supreme irony, since the purpose of the critical philosophy [of Kant] was to defend the validity and universality of knowledge" (*The Aims of Interpretation*, pp. 45–46, pp. 37–38, respectively).

28. Hirsch, *Validity in Interpretation*, p. 252.

29. Hirsch, *The Aims of Interpretation*, p. 39.

30. Hirsch, *Validity in Interpretation*, pp. 260, 256, respectively.

31. Hirsch, *The Aims of Interpretation*, p. 45.

32. Ibid., p. 36.

33. Jean Grondin, "Hermeneutics and Relativism," in *Festivals of Interpretation: Essays on Hans-Georg Gadamer's Work*, ed. Kathleen Wright (Albany: SUNY Press, 1990), p. 46.

34. Ibid., p. 53.

35. Ibid.

36. Trigg, *Rationality and Religion*, p. 117.

37. Trigg, *Philosophy Matters*, p. 12.

38. On this, see John R. Searle, "Rationality and Realism, What Is at Stake?" in *Daedalus* 122:4 (Fall 1993): 55–83, especially p. 67. In my judgment, Richard Rorty has a deeper grasp of the issue before us than Grondin when he explains that the real issue at stake for critics of relativism is about explaining "why our framework, or culture, or interests, or language, or whatever, is at last on the right track—in touch with physical reality,

or the moral law, or the real numbers, or some other sort of object." "So the real issue," adds Rorty, "is not between people who think one view is as good as another and people who do not. It is between those who think our culture, or purpose, or intuitions cannot be supported except conversationally, and people who still hope for other sorts of support." Richard Rorty, "Pragmatism, Relativism, and Irrationalism," in *American Philosophical Associations, Proceedings and Addresses* 53 (1979/1980), p. 728.

39. For this quote, see Allen Wood's "Relativism."

40. At one point in his article, "Hermeneutics and Relativism," Grondin alludes to the distinction between the epistemic notion of believing something to be true and the non-epistemic notion of being true, what is true in itself, and asks whether it is possible to make this distinction. His answer: "Ideally, perhaps. Nevertheless, what alleges to be true in itself must appear to us to be such; it must convince us of its objectivity" (p. 51).

41. Roger Trigg sees the fallacy in this way of thinking: "Reality is in no sense an indubitable foundation for knowledge as envisaged by traditional foundationalism. The certainty demanded by the latter cannot always be guaranteed by realism. . . . It runs together the reasoning by which we arrived at our beliefs with what our beliefs purport to be about. If we wish to retain the questionable image of foundations, the foundations of our knowledge may be said to be distinct from the metaphysical foundations on which our knowledge has to be built" (*Rationality and Religion*, p. 116).

42. Ibid., p. 192.

43. Grondin, "Hermeneutics and Relativism," p. 57: "To renounce an absolutist or metaphysical point of view is equivalent to recognizing the fallibility of our opinions."

44. On the epistemological points made in this paragraph, see Jeffrey Stout, *Ethics after Babel* (Boston: Beacon Press, 1988), p. 25. I have also profited from Allen Wood's "Relativism."

45. For this quote, see Allen Wood's "Relativism."

46. I owe this phrase to Henry Pietersma, "Truth and the Search for It," *University of Toronto Quarterly* 52:3 (Spring 1983): 221–34, and especially p. 229.

47. Hans-Georg Gadamer, "Hermeneutics as Practical Philosophy," in *Reason in the Age of Science*, trans. Frederick G. Lawrence (Cambridge, MA: MIT Press, 1981), pp. 88–112, and especially p. 105.

48. Hans-Georg Gadamer, "The Problem of Historical Consciousness," in *Interpretive Social Science: A Reader*, ed. Paul Rabinow and William M. Sullivan (Berkeley: University of California Press, 1979), pp. 151–52, 154.

49. Gadamer, "Hermeneutics as Practical Philosophy," p. 98.

50. Hans-Georg Gadamer, "What Is Truth?" in *Hermeneutics and Truth*, ed. Brice R. Wachterhauser (Evanston, IL: Northwestern University Press, 1994), p. 44.

51. Hans-Georg Gadamer, "The Universality of the Hermeneutical Problem," in *Philosophical Hermeneutics*, trans. and ed. David E. Linge (Berkeley: University of California Press, 1976), p. 11.

52. Ibid.

53. Gadamer correctly notes, "It is quite artificial to imagine that statements fall down from heaven and that they can be subjected to analytic labor without once bringing into consideration why they were stated and in what way they are responses to something. That is the first, basic, and infinitely far-reaching demand called for in any hermeneutical undertaking. Not only in philosophy or theology but in any research project, it is required that one elaborate an awareness of the hermeneutic situation. That has to be our initial aim when we approach what the question is" ("Hermeneutics as Practical Philosophy," p. 107).

54. Wolfhart Pannenberg, "Hermeneutic and Universal History," in *Basic Questions in Theology*, vol. 1, trans. George H. Kehm (Philadelphia: Fortress Press, 1970), p. 126. Also helpful to me in understanding the role of propositions in Gadamer's hermeneutics are two essays by Jean Grondin, "From Metaphysics to Hermeneutics" and "The Hermeneutical Intelligence of Language," in *Sources of Hermeneutics* (Albany: SUNY Press, 1995).

55. Hans-Georg Gadamer, "What Is Truth?" in *Hermeneutics and Truth*, pp. 33–46, and especially pp. 36–37. See also in the same collection Gadamer's essay, "Truth in the Human Sciences," pp. 25–32.

56. On this, see Rene van Woudenberg, *Filosofie van taal en tekst* (Budel: Damon, 2002), pp. 82–95.

57. Pannenberg, "Hermeneutic and Universal History," p. 126.

58. Gadamer, "Hermeneutics as Practical Philosophy," p. 105.

59. Ibid.

60. Hans-Georg Gadamer, "The Nature of Things and the Language of Things," in *Philosophical Hermeneutics*, pp. 74–75.

61. Ibid., p. 75.

62. Hans-Georg Gadamer, "On the Scope and Function of Hermeneutical Reflection," in *Philosophical Hermeneutics*, trans. and ed. by David E. Linge (Berkeley: University of California Press, 1976), p. 33.

63. Ibid.

64. Ibid., p. 34.

65. Hans-Georg Gadamer, "The Problem of Historical Consciousness," in *Interpretive Social Science*, p. 156. Gadamer says the same in *Truth and Method* in it earliest editions (298), but in the fifth edition (1986) Gadamer softens his claim from "only temporal distance can solve the question of critique in hermeneutics" to "often temporal distance can . . ."

66. Grondin, "Hermeneutics and Relativism," p. 56.

67. Wachterhauser, "Gadamer's Realism: The 'Belongingness' of Word and Reality," pp. 152, 157.

68. Nicholas Wolterstorff, "Between the Pincers of Increased Diversity and Supposed Irrationality," in *God, Philosophy and Academic Culture*, ed. William Wainwright (Atlanta, GA: Scholars Press, 1996), pp. 13–20, and for these two terms, see pp. 18 and 19, respectively.

69. Nicholas Wolterstorff, "The Promise of Speech-Act Theory for Biblical Interpretation," in *After Pentecost: Language and Biblical Interpretation*, ed. Craig Bartholomew, Colin Greene, Karl Moeller (Grand Rapids, MI: Zondervan, 2001), pp. 77–78.

70. Ibid., p. 80.

71. Grondin, "Hermeneutics and Relativism," pp. 55–56.

72. Pannenberg, "Hermeneutic and Universal History," p. 128.

73. Ibid.

74. On this important distinction, see Hans-Joachim Kraemer, "The Concept of Hermeneutical Experience: Alternatives to Gadamer," *Graduate Faculty Philosophy Journal* 24:1 (2003): 5–18, and for this distinction, pp. 10–11.

75. Wolterstorff, "The Promise of Speech-Act Theory for Biblical Interpretation," p. 82.

76. I am indebted to Rene van Woudenberg for these helpful distinctions between the different meanings of meaning. On this see, *Filosofie van taal en tekst*, pp. 106–114.

77. I am paraphrasing Roger Trigg's argument. On this, see his work *Philosophy Matters*, p. 60.

78. Hilary Putnam, *Realism and Reason*, Philosophical Papers, vol. 3 (Cambridge: Cambridge University Press, 1983), p. 288.

79. Trigg, *Philosophy Matters*, p. 62.

80. In this connection, I have found very helpful Emil L. Fackenheim's 1961 Aquinas Lecture, *Metaphysics and Historicity* (Milwaukee: Marquette University Press, 1961), pp. 62–66.

81. Emil L. Fackenheim, *Metaphysics and Historicity*, p. 62, n. 34.

82. The Trigg quotes in this paragraph are from his book *Philosophy Matters*, pp. 60–62.

83. Ralph McInerny, *Characters in Search of Their Author*, The Gifford Lectures, 1999–2000 (Notre Dame, IN: University of Notre Dame Press, 2001), p. 48.

84. Aristotle, *Metaphysics* 1011b.

4

"The Knowledge That One Does Not Know"

Gadamer, Levertov, and the Hermeneutics of the Question

Christina Bieber Lake

The book of Job is something of a playground for scholars interested in hermeneutics. Not only is it a hermeneutical conundrum itself, providing as it does many options for how we should interpret it, but it is also primarily a tale *about* interpretation. Job's life is the text, and many "readers"—Elihue, Bildad, Eliphaz, and Job's wife—all want to weigh in on its interpretation. But when God finally enters the dialogue, he surprises everyone (to nobody's surprise). For God, interpretation of the text of Job's suffering does not look like an interpretation at all. Instead, he asks more questions, questions that serve to show God's inscrutability and Job's ultimate finitude. In essence, God's "answer" gives hermeneutical priority to the question itself. Job's only good choice in response is to maintain open dialogue with God in all his mysterious otherness.

When Hans-Georg Gadamer approached the problem of hermeneutics in *Truth and Method*, he did it with a view of language that presupposes human finitude and insists on the priority of the question.[1] He described the romantic hermeneutical confidence that a reader could "understand a writer better than he understood himself" as a dangerous idea that ignores our historical contingency.[2] Our historicity ensures that we can never achieve identity with a writer; indeed, "all understanding inevitably involves some prejudice."[3] But far from being a problem, the temporal distance between author and reader forces us to enter a true conversation, a conversation that constantly tests our prejudices. This creates an "infinite process" of finding meaning in a text, a process that Gadamer describes as a "fusion of horizons." The "horizon of the present cannot be formed without the past," Gadamer argues, because "understanding is always the fusion of these horizons supposedly existing by themselves."[4]

This famous fusion is more shifting than it is stable—it is "continually in the process of being formed."[5] It is utterly dependent upon our continuing to think productively in spite of our prejudices—or rather, through them. And the way to think productively, for Gadamer, is to give hermeneutical priority to the question. To engage in hermeneutics is to engage in a dialogue with a text, to be open to it. It is to believe that it has something to say to us, something that we do not already know—even, in our finitude, something that we need. We indicate our openness by asking authentic questions, questions that we hope can be neither leading nor slanted, but that make room for us to be surprised by the answer.

What makes these views especially interesting to literary critics is their affinity with the goals of poetry.[6] Denise Levertov, to choose just one example, believed that the surprise inherent in the process of asking questions is the province of poetry. Poetry can teach the receptive humility of Job. It asks questions of the world, striving at all times for continued openness to new answers and new questions. For Levertov, understanding comes through the communion of authentic dialogue, first between poet and world, and by extension, between poem and reader.

It is not my intention in this paper to weigh in on the philosophical disputes over Gadamer's contributions to hermeneutics. Rather, my goal is to briefly unpack and then apply to Levertov's poetry three relevant concepts that Gadamer develops to describe the hermeneutical priority of the question. These concepts are: (1) the alterity of all authentic experience; (2) the inherent openness of the question; and (3) understanding as communion achieved by language. As I will go on to demonstrate, these three concepts are central to Levertov's poetry, which has the question at its heart as it encourages open, ongoing dialogue.

1. *The alterity of all authentic experience*. Gadamer believes in the hermeneutical priority of the question because he believes in the value of true dialectic. True dialectic involves respect for opposing points of view and experiences, and welcomes challenges to one's own opinion. And for Gadamer, as soon as we have an experience of otherness, we necessarily put questions to that experience. "The structure of the question is implicit in all experience," he writes. "We cannot have experiences without asking questions. Recognizing that an object is different, and not what we first thought, obviously presupposes the question whether it was this or that."[7] Socrates recognized the true value of questioning when he insisted on the difference between authentic and inauthentic questions. Authentic questions are posed out of the *need* for insight, and inauthentic questions are posed only to prove oneself right. In other words, the asker of authentic questions presupposes that we experience otherness as otherness—as something we cannot fully expect or predict.

When this logic of alterity is extended to textual interpretation, we assume that the text has something potentially mind-changing to say to us and that we will not truly understand that text unless we are open to it. Gadamer writes:

> Understanding begins, as we have already said above, when something addresses us. This is the first condition of hermeneutics. We now know what this requires, namely the fundamental suspension of our own prejudices. But all suspension of judgments and hence, a fortiori, of prejudices, has the logical structure of a *question.*[8]

To suspend one's prejudices is emphatically not the same thing as to believe that they can be completely overcome, as Gadamer criticized proponents of enlightenment hermeneutics for believing. In fact, to recognize that a text is truly other and to enter into dialogue with it is necessarily to recognize human finitude and our corresponding need for the other's perspective. In short, to be able to ask questions at all, Gadamer insists, "one must want to know, and that means knowing that one does not know."[9]

2. *The inherent openness of the question.* It is not enough for Gadamer that we acknowledge the essential alterity of texts and of all experience. We must also strive, through the hermeneutic priority of the question, to keep the possibilities of meaning open. It is only if our orientation toward experience is structured like a question and not like an answer that we can avoid dogmatism. Gadamer contrasts the dogmatic person to the experienced person. The more experienced a person is, the more open he is to additional experiences and to learning new things from them. He is engaged in the "dialectic of experience," and this dialectic "has its proper fulfillment not in definitive knowledge but in the openness to experience that is made possible by experience itself."[10]

Gadamer's language is interesting here—the consummation, the fulfillment of all experience is not understanding or insight, but rather a state of being open to new experiences. We lose this productive openness the minute we stop asking questions and start asserting opinions. Asking questions is thus not a method, but an *orientation* toward knowledge. Gadamer even goes so far as to say that asking questions, far more than finding answers, is what thinking is. "The art of questioning is the art of questioning even further—i.e., the art of thinking."[11] It is also very important to note that Gadamer's definition of thinking as dialogue is radically focused on the other; it is not dialogue with oneself. Gadamer mentioned that his thinking about the other was something he learned from Kierkegaard. "According to Kierkegaard, it is the other who breaks into my ego-centeredness and gives me something to understand. This Kierkegaardian motif guided me from the beginning."[12] This insistence on the other, as Donald Marshall points out, shows that Gadamer's ideas more clearly resemble those of Levinas than those of Plato. Marshall argues that Gadamer's "citation of Plato's description of dialogue as thinking intends to show the sense of Greek *logos*-philosophy, not to validate dialogue with the self over that with the other. Gadamer insists that even the 'inner word' that Aquinas takes from the Stoics (through the early Fathers) is not formed by a reflective act, but is always already turned toward the other. Thinking reserved from actual dialogue is unreal."[13] James Risser also takes care to separate Gadamer's interest in the "dynamics of conversation" from the dialectic of German Idealism, arguing that Gadamer "takes language to be living language, the language of speaking of one to another. This means for Gadamer that it is always the language of the voice and, as dialogical, the voice of the other that constitutes the field of hermeneutic understanding."[14]

3. *Understanding as communion achieved in language.* While one might be tempted from the above description of the dialectic of experience to conclude that Gadamer wants us to float continually in indeterminacy, that would be a mistake. Gadamer does believe that understanding is possible. But understanding is never a place at which we fully arrive; instead, it is a kind of living communion between writer and reader, a communion that acknowledges, without trying to overcome, the distance between our experience and the writer's, our age and the writer's. This communion is Gadamer's famous "fusion of horizons." There is a *fusion*—not just a meeting—because we never leave the encounter unchanged. Understanding involves transformation. "To reach an understanding in dialogue is not merely a matter of putting oneself forward and successfully asserting one's own point of view, but being transformed into a communion in which we do not remain what we were."[15]

Gadamer's emphasis on the reader's transformation draws together the notions of alterity and openness to the question that I just described. Because all readers are finite beings, we need others and cannot afford to come to a text—or to any experience—inviolate and inviolable. As Manfred Frank writes, in Gadamer's conception "the narcissism of a self-reflexive, self-understanding epistemological subject is already banished at the outset: self-understanding is always beforehand a being referred to the speech of the other, a speaking which, on its side, does not go away from the conversation unchanged, for it was fused with the alien horizon of its partner. Meaning arises in the reciprocity of an agreement in understanding that cannot be anticipated in advance."[16]

This sense of interpretation as ever evolving is what links it inexorably to the shifting, surprising, and ever fluid properties of language itself. Gadamer's insistence that "all interpretation is essentially verbal" leads us to pay special attention to literary language because of its deliberate indeterminacy, its invitation to read and reread, to be changed and then return to the text for more. Gadamer argues that a linguistic work of art "not only strikes us and deals us a blow but also is supposed to be accepted, albeit it with an assent that is the beginning of a long and often repeated effort at understanding. Every reading that seeks understanding is only a step on a path that never ends."[17]

To describe understanding as a fluid and very human achievement of language is to disabuse hermeneutics of the notion that it can behave according to the methodism of science. And this, of course, is what the poet has always known. For the poet, one of the most provocative formulations in *Truth and Method* is when Gadamer insists that "in fact we have experiences when we are shocked by things that do not accord with our expectations. Thus questioning too is more a passion than an action. A question presses itself on us; we can no longer avoid it and persist in our accustomed opinion."[18]

It is this idea that the question is more a passion than an action that leads me to Denise Levertov and her description of poetry.[19] For Levertov, poetry thrives in open-endedness, receives its form from the world it engages, and strives to have its readers experience what it notices about the world. In other words, poetry lives by the logic of the question. Levertov would have been very interested in the hermeneutical conundrum of Job's life, because she described her own journey to faith as a need to make sense of the suffering of innocent people. Many of her poems illustrate a question-driven, intellectual movement between faith and doubt. Indeed, Levertov's poems effect just the kind of dialectic that Gadamer insists describes what it means to think. She often writes poems in the second person, addressed to God or to famous mystics such as Julian of Norwich and Thomas Merton. In each of these dialogues Levertov engages human experience by asking questions—with or without a question mark. These questions fit Gadamer's definition of an authentic question—one that "breaks open the being of the object."[20]

There is a way in which all of Levertov's poems could be entitled "Primary Wonder."[21] This poem insists that poetry is born out of the need to ask questions; particularly, to ask God—through asking the world—why it is that there is something rather than nothing. In the first stanza, the speaker reports that the banality of life has distracted her from contemplating the mystery of being. In short, the speaker has forgotten to think poetically:

> Days pass when I forget the mystery.
> Problems insoluble and problems offering
> their own ignored solutions
> jostle for my attention, they crowd its antechamber
> along with a host of diversions, my courtiers, wearing
> their colored clothes; cap and bells.

Poetry for Levertov is always about attention. Here the speaker is distracted and unable to pay attention to the mystery of being. But when she opens herself anew to the otherness of the mystery, her resultant praise constitutes the poem's *raison d'etre*, given in the second stanza:

> And then
> Once more the quiet mystery
> is present to me, the throng's clamor
> recedes: the mystery
> that there is anything, anything at all,
> let alone cosmos, joy, memory, everything,
> rather than void: and that, O Lord,
> Creator, Hallowed One, You still,
> hour by hour sustain it.

The primary wonder of "Primary Wonder" is the question of being—why there is something rather than nothing. The mystery of being is something that a poet always *receives* first and *achieves* later, in response. This is what it means to say that a question is more a passion than an action. To the question of the mystery of being the only answer is the poem itself, which ends up asking the same questions about its own ontology. The only answer to the question of why there is something rather than nothing is to assert another verbal something against the void that is the blank page, so that the reader is confronted inexorably with that presence and begins her own questioning. This is partly what Gadamer meant, I think, when he wrote that "the *way* that understanding occurs . . . is the coming-into-language of the thing itself."[22]

A particular poem that illustrates the hermeneutical priority of the question in human experience is Levertov's "The Beginning of Wisdom."[23] Levertov writes this deceptively simple poem in the second person to emphasize that dialectical movement motivated by the question is at the heart of wisdom. Here the speaker's "I" is addressing God—the poem's "You." Although the poem is a questioning monologue, it does posit two participants, and the poem's seven clearly demarcated stanzas nearly perfectly alternate between the I and the You. For example, "You have brought me so far" reads stanza one, while stanza two responds with the consequent, "I know so much."

This I/Thou structure emphasizes that for this speaker, poetry begins with the otherness that is the universe. Not just the otherness of God, but of his creation and of all the works of art that come from the contemplation of that creation. It is, after all, the "You" that has brought the "I" so far. The poet, in Gadamerian terms, has experienced the shocking alterity of the world. And here the speaker is clearly overwhelmed by the world's givenness: "I know so much. Names, verbs, images. My mind / overflows, a drawer that can't close" (ll. 2–3). This moment in the poem parallels what Levertov describes in her essay "Some Notes on Organic Form" as the starting point for poetry. "First there must be an experience," she writes, "a sequence or constellation of perceptions of sufficient interest, felt by the poet intensely enough to demand of him their equivalence in words: he is *brought to speech.*"[24] The experience demands a verbal response, and this response becomes something that readers can experience. Recall that Gadamer argued that understanding is communion by the achievement of language; here, the poet's cup runneth over with words that indicate that this communion has begun. But stanza three also indicates that the poet's best efforts feel light against the shocking alterity of creation, and particularly its unanswered questions:

> Unscathed among the tortured. Ignorant parchment
> uninscribed, light strokes only, where a scribe
> tried out a pen. (ll. 4–6)

In this dialectic between God and poet, the experience of the world's alterity brings the poet exactly to the place that Gadamer describes—to a recognition of human finitude and limitation.[25] This poem is not an assertion of the powerful ego of the romantic poet.[26] In particular the speaker recognizes that she and, by extension, the "light strokes" of her pen are specks of dust passing through a particular world that is itself a small part of the universe:

> I am so small, a speck of dust
> moving across the huge world. The world
> a speck of dust in the universe. (ll. 7–9)

It is no surprise that this movement into the limitations inherent to the speaker's historicity would produce questions. And it is also no surprise that the questions come out of the speaker's smallness:

> Are you holding
> the universe? You hold
> onto my smallness. How do you grasp it,
> how does it not
> slip away? (ll. 10–14)

The speaker wants to know how it is that her speck of being should exist at all, that it should also be somehow responsible to the array of images that flood her consciousness and themselves beg for expression.[27] The questions that she asks of God open her out exactly the way that Gadamer said a good question should: to the knowledge that one does not know. The "I know so much" of stanza two is thus controverted, vis-à-vis these unanswerable questions, by the "I know so little" of stanza six. The silences on either side of this very short line speak louder than the words themselves. Like Job in the face of God's questions, the speaker has nothing to say except to acknowledge that to be brought to the point of knowing that we know so little is to be brought very far indeed.

It is the passion and province of the poet to be confronted by the mystery of being and be left with nothing to say. Nothing, that is, but the poem itself. It is the need for humility in the face of this essential irony that led Levertov to insist on a kind of free verse form that she preferred to call "open" or "exploratory" forms. These forms are open because they insist that poetry dwells in limitless possibility—that it is always in process. In her essay "On the Function of the Line" Levertov asks:

> In what way is contemporary, nonmetrical poetry exploratory? What I mean by that word is that such poetry, more than most poetry of the past, incorporates and reveals the process of thinking/feeling, feeling/thinking, rather than focusing more exclusively on its *results*; and in so doing it can explore human experience in a way that is not wholly new but is (or can be) valuable in its subtle difference of approach: valuable both as human testimony and as aesthetic experience.[28]

For Levertov, contemporary poetry uniquely achieves the openness of the question because of the pauses in its line breaks. Levertov argues that closed forms such as the sonnet suggest that the poet has found the answer to the meaning of some aspect of existence and is now merely presenting it whole for the reader's consumption. But exploratory verse illustrates the pauses and indeterminacies inherent to the questioning process, and these pauses invite readers to think of their own interactions with the mystery of being. Levertov continues:

> What is the nature of the alogical pauses the linebreak records? If readers will think of their own speech, or their silent inner monologue, when describing thoughts, feelings, perceptions, scenes or events, they will, I think, recognize that they frequently hesitate—albeit very briefly—as if with an unspoken question—a "what?" or a "who?" or a "how?"—before nouns, adjectives, verbs, adverbs, none of which require to be preceded by a comma or other regular punctuation in the course of syntactic logic.[29]

Levertov's emphasis here on what the reader experiences in the open forms of her poetry reveals the most important idea she hopes for us to take from the poem "The Beginning of Wisdom." By effecting an open, questioning dialogue between the speaker and God, Levertov also invites the reader to dialogue with her poem *in the same way.* Hermeneutics is not just the dialogue between poet and God, but also, of course, the dialogue between reader and poet. The fundamentals of that process are revealed when we change the "You" we had been reading as "God" to "You: the poet." The "I" becomes the reader of the poem, facing all the otherness that is aesthetic experience. "You have brought me so far" says the reader to the poet. And the monologue might proceed as follows: "Indeed, that is why I read—I long for shocking experiences of otherness that will alter me. You show me the mystery of the world's being until my mind overflows and I am moved to language myself, to asserting something against the blank of the page. And by the time I finish reading this poem I see how small I truly am, and therefore how amazed I am that language, this specific poem, can speak to me. It describes me in my smallness, which makes me feel both as insignificant as a speck of dust, but also significant enough to be written about—inscribed as I am on the pages of the world. You, Poet, have indeed brought me so far." What we are brought to in Levertov's poetry is our own transformation. Gadamer insists that to enter a true dialogue is to be open to transformation; Levertov believes that the poet shows us the way. As Breslin argues, in Levertov "[t]he self, hungrily taking in new experience, becomes a continually moving and constantly *re*formed center"[30]

The special gift of Levertov's poetry is the gift of this transforming encounter with the world. It is a sense of wonder that is sacramental, not romantic, as Albert Gelpi explains: "In Denise Levertov nature is not absorbed by the centripetal force of mind. She deliberately maintains the tension of the meeting of mind and nature. In this sense hers is a sacramental notion of life; experience is a communion with objects which are in themselves signs of their own secret mystery."[31] Levertov sets up many dialogues like the one in "The Beginning of Wisdom" to emphasize what we have to learn about the power of poetry to reveal—but never to contain—the mystery of the universe. The most exemplary of these dialogues might be the poem "The Showings: Lady Julian of Norwich."[32] In this poem, Levertov speaks to Julian as a poet of our day, insisting, as she does, that the mystery of being can be seen in a hazelnut. The poet begins her questioning of Julian by a kind of lament about how much there is to describe and process in the world. The speaker tells Julian that "there's the dizzying multiplication of all / language can name or fail to name, unutterable / swarming of molecules." Indeed, the speaker continues, there is so much to our daily, earthy, particular history,

And you ask us to turn our gaze
inside out, and see
a little thing, the size of a hazelnut, and believe
it is our world? Ask us to see it lying
in God's pierced palm? That it encompasses
every awareness our minds contain? All Time?
All limitless space given form in this
medieval enigma?
Yes, this is indeed
what you ask, sharing
the mystery you were shown: all that is made:
a little thing, the size of a hazelnut, held safe
in God's pierced palm. (ll. 15–27)

For Levertov as well as for Gadamer, true understanding requires that we stand in awe of the vast otherness of experience, an otherness that the passion of the poet reveals but never contains. Thus poetry, following as it does the passion of the question and not the activity of the argument, teaches us how to be wise. This is why Levertov's title references Proverbs 9:10, which reads: "The fear of the Lord is the beginning of wisdom, and the knowledge of the Holy One is understanding." The poem in its openness to experience teaches us that wisdom is not fundamentally a collection of knowledge, but is rather an *orientation* toward the otherness of being and, ultimately, toward the otherness of God. Wisdom begins when we stand in awe of all that we do not know. This conviction is ultimately why Levertov stands worlds apart from such deifiers of the imagination as Wallace Stevens. "Poems present their testimony as circumstantial evidences, not as closing argument," she writes. "Where Wallace Stevens says, 'God and the imagination are one,' I would say that the imagination, which synergizes intellect, emotion and instinct, is the perceptive organ through which it is possible, though not inevitable, to experience God."[33]

NOTES

1. As P. Christopher Smith argues, Gadamer's "philosophy of human finitude presupposes that whatever human beings might do or say is sustained by something which transcends them and in which they are embedded. Speakers are subordinate, namely, to the language that they speak" (P. Christopher Smith, *Hermeneutics and Human Finitude: Toward a Theory of Ethical Understanding* [New York: Fordham University Press, 1991], p. xix).

2. Hans-Georg Gadamer, *Truth and Method*, trans. Joel Weinsheimer and Donald G. Marshall, 2nd rev. ed. (New York: Continuum, 2002), p. 192.

3. Ibid., p. 270.

4. Ibid., p. 306.

5. Ibid.

6. James Risser argues that the topic of art is central to Gadamer's philosophical project. The experiences of philosophy and art "are hermeneutical, both engage in the experience of understanding, both are caught up in interpretation in which the world becomes larger not smaller" (James Risser, *Hermeneutics and the Voice of the Other: Re-Reading Gadamer's Philosophical Hermeneutics*, ed. Dennis J. Schmidt, SUNY Series in Contemporary Continental Philosophy [Albany: SUNY Press, 1997], p. 186).

7. Gadamer, *Truth and Method*, p. 362.

8. Ibid., p. 299.

9. Ibid., p. 363.

10. Ibid., p. 355.

11. Ibid., p. 367.

12. Hans-Georg Gadamer, "Reflections on My Philosophical Journey," in *The Philosophy of Hans-Georg Gadamer*, ed. Lewis Edwin Hahn (Chicago: Open Court, 1997), p. 46.

13. Donald G. Marshall, "Dialogue and *Ecriture*," in *Dialogue and Deconstruction: The Gadamer-Derrida Encounter*, ed. Diane P. Michelfelder and Richard E. Palmer (Albany: SUNY Press, 1989), p. 213.

14. Risser, *Hermeneutics and the Voice of the Other*, p. 159.

15. Gadamer, *Truth and Method*, p. 379.

16. Manfred Frank, "Limits of the Human Control of Language: Dialogue as the Place of Difference between Neostructuralism and Hermeneutics," in *Dialogue and Deconstruction: The Gadamer-Derrida Encounter*, ed. Diane P. Michelfelder and Richard E. Palmer (Albany: SUNY Press, 1989), p. 157.

17. Hans-Georg Gadamer, "Reply to Jacques Derrida," in *Dialogue and Deconstruction: The Gadamer-Derrida Encounter*, ed. Diane P. Michelfelder and Richard E. Palmer (Albany: SUNY Press, 1989), p. 57.

18. Gadamer, *Truth and Method*, p. 366.

19. Levertov was born in England in 1923. In 1947, she married an American and moved to the United States, where she wrote and taught until her death in 1997.

20. Gadamer, *Truth and Method*, p. 362.

21. Denise Levertov, *The Stream and the Sapphire: Selected Poems on Religious Themes* (New York: New Directions Books, 1997), p. 33.

22. Gadamer, *Truth and Method*, p. 378.

23. Levertov, *The Stream and the Sapphire*, p. 28.

24. Denise Levertov, *New and Selected Essays* (New York: New Directions, 1992), p. 68.

25. As James E. B. Breslin argues, the "acceptance of limits—physical, temporal, domestic—becomes intergral to her definition of the creative process" (James E. B. Breslin, "Denise Levertov," in *Denise Levertov: Selected Criticism*, ed. Albert Gelpi [Ann Arbor: University of Michigan Press, 1993], p. 63).

26. As Diana Collecott illustrates, the difference between Levertov's definition of the imagination and that of the romantic poet illustrates the connection between Levertov and Charles Olson's "Objectism." Objectism "is the getting rid of the lyrical interference of the

individual as ego, of the 'subject' and his soul, that peculiar presumption by which western man has interposed himself between what he is as a creature of nature . . . and those other creations of nature which we may, with no derogation, call objects" (quoted in Diana Collecott, "Inside and Outside in the Poetry of Denise Levertov," in *Critical Essays on Denise Levertov*, ed. Linda Wagner-Martin [Boston, MA: G. K. Hall, 1991], p. 67).

27. For Levertov, the imagination's role is always to discover what is there, not to invent or reanimate. She said in an interview with Ian Reid that "one way in which I could define the imagination might be to say it is the power of perceiving analogies and of extending this power from the observed to the surmised. Where fancy supposes, imagination believes, however; and draws kinetic force from the fervor of belief . . . rather than breathing life into the dust, though, I see it as perceiving the life inherent in the dust" (Denise Levertov and Jewel Spears Brooker, *Conversations with Denise Levertov, Literary Conversations Series* [Jackson: University Press of Mississippi, 1998], p. 71).

28. Levertov, *New and Selected Essays*, p. 79.

29. Ibid., pp. 79–80.

30. Breslin, "Denise Levertov," p. 78.

31. Albert Gelpi, "Two Notes on Denise Levertov and the Romantic Tradition," in *Denise Levertov: Selected Criticism*, ed. Albert Gelpi (Ann Arbor: University of Michigan Press, 1993), p. 92.

32. Levertov, *The Stream and the Sapphire*, pp. 50–51.

33. Levertov, *New and Selected Essays*, p. 246.

PART 2

Derrida and Deconstruction: Haunted Hermeneutics and Incarnational Iterability

5

Hauntological Hermeneutics and the Interpretation of Christian Faith

On Being Dead Equal before God

John D. Caputo

We dance round in a ring and suppose,
But the Secret sits in the middle and knows.
—*Robert Frost*

In what follows I will advocate a theory of interpretation as a conversation with the dead. By this I do not mean reading the works of dead white European males, but simply conversing with the dead, with the ones you would meet (or not quite meet) in any graveyard. So if the theme of our deliberations here is hermeneutics at the crossroads, then think of this as a discourse on hermeneutics at the cemetery, as if in coming upon the cross in the road we were to find a cemetery. I will maintain that the creative conflict of interpretations arises from the ambiguity of this conversation, from the difficulty we have in making out just what the dead are saying, for their voice is ever soft and low, almost absolutely silent. One might say, if one were of a mind to say such things, that only as "hauntology"—to deploy an impish Derrideanism—is hermeneutics possible.[1] It is in this general hauntological hermeneutical framework that I will insert in particular the interpretation of Christian faith. I offer thus a contextualization of Christian faith such that the inspiration that comes from the Holy Ghost is itself breathed upon by another ghostly aspiration.

Conversations in a Danish Church Yard

Kierkegaard and his pseudonyms liked to stress that before God, *coram deo,* we are all equal. When it comes to the God relationship, which is the absolute relationship to the absolute, no one has an inside track, a privileged angle, special access. You can't buy yourself "access" and "influence" with God by way of big contributions to the church, the way big contributors to presidential campaigns get to sleep in the Lincoln Bedroom in the White House, while the rest of us middling contributors sleep in our own humble beds at home. Nor is the absolute relationship to the absolute a matter of good luck, as if the God relationship depends upon having the good fortune to be standing in the right place at the right time just as the divine motorcade goes speeding by so that you catch a glimpse of the God not afforded other unfortunate chaps who were not around at the time. The *coram deo* is a great white light, an absolute and punishing leveler of human differences and human advantages, which mercilessly exposes the various masks and costumes that are donned in time and relativity. In divine matters, there are no lucky breaks, no inside traders, no special discounts for members of the family of the owner. Those are the corrupt ways things are done in the world, in a market economy, in a market town. Kierkegaard continually chided the residents of "*Koben-havn,*" the "merchant harbor town," who like the Dutch love nothing more than a bargain, with the thought that you cannot cut a special deal with God. God does not offer special discounts; the God relationship cannot be had on the cheap. When it comes to the absolute relationship to the absolute, all dealings are on the absolute up-and-up.

For example, in the *Philosophical Fragments,* Johannes Climacus spends a good deal of time arguing that, vis-à-vis the Paradox, there is no special advantage in belonging to the generation that was contemporary with the God/Man and no special disadvantage in coming along 2003 years later (well, he said 1843 years, but that was 160 years ago).[2] True, the contemporary generation had the advantage of seeing the man in the flesh, of hearing his words, of knowing the apostles and his family. But whatever advantage there was in that was offset by a terrifying disadvantage, by the "jolt," that is, the stunning, unthinkable, and to a Jewish mind blasphemous thought that this man of temporal flesh and bone was the Eternal one come into time. That jolt was revolting; it repelled and repulsed the contemporary generation, constituting a stumbling block to some and a scandal to others. We later generations have enjoyed the "consequences," the interlude of the intervening 2003 years. We have had the history of theology and the church, the history of Christian art and literature, excellent sermons, comfortable, padded pews and well appointed churches, a flood of musical compositions, and even a Hollywood film or two to ease the jolt and tease us into the idea. But that advantage of ease is exactly our disadvantage, for we have lost the difficulty and taken the idea for granted. We are all convinced that we are Christian because we most certainly are not Moslems, Hindus, or Zen Buddhists. The point is, Climacus said, in whatever generation we were born, we each bear the same infinite responsibility to make the movements of faith, to intensify existence to the point of absolute *pathos*, to reach the point of infinitely passionate existence. Before God, *coram deo*, we are all equally in need of maintaining an absolute passion for the absolute *telos* and a relative passion for any merely relative *telos*.

When it comes to the *unum necessarium*, the one thing necessary, which is the one-to-one relationship with God, we are all dead equal. If you doubt it, he says in the "Work of Love in Recollecting One Who Is Dead," near the end of *Works of Love*, take a trip to the cemetery and consult with those silent, still, and steady fellows lying just below the sod. They will not lie to you; a false word will never cross their lips. They are steadfast chaps and true, to a man. Kierkegaard spent a lot of time hanging around the lovely cemetery outside the nineteenth-century city limits, which was a deeply autonymic operation for him. His very name was funereal, *Kirke* + *gaard*, church yard, cemetery. While other fellows took their girlfriends there for a picnic, Kierkegaard went there to be alone and commune with these silent, solitary shades. To be a Kierke-gaardian then is to be a Church-Yardian, to adopt the view, not from nowhere, but from the "no more." No thinker can think life through like these fellows, he says, those "masterful thinkers" who cut right to the chase. They see through every illusion and offer the shortest and most succinct summary of life. If you are dazzled by all the different paths life may take, go the cemetery, "where all paths meet" and finally end up. If you are dizzied by all the dissimilarities in life, then go out and talk to these dead folk, where all men are equal, just as the political theorists say. In life we may deny that we are all of one blood, but in death we cannot deny the kinship of clay. Best of all, he urges us, go there in the morning, when the birds are chirping and the garden is lush and beautiful, when "the profusion of life out there almost makes you forget" all those chaps lying quietly six feet under the surface. Then you will see that only there do we actually attain "equal distribution"—Kierkegaard was writing this in the midst of the revolutions of 1848—where each family ends up with about the same square footage and share of the sun. Of course it is true that the plot of the wealthier families is about a foot or a half a foot bigger, and death's summary would not be accurate if it did not reflect that. The dead are deadly honest brokers. They tell us succinctly, in their wry and taciturn but loving way, in "an earnest jest," that this is all worldly advantage amounts to—about half a foot. Here, Søren Churchyard says, the prolixity of life is brilliantly and briefly summarized. In the view from the churchyard, we are all equal. Dead equal.[3]

In another place in the *Works of Love*, he makes the same point about absolute equality by way of the parable of the wedding feast. Suppose a man had a banquet and invited the lame and the beggars but not his friends? The world would call that not a banquet but an act of charity. Yet that is just what Jesus said to do, so that in the kingdom the banquet is given precisely for the "neighbor," for love (*agape*) of the neighbor—which means, for each and every one, as opposed to a dinner for a short list of one's closest friends (*philia*) or to an intimate dinner date with one's lover (*eros*). To be sure, the world would laugh at such a banquet; it would be madder than the mad hatter's party. But that is because the world can see only the worldly "dissimilarities" but cannot see the "neighbor" in each man, which is the essentially human and the essentially equal. After all, he says, these earthly differences among people are like the roles actors play, while the real person behind the role is the neighbor. When the curtain goes down, the one who plays the king and struts about the stage ordering everyone hither and yon and the one who plays the beggar pleading for a morsel of bread are just a couple of actors who remove their costumes and go out together for a drink. We would think these fellows mad if they started believing they really were in actuality His Royal Highness or the Emperor of Japan. So, Kierkegaard says, do not lace "the outer garments of dissimilarity" too tightly lest you cannot remove them when the play is over. In the play, we are entertained by the illusion and do not want to see the person beneath the role; acting is the art of deception. But Eternity—or God or death—is not deceived. Thus, if dissimilarity is temporality's mark, equality is the mark of eternity.[4]

We are indeed all equal, he says elsewhere in *Works of Love,* but not all the same.[5] The essentially human, the species-wide difference that sets us above the animals but a little lower than the angels, is not the highest. For beyond the universally human there is also what is most often forgotten: that within the species, each individual is essentially different. If one upright individual cannot do the opposite of what another upright individual would do under the same circumstances, then the God relationship—which is one-to-one—would be abolished. If every human being would be judged by a universal criterion, then everything would be completed in our public secular social life. Then everything would be easy and empty, having removed the depth that comes of the one-to-one relation with God. We are all equal, but all equally different, before God, like so many points on the circumference of a circle, all equidistant from the center, yet each point with its own defining, singularizing, uniquely proper one-to-one radius to the center.

But to whom, then, are the *Works of Love* addressed? To the Danes? To all Christendom? If they are to be themselves a work of love, as Kierkegaard plainly suggests,[6] and if the works of love concern the neighbor *in* each and every one of us, then not only are they *about* the neighbor, about defining this concept as a central idea of love, but they must also be addressed *to* the neighbor: that means to everyone without order of rank, not simply to a closed circle of friends on the invitation list. *The Works of Love* is a word of love sent out to Copenhagen and beyond, to all Christendom; to all Christendom and beyond, to everyone, that is, to the neighbor, with the unconditional and universal word that before God we are all equal, dead equal, and equally worthy of love.

That is the surprisingly cosmopolitan view from a relatively provincial church yard of a merchant harbor town[7]—and this provides the setting for my cosmopolitan hermeneutics at the cemetery.

Before the Secret

What I am going to call "hauntological hermeneutics" owes a thing or two to Jacques Derrida, who is, let us say, its guardian angel or Dutch uncle.[8] To be sure, the name "Derrida" is the name of the devil himself in certain quarters, of the devil of "relativism" and other forms of Franco-American postmodern *décadence.* This demonizing of Derrida is the issue of a deep-seated fear of difference and of an insecurity about the absolutist stance his critics have adopted, which is a matter I cannot take up now. Here I hope only to make it plain that, far from being a form of relativism, this hauntological hermeneutics he inspires in fact reproduces the religious structure of the absolute relationship to the absolute, or an absolute passion for the absolute, a passion for "the impossible." An absolute relationship to the absolute "transforms the whole existence of the existing person," Climacus says,[9] as opposed to a merely aesthetic *pathos,* in which one would be perfectly content to have a "correct idea" but without having to do anything about it. Having one's existence transformed all the way down is just about what Derrida means by having an "experience of the possible," whereas those who are content to play within the domain of the possible have to content themselves with a merely relative *pathos.*

So my quasi-Derridean hauntological hermeneutics shares this Church Yard wisdom, this word from the dead, who can be trusted never to let a false word cross their lips and to steadfastly abide by their views. We might even regard this hermeneutics as a postcard from the dead to the living, as a way to recollect the dead, to mourn their death, and in so doing to ensure that we all remain dead equal before God. Dead equal before God or death. Before God or death or eternity. These three limit structures—God and death and eternity—are, from a hauntological and structural point of view, the same—an aside that itself stands as worthy of a fuller investigation. But suffice it to say for the present purposes that what God and death and eternity have in common is a certain intractable, irrefragable unknowability, a certain coincidence of irreducible elusiveness. They are slippery fellows all, representing as they do the *passage aux frontières,* a passage to the limit. God and death and eternity dwell just outside our reach and just beyond our grasp, ever so slightly but infinitely on the other shore. Death lies just across the line of life, eternity just over the edge of time, God just beyond the border of the world, even as together they all lie just across the boundary of language. Impossible experiences, experiences of the impossible. *Le pas au-dela.*

That is why we can briefly but without injustice succinctly summarize all three under the name of the "secret," the secret that we have no secret access to the secret, and why we ourselves can be defined in terms of having to maintain an absolute relation to the absolute secret, which is what Climacus would call our highest passion. Think of the secret as a shroud placed over things that conceals our view. Before the secret, we are all dead equal, the secret for which "God" and "death" and "eternity" are among our most venerable and prestigious names. Here we are all equally at a disadvantage, all at an equal remove. No one is hardwired to the secret; no one has secret or privileged access to it. If *they* know it, they are not saying, they who lie there calmly, hands crossed, in solemn silence, unwilling to impart a hint or trace of what they know or do not know, unwilling to give anyone a special advantage. If they know it, we have not yet found a language in which we can communicate with them about it. For while the Babelian multiplicity of languages has been stilled there, and while there is but one common tongue there, it is a dead language that we cannot decipher. Indeed the dead can almost be defined by their reticence on the subject of the secret, as the ones who know but do not say, while *we* who visit them of a sunny Sunday afternoon, who stroll about on the grass above their heads, are really walking around in the dark. We lack both the vocabulary and the grammar of the secret, as we lack the language of the dead. Our hauntological hermeneutics is as convinced as any Christian spiritual writer that all temporal differences belong to the "garments of dissimilarity" that are donned in mundane life but are doffed at death, where our common nudity before the secret is exposed. But in this hermeneutics the white light of death, the funereal leveler of differences, the knight of absolute equality, goes under the name of the secret.

But do not despair. For the secret does not paralyze us but provokes us; it does not dispirit us but animates us. Indeed it inspires a dance, a ring dance, which is of course to move in circles. "We dance round in a ring and suppose," the poet says, "But the Secret sits in the middle and knows."[10] The secret sends us scurrying about in circles, drawing hermeneutic rings around its center, while it sits calmly in the middle and knows. The secret does not reduce us to silence but provokes interpretation, evoking multiple and conflicting interpretations, a flood of discourses, a multiplicity of poetic, religious, and philosophic discourses. Before the secret we are like those loquacious mystical preachers and prolific negative theologians who cannot manage to say enough about the ineffable, unspeakable mystery of God. For the nameless secret has many names—too many. The *deus innominabile*, said Meister Eckhart, is *omninominabile*. The unnameable is omninameable. If there will never be enough names to name God or death, that is because we do not know their name. The condition brought on by the secret is not the lack of names but the excess, not the defect of names but the surplus. We cannot stop up this excess; we cannot staunch the flow of names that flow like blood from an open wound. For in the end, the silence of the dead, like every silence, is ambiguous; we cannot quite make out what they are or are not saying. Hauntological hermeneutics takes up residence in this excess, in the polynymic, polymorphic overflow, in the uncontainable stream of names, which represents a condition of unstoppable translatability and inexpungible unknowability. We never reach the high ground from which to survey the whole; never attain the authority to pronounce the final word, the master name that stills the play of names that surges from the hidden depths of the secret sitting in the center. The secret is imperturbably dark and deep, like a tomb. It lies there calmly, silently, aswarm in the endless swell of interpretations that sweep over it up above, the subject of endless disputes, to which it never replies except with the ironic smile of the dead, itself the creation of a funereal art.

The secret provokes us with a bottomless undecidability, which constitutes a bottomless hermeneutical provocation. Whence the origin of hermeneutics in the cemetery, where endless interpretations of these matters of ultimate concern, as Tillich called them, flit about like ghosts on All Hallows' Eve. The secret is the source of the multiplicity of interpretations, of interpretation itself, for if we knew the secret, there would only be one interpretation, and if there were only one interpretation, there would not be any interpretations but only one uninterpreted fact of the matter, one uninterpreted absolute truth, which would also be the name of absolute terror. If we knew the secret—and this is to make the same point—to whom could we entrust it?

The Messiah

Driven on as it is by the secret, hauntological hermeneutics is therefore not despair but hope, not negation but affirmation, indeed, infinite, absolute, unconditional affirmation, yes, yes. But it subjects this unconditional and unlimited affirmation to certain limits, to certain conditions. It feels compelled to tip its hat to the undecidability in things, confessing in a certain Augustinian spirit that it does not quite know what it affirms, or what it desires, or what it loves, which is always inscribed within the secret. It loves with an everlasting love (almost) something, it does not know quite what. Even as it loves what it seeks, it is always seeking what it loves. So just as the pseudonyms enjoin maintaining an absolute relation to the absolute *telos* and a strictly relative relationship to a merely relative *telos*, so a certain pseudonymous "Jacques"—that is not his name, it's all a jest, but an earnest jest—insists on an absolute and unconditional affirmation of the undeconstructible, of something I do not quite know what, while making a strictly relative affirmation of everything deconstructible. That is the structure of what, following Johannes Climacus, we might call a certain religious *pathos* in deconstruction, what Derrida called a religion without religion.[11] For our hearts are restless, and they will not rest in whatever makes itself known and present, which is deconstructible—we look on these things and they say *ipse fecit nos*,[12] which means they have been constructed. Our hearts will not rest until they rest in the undeconstructible, *s'il y en a*, which is the object of a desire beyond desire, which is neither known nor present. Our hearts rise up or surge past what is given and presented in the phenomenological field. What is given is not it, not the impossible secret, which lies just on the other side of knowledge and the impossible. What is given and present is deconstructible in the dark light of the unknowable and unrepresentable secret, which is never given, because the dead won't give it up.

Now if we locate the heart of a certain religious desire in the desire for the coming of the Messiah, in the dream of the coming of the messianic age,[13] then from a hauntological point of view what else can one say but *viens, oui, oui*? What else can we do but engage this passion absolutely, to allows one's existence to be entirely transformed by this affirmation? Entirely, unconditionally, infinitely, absolutely—but with one little proviso or condition. That is, one must make room for a certain coefficient of undecidability, which means, tip one's hat to the secret, *memento mori*. Remember the word from the dead, who silently observe all the fuss up above, who remember well all life's passion and agitation but who now take a cooler and more dispassionate look at things, practicing a colder hermeneutics. That reminder is observed by offering a modest little distinction, which we might take as a word to the wise, as a word from the dead, who know whereof they do not speak. This accommodation is made by introducing a distinction, small, lame, and wooden though it is, between absolute passion, let us say, the "messianic" passion itself, if there is such a thing, in which we love and affirm unconditionally, and the various ways this absolute passion is given flesh and blood, brought down to earth in one place or the other, incarnated in one or another historical language and tradition (the "concrete messianisms"). That is, we are introducing a distinction between an undeconstructible and absolute relation to the undeconstructible (the impossible) and a relative and deconstructible relation to the deconstructible (possible). To observe that distinction is to do no more than recollect the dead, which is a work of love, for the dead have their eye on us. *They* know that *we* do not know the master name, certainly not the way *they* do.

In hauntological hermeneutics undecidability and undeconstructibility go hand in hand. Think of it as all slightly Jewish, arising from a deeply Jewish distrust of idols.[14] So from a strictly hauntological point of view, the Messiah is a shady character, slipping like a shade among various concrete messianic traditions, showing up here, deferring his presence there, taking different messianic forms, never settling on just one shape, the multiplicity of which keeps the figure of the Messiah in play, alive, in the world, but none of which stills the undecidable messianic dance, for the mysterious figure of the Messiah is likewise involved in a hermeneutic dance around the center. The Messiah is the figure of the *à venir*, of what is always and essentially to come, the *arrivant*, whom we affirm unconditionally, absolutely, undeconstructibly, while everything presently passing itself off as concrete messianic goods is deconstructible. Do not confuse the coming (*venue*) of the Messiah with his *présence*, with his real givenness or actual presence, for the Messiah is the very structure of hope and expectation, of the future, wherever there is a future. That is why even where it is believed the Messiah has already come, in Christianity, what is desired if not a repetition, the hope and expectation that he will come *again*? That is what it means to have a history. Christianity, the history of Christianity, which is a redundancy—for "Christianity" *is* the history that resulted from the deferral of the second coming. The earliest Christians did not expect to *have* a history. The history of Christianity is lived out in the *différance* between two comings, which is why the interpretation of Christian faith is inscribed within *différance* and undecidability. History is always a history of deferred presence, of what is groaning to come into presence, but any history worthy of its name is inwardly disturbed by the coming into presence of something unforeseeable, unpresentable, unrepresentable. Whatever is historically given is deconstructible, strained to the breaking point to bring forth the undeconstructible, *s'il y en a*, something I do not know quite what. *Memento mori.* If in love we recollect the dead, who are watching us, and if we do not forget the secret, before which we are all dead equal, the dead will return our love by reminding us that we do not have access to the final word or master name for what we desire, that even the name of the Messiah is the name of something whose name we do not quite know.

The various concrete messianisms are all "inhabited" by the Messiah, animated by his spirit, and one might even say—and this is the way I prefer to put it here—that they are spooked by his (holy) ghost.[15] That is why I am positing another not as holy ghost that haunts the Holy Ghost, a spirit spooking the Holy Spirit. To be haunted by a holy ghost is on the whole a holy and wholesome thing, a salutary reminder from the dead that we do not know the secret, although we have many interpretations. Only as hauntology is a holy hermeneutics possible. On the one hand, the pure messianic without the messianisms is a spook, a bodiless, ghostly, disincarnate specter. But on the other hand, if the concrete messianisms are not spooked by the messianic ghost, they become a danger to themselves and to others, a menace constantly exposed to the terror of absolute truth, the deadly terror that springs from the death of interpretation. The messianic and the messianisms interlace chiasmically, the messianisms giving the messianic flesh, the messianic keeping the messianisms on the move. The messianic disturbs the sleep of the concrete messianisms by whispering ghostly thoughts in their ear that all paths end in the silence of the Church Yard, that before the Secret we are all equal, all equi-distant from the secret that sits silently in the center and will not say what it knows. For we are all equally one-to-one with God, with death, with eternity. The messianic reminds the messianisms that if one individual cannot do the opposite of what another good individual would do in the same circumstances, the God relationship is abolished, for the God relationship is one-to-one, which is why there is more than one concrete messianism.

The Weak Messianic

Now let us see what this hauntological model means in the concrete, in the flesh, if I may say so, what effect it has on those of us who inhabit one of the concrete messianisms. The thing that characterizes inhabiting one of the concrete messianisms, or so it should, is that you believe them with all your heart and you cannot be half-hearted about it. Being half-heartedly in love with something has all the makings of what Johannes Climacus called a mediocre fellow.[16] The whole idea is to have a full-throated, whole-hearted, red-blooded living faith. But the very idea of a ghost is to haunt all that living vitality with an uncanny thought or two that comes to us in a church yard. So the messianic specter disturbs the concrete messianisms with the spectral thought that they are a historical garment, each its own way of naming the secret that has no name, since the dead won't give it up. It is all about the historical point of departure for eternal happiness, just as Johannes Climacus said. Were we born in another time, another place, another world, we would inevitably believe and hope and love something different, giving our messianic passion another form, or maybe even giving passion another form than messianic, or maybe even in another way than desire, and this with no disadvantage to our absolute relation to the absolute secret. There are many ways to actualize the passion of existence, and God does not play favorites. The God-relationship is not a matter of being in the right place at the right time, just when the divine motorcade is passing by.

To haunt the concrete messianisms with this disturbing thought is to bedevil them, to make productive trouble for them, not to destroy or to disable them, but to prevent them from circling in upon themselves, from setting themselves up as closed circles, to prevent their sleeping soundly at night. It is to force them to continue to dance in a ring on the edge and not to think that they have somehow found a way to slip surreptitiously into the center when no one else was looking. This spectral thought roams about the houses of the concrete messianisms and spooks them, keeping them up at night worrying about the contingency of their vocabularies, of their circumstance, of their time and place and language and historical setting. Or, to switch to another figure who is important for Kierkegaard, the Messiah is a kind of Jewish gadfly, like a Socrates who speaks Yiddish, who keeps the concrete messianisms in question, loose, unnerved, and open-ended, on their messianic toes, reminding them of the contingency of their birth and circumstance, reminding them that before the secret, we are all equal and no one enjoys special privileges. The pure messianic fills the concrete messianisms with fear and trembling, reminding them that the invitation to the heavenly banquet is not sent out to the special friends of God, to those inside God's inner circle with whom God has cut a special deal, but to the "neighbor," that is, to everyone, which includes, indeed which *refers especially* to, the outsiders. *Tout autre est tout autre.*

To be a Christian is to believe Christianity with all one's heart, but to believe is to say I do not know; *il faut croire.* The limitation does not lie in Christianity, which one believes entirely, but in belief.[17] Believing with your whole heart is only half the story, not all there is to it. It does not close down the undecidability; indeed, believing depends upon and presupposes the undecidability; otherwise it would be not believing but knowledge. Many different people believe different things with all their heart, and to suppress that is to suppress the one-to-one God-relationship. Believing with all your heart does not touch the cold and heartless heart of the secret. The secret is the seat of the undecidability and the undecidability is irreducible, which is why the other half of believing with your whole heart is to acknowledge the undecidability. The undecidability sits silently in the center, while believing with all your heart is a ring dance around the edge. After all, believing with all your heart does not get a rise out of the dead, does not move those unmoved movers so far removed from us, though they lie but six feet away. Believing with all your heart does not break their silence, cause them to rise to their feet and speak their mind. Nothing does. They remain unmoved. Like a tomb.

The pure messianic floats or hovers over the concrete messianisms, coming from beyond or otherwise than being—like a ghost. The messianic specter is not more than being but less, a half or demi-being. It differs from the concrete messianisms as the weak—Benjamin had spoken of a "weak messianic power"—differs from the strong.[18] That is because the concrete messianisms are hale and healthy beings, living, thriving confessional faiths with determinate and proper names, historical languages and institutions, sacred places, sacred texts, sacred languages, theological traditions, national and international headquarters, conference centers, hymnals, liturgies, candles, hearses and official pallbearers, and even—here is an advantage not to be denied—silver collection plates and professional bookkeepers. But the pure messianic has not the wherewithal to lay down its head and wanders in ankhoral night, like a desert nomad dependent upon the hospitality of those who will take it in. The concrete messianisms are strong and robust, full-bodied presences, while the messianic is a ghost of a thought, a ghost of a chance, at best a demi-being who disturbs our sleep.

A Quasi-Transcendental Ghost

On this hauntological model, the pure messianic haunts but it does not judge; it spooks but it does not command. Far from supposing that in virtue of its pure messianicity the messianic exerts a transcendental authority over the concrete messianisms, as if it were a transcendental monitor or judge, as if it were an *Aufklärer* passing judgment on them from above, the most the pure messianic can do is to exercise a spectral, haunting, graveyard function. The pure messianic is a voice from the dead, a voice in the dark, not the light of the Enlightenment or some sort of religion of pure reason, which looks down upon historical Christianity as an instance or token of the pure ahistorical messianic type and therefore as entirely governed by a priori laws set forth from on high. The pure messianic is more like that Swedenborgian *Geist*/ghost that Kant was worried about than the pure reason he defended. Do not mistake the conceptual status of the "messianic" as a strong Enlightenment universal rather than as a weak or minimalist hauntological shade, as a strong transcendental condition rather than as a poor, weak quasi-transcendental ghost. The pure messianic is just a demi-being, and it is neither a concrete historical presence, a full-blooded living being like Christianity or Judaism or Islam, nor is it a pure transcendental form. It arises from and confesses our common weakness and poverty, avowing our blindness and powerlessness before the secret. It is a hauntological confession, without ontological or transcendental pretension. It does not take the form of a formal a priori that professes a transcendental ideal but of a confession that I do not know the secret.

If we want to give this hauntological structure an ontological account, then we should say that it is not a true universal in the logical sense but rather more like a "formal indication" in the Heideggerian sense,[19] which can do no more than point to something, I do not know quite what, something that assumes flesh and blood in living individuals and living traditions. The ghostly formality of this desert-like messianicity does not transcend the concrete messianisms but falls short of them; it does not surpass the concrete messianisms but does get that far. The concrete messianisms go where the messianic does not go. The messianic is not a formal abstraction of which the concrete messianisms are material instances. A formal universal contains its subalternates under it, the way the universal "dog" contains the various subspecies of dogs within it. But a "formal indication" is not a transcendental form but a kind of weak schematic and indeterminate pointing in the direction of certain concrete actualizations that can be realized only *in actu exercitu*, that is, in the realizing acts in which they are taken up in the concrete by concrete individuals or communities. The messianic is not as sure-footed as the messianisms, but more lost; it is not as reflectively clear about itself as the messianisms, but more befuddled by the cloud of unknowing. The pure messianic has no history of its theology or defenders of the faith, no saints or apostles, no official publications, and no vestments, hearses, or hymnals.

Accordingly, like any ghost worthy of the name, the pure messianic needs a house to haunt, or, to revert to an earlier Derridean figure, the pure messianic is like a parasite that requires a living body to inhabit, not in such a way as to make them ill and lay them low, but just in order to keep them on their toes, on the *qui vive.* So by thus haunting or inhabiting the concrete messianisms, the messianic thereby acquires a certain concretion or incarnation for itself. It is perfectly true that all our prayers and desires and our faith require content; they must, in virtue of the law of intentionality, intend something, which means, be *for* or *of* or *in* something.[20] They must, in virtue of their facticity, belong to and draw upon the founding narratives of their traditions. Messianic passion must always have content. In what I would like to call *the first messianic movement*, the messianic always initially takes the form of a desire for or faith in something relatively determinate and nameable—for a democracy or a justice to come, a gift or a forgiveness to come, a hospitality or a friendship to come. These are the topics of Derrida's later seminars, which turn on what are for Derrida tremendously evocative words, words that are very much like what Heidegger would call "the force of the most elemental words in which Dasein expresses itself,"[21] all of which are words that we have inherited from our traditions. Derrida does not affirm an oligarchy or a National Socialism or an antisemitism to come,[22] although it is true that he is haunted by their menace, disturbed that that is what may indeed come, kept awake by the nightmare that what will come will be not the Messiah but the Monster, not the messianic age but the catastrophe. He is haunted by the fear that such will be the upshot of all our promises, but that is not what he desires and affirms.

Messianic passion always has a concrete, historical *terminus a quo.* We begin where we are; where else could we begin? But the *second messianic movement* is to circumcise this content, to cut it open in order to give it a future, to keep the future open to something coming, I do not know quite what, something indeterminate, an open-ended *terminus ad quem.* Remember the dead, who remind us that *we* do not know what *they* know and hence that we do not know the name of what we desire. This second messianic movement is thus a work of carrying to an unforeseeable infinity the movement of what is astir in these words. For these are the least bad words we have *today* for something shrouded by the deathly secret, something *to come*, something unforeseeable, something that cannot be contained by those words that we use in the present to name justice or the gift. The second messianic movement evokes the spectral possibilities that haunt but also animate these words, like a good spirit or a guardian angel or a holy ghost, or even like a devilish fellow who prods these words and gives them no rest. "Democracy" and "justice" are words that invoke an open-ended future rather than describe the present, words of unconditional passion for which there are all around us only contingent and conditional realizations. *Inquietum est cor nostrum*, our hearts are restless with an infinite restlessness that is not quenched by anything that is present.

The relationship of the messianic to the concrete messianisms is not *logical* but *hauntological*. It is not a matter of the formal relationship of the universal to the particular, or the superalternate to the subalternate, of the pure to the empirical, which are the categories of formal or transcendental logic, but rather as a hauntological difference between a living presence and the specters by which it is inhabited. We might also say that the relationship between them is not logical but *confessional* or better *circumfessional*, where we would distinguish between a more strictly Augustinian confession, which is also a confession that professes, and a confession that circum-fesses but without a profession. For the concrete messianisms have proper names to profess, untranslatable names, names that are above every other name, at the sound of which everyone's knees are to bend, names that they believe with their whole heart. But in the weak, ghostly circumfessional messianic one gives up the idea that there is a final vocabulary for its desire, that there are final unrevisable, untranslatable terms in which my absolute passion can be cast. The weak messianic confession is a confession of its weakness. So the messianic is only a quasi-Augustinian confession, where I am always asking what I love when I love my God and I am always in the dark about the answer, because the dead won't give it up. Here I am haunted by the idea that in the name of God, or of the love of God, or of the God of love, two good people may do opposite things, might believe with all their heart opposite things. So one might well argue that this weaker messianic confession is an even greater confession, for it has more to confess, is more at a loss, is more radically cut and adrift, more radically a question unto itself than in the confessional confessions, where one has all the benefits of churches and synagogues, hymnals and long robes, canons of orthodoxy and honorary degrees, by observing which professional clerics can earn a profitable living professing with an unnerving certainty what they profess not to know but to believe, while holding suspect those who believe differently. To suspect a good man who does the opposite of another good man is to abolish the God-relationship—in the name of God! It was ever thus.

A Haunting Conclusion

I have called upon a hauntological hermeneutics to contextualize Christian faith. I have not engaged in a contest between deconstruction and Christianity, which makes no sense, since deconstruction is not a position to take but a certain way of having a position (or de-position), Christian or otherwise. I have not chosen Derrida over Kierkegaard, because it is not a matter of choosing between them.

But I have invoked the hauntological structure of undecidability as the framework or context in which the leap of faith, Christian faith to be sure, but any faith, takes place. I have thus allowed the Holy Ghost to be disturbed by another ghost, a spectral figure of the secret, a ghost who prowls about in a deathly shroud trying to unsettle everyone. I have done all this not out of impishness or impudence or impiety but in the name of God, or in the name of the absolute equality of each individual before God. Before God, or death, or the absolute secret, before which we are equal, dead equal. God does not cut inside deals with favorites, does not engage in insider trading. God's covenant is a fair deal, on the up-and-up, and if a banquet is thrown in the mad-hatter, topsy-turvy kingdom of God, then it is one in which the outsiders are in and insiders are out. That means God's covenant is cut with everybody. Or else "God" is an idol, a narcissistic image we project in the name not of love of the neighbor but of self-love, which is the very opposite of the love advocated in the *Works of Love*. When the invitations go out to what is called the "neighbor" in the *Works of Love*, that means they go out to *everyone*, which means the other, *tout autre*, not to a short list of insiders and special friends, which means the same.

In hauntological hermeneutics, the "before God," *coram deo*, shades off into before death, *coram morte*. We are all equal before God or death, which means, all equi-distant from the secret, absolutely related to and removed from the absolute secret, equally deprived of transcendental credentials, cut off and circumcised from the secret that sits in the middle and knows. We are dead equal, equally driven by a passion for the undeconstructible, equally haunted by the hope of things to come, equally disturbed by the midnight thought that, were we born at another time, in another place, in another language, we would have formulated our absolute passion relatively differently, and with no absolute disadvantage before God.

Remember the secret. It does not paralyze us or reduce us to silence. On the contrary, it multiplies interpretations, sending us round and round the ring of interpretation. It multiplies discourses, so that names fly up like sparks in the cold night air of the secret. Let there be many dances, many names for God, omninameable, or death, God or death, so long as all of them are true.

Remember what Kierkegaard said in the *Works of Love*, that if one good individual cannot do the opposite of what another good person would do in the same circumstances, the God-relationship is abolished and everything is reduced to the public and the universal and the same. That is because for both individuals, the question is raised about what they love when they love their God and for both in absolute passion.

Remember that there are many ways to have an absolute passion for the absolute, and a relative passion for the relative. Let there be many ways to actualize the absolute passion for the absolute, many ways to charge existence to infinity, so long as all of them are true. Let there be many ways to transform our whole existence, inside and outside Christianity, many ways to bend our knee in absolute passion, so long as all of them are true.

Above all, remember the dead. Nothing moves them to speak out, or causes them to intervene in our disputes, or motivates them to take a stand in our endless interpretations of the secret, which we may assume they would surely do were one of us up above to hit upon the secret that they know but will not say. We cannot but wonder what is running through their minds as they lie there, calmly listening to the bustle and buzz overhead. They well remember all the passion of the ring dance up above. They well remember the diverse and colorful garments of dissimilarities they wore on the stage of life. They cannot but smile when they recall this fellow Hans, a few plots over, who strutted about like quite a prosperous fellow up there, and that poor chap Nielson, several plots down, who could never make ends meet up above. A man here, a woman there; a rich man here, a poor man there; a famous judge here, a humble pastor there; a very ardent Christian here, an equally passionate Moslem there. But down here, down below, they are all equal and they are all neighbors, of common kin and clay. These masterful thinkers teach us, in the succinct and silent seminar they conduct down below, that we are all equal, all equally removed from the secret by the small but infinite distance of six feet of earth.

Meanwhile, back in the cemetery, Magister Kierkegaard, the Church Yard philosopher, that master of conversations with the dead, can be found concealed behind a tree on a sunny summer morning, while all the birds are chirping, making notes for a new upbuilding discourse. In it, he intends to remind all of Copenhagen, nay, all of Christendom, nay, everyone, the whole world, *urbi et orbi*, for we are all neighbors, everyone without exception, that before God, *coram deo*, we are all equal.

Dead equal.

NOTES

1. I am borrowing the figures of the "specter" and of a "hauntology" from Jacques Derrida, *Specters of Marx: The State of the Debt, the Work of Mourning, and the New International*, trans. Peggy Kamuf (New York: Routledge, 1994).

2. See *Kierkegaard's Writings*, volume 7: *Philosophical Fragments, or A Fragment of Philosophy* and *Johannes Climacus, or De Omnibus dubitandum est*, trans. and ed. Howard and Edna Hong (Princeton: Princeton University Press, 1985), chs. 4 and 6.

3. *Kierkegaard's Writings*, XVI, *Works of Love*, trans. and ed. Howard and Edna Hong (Princeton: Princeton University Press, 1995), pp. 345–46.

4. *Works of Love*, pp. 81–89.

5. *Works of Love*, p. 230.

6. *Works of Love*, pp. 359 ff.

7. A final note on Kierkegaard: The motif of the absolute equality of each individual before God in Kierkegaard and the pseudonyms competes with and disrupts his Christo-centrism, that is, his central motif that only before the Paradox of the God/man, and hence only in Christianity, can existence achieve absolute passion. But this Christo-centrism privileges Christians over non-Christians in a way that is disturbed by the theme of absolute equality, for the God-relationship would be destroyed if two men could not achieve ab-

solute passion by doing the opposite of one another (*Works of Love*, 230), that is, the one being Christian, the other not. For a penetrating account of the universally human in *Works of Love* and the upbuilding discourses, see George Pattison, *Kierkegaard's Upbuilding Discourses: Philosophy, Literature and Theology* (London: Routledge, 2002).

8. Here, as always, I argue that although Derrida is a critic of the word "hermeneutics," which he takes to mean decoding or deciphering a master meaning, deconstruction has in fact all the makings of a hermeneutics more radically conceived.

9. *Kierkegaard's Writings*, XII.1, *Concluding Unscientific Postscript to "Philosophical Fragments,"* trans. and ed. Howard and Edna Hong (Princeton: Princeton University Press, 1992), p. 387.

10. Robert Frost, "The Secret Sits," in *Poetry of Robert Frost*, ed. Edward Connery Lathem (New York: Vintage Books, 2001), p. 362.

11. Derrida, *The Gift of Death*, trans. David Wills (Chicago: University of Chicago Press, 1995), p. 49.

12. Augustine, *Confessiones*, X, 6.

13. Messianic desire would apply to the "religions of the Book," to the three great monotheisms. How to identify religious desire outside these religions is a more difficult problem and may perhaps involve something other than passion or desire, e.g., the passion or desire to detach oneself from passion or desire. There is no one thing called "religion," which is a Western, Latin word for something, I do not quite know what.

14. That is a motif which has been nicely improvised upon in Bruce Benson, *Graven Ideologies: Nietzsche, Derrida and Marion on Modern Idolatry* (Downers Grove, IL: Inter-Varsity Press, 2002).

15. Christianity for Derrida is one of the "concrete messianisms," one of the historical garbs assumed by the figure of the Messiah. He mentions several such messianisms, both religious and philosophical: the three great religions of the Book, Judaism, Christianity, and Islam, and the three great philosophical eschatologies of Hegel, Marx, and Heidegger. The messianic or messianicity, on the other hand, is a pure, formal, open-ended hope, a hope not in some determinate outcome to history, like the hope in the second coming of Jesus in Christianity, or the repetition of the first Greek beginning in Heidegger, or the Absolute's return to itself in pure self-knowledge, but a hope in the future itself, in the very idea of the *à venir.* The *venue*, the coming of the Messiah, is thus to be distinguished from the historically given ways in which the messianic figure is concretely represented. The real and actual history of the concrete messianisms is so many ways for the Messiah to come, so many ways the Messiah enters time and history. These matters are discussed in some detail, with extensive references to their textual sources, in *Deconstruction in a Nutshell: A Conversation with Jacques Derrida* (New York: Fordham University Press, 1977), ch. 6. Climacus was flirting with something like this distinction when he spoke about the relationship between the *Fragments* and the *Postscript.* In the *Fragments* he was describing the formal structure of the relationship to the Teacher, but in the *Postscript* he gave that nude and formal structure its concrete "historical costume" (*Postscript*, p. 10), fleshed it out in all of its historical particularity. The *Fragments* were describing a ghost of a possibility, an ethereal thing, and were all about "the god," which does not exist, while Christianity is its concrete and historical embodiment.

16. *Fragments*, p. 37.

17. If I know something to be true, I also believe it. But from the fact that I believe something, it does not follow that I know it to be true; it is in that sense that I speak of belief, which is a faith, not a knowledge.

18. The Messiah is a figure Derrida clearly inherited from the religions of the book, but the immediate source from which Derrida borrowed the idea was Walter Benjamin, for whom the figure was not only a figure for the future but also a figure of memory and mourning, thus containing a reference to the dead. On Benjamin's use of the idea, we today are the messianic generation whom the dead awaited, whom they were expecting to right the world's wrongs, so that we bear an infinite responsibility to them to bring about the messianic age. See Walter Benjamin, "Theses on the Philosophy of History," in *Illuminations: Essays and Reflections*, trans. Harry Zohn, ed. Hannah Arendt (New York: Schocken Books, 1969), pp. 253–64; cf. Derrida, *Specters*, pp. 180–81 n2.

19. See Martin Heidegger, *Phänomenologische Interpretationen zu Aristoteles. Einführung in die phänomenologische Forschung*, WS 1921/22, *Gesamtausgabe*, vol. 61, Hg. W. Bröcker and K. Bröcker-Oltmanns (Frankfurt/Main: Klostermann, 1985), pp. 33–34, 60–61 et passim. See Daniel O. Dahlstrom, "Heidegger's Method: Philosophical Concepts as Formal Indications," *Review of Metaphysics* 47 (1994): 775–95; and John van Buren, *The Young Heidegger* (Bloomington: Indiana University Press, 1994).

20. However, intentionality does not guarantee a determinate object. Husserl points out that it is possible for an intentional act to be directed at an indeterminate object, in which case indeterminacy is what specifically or determinately characterizes the essence of the act. See Edmund Husserl, *The Shorter Logical Investigations*, trans. J. N. Findlay, ed. Dermot Moran (London: Routledge, 2001), p. 228. In Heidegger and Kierkegaard, the feeling of anxiety is determinately differentiated from fear precisely by the indeterminacy of its object.

21. Martin Heidegger, *Being and Time*, trans. Edward Robinson and John Macquarie (New York: Harper and Row, 1962), p. 262.

22. See "De l'antisémitisme à venir," in Jacques Derrida and Elisabeth Roudinesco, *De quoi demain . . . Dialogue* (Paris: Fayard/Galilée, 2001), pp. 175 ff.

6

Limited Inc/arnation

Revisiting the Searle/Derrida Debate in Christian Context

James K. A. Smith

Propaedeutics: On Confessional Theology and Scriptural Authority

The hermeneutical question of authorial intent simply cannot be circumvented for a tradition that receives the Scriptures as the Word of God.[1] If the Scriptures are to function as an *authority* for faith and practice, that authority must derive from the divine Author in some way. As articulated in the Belgic Confession, we receive these holy books as "regulating, founding, and establishing our faith . . . because the Holy Spirit testifies in our hearts that they are from God."[2] Or as formulated by the Westminster Confession, "[t]he authority of holy scripture, for which it ought to be believed and obeyed, dependeth not upon the testimony of any man or church, but wholly upon God, (who is truth in himself,) the author thereof; and therefore it is to be received, because it is the word of God."[3] The reception of the Scriptures as the Word of God—and the reception of them as binding upon faith, thought, and practice—is thus directly linked to their ability to communicate to us God's will for his covenant people.[4] Authority, then, is linked to authorship, and more specifically, to the communication of the Author's will (intention) to the community. The special case of biblical interpretation and authority for a confessional community, then, raises larger questions regarding interpretation, authority, and authorial intent. While the case of scriptural authority is the catalyst, my primary interest here is that set of larger questions.

Given this sine qua non, it would seem that the radical semiotics of Jacques Derrida must be the target of Christian critique. And indeed, a number of criticisms have been leveled at Derrida by Christian philosophers and theologians, echoing the earlier critique articulated by John Searle. In this chapter, I want to argue that these Christian critiques of Derrida are misguided, precisely because they follow (or at least parallel) Searle's misguided critique of Derrida.[5] Thus, I will revisit the Derrida/Searle debate within a specifically Christian context. In particular, I will demonstrate (1) that Derrida's account of the "iterability" of the sign is consistent with the finitude of a good creation, and (2) that Derrida's account does not jettison the role of authorial intent, but only mitigates the power of the author to "govern" all interpretation. In other words, Derrida does *not* deny that language *communicates* (contra Searle). I will then argue that the latter aspect is consistent with God's revelation of himself in Christ to finite (and free) interpreters. God's self-revelation—whether in Scripture or in the Incarnation itself—follows an "incarnational logic" that is consistent with Derrida's account of semiotic operation.[6] In other words, the Incarnation itself—as God's communication to humanity—is iterable according to Derrida's account.

The "Received" Derrida: Searle and His Christian Heirs

Derrida's Religious Despisers

Many evangelical philosophers and theologians have taken Jacques Derrida to be some form of the prophet of the Beast—the anti-Author with respect to interpretation and authorial intent.[7] The common understanding of Derrida—which I will describe as the "received" Derrida, mediated by American English departments—is that his semiotics (his accounts of language as *signs*) spells the impossibility for texts to communicate the intentions of their authors. As a result, according to the "received" Derrida, interpretation is a wholly arbitrary endeavor—a creative game with the play of signifiers where the reader is Lord of the dance. Even some of our best theologians are purveyors of this reading. For instance, Nicholas Wolterstorff suggests that in "deconstructionist [. . .] play-of-interpretations style of interpretation" there is no constraint on interpretation save "imagination." This supposedly "deconstructionist" approach is then set up in opposition to what he calls "authorial discourse interpretation," which is interested in understanding just what an author means when she writes something. The opposition comes to the fore when, to follow Wolterstorff's example, you have something like a *promise:* if my wife makes me a promise—"I promise we'll go golfing on Saturday"—my interest as interpreter of her utterance is just what she *means* when she says that: This Saturday? Nine holes or eighteen? At Saskatoon or Indian Trails? Rain or shine? But for Wolterstorff, Derrida's "play-of-interpretations" hermeneutic precludes such questions—such an approach "does not get one in touch with what someone said."[8] Wolterstorff then goes on to draw the analogy between the promise and the Scriptures as a covenantal communication or medium of "divine discourse": "If you do believe that the Scriptures are a medium of divine discourse, then what is wanted is authorial discourse interpretation. Nothing else will do. Not textual-sense interpretation [à la Ricoeur], and not play-of-interpretations interpretation [à la Derrida]."[9]

A similar opposition is set up by Kevin Vanhoozer: Taking Derrida to be a "hermeneutic nonrealist" and "literary atheist,"[10] Vanhoozer claims that deconstruction signals the impossibility of communication. Since "meaning is located in the author's intention to convey a particular message through signs," and since "[a]ccording to Derrida . . . the notion of a mental intention is a metaphysical chimera," then it follows, according to Vanhoozer's logic, that Derridean semiotics preclude authorial intent in their consideration of meaning.[11] Vanhoozer goes on to formulate his reading of Derrida in terms of "presence" and "absence"—an important theme to which we will return below. According to Vanhoozer, Derrida's analysis of language "destroys the ideal of pure presence"; presence "is only a mirage." Because Derrida denies "that there is *any* presence," Vanhoozer concludes that "[a]bsence is the first and last word."[12] What exactly does this mean? Take Vanhoozer's example: if I want to understand the Gospel of Mark, according to Derrida the "meaning" of Mark's Gospel does not rest on an author "Mark" because we "never do reach the authorial presence of Mark."[13] Because Derrida's semiotics precludes *full presence,* Vanhoozer concludes that it precludes *meaning* insofar as meaning is linked to authorial intent, and authorial intent is linked to the full presence of the author (to himself and to us). Deconstructionist accounts of language, then, would preclude the very reception of the Scriptures *as* the authoritative Word of God insofar as they cut off any access to the Author. As such, it would seem that we are left with the (false) disjunctions articulated by Brian Ingraffia: postmodern theory *or* biblical theology; Derrida *or* meaning; deconstruction *or* authorial intent.[14]

What is the genesis of such a reading of Derrida? I want to here demonstrate that this understanding of Derrida—the "received" Derrida—moves in the wake of Searle's Derrida, generated by his *mis*reading of Derrida's claims. After summarizing Searle's reading, I will move on to demonstrate why it is a *mis*reading, then offer an alternative account of Derrida's claims in a concluding section.

A Genealogy of the "Received" Derrida: Searle's "Reply"

The key text in this genealogy[15] of the "received" Derrida is Searle's "Reply"[16] to Derrida's "Signature Event Context,"[17] both appearing in the first issue of *Glyph: Johns Hopkins Textual Studies.* Derrida's essay—which I'll comment on below—was originally delivered to a conference in Montreal on the theme of "Communication" in 1971. As such, the very notion and possibility of communication is central to the discussion. But I would argue that Searle's "Reply" indicates a serious *mis*communication—one that Derrida carefully demonstrated.

Is this a performative contradiction on Derrida's part? Doesn't deconstruction in fact *glorify* miscommunication? And therefore doesn't Derrida's protest about being *mis*understood run counter to his own theoretical claims? Or instead, does the fact that Derrida protests this misreading signal that "deconstruction" perhaps is not claiming what we thought? Could it be that Derrida's insistence on being read *well* alerts us that his account of interpretation might not be what we thought?[18] In other words, I want to suggest that the "received" Derrida—the "Searlean" Derrida—is not the "real" Derrida.

If Searle is Dr. Frankenstein to this monstrous "received" Derrida, how did this creature come about? And what are some of its anatomical features? First, in general, I would argue that the "received" Derrida is generated by Searle's confusion about just what is at stake for Derrida (in SEC). Searle's essay restates Derrida's position—his supposed "general attack on the idea of communication as the communication of intended meanings" (R, p. 199)—as follows: "The argument [of SEC] is that since writing can and must be able to function in the radical absence of the sender, the receiver, and the context of production, it *cannot* be the communication of the sender's meaning to the receiver" (R, p. 199; emphasis added). He goes on to conclude that since all statements must be "iterable,"[19] according to Derrida, then it must follow that "the horizon of communication is *not* the communication of consciousnesses or presences nor is it the transport of the intended meaning (*vouloir dire*) of the author" (R, 199; emphasis added). Finally, he suggests that Derrida wants to show that "writing is *not* a vehicle of intentionality" or that "intentionality is *absent* from written communication" (R, 201; emphasis added). In sum, Searle concludes that Derrida's account of iterability is mutually exclusive with respect to discerning authorial intent; in other words, if Derrida were right, communication would be impossible. Searle sets this up as an either/or disjunction: *either* we concede that language is iterable and give up the very hope for communication, *or* we believe in the possibility of communication and reject Derrida's semiotics. Either we side with Searle and believe that communication is possible, or we side with Derrida and conclude that communication is impossible. Thus we can deduce that Searle, like some of his theological heirs, adopts a dialectical disjunction between presence and absence: presence *or* absence, *full* presence or *complete* absence. But below I will argue that a logic of incarnation refuses this disjunction.

By construing the issue in terms of the *either/or* of communication, Searle takes the question to be *whether* intentions can be communicated. But this is not Derrida's point in SEC. He is not asking whether communication is possible at all. Rather, Derrida is asking: *to what degree* can an author's intentions be communicated? Perfectly? Transparently? Immediately? At root, what is at stake are the *conditions* of possibility of communication, not the *possibility* of communication. Granted, Derrida will argue that the conditions of possibility for communication—especially iterability—also make *mis*communication possible; but this certainly does not entail that communication is *im*possible.

Perhaps we can get a handle on the issue here by going back to an old Augustinian distinction in his discussion of original sin. We might recall that Augustine argues that, with respect to sin, Adam in paradise is *posse non peccare*, able not to sin; postlapsarian Adam is *non posse non peccare*, not able not to sin; finally, the redeemed Adam in the eschaton is *non posse peccare*, not able to sin. I think we could distinguish between Searle's Derrida and Derrida's argument in a similar manner: the Searlean or "received" Derrida suggests that language is *non posse communicare*, not able to communicate;[20] but in fact Derrida's claim is that language is *posse non communicare*, able *not* to communicate, but also able *to* communicate.[21]

Rereading Derrida: Iterability and the Structure of Creation

The burden of this section is to demonstrate the claim I've made above, namely, that Derrida's claim with respect to communication is both weaker and more positive than Searle has construed it. My interest is not primarily to defend Derrida because I am a "Derridean."[22] Rather, I believe that the early Derrida—Derrida the phenomenologist—rightly discerned some of the structural features of language and as such grants us insight into the "grain of the universe" and the structure of creation.[23] In this section I would like to provide an exposition of Derrida's claims about language, communication, and interpretation in "Signature Event Context" and his later reply to Searle in *Limited Inc.* There is, of course, an entire Derridean lexicon relevant to these matters, but I will try to confine myself to explaining just three key themes: (1) the issue of context; (2) Derrida's notion of "iterability"; and (3) what I'll call the semiotic conditioning of consciousness or experience.[24]

The "Problem of Context"

At the opening of SEC, given to a colloquium on "communication," Derrida suggests that the word *communication* is equivocal—it covers, as it were, a vast "field." This vast field is "reduced massively by the limits of what is called a *context*" (SEC, p. 310).[25] Here Derrida announces that the issue of his essay is "the problem of context." It is context that determines the meaning of the word *communication*; so, for example, in the context of a philosophy colloquium held in French, we have a "conventional context, produced by a kind of implicit but structurally vague consensus" that "prescribes" that one address the *theme* of communication *in a certain way*.

Given that the central problematic in this essay is *context*, Derrida here opens what is for him the central question of the colloquium: "But are the prerequisites of a context ever absolutely determinable? Fundamentally, this is the most general question I would like to attempt to elaborate. Is there a rigorous and scientific concept of *context*?" Derrida's goal is "to demonstrate why a context is never absolutely determinable, or rather in what way its determination is never certain or saturated" (SEC, p. 310). He describes this as a "structural nonsaturation" that has two effects: (1) a critique of the usual concept of context (inherited, for instance, from Schleiermacher or Dilthey); and (2) "a rendering necessary of a certain generalization and a certain displacement of the concept of writing" (it is not immediately clear how [2] follows). Derrida argues: If communication is understood "in the restricted sense of the transmission of meaning," then writing can no longer be included in the category of communication (presumably because writing does not transmit meaning—but at this point, this remains an enthymeme) (SEC, p. 310).[26]

Now, if one takes the notion of writing "in its usually accepted sense," then it must be seen as a *means of communication*[27]—even as one that extends the field of oral or gestural communication (SEC, p. 311).[28] But what is the nature of this *extension*? Is it just a neutral enlargement of a homogeneous space of communication—a mere difference of *degree* ("a simple gradation," p. 313)? What is presupposed[29] in this notion of extension? Derrida takes this notion of extension to be the dominant "philosophical interpretation of writing" (SEC, p. 311). While elsewhere he considers the model as it is proffered by Rousseau or Plato,[30] in SEC the example he chooses is Condillac (pp. 310–11). In Condillac there is an account of progression from action to writing: (1) language of action→[31](2) language of sound →(3) written signs. The written is invented to make "ideas" known to *absent* persons (p. 312); thus language is re-presentative (p. 312). Writing is merely an extenuation of presence, supplementing presence (p. 313).

But what of the role of *absence* in Condillac's account (p. 313)? "How is it determined?" It is "the absence of the addressee." Obviously then, once the communiqué is received, it is the address*or* who is absent to the recipient. This absence is never examined by Condillac; Derrida, on the other hand, will argue that this absence (a) belongs to the structure of all writing and (b) belongs to the structure of all language in general. Thus Derrida advances two hypotheses:

[1] Every sign supposes a certain absence—because "absence in the field of writing is of an original kind" (SEC, p. 314).

[2] If the "absence proper to writing" were "found to suit every species of sign and communication," it would follow that "writing would no longer be [merely] a species of communication" (p. 314); rather, communication would always already be a kind of writing, and thus constituted by the same absence proper to writing.

Iterability and the Conditions of Possibility of Communication

Derrida goes on to "characterize [this] absence" (p. 315). In the traditional view (that of Plato, Condillac, and Rousseau), this absence is only one of extension—the absence is "only a presence that is distant, delayed" (p. 315)—a St. Paul who can't make it to Rome. But Derrida argues that in order for the structure of writing to be constituted, "this distance, division, delay, *différance* must be capable of being brought to a certain *absolute* degree of absence" (emphasis added). In other words, such absence is not accidental; it is essential—or as Derrida would prefer to say, structural. What does Derrida mean by this?

"My 'written communication' must, if you will, remain legible despite the absolute disappearance[32] of every determined addressee in general for it to function as writing" (SEC, p. 315). That is, in order for writing to operate as a means of communication it must participate in a system of inscription that does not depend upon any particular recipient (even a secret code could be broken); in order to be "legible," it must utilize a public system of marks that is not the product of—or under the control of—any particular addressee (or addressor). Derrida describes this condition as *iterability*: "This iterability [. . .] structures the mark of writing itself" (p. 315).[33] Iterability, or what we might call *structural legibility*, requires a certain disconnection from particular ("empirically determined") addressees (and addressors). Another way of putting this: writing always already implies the insertion of a *third party*.[34] "The possibility of repeating, and therefore identifying, marks is implied in every code, making of it a communicable, transmittable, decipherable grid that is iterable for a third party, and thus for any possible user in general" (p. 315).

Thus Derrida concludes that "[a]ll writing, therefore, in order to be what it is, must be able to function in the radical absence of every empirically determined addressee in general" (pp. 315–16). But the upshot of this is central to Derrida's argument: this absence is not merely accidental, not merely deferred or delayed (a "modification of presence"); it is a *structural*, even "absolute," absence ("a break in presence, 'death,' or the possibility of the 'death' of the addressee, inscribed in the structure of the mark" [p. 316]). This will then entail an important consequence to be unpacked: "the radical destruction . . . of every *context* as a protocol of a code" (p. 316).

Derrida then demonstrates why what is true of the addressee (radical absence as condition of writing) must also be true of the *sender*: "For the written to be written, it must continue to 'act' and to be legible even if what is called the author of the writing no longer answers for what he has written, for what he seems to have signed, whether he is provisionally absent, or if he is dead, or if in general he does support . . . the plenitude of his meaning" (p. 316).[35] With respect to writing, the situation of the author and reader is "fundamentally the same" (p. 316). Derrida describes this as an "essential drifting due to writing as an iterative structure cut off from all absolute responsibility, from *consciousness* as the authority of the last analysis, writing orphaned, and separated at birth from the assistance of its father" (p. 316). And of course, it is just this orphaning of writing that Plato condemns in the *Phaedrus*.

The Semiotic Conditioning of Consciousness

Now Derrida makes his central move (and precisely the one that distinguishes him from Plato): to demonstrate that these characteristics of writing are in fact characteristic of language per se, indeed of experience itself. "I would like to demonstrate that the recognizable traits of the classical and narrowly defined concept of writing are generalizable. They would be valid not only for all the orders of 'signs' and for all languages in general, but even, beyond semiolinguistic communication, for the entire field of what philosophy would call experience" (pp. 316–17). First, what are these "traits?"

1. *Repeatability:* A written sign is a "mark which remains" and thus which can give rise to an "iteration" in the absence of the "empirically determined sub-

ject who, in a given context, has emitted or produced it" (p. 317). Traditionally, this is how written communication is distinguished from spoken communication, but Derrida argues that this is a feature of language *as such*.

2. *Decontextualization:* As a result of [1], it follows that "a written sign carries with it a force of breaking with its context" (p. 317)—unhitching it, as it were, from the original conditions of its inscription. But "[t]his force of breaking is not an accidental predicate, but the very structure of the written" (p. 317). Thus the inscription is not controlled or "enclosed" by its context: "one can always lift a written syntagma from the interlocking chain in which it is caught or given without making it lose every possibility of functioning, if not every possibility of 'communicating,' precisely" (p. 317).

3. This force of breaking or "rupture" is due to *spacing* (p. 317): a spacing that separates it both from other elements of "the internal contextual chain" and "from all forms of a present referent." This spacing is "not the simple negativity of a lack, but the emergence of the mark" (p. 317).

Now, are these three traits characteristic only of *writing*—of "written *communication*?" "Are they not also to be found in all language, for example in spoken language, and ultimately in the totality of 'experience'"[36]—since experience itself is constituted by a system of marks, spacing, and deferral?

Consider any element of spoken language: in order for it to "function," it must have a "certain self-identity" in order to be recognized and repeated (p. 318). In other words, even the phoneme must be characterized by *iterability*, "the possibility of being repeated in the absence not only of its referent," but also "of a determined signified or current intention of signification" (p. 318). Thus the spoken word is able to function only insofar as it is iterable; and insofar as it is iterable, it is characterized by the "structural *possibility* of being severed from its referent or signified (and therefore from communication and its context)" (p. 318, emphasis added). "I will extend this law even to all 'experience' in general, if it is granted that there is no experience of *pure* presence, but only chains of differential marks" (p. 318).

The Problem of Context Revisited

In order for signs—whether written or spoken—to communicate (roughly, transfer meaning across a web of relations) it is necessary that such signs be *iterable*, formally or structurally discernible by a plurality of both addressees and senders. But insofar as signs are iterable, they are also decontextualizable—they can be unhitched from a particular context and understood differently. Since iterability is a necessary condition for communication, the possibility of decontextualization necessarily attends language. As such, every utterance and text is susceptible to different interpretations. But just what is it that changes in such cases? Here we see again the importance of *context* in determining the meaning of a text or utterance. In other words, what a text *means* depends upon the determination of a context. Here Derrida appeals to an example of "ungrammaticality" from Husserl's *Logical Investigations:* the phoneme *le ver est ou*, which could be *heard* as the ungrammatical "green is or," or understood as one of two questions: "Where has the green [of the grass] gone?" [*le vert est où?*] or "Where has the glass gone?" [*le verre est où?*]. The point is simply that even the supposed ungrammaticality of the phrase is dependent upon a context. As Derrida points out: "it is only in a context determined by a will to know, by an epistemic intention, by a conscious relation to the object as an object of knowledge within a horizon of truth—it is in this *oriented contextual field* that 'green is or' is unacceptable. But, since 'green is or' or 'abracadabra' *do not constitute their own context in themselves*, nothing prevents their functioning in another context as signifying [*i.e.*, meaningful] marks" (SEC, p. 320, emphasis added). Because of the necessary structure of iterability (p. 321), there is always a "possibility of extraction" and the possibility of a "break within every given context" (SEC, p. 320). Thus Derrida concludes that "there are only contexts" (SEC, p. 320). This must be read as a correlate of his more famous claim that "*il n y a pas de hors-texte* [There is no outside-text]" (*Of Grammatology*, p. 158). This "does *not* mean," Derrida insists, "that all referents are suspended, denied, or enclosed in a book, as people have claimed, or have been naïve enough to believe and to have accused me of believing" (A, p. 148). Rather, the point is that "every referent, all reality has the structure of a differential trace, and that one cannot refer to this 'real' except in an interpretive experience" (A, 148). "There are only contexts" means that "meaning" is inextricably linked to contexts at the same time that signs are characterized by a decontextualizability (or, roughly, "undecidability" [A, p. 115 ff.]). But it is important to note, *contra Searle*, that these are structures of *possibility*, not impossibility. Yes, decontextualizability does mean that it is possible for my utterance to be "taken out of context" and *mis*understood; but it does *not* entail that communication is impossible.[37] I *can* communicate via iterable signs—but those very signs are also the condition of possibility for being *mis*understood.[38] The question, then, is what would constitute the criteria for being "properly understood?"

Here two crucial aspects follow from Derrida's claim that "there are only contexts": first, the matter of how contexts are *determined*, and second, the role of *community* in such determination. Let's begin with what Derrida calls the "problem of determination" (A, p. 155 n. 4). In both SEC and A, Derrida argues that the meaning of a text is linked to the determination of a contextual field (SEC, p. 320; A, p. 131 ff.). Now, it is certainly the case that when discussing just how contexts get "fixed" (A, p. 131), Derrida emphasizes the extent to which contexts *cannot* be fixed or stabilized; context goes all the way down. While the "reconstitution of a context . . . is a regulative ideal in the ethics of reading, or interpretation, or of discussion," it must be conceded that "this ideal is unattainable, for reasons which are essential" (A, p. 131). Thus what Derrida rejects is Austin's notion of a "total context" (SEC, p. 322); indeed, here we recall that Derrida's stated project at the beginning of the essay was to demonstrate "why a context is never absolutely determinable, or rather in what way its determination is never certain or saturated" (SEC, p. 310; cf. A, 137). A context can never be completely saturated or determined because there is always a dual element of *absence:* of senders from receivers, but also of senders from themselves.[39] "[T]his essential absence of intention [. . .], this structural unconsciousness if you will, prohibits every saturation of a context. For a context to be exhaustively determinable, in the sense demanded by Austin, it at least would be necessary for the conscious intention to be totally present and actually transparent for itself and others" (SEC, p. 327). But it is precisely the semiotic conditioning of consciousness that precludes such. This "absence" is simply synonymous with the structural distance between finite beings, as well as the plenitude of consciousness that exceeds "pure" or "full" presence (A, pp. 128–29),[40] both of which entail decontextualizability. So, for instance, what is called "objective" is, in fact, determined by a context—just a vast, very old one (A, p. 136). Thus Derrida concludes that "[o]ne of the definitions of what is called deconstruction would be the effort to take this limitless context into account, to pay the sharpest and broadest attention possible to context, and thus to an incessant movement of recontextualization" (A, p. 136).

But are there *limits* to this recontextualization? Or perhaps better: could we be justified in *halting* this play of recontextualization? Does this incessant movement of recontextualization mean that the function of texts cannot be stabilized? To be more specific: could we ever be justified in "fixing" the context, and hence meaning, of a text (such as the Scriptures)? Or could one legitimately protest that John Searle has *mis*understood one's texts?

Despite emphasizing the impossibility of a total context, Derrida does not decry the determination of context *as such.* In fact, Derrida is not even opposed to "interpretive police" as such; rather, he patiently describes the way in which the determination of a given community can then determine the context of utterance, thus producing criteria for good and bad interpretations, true and false interpretations (cf. A, p. 146). "Otherwise," he notes, "one could indeed say just anything at all and I have never accepted saying, or encouraging others to say, just anything at all, nor have I argued for indeterminacy as such" (A, pp. 144–45). What Derrida is opposed to, then, is not the determination of communities *as such,* but rather to the naïve assumption that no such determination has taken place—that these communities or rules are "natural" or "self-evident" (A, p. 146). So, for instance, the academic community is defined by a certain *telos,* certain procedures, a certain consensus. "I believe that no research is possible *in a community* (for example, academic) without the prior search for this minimal consensus" (A, p. 146; emphasis added). Therefore, with the determination of the community, we have in place certain rules that are to "govern" interpretation, and it is these "rules" that Searle has violated ("Afterword," p. 146).

It is in this context that Derrida speaks in a positive manner regarding a kind of interpretive police. A question put to him by Gerald Graff seems to equate the "political" with the "repressive," suggesting that any determination of rules must be inherently repressive and a function of a kind of police-state (A, p. 131). Derrida, however, rejects this equation: "I would hesitate before associating the police, directly and necessarily, as you seem to do . . . with a determinate politics, and in particular, with a repressive politics" ("Afterword," p. 132). Restrictions and rules as such, enforced by police, are not inherently repressive; as he mundanely notes, "[a] red light is not repressive" (A, p. 132; cf. A, pp. 138, 139). Certainly such restriction is not *neutral*—it is a political gesture (A, pp. 132, 135–36)—but such non-neutrality should not be confused with repression. Indeed, Derrida explicitly notes that not all determinations of context are repressive: "I never said that the police as such and a priori, or 'the very project of attempting to fix the context of utterances,' is 'politically' suspect. *There is no society without police*" (A, p. 135, emphasis added). So also, "one cannot do anything, least of all speak, without determining . . . a context" (A, p. 136). So communities "fix" contexts and contexts determine "meanings"—in the sense that they can choose to halt the play of recontextualization.[41]

With this account of context in place we can return to the question of authorial intent: what is the link between the determination of meaning by communal contexts and the discernment of authorial intent? Does Derrida's account of iterability preclude authorial intent? Simply, no; rather, Derrida would emphasize two points: first, the author's intention(s) is one of an array of possible meanings for a given utterance. This follows from iterability and the structural possibility of decontextualization that is a necessary condition of possibility for language. Thus, when the author of the "Song of Songs" pens the line "Your hair is like a flock of goats" (6:5), the author's *intended* meaning is one of many possible meanings of this grapheme (and whether the Puritans' interpretation was included in the author's intention would be a matter for discussion). But second, there *can* be a determination of one (or several) meanings *as* the author's intended meaning *within the consensus of a communal determination.* The author's intent is not something that is "perspicuous" or *Zuhanden,* to be simply read off the lines of a text. Discerning the author's intentions can only unfold as a communal discernment, insofar as the community "saturates" a context, to use Derrida's term. In other words, the author's intention is not something that exclusively occupies the space of an utterance, or self-evidently inheres in a given text.[42] But it is something that can be communicated via a text or utterance and would be discerned from *within* the determination of a particular community. The "author's intention," then, is not some magical hermeneutic grail that escapes the conditioning of context and textuality; but neither is it sheer myth. While Derrida's semiotics emphasizes the necessary mediation of authorial intent (as well as its discernment), it does not preclude the communication of the author's wishes and desires. "In this typology," he notes, "the category of intention will not disappear; *it will have its place,* but from this place it will no longer be able to *govern* the entire scene and the entire system of utterances" (SEC, p. 326; emphasis added). Communication involves risk precisely because I cannot govern the way in which my utterances and texts are interpreted; there is no simple recourse to the author's intentions to halt such recontextualization. There is this "risk" and lack of governance because "the intention which animates utterance will never be *completely* present in itself and its content" (SEC, p. 326; emphasis added). Note, however, that Derrida does not say it is completely *absent,* either; he simply does not deny the possibility of communication as Searle suggests. This is because, unlike Searle (as noted above), he does not operate with a dialectic of pure absence or full presence, but rather is attentive to *degrees* or *intensities* of presence. In the utterance, the author is *both* absent *and* present; we might say that what Derrida describes is not full presence (or absence) but *real* presence: the author is *really* present, but not fully present—she also remains withheld from or beyond the utterance.[43] As such, Derrida's account of authorial intention echoes what I have described elsewhere as a "logic of incarnation," which refuses the either/or of full presence or complete absence (adopted by Searle), but rather provides an account of the *real* presence and yet necessary absence of the author in the text—just as Christ manifests to us the fullness of God, without God's transcendence being reduced *to* the manifestation.

"This way of thinking of context," Derrida contends, "does not, as such, amount to a relativism" (A, p. 137). So, while the text from Song of Songs above can be read in many different ways, the community of which I am a part—Reformed Christianity, which includes the Puritans as part of the community—has discerned that one of the Author/author's intended meanings included a picture of the Church as the Bride of Christ. Such a discernment of authorial intention is in no wise precluded by Derrida's semiotics.

A Critique of Derrida: On Staying with the Posse Non

While above I have tried to demonstrate that Searle's reading of Derrida actually *mis*reads Derrida's account, I do think that Derrida bears some responsibility for Searle's either/or approach. In particular, I think that in places Derrida overdetermines the situation of decontextualization and the possibility of miscommunication by suggesting that miscommunication is somehow *essential*. Invoking an ideal of "purity," Derrida at times seems to assert what Searle hears him saying: that communication is impossible. For instance, Derrida concludes that "the condition of possibility for these effects is simultaneously, once again, the condition of their impossibility, of the impossibility of their rigorous purity" (SEC, p. 326). And he appeals to such a notion, "purity," precisely when he lapses into what appears to be a dialectics of *either* presence *or* absence, suggesting an "essential absence of intention" (SEC, p. 327) such that "communication, if one insists upon using the word, is not the means of transport of sense, the exchange of intentions and meanings" (SEC, p. 329).

But here Derrida oversteps the evidence, drawing a conclusion that does not necessarily follow from the semiotics he has unpacked.[44] In fact, the genius of his account is the refusal of a simplistic opposition or disjunction between presence and absence—between either "full" presence or "complete" absence. Instead, he offers an account that recognizes varying degrees of presence/absence—a varying intensity of presence. "Every sign," he says, "supposes a *certain* absence" (SEC, p. 314; emphasis added); as such, "the intention which animates utterance will never be *completely* present in itself and its content" (p. 326; emphasis added). But for the same reason, it will never be *completely* absent either. While absence is essential, it is also *partial*; and while a context cannot be "saturated" precisely because it can never be "totally present" (SEC, p. 327), this does not mean that the context cannot be "relatively" determined (p. 327). On Derrida's own account, he should refuse the (Cartesian)[45] criterion of "purity" that leads him at times to suggest that communication is *non posse;* instead, and more consistently, his (almost incarnational) semiotics of a present absence and absent presence should stick with the *posse non* account of communication.

Revelation, Incarnation, and Iterability: The Risk of Communication

My primary interest, as indicated in the introduction, is propadeutic: I wanted to return to the Searle/Derrida debate in order to consider the account of authority intention that is generated by Derrida's semiotics. As indicated in the opening, the catalyst for this more formal question is the special question of scriptural authority and interpretation. Space does not permit a full account of this specific case, but permit me to offer a sketch of where such work should go—where we Christian interpreters might proceed from this crossroads.

The Iterability of the Incarnation

I think what Derrida's account of language and interpretation gives us is not a sense of the *impossibility* of communication, but rather a sense of the *risk* of communication: to speak is to venture into the play of signs, and thus to risk decontextualization and misunderstanding. But such a risk is the necessary condition for communication.

It is in this sense that we can see God's own speaking and "communication" as operating under the (creational)[46] conditions sketched by Derrida. Insofar as revelation is a communication to finite embodied beings, God's speaking must operate under the conditions of finite language. In the beginning was the Word, and the Word was iterable, since such is the condition of possibility for communication. As such, the Word was a matter of interpretation, subject to decontextualization and the play of meaning. It is in this sense that he came to his own and his own did not receive him. This means, of course, that they did not receive him as the Word spoken by the Father; rather, they construed him otherwise. Thus, other readings of the Word are possible, but not all are judged to be the Author's intention: to "read" Jesus as anything less than the Incarnation of God is to *mis*read him. Of course, such misreadings are possible given the structure of communication; that is a necessary risk. Moreover, the determination of the Author's intention is determined *by* and *from within* the community of the Church, both globally and across time. The ecumenical councils, of course, were the early Church's communal efforts to discern the authorial intent, we might say, of the Incarnation. Some "readings" of the Incarnation—those of the Docetists or Arians—were ruled "out of bounds"' by the interpretive police. That's not to say that such readings couldn't be generated by the signifiers at issue, but only that the community's determination concluded that such meanings were *not* those intended by the Author. However, while I am arguing that the Incarnation and the Scriptures operate under the conditions of iterability, I also think that there is a sense in which the text of Scripture—and the "text" of the Incarnation to which it attests—is unique and does require a "special" hermeneutic.

On the Necessity of a Special Hermeneutic for Scripture

My account of the Incarnation above echoes both the Prologue to John's Gospel and Kierkegaard's *Philosophical Fragments.*[47] If we follow Kierkegaard's analysis, we will see the need for a "special hermeneutic" as something of a supplement to the "creational" hermeneutic sketched above.[48] This is because only with respect to Scripture do we have a situation where the Author also indwells the reader—or better, the reading community—to illumine the text (1 Cor 2:10–16). Or, in the terms of Kierkegaard's *Fragments*, the Teacher is also the One who provides the condition for the reception of the teaching in the heart of the learner. As such, as the community of the faithful discern the Author's intention, they are indwelt and led by the Spirit of the Author. This would not be a "God of the gaps," deus ex machina appeal to a new immediacy nor a magical access to authorial intent. Rather, this special, pneumatological hermeneutic would be an extension of the account of context provided above.[49] In other words, our hermeneutics of Scripture will require, first and foremost, an ecclesiology.

NOTES

1. It will become clear below that my primary interest in this essay is the hermeneutics of *Scripture*, and I will conclude that we do need something like a "special hermeneutic" for the Bible—not because its language is different, but for other reasons (see the section "Revelation, Incarnation, and Iterability" below). However, I think the basic point of this essay holds for a general hermeneutics, namely, that interpreting for a speaker/author's intention cannot be simply jettisoned. There are all kinds of texts, utterances, and contexts where discerning authorial intent is of paramount importance (e.g., promises, contracts, interviews, etc.).

2. *Belgic Confession*, art. 5, in *Ecumenical Creeds and Reformed Confessions* (Grand Rapids, Mich.: CRC Publications, 1988).

3. *Westminster Confession*, I.iv.

4. *Belgic Confession*, art. 7; *Westminster Confession*, I.vi.

5. My focus here will be Searle's reading, noting only representative examples of Christian critique. Insofar as these follow or parallel Searle, I will take it that they are guilty by association.

6. I have unpacked this incarnational logic in more detail in James K. A. Smith, *Speech and Theology: Language and the Logic of Incarnation*, Radical Orthodoxy Series (London: Routledge, 2002), pp. 153–82. See also Smith, "A Principle of Incarnation in Derrida's (*Theologische?*) *Jugendschriften*," *Modern Theology* 18 (2002): 217–30.

7. Ronald Hall links this to demons, claiming that "the spirit of writing for Derrida is a demonic perversion of spirit" (in *Word and Spirit: A Kierkegaardian Critique of the Modern Age* [Bloomington: Indiana University Press, 1993]). Kevin Vanhoozer describes Derrida (equating him with Roland Barthes) as a "countertheologian" for whom "there is noth-

ing outside the play of writing, nothing that guarantees that our words refer to the world" (Vanhoozer, "The Spirit of Understanding: Special Revelation and General Hermeneutics," in *Disciplining Hermeneutics*, ed. Roger Lundin [Grand Rapids: Eerdmans, 1997], p. 136). I will argue below that this reading of Derrida as some kind of linguistic idealist (or "textual Gnostic," as Vanhoozer puts it) is a serious *mis*reading, as Derrida himself notes in "Afterword."

8. Nicholas Wolterstorff, "The Importance of Hermeneutics for a Christian Worldview," in *Disciplining Hermeneutics*, p. 43. Wolterstorff goes on to utilize another common strategy in these contexts: the claim of performative contradiction on Derrida's part. "It is worth adding," he notes, "that Derrida, the master deconstructionist, insists that when we interpret *his* texts, we must interpret for *what he said*" (p. 43). Well, could that perhaps be a clue that he is *not* claiming what has just been laid at his feet?

9. Ibid., p. 43.

10. Kevin Vanhoozer, *Is There a Meaning in This Text?* (Grand Rapids: Zondervan, 1998), pp. 26, 30.

11. Ibid., pp. 43–44.

12. Ibid., pp. 61, 63 (emphasis added), 62.

13. Ibid., p. 63. He later describes this as the "unique presence" of Mark (p. 65). Of course, behind this are also some assumptions about a kind of dual authorship of Mark—that there is a sense in which God is also (and perhaps most importantly) the author of the gospel according to Mark. For a summary discussion of the inspiration of Scripture, see Donald G. Bloesch, *Holy Scripture: Revelation, Inspiration, and Interpretation*, Christian Foundations Series (Downers Grove, IL: InterVarsity Press, 1994), pp. 85–160, and John Webster, *Holy Scripture: A Dogmatic Sketch* (Cambridge: Cambridge University Press, 2003), pp. 30–39. For a pneumatological account, see Amos Yong, *Spirit-Word-Community: Theological Hermeneutics in a Trinitarian Perspective* (Burlington, VT: Ashgate, 2002), pp. 241–44.

14. Brian Ingraffia, *Postmodern Theory and* [it seems to me this conjunction should be a disjunction: *or*] *Biblical Theology: Vanquishing God's Shadow* (Cambridge: Cambridge University Press, 1995), p. 241 (cf. p. 14). I have critiqued Ingraffia's model in my "A Little Story About Metanarratives: Lyotard, Religion, and Postmodernism Revisited," *Faith and Philosophy* 18 (2002): 353–68.

15. I am proceeding by means of a regressive procedure here: beginning with the "received" Derrida of Searle's reply, then going back to Derrida's initial essay and later response in order to discern the shape of the "real" Derrida.

16. John R. Searle, "Reiterating the Differences: A Reply to Derrida," *Glyph* 1 (1977): 198–208. Henceforth abbreviated in the text as R.

17. Jacques Derrida, "Signature Event Context," in *Margins of Philosophy*, trans. Alan Bass (Chicago: University of Chicago Press, 1982), pp. 309–30, first published in *Glyph* 1 (1977) and also reprinted in *Limited Inc.* Henceforth abbreviated as SEC.

18. Derrida certainly thinks that readings can be "on the right track," and thus others on the wrong track. As he later articulates this point: "For of course there is a 'right track' [*une 'bonne voie'*], a better way, and let it be said in passing how surprised I have often been, how amused or discouraged, depending on my humor, by the use or abuse of the following argument: Since the deconstructionist (which is to say, isn't it, the skeptic-relativist-nihilist!) is supposed not to believe in truth, stability, or the unity of meaning, in intention or 'meaning-to-say,' how can he demand that his own text be interpreted correctly? How can he accuse anyone else of having misunderstood, simplified, deformed it, etc.? [. . .]

The answer is simple enough: this definition of the deconstructionist is *false* (that's right: false, not true) and feeble; it supposes a bad (that's right: bad, not good) and feeble reading . . ." See Jacques Derrida, A, in *Limited Inc* (Evanston, IL: Northwestern University Press, 1988), p. 146. Henceforth abbreviated in the text as A.

19. Iterability is defined in more detail below. Roughly, it denotes a kind of structural legibility that requires an essential dissociation from a particular consciousness or communicative agent.

20. I have used this earlier, in a discussion of Derrida's *Post Card*, in my "How to Avoid Not Speaking: Attestations," in *Knowing Other-wise*, Perspectives in Continental Philosophy Series, ed. James H. Olthuis (Bronx, N.Y.: Fordham University Press, 1997), pp. 217–34. There I noted Derrida's tendency to slide toward a *non posse non* position, and I would concede that there is some slippage in that direction in SEC. But I would argue that this is *not* a necessary conclusion from Derrida's semiotics, but an instance of overdetermination on his part.

21. Is it perhaps Searle's position that language is *non posse non communicare*, not able not to communicate? For my criticism of such immediacy models, see "How To Avoid Not Speaking."

22. For my marked and clear distance from Derrida, see *The Fall of Interpretation*, ch. 4; "Determined Violence"; and "Re-Kanting Postmodernism."

23. The burden of my argument in *The Fall of Interpretation* is that language is a *created*, prelapsarian reality, constitutive of the finitude of creaturehood, and thus also included in the pronouncement of creation's "goodness" (Gen 1:31).

24. This is particularly the focus of *Speech and Phenomena*. I think it is helpful to see Searle/Austin and Husserl as analogues in this respect (see A, p. 121).

25. This is consistent with his later claim, in *Limited Inc*, that *il n y a pas de hors-texte* means nothing other than "there is nothing outside of context" (A, p. 136).

26. Below we will return to such claims as one of the reasons that Derrida is, in some sense, responsible for Searle's misreading.

27. Where "meaning" is the "content" of the semantic message (SEC, p. 311).

28. I think it is important to note that Searle, in his "Reply," almost completely ignores this section of the essay.

29. Ultimately Derrida thinks it presupposes a "simplicity of the origin" (p. 311); so what is *really* at stake is the conception of *speech*.

30. On Rousseau, see Derrida, *Of Grammatology*, pp. 141–94; on Plato, see Derrida, "Plato's Pharmacy," in *Dissemination*, trans. Barbara Johnson (Chicago: University of Chicago Press, 1981), pp. 61–171.

31. This relation signified by the arrow is almost always a relation of *supplementation* in Condillac (313 n. 3). On the logic of "supplementation," see Derrida, *Of Grammatology*, pp. 141–64 and *Speech and Phenomena*, pp. 88–104.

32. I think it's helpful to see Derrida here engaged in a kind of thought project analogous to Husserl's account of the "destruction of the world" in *Ideas* I. The "death of the author" (and recipients) is a thought project intended to unveil the *structure* of writing. It has nothing to do with the biological death of authors (as Searle seems to think).

33. Here Derrida inserts a very important parenthetical remark, noting that *iter* comes from *itara*, meaning *other* in Sanskrit—"and everything that follows may be read as the exploitation of the logic which links repetition to *alterity*" (p. 315; emphasis added). I would argue—especially from *Speech and Phenomena*—that "absence" signifies an alterity, even transcendence, for Derrida. It is not an absence of lack, but excess (cf. p. 317).

34. Derrida offers this when considering the hypothesis of a secret code shared by only two subjects. I think this context helps us to see how and why Wheeler argues that Derrida's argument is akin to Wittgenstein's critique of the notion of "private languages" (see Wheeler, *Deconstruction as Analytic Philosophy*, pp. 3, 211).

35. Derrida, of course, does not think this is true only if authors actually die, nor even if they are not here in the room with me ("provisionally absent"). Because this is a structural matter, even the presence of the author does not mitigate the structure ("interviews" with the author don't eliminate this absence). For an enactment of this, see "Passions," in *Sauf le nom*, included in *On the Name*, ed. Thomas Dutoit (Stanford: Stanford University Press, 1995), pp. 3–31.

36. This must be understood within a phenomenological context.

37. Derrida alerts us to the danger of over-reading his conclusions here: "Above all, I will *not* conclude from this that there is no relative specificity of the effects of consciousness, of the effects of speech (in opposition to writing in the traditional sense), that there is no effect of the performative, no effect of ordinary language, no effect of presence and of speech acts. It is simply that these effects do not exclude what is generally opposed to them term by term, but on the contrary presuppose it in dyssymmetrical fashion, as the general space of their possibility" (SEC, p. 327; emphasis added). Texts and utterances *can* be effective. Cf. SEC, p. 326: "You cannot deny that there are also performatives that succeed."

38. Or as he states elsewhere, "'forgery' is always possible, the *possibility* of transgression is always inscribed in speech acts (oral or written)" (A, p. 133). Again, note the emphasis on *possibility*.

39. This point is the burden of Derrida's analysis in *Speech and Phenomena:* because consciousness itself is linguistically or semiotically conditioned, there is a sense in which we are never fully present to ourselves. As speakers, we are not masters of our intentions. I have discussed this in more detail in my "A Principle of Incarnation in Derrida's (*Theologische*?) *Jugendschriften*," *Modern Theology* 18 (2002): 217–30.

40. Cf. SEC, p. 316. This claim—that consciousness is not characterized by full presence—is more explicitly developed by Derrida in *Speech and Phenomena.* I have tried to demonstrate an Augustinian parallel to this anthropology in chapter 4 of my *Speech and Theology.* This is also a central point of disagreement between Searle and Derrida. Searle, like Husserl, seems to assume the full presence of consciousness to itself (see R, p. 199); in other words, Searle is much more confident that authors know what they mean (R, p. 201).

41. I take these Derridean conclusions to be roughly equivalent to postliberal accounts of biblical interpretation, as found in Hauerwas and others.

42. If it did, there would be no disagreement about the author's intention in a given text. But obviously within even scriptural interpretation there is deep disagreement about just what the Author intended. When, for instance, we are told to "love our enemies," some take this statement to nevertheless permit bombing campaigns intended to "shock and awe"; I take it to mean that violence is a sin. Both of these interpretations depend upon a *context* determined by a *community.* Of course, what remains to be asked is how we judge *between* communities.

43. I have earlier suggested the model of "real presence" (drawing on Calvin) to think about Derrida in my "A Principle of Incarnation in Derrida's (*Theologische?*) *Jugendschriften.*"

44. In my "How To Avoid Not Speaking," I have argued that Derrida makes a similar move of overstepping in *The Post Card.*

45. Elsewhere I argue that this is also a Kantian gesture, invoking a kind of regulative ideal. See James K. A. Smith, *Deconstructing Myths of Religious Violence: Derrida and the*

Logic of Determination (forthcoming). It is a similar ideal of "purity" that leads him to link interpretation with an essential "violence" in A.

46. By this I mean that I believe Derrida's account of language has rightly discerned aspects of the structure of creation.

47. I have considered the "logic of incarnation" of both of these more carefully in my *Speech and Theology*, ch. 5.

48. In my *Fall of Interpretation,* I argue that Derrida's account coincides with what I describe as a "creational" hermeneutic.

49. For a lucid discussion along these lines, see Amos Yong, *Spirit-Word-Community: Theological Hermeneutics in Trinitarian Perspective* (Burlington, VT: Ashgate, 2002), pp. 275–310.

PART 3

Literature's Contribution to Christian Understanding: Pointing, Witnessing, Exchanging

7

Meeting at the Modern Crossroads

Fiction, History, and Christian Understanding

Roger Lundin

"Wait!" cries Canadian-born Shreve McCannon to his Harvard roommate on a bitter night in the winter of 1910. For hours, that roommate, Quentin Compson, has been unburdening himself to Shreve, telling him a convoluted yet compelling story about a drama that had unfolded decades before in Quentin's native Mississippi. This particular conversation has been prompted by a letter to Quentin from his father, reporting the death of Rosa Coldfield, the sister-in-law of Sutpen and the last surviving actor in a nineteenth-century drama that is the focus of Quentin's obsession.

This grand, gothic drama is at the heart of William Faulkner's greatest novel, *Absalom, Absalom!* It involves the story of Thomas Sutpen, a man who, in 1833, "out of quiet thunderclap [. . .] abrupt[ed] (man-horse-demon) upon a scene peaceful and decorous as a schoolprize water color, faint sulphur-reek still in hair clothes and beard."[1] Having arrived in Jefferson, Mississippi, "out of no discernible past," Sutpen built a garish mansion, married the daughter of the town's most respectable shopkeeper, fathered a son and daughter, went off to fight in the Civil War, returned to discover that his son had killed his daughter's suitor, set about rebuilding his ravaged plantation, fathered another child by his hired hand's granddaughter, and was then cut down with a rusty scythe by that same hired hand on a summer's day in 1869. For decades after his death, Sutpen's legitimate daughter and illegitimate daughter lived within the rotting mansion he had left behind, only to have that mansion torched by that illegitimate daughter in a final suicidal act in 1909.

What could all of this possibly mean? "It's just incredible," Quentin's father, Jason Compson, tells him one night in the summer of 1909, shortly before the son leaves for his freshman year at Harvard. "It just does not explain.[. . .] We have a few old mouth-to-mouth tales; we exhume from old trunks and boxes and drawers letters without salutation or signature, in which men and women who once lived and breathed are now merely initials or nicknames [. . .]." Of the people in that past, Mr. Compson complains, "they are there, yet something is missing; they are like a chemical formula exhumed along with the letters from that forgotten chest." You pore over those letters, trying to discover their meaning. Yet even though you "bring them together again and again nothing happens: just the words, the symbols, the shapes themselves, shadowy inscrutable and serene, against that turgid background of a horrible and bloody mischancing of human affairs" (*AA*, p. 80).

As he describes these imaginary letters, Jason Compson sounds like a textual scholar cautiously sifting through the papyri and codices of the ancient scriptures. The paper is "old and faded and falling to pieces," the writing "faded, almost indecipherable," and the text mysteriously unfathomable, "shadowy inscrutable and serene." The script is "familiar in shape and sense," but the meaning of the text remains opaque and oblique.

This is the stuff of hermeneutics, these the problems of historical understanding and textual interpretation. Hermeneutical issues vexed and inspired Faulkner, and it is to his preoccupation with these matters that we owe many of his stylistic discoveries and thematic concerns. In his early fiction, this master of modernist innovation explored this territory through the use of multiple first-person narrators and radical shifts of time and perspective. In *Absalom, Absalom!* he pushed the hermeneutical problem even further by placing the crucial activity of the novel in the nineteenth century and its narration in the twentieth. To understand Sutpen and the ruin in his wake, Faulkner gives us "a few old mouth-to-mouth tales" and "letters without salutation or signature." From these we, and the narrators in the novel, must make our judgments about the meaning of this man and his historical moment.

With the exception of the Canadian Shreve, the narrators in *Absalom, Absalom!* make the telling of Sutpen's story an occasion for self-understanding and cultural interpretation. As southerners sharing the horrible history of slavery, the Civil War, and reconstruction, they fix upon questions of failure, loss, and fate, all of which seem encapsulated in the career of Thomas Sutpen. Where their northern counterparts set their eyes on a bright future, these heirs of the "lost cause" stare into an obscure past. For them, as for their creator William Faulkner, "the past is never dead. It's not even past."

This is particularly the case for Quentin Compson, whose dilemma Faulkner first examined in *The Sound and the Fury*, published seven years before *Absalom, Absalom!* In that earlier work, Quentin is tormented by his family's demise and by his inability to defend its honor. As the story of Sutpen then unfolds for him in the fall and winter of 1909, he can only listen with amazement to this drama filled with heroic actions and tragic deeds. He hears of how Sutpen's son, Henry, makes a wrenching decision to kill his own half-brother, Charles Bon, to keep him from marrying their sister, Judith. For the impotent Quentin, this account of tragic and heroic action is "something which he [. . .] could not pass" (AA, p. 139). He wrestles with Sutpen's story as though his own emotional life was at risk. The last lines of the novel find Quentin responding to Shreve's question—"Why do you hate the South?"—with a vehement denial: "'I dont hate it,' Quentin said, quickly, at once, immediately; 'I dont hate it,' he said. *I dont hate it,* he thought, panting in the cold air, the iron New England dark: *I dont. I dont! I dont hate it! I dont hate it!*" (AA, p. 303). Less than five months later, as readers of *The Sound and the Fury* know, Quentin will put weights on his ankles and drown himself in the Charles River. Though he may not hate the South, he can neither fathom nor endure its history.

To be sure, Quentin Compson is a character in a work of fiction and not a player on the stage of intellectual history. Yet if we step back from the novel, we can view his desperate efforts to understand the past as one episode in a long drama of modern self-understanding. The debates about the meaning of the past in *Absalom, Absalom!*, for example, call to mind several of Søren Kierkegaard's provocative discussions of hermeneutics and the Christian tradition. As a case in point, near the beginning of *Concluding Unscientific Postscript*, the Danish ironist describes Gotthold Ephraim Lessing's objections to the doctrine of revelation. Lessing questioned the wisdom of grounding the authority of the Christian faith in the purported revelatory events of an ancient past. How can belief depend upon historical revelation, which is particular in its scope and limited in its reach?[2] "The core of the problem," explains Helmut Thielicke, "is that for Lessing the unconditioned or absolute cannot occur in history because history is an accumulation of the accidental and irrational."[3]

"Lessing has said that accidental historical truths can never serve as proofs for eternal truths of the reason," Kierkegaard claims, "and that the transition by which it is proposed to base an eternal truth upon historical testimony is a leap." As Kierkegaard asks in discussing Lessing's dilemma: "Is it possible to base an eternal happiness on historical knowledge?"[4] Convinced that the necessary truths of reason provide more support than the shaky pillars of historical revelation, Lessing believed it possible to dismiss as "on principle irrelevant" any challenge to truthfulness of the biblical record or the plausibility of the accounts of miracles.[5] In the end, he held, it should not matter what happened in the historical past, if we can acquire certainty in the rational present.

Lessing's concerns uncover key fault lines running beneath the surface of modern hermeneutics. In the early centuries of the Protestant era, the ground had already begun to shift noticeably on questions concerning the trustworthiness of the Bible and the possibility of recovering its meaning across the centuries stretching between us and the originating events. With their understanding of historical mediation, Eastern Orthodoxy and Roman Catholicism could account more readily for the productivity of those centuries. Because of its individualist slant and singular focus upon the Bible, frequently to the exclusion of the church, Protestantism found it more problematic to treat history as a productive theological reality. "As a result," writes Jaroslav Pelikan, "when, in the modern age, a radical historical criticism undertook to examine the origins and development of cherished institutions, persons, and ideas, 'the system began to give way, with a dazzling and perplexing, because unaccustomed, light.'"[6] If historical distance could not mediate our understanding of the text, that distance had to be obliterated.

In the eighteenth century, the effort to overcome historical distance most frequently took the form of a search for the text's original plain sense, which, not surprisingly in that enlightened era, turned out to be a rationalistic sense. Thomas Jefferson, for example, was confident that he could prune away from the biblical record the excesses and distortions that had secured themselves to the simple message of Jesus. This first-century Nazarene propounded a "system of morality [that] was the most benevolent & sublime probably that has ever been taught." Yet unfortunately, "his character & doctrines have received still greater injury" through the ages from those who "pretend to be his special disciples." Selfishly, they "have disfigured and sophisticated his actions & precepts, from views of personal interest."[7] Only through the paring away of historical accretions would it be possible to recapture the pristine, original message of the Scriptures.

In the nineteenth century, the quest for scriptural purity and origins took a number of forms. In some quarters, it became the drive to recover the exact mental state of the author (Schleiermacher), while in other instances, it involved a search for the unadulterated historical Jesus (Strauss, Renan, and others). Here again, the liberal Protestant temperament sought a means of separating the wheat from the chaff, the essence from the excess. Though they differed dramatically on what they took that essence to be, the eighteenth- and nineteenth-century critics shared the conviction that it could be found, whether through a discipline of historical reconstruction or an art of imaginative empathy.[8]

In what is surely one of the great shifts in modern intellectual history, during the second half of the nineteenth century, the drive to recuperate the past began to give way to the desire to abandon it. Nietzsche is a key figure here, both as a nineteenth-century original and as a late-twentieth-century influence. In an early (1874) essay, he set it as his goal "to show [. . .] why history as a costly superfluity and luxury must, to use Goethe's word, be seriously hated by us." We have a need and use for history, but "only to the extent that history serves life." Left unchecked, history has the power to make life become "stunted and degenerate."[9]

To learn the benefits of hating history, we need only "consider the cattle, grazing as they pass" us by; they do not know the meaning of yesterday or today, for they are "fettered to the moment and its pleasure or displeasure, and thus neither melancholy nor bored" (*UM*, p. 60). The human being who stares at the animals "wonders at himself, that he cannot learn to forget but clings relentlessly to the past: however far and fast he may run, this chain runs with him." The phrase "it was" is that great chain, "that password which gives conflict, suffering and satiety access to man so as to remind him what his existence fundamentally is—an imperfect tense that can never become a perfect one" (*UM*, p. 61). To live in happiness, we must acknowledge that "forgetting is essential to action of any kind." We must forsake the effort to find an elusive meaning in the past. Whether we examine events in the past or objects in the present, what we see are our own ideals staring back at us, for "man really mirrors himself in things, that which gives him back his own reflection he considers beautiful."[10]

Is the past, then, a mine in which the truth lies buried, or a mirror in which the present is reflected? Faulkner considered both alternatives extreme and sought instead a middle ground, as he explained to students at the University of Virginia in 1958. "No, it's Sutpen's story," he replied to a student who had asked whether *Absalom, Absalom!* was Quentin Compson's tale rather than Thomas Sutpen's. The character of Sutpen was the germ for the story; the development of his outlandish scheme riveted Faulkner's attention, and the tragic legacy of slavery as well as the destructive arc of Sutpen's vanity fascinated and oppressed him. "But, then," Faulkner added, almost as an afterthought, the novel is, after all, in many ways Quentin's story, for "any time any character gets into a book, no matter how minor, he's actually telling his biography, talking about himself, in a thousand different terms."[11]

So whose story is being told in *Absalom, Absalom!*? Sutpen's? Quentin's? Rosa's? How is a reader to know the truth about Sutpen, if everything we learn of him comes from the mouths and minds of idiosyncratic narrators? Are we perhaps left with nothing but a series of contingent stories that are radically different versions of the unknowable Thomas Sutpen? Faulkner was alert to this interpretive possibility, but he resisted the conclusion in the end. Alluding to a well-known poem by Wallace Stevens, a student at the University of Virginia asked him whether any narrator in *Absalom, Absalom!* "had it right." Or "is it more or less a case of thirteen ways of looking at a blackbird with none of them right?" Faulkner welcomed that interpretive option: "That's it exactly. I think that no one individual can look at truth. It blinds you." This is especially the case with Thomas Sutpen, for "the old man was himself a little too big for people no greater in stature than Quentin and Miss Rosa and Mr. Compson to see all at once." Yet though it may be a matter of "thirteen ways of looking at a blackbird," the truth about Sutpen is more than a sum of those parts. "But the truth," he concludes, "I would like to think, comes out, that when the reader has read all these thirteen different ways of looking at a blackbird, the reader has his own fourteenth image of that blackbird which I would like to think is the truth."[12]

Faulkner's response to this particular question and his more general treatment of human understanding in *Absalom, Absalom!* show remarkable parallels to the work of Hans-Georg Gadamer, an exact contemporary whom Faulkner certainly never read. In uncanny ways, Gadamer's *Truth and Method* provides us with a way of reading *Absalom, Absalom!* as a trenchant meditation on human understanding and the search for truth. In its focus upon play as a clue to ontological explanation, in its comprehension of the interpretive significance of tragedy, and in its determined insistence on the productive power of historicity, *Truth and Method* articulates the complex hermeneutical concerns that Faulkner creatively imagines in *Absalom, Absalom!*

This brings us back to Shreve McCannon, who at the beginning asked us to "wait." But Shreve is content with waiting. He is a patient man, one eager to hear a story elaborated and to have its ending delayed. "No, you wait," he implores Quentin at the midpoint of their conversation. "Let me play a while now" (*AA*, p. 224). And play they do, concocting events and fabricating conversations to explain this "horrible and bloody mischancing of human affairs." Working at times without even evidence to inform their imaginings, Shreve and Quentin construct elaborate dialogues between Sutpen's sons, Henry and Charles Bon. At times they impute complex motives and attribute labyrinthine self-understandings to minds to which they had no access and about which they know little. In key instances, they imagine meetings, conversations, and confrontations that almost certainly never took place.

Yet there is more than pointless fantasy in their endless talk. Somehow, in the midst of their mannered and fanciful elaborations of the Sutpen story, Shreve and Quentin recuperate twentieth-century truth about a nineteenth-century tragedy. A key to understanding how they accomplish this comes from their mutual requests to be allowed to "play a while" in telling the story. With this demand, they uncannily anticipate Gadamer, who, near the beginning of *Truth and Method*, conducts an extended discussion of "Play as the Clue to Ontological Explanation."[13] Seeking to free the concept of play from its subjective meaning in philosophy since Kant, Gadamer defines it as being neither a frivolous diversion nor an activity in which the subjectivity of the player is a primary concern.[14] In his words, "the actual subject of play is obviously not the subjectivity of an individual . . . but is instead the play itself."[15]

Gadamer draws upon the foundational work of Johan Huizinga, who discovered "the curious indecisiveness of the playing consciousness, which makes it absolutely impossible to decide between belief and non-belief" (*TM*, p. 104). In Huizinga's view, there is in the "holy play" of primitive peoples "no conceptual distinction between being and playing," so in a genuine "concept of play the difference between belief and pretense is dissolved" (quoted in *TM*, p. 104). Where the Cartesian tradition places a premium upon self-awareness in human understanding, "the structure of play absorbs the player into itself, and thus frees him from the burden of taking the initiative, which constitutes the actual strain of existence" (*TM*, p. 105). This is a particularly welcome freedom for the neurotically self-conscious Quentin Compson, who feels acutely "the actual strain of existence."

It is "characteristic of human play that it plays *something*" Gadamer explains. "That means that the structure of movement to which it submits has a definite quality which the player 'chooses'" (*TM*, p. 107). To enter the game is to submit oneself to the rules that constrain the possibilities within it. You discover yourself by losing yourself, by giving yourself up to the uncertainties and boundaries of the game. Robert Frost said he considered the writing of free verse to be like "playing tennis with the net down." You would never experience the frustration of hitting a shot into the net, but what would be the significance of the accomplishment? It is the constraints of the game, in the end, that make play productive.[16]

Quentin and Shreve strain against those constraints in their conversation, during which they enter so completely into the play of the story that they fuse with the objects of their attention. As they conjure images of Henry Sutpen and Charles Bon, Faulkner writes, it is "not two of them there and then either but four of them riding the two horses through the iron darkness" (*AA*, p. 237). When Shreve stops talking at one point, Faulkner's book reports, "Shreve ceased. That is, for all the two of them, Shreve and Quentin, knew he had stopped, since for all the two of them knew he had never begun, since it did not matter (and possibly neither of them conscious of the distinction) which one had been doing the talking" (*AA*, p. 267).

Such is the genius of true conversation, Gadamer argues: "The more genuine a conversation is, the less its conduct lies within the will of either partner." We never quite have the conversation we set out to have, for "we fall into conversation. . . . No one knows in advance what will 'come out' of a conversation." In the mystery of language, "a conversation has a spirit of its own, and . . . the language in which it is conducted bears its own truth within it—i.e., . . . it allows something to 'emerge' which henceforth exists." Understanding does not involve transposing ourselves into another person, Gadamer argues; instead, "to understand what a person says is . . . to come to an understanding about the subject matter, not to get inside another person and relive his experiences" (*TM*, p. 383).

Gadamer seems here to have hit upon what Faulkner struggled to describe to his Virginia students. The "fourteenth way" of looking at the blackbird puts the reader into a conversation with the novel's narrators. "To conduct a conversation," Gadamer asserts, "means to allow oneself to be conducted by the subject matter to which the partners in the dialogue are oriented" (*TM*, p. 367). For the author, character, and readers, Thomas Sutpen and all that he entails—including the disastrous legacy of slavery—form the subject matter to which the author, characters, and readers of the novel are oriented. We play at possibilities, suspending our judgments and waiting for the story to unfold; and we hypothesize about this man and his tragic life.[17]

As confusing as the interpretations offered by narrators of *Absalom, Absalom!* may appear to be, Faulkner does provide facts to mark the boundaries of the conversational play. As a number of critics have observed, *Absalom, Absalom!* possesses the qualities of a detective story. This makes it, in the words of Cleanth Brooks, "a nice instance of how the novelist works, for Shreve and Quentin both show a good deal of the insights of the novelist and his imaginative capacity for constructing plausible motivations around a few given facts." Using those facts creatively, Quentin and Shreve conduct their freewheeling conversation in such a manner that they provide, Brooks claims, a "persuasive commentary upon the thesis that much of 'history' is really a kind of imaginative construction."[18]

The most important interpretive constraint is provided by the knowledge Quentin acquires when he travels out to Sutpen's rotting home with Miss Rosa on a September evening in 1909. In a shuttered room, Quentin confronts the shattered Henry Sutpen, who has come home to die. From Henry, Quentin learns that Charles Bon was Henry's half-brother and the son of Thomas Sutpen. The possibility of miscegenation and incest accounts for Sutpen's fear of Bon's courtship of Judith as well as Henry's tragic decision to shoot the friend who is in fact his brother. The earlier conversations of the novel, those involving Mr. Compson and Rosa Coldfield, took place when none of the discussants knew Bon's identity. All the conjectures in the second half of the book—the January 1910 conversation between Quentin and Shreve—unfold in the light of that fact of sonship and brotherhood.

As a conversational partner with Shreve, Quentin provides a further constraint through his understanding of the tragic dimensions of Sutpen's story. Where Shreve sees this story as a grand spectacle, Quentin reads it as a devastating drama of moral blindness and cultural ruin. His reading of tragedy is weighted toward Hamlet-like struggles with identity and heroic action; he fixes upon the question of incest, almost to the exclusion of the matters of slavery and racism. Yet though his interpretation is partial, it does comport with a tragic understanding of the human condition and illuminates Gadamer's exposition of the relationship between tragedy and interpretation.

In *Absalom, Absalom!*, talk of tragedy begins at the novel's midpoint, as Quentin and Shreve set out on their late-night interpretive journey. "His trouble was innocence," Quentin says of Sutpen. Turned away as a boy from the front door of the mansion owned by his father's sharecropping master, young Tom Sutpen leaves home to pursue his "design."[19] He determines to revenge this slight by acquiring his own plantation, from whose door no child of his will ever be turned away. To that end, he travels to the West Indies, marries the daughter of a wealthy planter, and fathers a son by her. Only later does he discover that his wife is of mixed blood; he disposes of her and their son, for they are no longer "incremental to his design." He eventually makes his way to Yoknapatawpha County, where once again he acquires property, a wife, and a son and daughter.

But then Sutpen's entire design threatens to shatter in an instant, when his Henry returns from the University with a friend, Charles Bon, Sutpen's abandoned son by his first wife. Quentin imagines the father standing on his porch that day in 1859, awaiting Henry's arrival. The moment he first saw Bon, "he must have felt and heard the design—house, position, posterity, and all—come down like it had been built out of smoke, making no sound, creating no rush of displaced air and not even leaving any debris." When Sutpen related this experience several years later to Quentin's grandfather, he did not call it, Quentin says, "retribution, no sins of the father come home to roost; not even calling it bad luck, but just a mistake: that mistake which he could not discover himself and which he came to Grandfather, not to excuse but just to review the facts for an impartial [. . .] mind to examine and find and point out to him" (AA, p. 215).

Quentin concludes that Sutpen could not understand his own experience because of his peculiar "innocence which believed that the ingredients of morality were like the ingredients of pie or cake and once you had measured them and balanced them and mixed them and put them into the oven it was all finished and nothing but pie or cake could come out" (*AA*, pp. 211–12). For Sutpen, life is a matter of technique, determination, and domination, and a sin is but a mistake, something to be blotted out and corrected. Lacking irony and an awareness of his own finitude and responsibility, Sutpen does not understand what he has suffered and endured; nor can he fathom all that he has made others suffer and endure and all the horrific pain that the system he employs—that of chattel slavery—inflicts upon its oppressed subjects. A man of impeccable methods, Sutpen has no clue about the truth.

In Gadamer's terms, Thomas Sutpen cannot interpret his experience correctly, because he has failed to learn from it. Experience "inevitably involves many disappointments of one's expectations and only thus is experience acquired.[. . .] Every experience worthy of the name thwarts an expectation," Gadamer claims, and "thus the historical nature of man essentially implies a fundamental negativity that emerges in the relation between experience and insight" (*TM*, p. 356).

The negativity of experience makes it productive; through reversal, we acquire a wisdom that has decidedly religious connotations for Gadamer. Discussing the Aeschylean claim that "man must suffer into truth," he observes that "what a man has to learn through suffering is not this or that particular thing, but insight into the limitations of humanity, into the absoluteness of the barrier that separates man from the divine. It is ultimately a religious insight—the kind of insight that gave birth to Greek tragedy" (*TM*, p. 357).

According to Gerald Bruns, Gadamer shares the tragedian's skepticism about the limits of method in human understanding: "Experience is always more important than principles, vocabularies, concepts, procedures, and rules.[. . .] Experience does not consist in positive knowledge; rather (useless as it sounds) being experienced consists in openness to experience, tragic as it often is, which is perhaps another way of characterizing the recognition of contingency."[20] Working within his rationalized design, Sutpen can neither make allowances for contingencies nor understand their meaning. For him, the contingent can only be random and purposeless, and there is no sense that can be made of Gadamer's argument that "experience is experience of human finitude. The truly experienced person is one who has taken this to heart, who knows that he is master neither of time nor the future" (*TM*, p. 357).

Experience teaches us, that is, how to read and how to know what is real, for "the genuine result of experience, then—as of all desire to know—is to know what is" (*TM*, p. 357). In terms that read like an indictment of Sutpen's self-understanding, Gadamer concludes, "the idea that everything can be reversed, that there is always time for everything and that everything somehow returns, proves to be an illusion" (*TM*, p. 357). This indeed was Sutpen's illusion to the very end; he believed that he had only made a "tactical mistake" and behaved "like a skirmisher who is outnumbered yet cannot retreat who believes that if he is just patient enough and clever enough and calm enough and alert enough he can get the enemy scattered and pick them off one by one" (*AA*, p. 216).

"Genuine experience is experience of one's own historicity," Gadamer concludes, and on this point he would find himself in close agreement with Faulkner (*TM*, p. 357). Judith Sutpen speaks to this matter, when she brings to Quentin's grandmother a letter she has received from Charles Bon. When Grandmother Compson asks, "You want me to keep it?" Judith responds, "Yes. Or destroy it. As you like it." She explains that a human life makes "so little impression" that when it ends "all you have left is a block of stone with scratches on it." So, Judith says, she has brought the letter, because

> if you could go to someone, [. . .] and give them something—a scrap of paper—something, anything, [. . .] at least it would be something just because it would have happened, be remembered even if only from passing from one hand to another, one mind to another, and it would be at least a scratch, something, something that might make a mark on something that *was* once for the reason that it can die someday, while the block of stone cant be *is* because it never can become *was* because it cant ever die or perish. (*AA*, pp. 100–101)

The historicity of the individual raises for Faulkner and Gadamer the question of the historicity of human consciousness itself. In *Truth and Method*, Gadamer provides a sharp critique of what he calls the "Enlightenment [. . .] prejudice against prejudice itself, which denies tradition its power" (*TM*, p. 270). It was the universal goal of the Enlightenment to provide through the critique of prejudice a means of extricating the rational self from history and its biases. But "a person who believes he is free of prejudices," argues Gadamer, "experiences the power of the prejudices that unconsciously dominate him as a *vis a tergo* [a force from behind]." Even more important, one who "does not admit that he is dominated by prejudices will fail to see what manifests itself by their light" (*TM*, p. 360). To understand anything and learn the truth about it, "historical consciousness must not rely on the critical method with which it approaches its sources, as if this prevented it from mixing in its own judgments and prejudices. It must, in fact, think within its own historicity. To be situated within a tradition does not limit the freedom of knowledge but makes it possible" (*TM*, p. 361). This is the point of Quentin's anguished comment to Shreve: "You cant understand it. You would have to be born there" (*AA*, p. 289).

Each of these points of congruence in Faulkner and Gadamer—of play as a clue to the understanding of reality, of tragic apprehension as central to human understanding, and of the historicity of individual life and historical consciousness (and God)—is potentially but not necessarily consonant with Christian belief. The realm of play, for example, speaks of the sphere of interpretive and cultural freedom that diverse Christian traditions acknowledge and celebrate. From the football coach who sees the gridiron as the crucible of Christian discipleship to the priest who celebrates the ritual of the Mass each week, the Christian faith is about people at play in deadly serious matters. The first epistle of John addresses its audience as people who are, regardless of their age, children at play: "Beloved, we are God's children now; what we will be has not yet been revealed. What we do know is this: when he is revealed, we will be like him, for we will see him as he is." As Huizinga summarizes the matter: "Instead of the old saw: 'All is vanity,' the more positive conclusion forces itself upon us that 'all is play.'" He notes that "in singular imagery the thought comes back again in the *Book of Proverbs*, where Wisdom says: 'The Lord possessed me in the beginning of his ways, before he made any thing from the beginning.[. . .] I was with him forming all things: and was delighted every day, playing before him at all times; playing in the world. And my delights were to be with the children of men.'"[21]

Play, then, is a vital element in the interpretation of texts and history, but in the Christian tradition, those who play must always keep an eye on the limits of their abilities and the waywardness of their natures. This is the point of works as diverse as Dante's *Divine Comedy*, Calvin's *Institutes*, Dostoevsky's *The Brothers Karamazov*, and the short stories of Flannery O'Connor, all of which offer views of the person that intersect tragedy's outline of the human condition and correspond at many points with the insights of Faulkner and Gadamer.

That is not to say that a tragic understanding of life, as Gadamer outlines it and Faulkner realizes it, is identical with the Christian doctrine of sin. Tragedy inclines toward an understanding of the impersonality of fate while the Christian faith affirms the personality of God and the responsibility of sinners. The distinctions between Gadamer and the confessional history of Christianity on this point are drawn nicely in a recent essay by Jens Zimmermann. In this work, which is based upon a conversation conducted two weeks before Gadamer's death, Zimmermann distinguishes between the German philosopher's passionate concern with the impersonal question of transcendence and the creedal affirmation of the personality of God. "For Gadamer," writes Zimmermann, an interest in Christian history and religion in general "does not mean a return to dogmatic religion but the exploration of transcendence, and transcendence is first and foremost the acknowledgment of our finitude" acquired through recognition of the limits of human knowledge.[22] The Gadamerian transcendent is neither personal nor self-revealing. The most we can say of it is that, in Gadamer's words, "transcendence 'is not simply to believe in God but it is something incomprehensible.'" Indeed, for Gadamer, the bedrock of transcendence is "*ignoramus*, the admitting of our non-knowing (*unser Nichtwissen*)."[23] In their appreciation of the absolute limit separating humanity from the divine, and in their awareness of the role that limit plays in human understanding, tragedy, as understood by Gadamer and Faulkner, and the Christian faith are in basic agreement.[24] In their understanding of the self-revealing possibilities of God, they are, perhaps irrevocably, at odds.

Finally, in their confidence in the power of truth to emerge through dialogue and over the course of history, Faulkner and Gadamer find genuine points of contact with the Christian faith. They reject the notion that the detached observer most clearly apprehends the truth and turn instead to possibilities of conversation, of question and answer. Gadamer speaks eloquently of the power of questions to draw out the truth of texts: "Questions always bring out the undetermined possibilities of a thing," he writes. "Anticipating an answer itself presupposes that the questioner is part of the tradition and regards himself as addressed by it. This is the truth of historically effected consciousness" (*TM*, pp. 375, 377). Quentin Compson is precisely this type of questioner. For him the story of Thomas Sutpen remains an intensely personal matter, because it is part of the history of Quentin's vexed culture, and Quentin is convinced that that history is integral to his own identity and self-understanding.

Yet here points of divergence emerge between Gadamer and Faulkner, on the one hand, and Christian understanding, on the other. In Gadamerian hermeneutics, it is difficult to imagine a place for a doctrine of revelation. For Gadamer, Scripture and tradition tend to be conflated and become a linguistic tradition that embodies the truth but does not point to it. In historic Christianity, truth does not only emerge within history; it is also something imparted to men and women from beyond history.

According to Barth, the "Bible lays such extraordinary stress on the historicity of the revelation recorded by it because by revelation it does not mean a creation of man." It makes this point emphatically, because what it offers is not an emergence of divine truth but "an impartation to men." The revelatory events of the Christian Scriptures "do not purport to be manifestations of a universal or an idea" that can then be "comfortably compared" with the idea and assessed in all their particularity. This is the manner of reading revelation in the Enlightenment tradition stretching from Lessing to Kant, Herder, and Hegel; "with its intolerable distinction between the eternal content and the historical 'vehicle,'" it represents for Barth the "nadir of the modern misunderstanding of the Bible." Gadamer would likely appear to Barth as a practitioner trained in this school of misunderstanding, yet another modern thinker who cannot acknowledge that "revelation comes vertically from heaven" and "befalls man with the same contingency with which, living in this specific place at this specific time and in these specific circumstances he is this specific man at this specific stage of his inner and outer life."[25]

Like Gadamer, Faulkner also presents an understanding of the human condition that is not so much antagonistic to Christian belief as it is partial. He has a profoundly Christian anthropology, but his eschatology is post- or sub-Christian. He treats Dilsey's Christianity, for example, without a hint of irony in the final section of *The Sound and the Fury*. "'I've seed de first en de last. Never you mind me.[. . .] I seed de beginnin, en now I sees de endin," Dilsey tells her daughter Frony.[26] Yet while Faulkner may admire her faith in the forgiveness of sins and the resurrection of the body, he does not share it.[27]

To borrow a figure from Barbara Packer's remarkable book on Emerson, the question for us is whether the hope offered in Faulkner and Gadamer "belongs among the visions from Patmos or the views from Pisgah; whether we are being shown the Jerusalem in which we will someday live, or the Promised Land we will never be permitted to enter."[28] Where have these two left us? Consider the following: they faced the problems of historicism and relativism directly, and they acknowledged unblinkingly the historicity of experience and the fragility of human understanding. At the same time, they believed that while we may know the truth only in part, what we know is more than what we have projected or imagined. In short, with their understanding of the playful search for truth, in their appreciation of the religious and hermeneutical significance of tragedy, and in their persistent belief in the power of the truth to emerge through the dialogical struggles of history, Gadamer and Faulkner point to Christian truth even if they do not fully embrace it. "If those who are called philosophers," St. Augustine instructs us, "have said things which are indeed true and are well accommodated to our faith, they should not be feared; rather, what they have said should [. . .] be converted to our use."[29] If Faulkner and Gadamer can help us scale the heights of Pisgah, who are we to fault them for their failure to lead us into the Promised Land? That final journey is left to us—and through the mysterious grace of God, perhaps to them—to take.

NOTES

1. William Faulkner, *Absalom, Absalom!* (1936; New York: Vintage, 1990), p. 4. Hereafter referred to as *AA*.

2. "It must be possible for everything the Evangelists and Apostles have written to be lost again, and for the religion they taught to remain notwithstanding. Religion is not true because the Evangelists and Apostles taught it, but they taught it because it is true. The tradition handed down to us in writing must be explicable by its inner truth, and no written tradition can give it inner truth if it does not contain any" (Lessing, quoted in Karl Barth, *Protestant Theology in the Nineteenth Century*, trans. Brian Cozens and John Bowden [Grand Rapids: Eerdmans, 2002], p. 241).

3. Helmut Thielicke, *Modern Faith and Thought*, trans. Geoffrey W. Bromiley (Grand Rapids: Eerdmans, 1990), p. 122.

4. Søren Kierkegaard, *Concluding Unscientific Postscript*, trans. David F. Swenson and Walter Lowrie (Princeton: Princeton University Press, 1941), p. 86. The Swiss theologian Emil Brunner writes that for the enlightened person of the eighteenth century, "historical revelation is the great scandal or stumbling-block [. . .]. To acknowledge historical revelation means to acknowledge that the truth is not in us, that the right relation to God cannot be established from our side; that the breach between God and us is of such a nature that we can do nothing about" (Emil Brunner, *The Scandal of Christianity: The Gospel as Stumbling Block to Modern Man* [Richmond: John Knox, 1965], p. 22).

5. Barth, *Protestant Theology*, p. 242. "Lessing is well acquainted with a proof of Christianity through history. But it must be 'the proof of spirit and of power.' That is, history does not prove any truth for us so long as it is the 'contingent truth of history' merely reported to us by others and not truth 'felt' and 'experienced' by ourselves. It becomes the 'necessary truth of reason,' i.e., truth that is necessary and real for us, when and to the extent that it is thus felt and experienced in the way 'the paralytic experiences the beneficent shock of the electric spark'" (Karl Barth, *Church Dogmatics*, 4 vols., 13 parts, ed. G. W. Bromiley and T. F. Torrance [Edinburgh: T. and T. Clark, 1956–62], 1.1.146; hereafter referred to as *CD*).

6. Jaroslav Pelikan, *Christian Doctrine and Modern Culture (Since 1700)*, vol. 5 of *The Christian Tradition* (Chicago: University of Chicago Press, 1989), p. 231.

7. Thomas Jefferson, *Writings*, ed. Merrill Peterson (New York: Library of America, 1984), p. 1121.

8. As I have suggested elsewhere, in the matter of historical recovery, the late-twentieth-century heirs of Protestant liberalism proved to be the conservative biblical critics. Though they differed from their forebears in their theological judgments and assertions, those later conservative critics appropriated as their own the earlier liberals' desire to recover the purified meaning of the Christian revelation.

9. Friedrich Nietzsche, *Untimely Meditations*, trans. R. J. Hollingdale (Cambridge: Cambridge University Press, 1983), p. 59. Hereafter abbreviated as *UM*.

10. Friedrich Nietzsche, *Twilight of the Idols* and *The Anti-Christ*, trans. R. J. Hollingdale (London: Penguin, 1968), p. 78. It is important to note that for Nietzsche "*the unhistorical and the historical are necessary in equal measure for the health of an individual, of a people and of a culture.*" The means of overcoming the debilitating power of history are readily at hand for the willful individual and culture: "The stronger the innermost roots of a man's nature, the more readily will he be able to assimilate and appropriate the things of the past; and the most powerful and tremendous nature would be characterized by the fact that it would know no boundary at all at which the historical sense began to overwhelm it; it would draw to itself and incorporate into itself all the past, its own and that most foreign to it, and as it were transform it into blood" (UM, pp. 62–63).

11. Frederick L. Gwynn and Joseph Blotner, eds., *Faulkner in the University: Class Conferences at the University of Virginia, 1957–1958* (Charlottesville: University of Virginia Press, 1959), p. 275.

12. Ibid., pp. 273–74.

13. David Minter makes a parallel point about Shreve's "playful" dialogue, albeit without employing the vocabulary of philosophical hermeneutics: "Like Quentin, Shreve moves through a kind of apprenticeship in which listening is the central human act toward moments in which listening gives way to talking. Following an extended collaborative dialogue with Quentin, in chapters 6 and 7, Shreve begins, first, to recall, then to repeat, and then slowly to rearrange and elaborate all he has heard and absorbed" (David Minter, *Faulkner's Questioning Narratives: Fiction of His Major Phase, 1929–42* [Urbana: University of Illinois Press, 2001], p. 77).

14. The Kantian subjectivization of aesthetics and play has had an extraordinary influence over the theory and criticism of the arts in the past two centuries. For a nuanced and appreciative exploration of Kant's understanding of the role of play, see Paul Guyer, *Kant and the Claims of Taste*, 2nd ed. (Cambridge: Cambridge University Press, 1997), pp. 60–105.

15. Hans-Georg Gadamer, *Truth and Method*, 2nd rev. ed., trans. Joel Weinsheimer and Donald G. Marshall (New York: Crossroad, 1989), p. 104. Hereafter referred to as *TM*.

16. Two vastly different works make a similar point about the necessarily limiting yet fruitful nature of the rule-governed domain of games; both works use the image of rooms. First, Kenneth Burke on the manner in which we learn: "Where does the drama get its materials? From the 'unending conversation' that is going on at the point in history when we are born. Imagine that you enter a parlor. You come late. When you arrive, others have long preceded you, and they are engaged in a heated discussion, a discussion too heated for them to pause and tell you exactly what it is about. In fact, the discussion had already begun long before any of them got there, so that no one present is qualified to retrace for you all the steps that had gone before. You listen for a while, until you decide that you have caught the tenor of the argument; then you put in your oar. Someone answers; you answer

him; another comes to your defense; another aligns himself against you, to either the embarrassment or gratification of your opponent, depending upon the quality of your ally's assistance. However, the discussion is interminable. The hour grows late, you must depart. And you do depart, with the discussion still vigorously in progress" (Kenneth Burke, *The Philosophy of Literary Form: Studies in Symbolic Action*, 3rd ed. [Berkeley: University of California Press, 1973], pp. 110–11).

The other passage appears near the conclusion of Don DeLillo's *White Noise*. It involves a confrontation between the protagonist, Jack Gladney, and a mysterious man he has been tracking down. When he confronts that man, the latter tells Jack:

"'By coming in here, you agree to a certain behavior,' Mink said.

"'What behavior?'

"'Room behavior. The point of rooms is that they're inside. No one should go into a room unless he understands this. People behave one way in rooms, another way in streets, parks and airports. To enter a room is to agree to a certain kind of behavior. It follows that this would be the kind of behavior that takes place in rooms. This is the standard, as opposed to parking lots and beaches. It is the point of rooms. No one should enter a room not knowing the point.'"

(Don DeLillo, *White Noise: Text and Criticism*, ed. Mark Osteen [New York: Penguin, 1998], p. 306).

17. The dialogic view of interpretation is associated with the work of Mikhail Bakhtin. Using Fyodor Dostoevsky's *The Brothers Karamazov* as his touchstone, Bakhtin developed a theory of the polyphonic novel: "A *plurality of independent and unmerged voices and consciousnesses, a genuine polyphony of fully valid voices is in fact the chief characteristic of Dostoevsky's novels.* What unfolds in his works is not a multitude of characters and fates in a single objective world, illuminated by a single authorial consciousness; rather a *plurality of consciousnesses, with equal rights and each with its own world,* combine but are not merged in the unity of the event" (Mikhail Bakhtin, *Problems of Dostoevsky's Poetics*, ed. and trans. Caryl Emerson [Minneapolis: University of Minnesota Press, 1984], p. 6).

Gary Saul Morson and Caryl Emerson explain: "[I]n a polyphonic work the form-shaping ideology itself demands that the author cease to exercise monologic control. This, then, is the second criterion of polyphony: a change in the author's position in the work. Polyphony demands a work in which several consciousnesses meet as equals and engage in a dialogue that is in principle unfinalizable.[. . .] The direct power to mean, which in a monologic work belongs to the author alone, belongs to several voices in a polyphonic work. By surrendering his monologic powers, Dostoevsky created a way to embody a dialogic conception of truth" (Gary Saul Morson and Caryl Emerson, *Mikhail Bakhtin: Creation of a Prosaics* [Stanford: Stanford University Press, 1990], pp. 238–39).

18. Cleanth Brooks, *William Faulkner: The Yoknapatawpha Country* (New Haven: Yale University Press, 1963), p. 311. In an appendix to *William Faulkner: The Yoknapatawpha Country*, Brooks provides a remarkable detailing of "What WE KNOW about Thomas Sutpen and His Children" (pp. 429–36). For my reconstruction of the events in *Absalom, Absalom!* I am deeply indebted to Brooks's efforts.

19. One of the most crucial questions of *Absalom, Absalom!* has to do with the nature of Sutpen's design. Just what was he seeking, when he set out from his Tidewater home to fashion an entirely new life for himself? Richard Godden provides a balanced and comprehensive examination of different critical assessments of Sutpen's "design." While inventively insightful, his own reading of Sutpen's design as a matter of "labor trauma" reads the story exclusively as an exercise in the repression of a materially bound consciousness

and truth. Godden considers it "a mistake to read the novel's difficulty as raising primarily epistemological questions [. . .] [including] some form of the unanswerable question, How can they (or we) know at all?" To Godden, such hermeneutical concerns miss the obvious Marxist point: "In *Absalom, Absalom!*, a novel designed to explore a repressive class 'design,' difficulty begs the altogether more answerable question, How can those who know so much, repress so much of what they know" (Richard Godden, "*Absalom, Absalom!*, Haiti and Labor History: Reading Unreadable Revolutions," *ELH* 61 [Autumn 1994]: 714).

20. Gerald L. Bruns, *Hermeneutics, Ancient and Modern* (New Haven: Yale University Press, 1992), p. 259.

21. Johan Huizinga, *Homo Ludens: A Study of the Play-Element in Culture* (1950; Boston: Beacon, 1955), p. 212.

22. Jens Zimmerman, "Ignoramus: Gadamer's 'Religious Turn.'" *Symposium: Journal of the Canadian Society for Hermeneutics and Postmodern Thought* 6 (2002): 203–17, p. 207.

23. Ibid., p. 208.

24. To be sure, there is an additional point of divergence between the tragic vision and the Christian faith. It has to do with the genre of comedy, which historically has been more closely associated with the Christian creeds and their central affirmations. Comedy speaks of a final resolution and reconciliation, a triumph over death and suffering as well as a healing of the divisions between men and women and God. Thus, in the words of Nathan Scott, "though there is no simple and absolute antithesis between the tragic vision and the Christian faith, the relation is, nevertheless, always one of strain. Indeed, *finally*, it is one in which what is tragically broken in life is taken up and absorbed into the great Eucharistic action of offering, consecration, and communion, whereby the self-oblation of the Church becomes one with Christ's own oblation of Himself for our redemption" (Nathan Scott, *The Broken Center: Studies in the Theological Horizon of Modern Literature* [New Haven: Yale University Press, 1966], p. 141).

25. CD, 1.1.329. There are a number of references to Barth sprinkled across Gadamer's works. Virtually all of them deal with the advent of dialectical theology at the close of WWI. In one instance, Gadamer treats Barth's work at greater length and draws a distinct parallel between him and Rudolf Bultmann. They were alike, Gadamer claims, and it was "Bultmann's combination of historical-critical research with theological exegesis and his reliance on philosophy (Heidegger)" that prevented "Barth from recognizing himself in Bultmann's method" (*TM*, p. 509).

According to Barth, the contrary was the case. In *Church Dogmatics* 2.1, he playfully but forcefully rejects his own earlier emphasis upon a radical time and eternity dialectic. Only when "P. Tillich with his Kairos-philosophy, and later R. Bultmann with his reduction of New Testament anthropology to the terms of existentialist philosophy, believed they could welcome me (Barth) as one of themselves" did the author of the *Church Dogmatics* realize how firmly he had to reject his own earlier distortions (CD, 2.1.635). Barth saw keenly that the similarities between him and Bultmann were a result of his own earlier distortions and Bultmann's eagerness to claim him for a view and venture that Barth had no desire to call his own.

26. William Faulkner, *The Sound and the Fury* (1929; New York: Vintage, 1990), p. 297.

27. Though he makes *Absalom, Absalom!* out to be a somewhat more explicitly Christian novel than most critics would allow, John Hunt in the end strikes a useful balance between the Christian affirmation contained in the novel and the Stoic denial affirmed at its core: in *Absalom, Absalom!* Faulkner "brings the Christian and Stoic alternatives together,

tips the theological balance in favor of the Christian, but does not break their essential tension" (John W. Hunt, "The Theological Center of *Absalom, Absalom!*" in *Religious Perspectives in Faulkner's Fiction: Yoknapatawpha and Beyond*, ed. J. Robert Barth, S.J. [Notre Dame: University of Notre Dame Press, 1972], p. 169).

28. B[arbara] L. Packer, *Emerson's Fall; A New Interpretation of the Major Essays* (New York: Continuum, 1982), p. 84.

29. St. Augustine, *On Christian Doctrine*, trans. D. W. Robertson Jr. (New York: Bobbs-Merrill, 1958), p. 75.

8

The Hermeneutics of Deliverance

Robinson Crusoe and the Problem of Witnessing

Brian McCrea

As I consider how a Christian perspective might articulate with recent developments in literary theory and interpretation, I would validate Christian interpretation not as part of a virtuous life (although it well may be), but as a better method. The great challenge for me as a Christian interpreter is to reopen an important work, to discuss it apart from conventional wisdom, to get beyond the impasses at which critics with differing methodologies frequently arrive. The post-structuralist heterodoxies of the 1980s and 1990s have become canonical in my place (a large research-university English Department) and my time (2004). Literary theory written from a Christian perspective might have a strong claim to be "the next new thing" if its practitioners can acknowledge and begin to answer at least three questions that these few sentences already have begged: What is Christian interpretation? What makes a work important? How does one "reopen" or advance criticism of an important work?

I suggest that Christian interpretation—at least of prose narratives—will center upon witnessing; as the Gospels and the Pauline letters bear complicated witness to the life of Christ, so prose narratives bear complicated witness to the events that they describe.[1] An important work interests readers and provides matter for debate between critics and thinkers over a long period of time. Critics who reopen important works find something new and significant to say about them when it seems that, thanks to the great American higher education publication mill, all that might be said has been said.

Daniel Defoe's *Robinson Crusoe* provides a useful example of an important work whose long history of significant commentary includes an impasse and a sophisticated Hegelian mediation of those critical differences. In what follows, I will reopen *Robinson Crusoe* via an account of Christian witnessing offered by Paul Ricoeur. The difficulties that befall Crusoe as he attempts to bear witness to his, it would seem, extraordinarily memorable experiences find a revealing (and liberating) counterpart in the witnessing of the Apostles. This Christian perspective upon Crusoe, insofar as it accounts for features of his narrative that Hegelian mediation cannot, gets readers beyond the terminus, however happy, at which criticism of Defoe arrived in the 1970s. The Christian perspective, in sum, enables a superior critique.

Crusoe's narrative includes two widely commented upon but still problematic features that offer an opportunity for this hermeneutics of witnessing to distinguish itself: Crusoe's journal and Crusoe's dream of a native who escapes execution by cannibals and finds sanctuary with him. Crusoe's dream does not quite correspond in its details to his rescue of Friday, and his journal bears an odd, sometimes equivocal, relationship to his narrative. While some critics might take these anomalies as signs of Defoe's sloppiness (Defoe is famous for his mistakes),[2] they instead may betoken his rich and, even by our standards, sophisticated sense of how difficult it is to witness the truth. Defoe's sensitivity to this difficulty is important in relation to a more general question that has a specifically Christian basis—Crusoe's "deliverance." In a narrative as multifarious as Defoe's, one hesitates to claim great significance for a single word. However, "deliver," "to deliver," and "deliverance" appear so frequently in *Crusoe* as to verge upon being omnipresent. Crusoe chances upon Psalm 50, verse 15 ("And call upon me in the day of trouble. I will deliver thee and thou shalt exalt me") as he fights a violent "feaver" that he fears will kill him.[3] When he recovers his health, he also claims to be spiritually renewed because he now understands what deliverance is—not rescue from his island, but freedom from sin. He will have difficulty maintaining this exalted understanding of deliverance and, in later uses of the word, can sound, to risk an anachronism, as if he is ordering a pizza rather than purging himself of material yearnings.

The full title of the book that we know as *Robinson Crusoe* is *The Life and Strange Surprizing Adventures of Robinson Crusoe of York. Mariner.* While the title page emphasizes "Adventures," Defoe, in his various prefaces, emphasizes "the religious and useful Inferences drawn from every Part."[4] He asks his readers to grant his narrative the status of a parable and asserts, "The Fable is always made for the Moral, not the Moral for the Fable."[5] For Defoe, *Crusoe* is more than an adventure story.

Subsequent commentators have not hesitated to disagree with Defoe—and with each other. Some have granted Defoe's claim to offer a spiritual autobiography of a prototypical protestant wayfarer. Others, perhaps most famously Karl Marx, have asserted that Crusoe's is, indeed, an "adventure" story, with the adventure residing in the discovery of the economic individualism that underlies capitalism. Marx humorously dismissed Defoe's claim that Crusoe's story had a religious "Application": "Of his prayers and the like we take no account, since they are a source of pleasure to him, and he looks upon them as so much recreation."[6] In his extraordinarily influential *The Rise of the Novel*, Ian Watt cites Marx, describes "Crusoe's religious life" as "somewhat gratuitous," and sees the narrative as shaped by "hypostasis of the economic motive."[7]

The Rise of the Novel was published in 1957. By the mid-1960s, critics were taking seriously Defoe's claim to be a writer of parables. George A. Starr placed Defoe's novels within the tradition of seventeenth-century spiritual autobiography, arguing, contra Marx and Watt, that "What affords him [Crusoe] peace of mind is not success in the role of *homo economicus*, but the discovery that he can rely on Providence for direction and support."[8] In his *The Reluctant Pilgrim*, J. Paul Hunter describes Crusoe's search for a divine pattern in his life, even as he points out how easily scholars can let their presuppositions control their interpretations:

> Defoe's library had been sold a few months before his death in 1731, and although the *Daily Advertiser* for November 13, 1731 mentioned a sale catalogue, no copy had been found before 1895, when George A. Aitken located one in the British Museum. The value of the find was considerably diminished, however, by the fact that Defoe's books were grouped with those of an Anglican clergyman, Phillip Farewell, and the catalogue failed to distinguish individual ownership. . . . Aitken proposed a partial list of Defoe's books, setting aside as Dr. Farewell's "the large array of theological and classical literature." He admitted that "in adopting this course we shall, no doubt, pass over not a few works of Defoe's, but this is unavoidable."
>
> Aitken listed more than three dozen travel books and maps as probably belonging to Defoe, and later source students seem to have trusted Aitken's list completely.[9]

If interpreters presuppose that Defoe was an inspired hack who wrote adventure stories, they will not question Aitken's guesses. If interpreters, in the wake of the work of Starr and Hunter, presuppose that Defoe's religion was more than "gratuitous," they well may suspect that some of that "theological and classical literature" belonged to him. Significant here is that both parties to the debate over Defoe share a critical method. Starr and Hunter do not offer a Christian interpretation of Defoe. Rather, they locate different sources for his writing than do Marx and Watt. They place Defoe within a tradition of devotional literature but do not raise questions about that tradition's source, about the testimony upon which it depends.

By the 1970s, then, the divisions in Defoe criticism were reassuringly clear and, seemingly, unbridgeable. As James Sutherland put the case in 1971, "Is *Robinson Crusoe* a simple story of adventure, or has it a deeper significance? In recent years critics have tended to concentrate attention on the character of Crusoe and to interpret the story in accordance with his ruling passion. More especially, they have dwelt upon that 'original sin' about which Crusoe himself expatiates at some length."[10] Sutherland did not emphasize that when critics narrowed their focus to

Crusoe's "original sin," they did not improve their chances of resolving the adventure story/spiritual autobiography split. If Crusoe's failure to heed the warnings of his father redacts Adam's Fall, then why is it that Crusoe discovers an Edenic bower only after he is shipwrecked? If Crusoe, to take another scriptural precedent that he cites, redacts the story of the Prodigal Son, how is it that he returns home to find his father dead and himself wealthy beyond his happiest imagining? If Crusoe's experiences at sea are comparable to Jonah's, why does the inner voice that warns him against taking another sea voyage direct him to a passage over land in which he is nearly devoured by wolves? Crusoe is quite good at citing scriptural precedents for his case, but he also is remarkably insensitive to the ways in which his story departs from those precedents.

Those eager to dismiss Defoe's claims to religious "Application" find in these departures powerful evidence for the preeminence of economic individualism. As Leopold Damrosch Jr. summarizes this view, whatever the "Affinities" between *Crusoe* and the Puritan tradition, Defoe's novel "in the end stands as a remarkable instance of a work that gets away from its author, and gives expression to attitudes that lie far from his conscious intention." Defoe may set out to "dramatize the conversion of the Puritan self"[11] but he cannot stay away from the excitement that economic success brings. Damrosch's comment is particularly helpful because it shows how the division between those who grant Crusoe his prayers and those who hypostatize his economic motive typically conflates with another: between those who grant Defoe control, even sophistication, as a writer and those who describe him as the greatest hack writer in literary history, a man who wrote for money and in a rush, and, somehow, along the way, happened to found the English novel.

In 1975 the Clarendon Press published John J. Richetti's *Defoe's Narratives: Situations and Structures.*[12] Richetti's great achievement was to find in G. W. F. Hegel's *Phenomenology of the Spirit* a version of consciousness that, once imputed to Crusoe, mediates between his economic and religious successes. Richetti outlines the division between Marx and Watt, Starr and Hunter, then claims

> we must concede the accuracy of both these descriptions; Crusoe is in my view neither exclusively a masterful economic individual nor a heroically spiritual slave. He inhabits both ideologies in such a way that he manages to be both at once and therefore to reside in neither. What we may call the *real* Crusoe, the existential Crusoe that *the novel aspires instinctively to deliver,* is the personal energy that experiences the contradictions implicit in mimetic narrative: control in a context of helplessness and helplessness in a context of control. (*DN*, p. 23; my emphasis)

This rapid summary may leave the mistaken impression that Richetti resolves the Crusoe paradox by magically waving the wand of Hegelian dialectic. Actually, Richetti moves so comprehensively between the different camps because he finds a new way to talk about Crusoe. Rather than focus upon Crusoe's material successes or his religious claims, Richetti argues that in his isolation, Crusoe "becomes . . . a contemplative consciousness who can literally observe himself at work, resembling in that fruitful split the master in Hegel's formulation who interposes the slave between the thing and himself and thereby achieves freedom" (*DN*, p. 35).

Richetti reopens the case of Crusoe's illness, a crucial event for critics in the Starr-Hunter vein. For Richetti the illness is important because during it Crusoe

> observes "himself," he achieves by sickness the perspective that Hegel called the "master." Part of himself remains the "slave," indeed the point is that part of him becomes for the first time entirely perceived in the narrative as the slave of circumstance, committed fully and clearly to a chain of events going back to his origins. He has always been part of that chain, but as readers of the sickness-conversion sequence we are being involved in the operative reality of the chain and in the simultaneous freedom implicit in our and Crusoe's consciousness of that necessity and co-operating with it. (*DN*, p. 44)

Crusoe's is a conversion of "consciousness." As a result of it, Crusoe can leave behind the "paranoid seclusion" of his early months after the shipwreck and "convert his island from a prison to a garden" (*DN*, p. 46). Crusoe finds his Eden only after his attitude changes.

In Richetti's account, illness—the physical weakness that Crusoe describes lengthily and repeatedly—is an experience of "pure passivity" that counterpoints the frantic activity of his early, fearful months on the island (*DN*, p. 46). Crusoe's "new condition," then, is not that of a born-again Christian, but rather "the synthesis which results from the thesis and antithesis of pure action and pure passivity." In one of his most perceptive and comprehensive analyses, Richetti observes that, after his illness, Crusoe becomes

> the perfect mediator. Having reconciled contradiction in himself, he moves among contradictions, resolving them. He discovers that the island has wet and dry seasons, he builds a "villa" for pleasure to balance his secure fortress for survival, he tames wild things (a parrot, then goats), he despises the surplus value of his gold and celebrates useful things but keeps his gold anyway, in effect reconciling two systems of value. He is able to speak jauntily "of my reign or my captivity, which you please." (*DN*, p. 47)

Beyond these specific mediations, Richetti points to a more general: "Crusoe sings a *contemptus mundi* tune even while we rejoice in his expanding and ever more orderly island." Crusoe keeps telling us that "things" really do not matter, even as his narrative generates interest by showing us how he learns to fire pottery and build boats, to bake bread and cure raisins. For Richetti this is not an inconsistency on Crusoe's part but rather a sign that he has achieved "Hegelian mastership; he has done with the thing and is not contained in its being but 'enjoys it without qualification and without reserve. The aspect of its independence he leaves to the servant, who labors upon it'" (*DN*, p. 47). For much of the narrative, Crusoe contains within himself both the master and the servant. However, "the sequence of his career," the shaping principle of his story, is his "elevation to higher and higher forms of mastery (the self, the environment, animals, natives, and Europeans)" (*DN*, p. 60). Crusoe's mastery becomes complete, not with his rescue of Friday, but with his leaving behind him Europeans who will tend to his island.

Richetti merits extended citation because of the insightfulness, comprehensiveness, and definitiveness (in the sense of its overcoming a long-standing critical impasse) of his interpretation. Taking his hermeneutic from Hegel, Richetti makes the parties to the earlier dispute, all of whom he treats with good grace, appear imperceptive. They all have missed something important. Not only does he synthesize the adventure story/spiritual autobiography split, he also, less obviously, moots the Defoe as inspired hack/Defoe as careful artist split. In this latter case, he relies upon some careful phrasing. Recall his claim, "What we may call the real Crusoe, the existential Crusoe that the novel aspires instinctively to deliver, is the personal energy that experiences the contradiction implicit in mimetic narrative." In Richetti's dialectic, the "novel" replaces "Defoe" as the agent for aspiration. As Richetti endows the novel with "instincts," the problematic figure of Defoe moves to the background, and Crusoe becomes a locus of "personal energy" rather than a character.

To offer an interpretation of *Robinson Crusoe* even more comprehensive than Richetti's Hegelian reading is a large challenge. But a Christian perspective upon the difficulties, the uncertainties and, finally, the importance of witnessing can account for features of the narrative that he finds hard to explain. In his most famous novel, Daniel Defoe, who trained to be a Dissenting minister before his life took many other turns,[13] creates a protagonist who claims to testify accurately to the events of his life. That Crusoe cannot get his story quite right may not be a sign of Defoe's sloppiness; rather, Crusoe's faulty witnessing may betoken Defoe's rich sense of how difficult it is, even in the most important or harrowing of matters, to say the truth.

Witnessing, of course, is a large and much discussed topic, one that cannot be fairly treated in this space. To narrow this discussion to a manageable focus, I will work from Paul Ricoeur's "Preface to Bultmann,"[14] which he wrote in the early 1960s. As Ricoeur, a philosopher first, theologian second, considers the hermeneutics of the "Christ-event," his commentary holds striking relevance to *Crusoe* and points a way for interpretation to get outside/beyond Richetti's dialectic. In Ricoeur's account, the "hermeneutic problem" with that event is that it is "already an interpretation of a preceding Scripture." Jesus is both "exegesis and exegete of Scripture"; even if we could somehow get back to the original Jesus, we would not escape the hermeneutic circle because we would be getting back to an interpretation (PB, pp. 382, 384).

Our position as interpreters of the "Christ-event" is particularly difficult because "We ourselves are no longer those witnesses who have seen. We are the hearers who listen to the witnesses: *fides ex auditu*. Hence, we can believe only by listening and by interpreting a text which is already an interpretation" (PB, p. 386). As Ricoeur describes the relationship between the Old and New Testaments, he raises a basic question that many Christians will find unsettling, one that Defoe redacts through Crusoe:

> So long as the New Testament served to decipher the Old, it was taken as an absolute norm. And it remains an absolute norm as long as its literal meaning serves as an indisputable basis on which all other levels of meaning—the allegorical, moral, and anagogical—are constructed. But the fact is that the literal meaning is itself a text to be understood, a letter to be interpreted. (PB, pp. 386–87)

That we cannot hope to witness directly the life of Christ is hardly a controversial or even unsettling claim. But that we cannot hope for literal meaning in the Scriptures—a meaning that resides apart from interpretation—is both. Defoe anticipates the uncertainty described by Ricoeur by building Crusoe's story upon this absence of the literal.

Not only does Ricoeur take from us our confidence in what we can witness, he also reminds us that the Gospels are belated rather than original texts. The Gospels are written at

> a distance, however minimal, from the event that . . . [they] proclaim. This distance always increasing with time, is what separates the first witness from the entire line of those who hear the witness. Our modernity means only that the distance is now considerable between the place I myself occupy at the center of a culture and the original site of the first witness. This distance . . . is given at the beginning. It is the very first distance between the hearer and the witness of the event.
>
> Thus the somehow accidental distance of a twentieth-century man, situated in another, a scientific and historical culture, reveals an original distance which remained concealed because it was so short, yet it was already constitutive of primitive faith itself. (PB, p. 387)

In perhaps the most influential recent account of this "distance," Paula Frederiksen notes that Matthew's "messianic lineage cannot be made compatible with Luke's, but this is no surprise: neither evangelist had access to actual historical information about Jesus' ancestry, or, probably, to each other's work."[15] The "salient details of Matthew's narrative cannot be matched to Luke's," and a similar tendency to "contradict" Luke appears in the Letters of Paul (*FJC*, pp. 36, 55). Those letters, even though Paul was not a disciple, are older than the Gospels, closer, at least chronologically, to the events of Christ's life. While "Paul cannot take us as close to the historical origins of the Jesus movement as we might expect . . . his letters do come from someone irrefutably acquainted with the leaders of the original community" (*FJC*, p. 52). They also have the virtue of coming "directly from Paul himself, without the vicissitudes of oral transmission that make criticism of the gospels so complicated" (*FJC*, pp. 52–53).

Frederiksen concludes, "the Pauline letters are the primary sources of the Christian tradition par excellence" (*FJC*, p. 53), but her claim only confirms how multifarious the words "origins" and "original" become in any discussion of the Scriptures. For all their power and influence, the Gospels are not "eyewitness" accounts; nor are Paul's epistles. In *Crusoe* Defoe offers an early modern redaction of this anxiety about origin. As time passes, Crusoe varies his accounts of the traumatic events that cause his exile. What Defoe finally "delivers" Crusoe from is not the island or sin; rather, Defoe frees his protagonist from the requirement that he provide an accurate, true-to-its-origins account of his "Adventures."

After several weeks on his island, Crusoe starts to keep "a journal of my every day's employment" (*RC*, p. 86). Richetti describes Crusoe as "only beginning to keep the journal after he had achieved some mastery of himself and of the island" (*RC*, p. 38). Crusoe himself admits that he did not write much from the beginning of his stay because "I was in too much hurry, and not only hurry as to labor, but in too much discomposure of mind" (*RC*, p. 86). For Richetti the journal mediates between the frantic activity that characterizes Crusoe's first days on the island and the inertness that befalls him during his illness. The journal thus marks a stage in Crusoe's developing self-control.

Christian interpreters who come to the journal from Ricoeur can point to it as Defoe's version of "an original distance that remained concealed because it was so short." In the journal a storm destroys Crusoe's ship twenty-five days after he arrived on the island; in the narrative, the storm comes in thirteen days (*RC*, pp. 75, 87). In the narrative, Crusoe claims that he offered thanks to God once he landed safely on shore; in the journal, he claims he did not (*RC*, pp. 65, 103–104). Apart from discrepancies of this sort, the relationship between journal and text becomes ever more obscure as Crusoe moves between them. Crusoe punctuates his narrative with remarks such as "to return to my journal" (*RC*, p. 95) and "I return to my journal" (*RC*, p. 111), but even the most attentive readers may have trouble saying when he left it.[16] Early in the journal, Crusoe's entries are dated and brief. Readers may guess that an expanded meditation upon an event or object comes from somewhere else. But as the journal entries become longer, this touchstone vanishes.

Shortly after the first anniversary of the shipwreck, Crusoe reports

> my ink began to fail me, and so I contented my self to use it more sparingly, and to write down only the most remarkable events of my life, without continuing a daily memorandum of other things. (*RC*, p. 117)

Besides placing the journal at the mercy of material circumstance, rather than associating it with Crusoe's developing "mastery" of himself and others, this information does not help readers who want to identify when, subsequently, Crusoe writes in his journal. The only principle of organization is his supply of ink. The journal is older than the rest of the text, which we assume Crusoe writes sometime after his return to England. Yet the journal is not original. Defoe takes care to emphasize that this document is at some distance from events, and its witness confuses matters rather than clarifying them. The journal does not discredit Crusoe, who, after all, is under extraordinary stress, but it does require readers to have "primitive faith" in him.

Richetti admits to difficulty in accounting for Crusoe's proleptic dream of an escapee from cannibals who finds his fortress and becomes his servant. Richetti describes the dream as "curiously unreal" and then offers, as he looks forward to the actual circumstances of Friday's arrival, "opportunity when it comes never matches plans" (*DN*, pp. 54, 55). This may be true enough. I remember my mother's offering of a similar commonplace. But it's not Hegel. Richetti also points out that, in the dream, "Crusoe does not really participate but simply watches with a cool detachment totally foreign to normal dream experience" (*DN*, p. 54). This link to Crusoe's earlier passivity, however, does not help Richetti's argument because the dream comes late in the story, after Crusoe, in Richetti's account, has achieved self-mastery and, through his synthesis of the roles of master and servant, control of the island.

Ricoeur and Frederiksen help us to understand this disparity between the dream and Crusoe's account of his rescue of the character whom we come to know as Friday. It betokens Defoe's recognition that not even the unconscious can provide us with an origin prior to or beyond interpretation. This disparity is much the same as the disparity between the journal and the rest of the narrative. The "prior" account does not agree completely with the "later." This disagreement, rather than indicating sloppiness or ineptness of Defoe's part, reveals that the putatively older text is as much an interpretation as the later. Originals, Defoe suggests and Ricoeur would agree, are prior to narrative, even though Crusoe and his readers may sometimes confuse narratives that are very old, very close to the original events, with the original.

Defoe subverts notions of origin when Crusoe, "his ink eeked out with water . . . till it was so pale it scarce left any appearance of black upon the paper," observes "a strange concurrence of days in the various providences which befell me." Put simply, Crusoe notes that the important events of his life have happened on the same date:

> the same day that I broke away from my father . . . the same day afterwards I was taken by the sallee man of war, and made a slave.
>
> The same day of the year that I escaped out of the wreck of that ship in Yarmouth Roads, that same day—year afterwards, I made my escape from Sallee in the boat.
>
> The same day of the year I was born on, viz. the 30th of September, that same day I had my life so miraculously saved twenty-six years after, when I was cast on shore on this island, so that my wicked life and my solitary life begun both on a day. (*RC*, pp. 143–44)

While Crusoe would suggest that all begins with/returns to the date of his birth, these special dates are different, and he calculates them only as his ink is "wasted." They do not fix the relationship between his journal and his narrative or between his narrative and his life on the island. For all the confidence with which he dates events here, Crusoe earlier admits that, despite all his care, he "lost a day in my accompt" of his time on the island. He suspects his mistake is owing to his sleeping through a day during his recovery from his illness, but admits he may have "lost it by crossing and re-crossing the line." In any case not until his "later" return to Europe does he understand that his earlier "accompt" is in error (*RC*, p. 109).

In the case of "deliverance"—the single most important word in *Crusoe*, I suggest—Crusoe's uses of it bear only the most problematic of relationships to scriptural precedents. In almost the same breath, Crusoe will speak of "deliverance" in the most exalted spiritual terms and then in the most quotidian. Richetti, of course, can read "deliverance" through his dialectic, but Crusoe's "consciousness" never advances to a point at which he uses the word uniformly and consistently. To cite only one example from the hundreds possible: near his story's end, Crusoe rescues an English ship captain and two other officers from mutineers. Prior to their rescue, he observes the group and compares their arrival on the island to his:

> As I knew nothing that night of the supply I was to receive by the providential driving of the ship nearer the land . . . so these three poor desolate men knew nothing how certain of deliverance and supply they were. . . . [S]o much reason have we to depend cheerfully upon the great Maker of the world, that He does not leave his creatures so absolutely destitute, but that in the worst circumstances they have always something to be thankful for, and sometimes are nearer their deliverance than they imagine; nay, are even brought to their deliverance by the means by which they seem to be brought to their destruction. (*RC*, pp. 250–52)

Is "deliverance" synonymous with "supply," or is it part of a "providential" enactment of the "great Maker's will"? At this point in the story, Crusoe's "consciousness" has become "contemplative," but his references to "deliverance" remain as multifarious as they were before and during his conversion. While he would claim that the "deliverance" about to befall these men follows the pattern of his "deliverance," the events of the two narratives bear only the slimmest of resemblances; only the scene is the same.

In his account of the change in Crusoe that illness brings, Richetti claimed that "the point is that part of him becomes for the first time entirely perceived in his narrative as the slave of circumstance, committed fully and clearly to a chain of events going back to his origins." Richetti also claimed that Crusoe "has always been part of that chain." Following Ricoeur and contra Richetti, I suggest that Crusoe is not delivered to a new "consciousness" of his "origins." Precisely the opposite occurs: he is delivered from the claims of a prior literal event. His narrative is confused, sometimes self-contradictory, but, for himself and for generations of readers, true. The narrative is ongoing—sequels will follow—and Crusoe is free to never quite say when and where he writes it. It, finally, is best read from a Christian as opposed to a Hegelian perspective, because the witness to its events is both exegesis and exegete. His life is an interpretation.

Like the authors of the Scriptures, Crusoe always stands at "a distance, however minimal from the event that . . . [he] proclaims." In the vicissitudes, both material and temporal, that surround his journal and in the skewed prolepsis of his dream, Crusoe "reveals an original distance which remained concealed because it was so short." No matter how close he seems to the events of the shipwreck, Crusoe could not write as they unfolded; he had to swim. That distance, once revealed, however, is not the enemy of faith but "constitutive" of it. Crusoe believes, and millions of readers have followed him in this, that he can recreate events and accurately define their moral significance. That critics are eager to outline his mistakes reveals the power that his claim to truth—both factual and moral—holds.

Defoe probably learned about this problematic "original distance" from a very early age. His education remains a subject few scholars, Christian or otherwise, have pursued. In a 1953 essay, "Defoe's Education at the Newington Green Academy," Lew Girdler pointed out that Defoe's school was "one of the best educational institutions in England," that its headmaster, Charles Morton, later president of Harvard College, "was one of the most pious, learned, and intellectually inquisitive Dissenters then alive." Girdler establishes the books that Defoe likely studied, including Richard Baxter's "Books of Controversies and Devotions."[17] Baxter's work, which Defoe would have read as a fifteen- to twenty-year-old blossoming intellectual, vindicates Protestantism over against Roman Catholicism by focusing upon the difficulties of witnessing. In his *The Life of Faith* (1670), he posits the following relationship between faith and the Scriptures:

> settle your belief of Christianity it self; that is, of so much as Baptism containeth or importeth: This is more easily proved, than the truth of every word in the Scriptures
>
> . . . [W]hen this is first soundly proved to you, then you cannot justly take any textual difficulties, to be sufficient cause of raising difficulty to your faith in the essentials.[18]

Baxter points out that the Gospels were written many years "after Christ's resurrection" (*LF*, p. 91), that the Apostles preached and baptized before they wrote, and, on this basis, that Protestants should avoid "a preposterous care of the Honour of the Scriptures, through an excessive opposition to the Papists who undervalue them" (*LF*, p. 92). An author who grew up reading Baxter likely would not make Crusoe's journal a definitive original text.

In his 1990 Tanner Lectures, Umberto Eco makes a casual reference to Robinson Crusoe as a prototypical, even incorrigible, literalist. In Eco's example, Crusoe receives a letter about figs, or, more precisely, a letter that once accompanied a basket of figs that has been stolen:

> Let us suppose now that not only was the messenger [accompanying the figs] killed but that his killers ate all the figs, destroyed the basket, put the letter into a bottle and threw it in the ocean, so that it was found seventy years after by Robinson Crusoe. No basket, no slave, no figs, only a letter. Notwithstanding this, I bet the first reaction of Robinson would have been "Where are the figs?"[19]

Richetti takes readers far beyond this easy dismissal of Crusoe as a man concerned only with things.[20] However, as readers become more sensitive to the problematic nature of Crusoe's witnessing, they may see beyond Richetti's dialectical account of Crusoe's "consciousness." A new literary history of Defoe's Christian education should investigate the status of the Scriptures in his readings, particularly as those readings, like Baxter's *Life of Faith*, deliver the Scriptures from impossible claims to be authentic, firsthand accounts.

Criticism written from a Christian perspective—interpretation that begins with the problem of Crusoe's witness to his "deliverance"—will not be satisfied with Richetti's account. Rather, Christian interpretation will see Crusoe as an extended anticipation of two of postmodernism's great themes: the problematic nature of any claim to have or to hear the "originary" word and the difficulty of finding a "literal" truth that exists prior to interpretation. Defoe—not the "novel" but Defoe—anticipates Ricoeur by incorporating in his narrative that "original distance which remained concealed because it was so short." Long before Jacques Derrida's *Of Grammatology*, Defoe suggests that we will find the truth, not by hearing the first word, but by studying our lives. For Defoe, the uncertain relationship between Crusoe's narrative and the events of his life does not threaten the truth of that narrative. Rather, following the precedent of the Gospels that Crusoe reads so intently, Defoe inscribes that "original distance" as faith's first condition.

NOTES

1. The reconstitution of Christian backgrounds—be they in the Scriptures or in devotional literature—has a long and worthy history in literary studies. In the field of eighteenth-century studies, Martin C. Battestin's *The Moral Basis of Fielding's Art: A Study of Joseph Andrews* (Middletown, CT: Wesleyan University Press, 1959) focused upon Henry Fielding's grounding in the works of Anglican Latitudinarian divines. Battestin initiated a discussion of "providential order" in seventeenth- and eighteenth-century narratives that continued through the 1960s and 1970s and received its most extended expression in Aubrey L. Williams, *An Approach to Congreve* (New Haven: Yale University Press, 1979). "Providential" readings became so popular that, by the early 1970s, critics of them referred to Battestin, Williams, and their followers as "the God Squad." In what follows, I do not define "Christian Interpretation" as the pursuit of sources and analogues or as the elaboration of thematic continuities. Instead, I propose that the problematic witnessing in which Christian interpretation begins has broad hermeneutic relevance to narratives that are avowedly religious, to narratives that are avowedly secular, and to narratives, like Defoe's, whose status is contested. For a compendious summary of his work on the Christian context for eighteenth-century fiction, see Martin Battestin, "The Critique of Freethinking: From Swift to Sterne," *Eighteenth-Century Fiction* 15 (2003): 341–420. For a balanced critique of "providential" readings, see Brian Corman's review of Williams's *Approach to Congreve*, in *Eighteenth-Century Studies* 13 (1980): 452–56.

2. Perhaps most famously, Defoe's Roxana claims to have had five, then six children by her first husband. On his first trip to the shipwreck, Crusoe pulls off his clothes to swim, then, once on board, fills his pockets with biscuits.

3. Daniel Defoe, *Robinson Crusoe*, ed. Angus Ross (Harmondsworth, England: Penguin Books, 1965), pp. 108–109. Hereafter abbreviated as *RC*; all subsequent references to *Robinson Crusoe* are to the Penguin edition; page numbers are given in parentheses in the text.

4. Daniel Defoe, "Preface," in *The Farther Adventures of Robinson Crusoe* (Oxford: Basil Blackwell, 1974), p. 2.

5. Daniel Defoe, "Preface," in *Serious Reflections during the Life and Surprising Adventures of Robinson Crusoe*, vol. 3 of *The Works of Daniel Defoe*, ed. G. H. Maynadier (New York: Crowell, 1903), p. 3.

6. Karl Marx, *Capital*, trans. Samuel Moore and Edward Aveling (Chicago: Charles H. Kerr, 1921), I.88–89.

7. Ian Watt, *The Rise of the Novel* (Berkeley and Los Angeles: University of California Press, 1957), pp. 81, 64.

8. George A. Starr, *Defoe and Spiritual Autobiography* (Princeton: Princeton University Press, 1965), p. 195.

9. J. Paul Hunter, *The Reluctant Pilgrim* (Baltimore: Johns Hopkins University Press, 1965), p. 10.

10. James Sutherland, *Daniel Defoe: A Critical Study* (Cambridge, MA: Houghton Mifflin, 1971), p. 139.

11. Leopold Damrosch Jr., *God's Plot and Man's Stories* (Chicago: University of Chicago Press, 1985), p. 187.

12. John J. Richetti, *Defoe's Narratives: Situations and Structures* (Oxford: Clarendon Press, 1975). Hereafter abbreviated as *DN*; page numbers for all subsequent references to Richetti will be given parenthetically in the text.

13. See Paula R. Backscheider, *Daniel Defoe: His Life* (Baltimore: Johns Hopkins University Press, 1989), pp. 14–15, for a summary of Defoe's education. He apparently pursued the "theological curriculum" at Newington Green Academy. Backscheider cites Defoe's claim in his *Review* for 22 October 1709 that he was "first . . . set a-part for, and then . . . set a-part from the Honour of . . . Sacred Employ."

14. Paul Ricoeur, "Preface to Bultmann," in *The Conflict of Interpretations: Essays in Hermeneutics*, ed. Don Ihde (Evanston: Northwestern University Press, 1974), pp. 381–401. Hereafter abbreviated as PB; page numbers for all subsequent references to the "Preface to Bultmann" will be given parenthetically in the text.

15. Paula Frederiksen, *From Jesus to the Christ: The Origins of the New Testament Images of Jesus* (New Haven: Yale University Press, 1988), p. 36. Hereafter abbreviated as *FJC*; page numbers for all subsequent references to *From Jesus to Christ* are given parenthetically in the text.

16. Crusoe's entry for July 4 (*RC*, pp. 110–11) summarizes nicely the problem that his readers face. He describes a morning of Bible study that leads him to meditate upon the true meaning of "deliverance." At the conclusion of the meditation, he writes, "But leaving this part, I return to my journal." At no earlier point does he indicate that he has left the journal; the entry for July 4 has been interrupted.

17. Lew Girdler, "Defoe's Education at the Newington Green Academy," *Studies in Philology* 50 (1953): 573, 583.

18. Richard Baxter, *The Life of Faith/In Three Parts/Sermon on Heb. II i./* pub. by King's Command (London: R. W. for Nevill Simmons, 1670), p. 93. Hereafter abbreviated as *LF*; page numbers for all subsequent references to the *Life of Faith* are given in parentheses in the text.

19. Umberto Eco, "Interpretation and History," *Interpretation and Overinterpretation*, ed. Stefan Collini (Cambridge: Cambridge University Press, 1992), pp. 41–42.

20. While in his commentary upon witnessing Ricoeur enables a Christian perspective that grants Crusoe hermeneutical significance, Ricouer, like Eco, writes out of a crit-

ical tradition in which Crusoe stands as a chauvinistic literalist. In his "Hermeneutics and the Critique of Ideology," Ricoeur briefly dismisses Crusoe as he comments upon Hans-Georg Gadamer's concept of the "*fusion of horizons*": "We exist neither in closed horizons, nor within a horizon that is unique. No horizon is closed, since it is possible to place oneself within another point of view and in another culture. It would be reminiscent of Robinson Crusoe to claim that the other is inaccessible" (Paul Ricouer, *Hermeneutics and the Human Sciences,* ed. and trans. John B. Thompson [Cambridge: Cambridge University Press, 1981], p. 75). Writing in the late twentieth century, both Ricoeur and Eco bear witness to Crusoe's enduring interest for readers and critics. That both of these major figures write so dismissively of Crusoe only emphasizes how much the Christian perspective that I propose here can add to our understanding of Defoe's achievement.

9

John Calvin's Notion of "Exchange" and the Usefulness of Literature

Michael VanderWeele

Today's discipline of literary studies too often neglects the moral and emotional community formed by reading. It moves between two competing interests, one in celebration of individual consciousness, the other in criticism of large, sometimes anonymous, political and economic forces. These two interests are not so far apart as first appears. They both assume a view of literature that is less and less helpful and, behind that, an anthropology that deserves our most careful scrutiny. The relationship of literary studies to anthropology has recently been remarked by Noam Chomsky in *Language and Politics.* Chomsky writes that a view of literature and what it does is rooted in some concept of human nature and human needs.[1] Chomsky doesn't stand alone. A similar claim is made by David Lyle Jeffrey when he states that within the scriptural tradition reading is subordinate to "a profoundly mediated theory of the 'meaning of person.'"[2] The celebration of individual consciousness and the criticism of political and economic forces share a certain unneighborliness, which raises questions about the anthropology that underlies them. Both approaches to literary study emphasize a freedom that, if won, could only be described as a lonely freedom, the freedom of Hamlet, able to recast himself but orphaned and outside of relationship with the rest of society.[3]

At the beginning of the twenty-first century, rather than the freedom of individual consciousness or the too-distant critique of political and economic forces, we need readings of literature that attend more to the neighborhoods and mediating structures of public life. Such readings will come out of a different anthropological understanding of the author-reader relationship. One resource for such an understanding can be found in John Calvin's notion of "exchange." In what follows, I will analyze two contemporary approaches to literature and then present an argument for an alternative approach I'll call rhetorical aesthetics. My approach takes its lead from the concept of human nature and human needs implicit in Calvin's description of exchange as both an economic and a theological value.[4] I will argue that it is also normative for the sophisticated social communication we call literature.

Two Contemporary Responses

The question of aesthetics' relationship to human consciousness is at least as old as Friedrich Schiller's *Letters on the Aesthetic Education of Man,* written at roughly the same time as the French Revolution.[5] Schiller thought the only true change would come from change of the mind. Change in consciousness over time, even a long time, would lead, he thought, to readiness for political and social change. Affecting consciousness was the goal of the early English Romantics, too, not only for political but also for religious reasons, hoping to instill the spirituality of Christianity without its doctrine. Spirituality without doctrine seemed to be the goal, still, of the mid-twentieth-century New Critics, such as Cleanth Brooks, John Crowe Ransom, Allen Tate, and others. It wasn't that they always wished to dismiss doctrine—several of them were confessing Christians—but that they wanted to preserve it outside the bounds of literary argument. They associated creative writing with disinterested pleasure. Literary texts had ontological being without rhetorical charge. In "Ars Poetica," Archibald MacLeish described the reader's appropriate stance toward the creative work in his famous lines, "The poem should not mean / but be."

The best literary students of human consciousness have measured its cost as well as its glory. The glory is singular: freedom. Our best example is Hamlet. We share in his orphan drift but also in his freedom to recast himself time and again.[6] Geoffrey Hartman saw clearly the costs of such freedom. He wrote about consciousness as "knowingly or unknowingly the result of a contract, as in *Faust,* of a conspiracy, as in the Fall, or of a covenant like the crucifixion." The economy of consciousness is costly, because historical, Hartman warns: "Such *liaisons dangereuses* implicate us, make us historical."[7] But they also "create in us a new and powerful awareness." In fact, that awareness is richer for the imprint of suffering and death. If he fears (this is still the 1960s) that we see "the expanse, not the expense, of vision," the expense has its own value, too. It makes our vision, which here means our consciousness, still richer (*BY,* p. 55). The freedom of a suffering but still to be self-determined consciousness: we seem still to live in this hope.

The concern to understand human consciousness through literature usually goes through form. Even in "Beyond Formalism," Hartman argues for the value of formal studies. "There are many ways to transcend formalism," he writes, "but the worst is not to study forms" (*BY*, p. 56). Such study has a "preparatory function" (*BY*, p. 57) for the daring use of critical and historical intuition. In his search for such daring use, Hartman looks to earlier biblical exegesis. "If our neo-scriptural activity of explication were as daring and conscious as it used to be when Bible texts had to be harmonized with strange or contrary experience, i.e., with history, no one could level this charge of puerility" (*BY*, p. 56). But Hartman raises the example of biblical exegesis in order, finally, to replace it. The mandate with which he closes "Beyond Formalism" couldn't be clearer about art's status as our new scripture: we need "to raise exegesis to its former state by confronting art with experience as searchingly as if art were scripture" (*BY*, p. 57). That confrontation, like a bittersweet fall, enriches consciousness. It also, in our modern world, can make consciousness lonely, for this consciousness is almost always construed as individual.

Closer to our own time, novelist/critic David Lodge's most recent nonfiction book, *Consciousness and the Novel*, marks a continuing interest in understanding consciousness through literary study. Lodge worries about the significance to novels of contemporary cognitive studies that suggest our lives are novels and the stability of the self an illusion created by language, but he still celebrates the novel as the "richest record of human consciousness we have" and the "best means of describing experience and depicting consciousness."[8]

A contemporary challenge to this goal of reading literature in order to understand human consciousness was launched by Martha Woodmansee in *The Author, Art, and the Market: Rereading the History of Aesthetics* (1994). Woodmansee links the goal of understanding human consciousness to early aesthetics' emphasis on disinterested pleasure. She analyzes the theological traces that encouraged disinterested instead of interested readings. She shows that the principle of "disinterested pleasure" traveled from theology to aesthetics through a quietist brand of German Pietism. Woodmansee quotes from Karl Philipp Moritz's description, in his 1785 autobiographical novel, of his father's group of extreme Pietists:

> [They] are concerned for the most part with that . . . total abandonment of the self and entry upon a blissful state of nothingness, with the complete extermination of all so-called *self-ness* [*Eigenheit*] or *self-love* [*Eigenliebe*], and a totally disinterested [*uninteressierte*] love of God, in which not the merest spark of self-love may mingle, if it is to be pure; and out of this there arises in them a perfect, blissful *tranquillity* which is the highest goal of all these strivings.

This summary of the religious goals of the extreme Pietists "is transported almost verbatim," Woodmansee writes, "into Moritz's theory of art, where it serves precisely to characterize what we now term the 'aesthetic attitude.'" This aesthetic attitude, with its principle of disinterestedness or of unselfish pleasure, suggested art's self-sufficiency rather than what Woodmansee calls its "instrumental" value. When Moritz wrote *Toward a Unification of All the Fine Arts and Letters under the Concept of Self-Sufficiency*, also in 1785, he used a language similar to his father's language for contemplating God; but now he turned it toward the ideal attitude for contemplating a work of art:

> As the beautiful object completely captivates our attention, it diverts our attention momentarily from ourselves with the result that we seem to lose ourselves in the beautiful object; and precisely this loss, this forgetfulness of ourselves, is the highest degree of pure and disinterested [*uneigennutzigen*] pleasure which beauty grants us. (*AAM*, p. 19)

Even as God had been seen as an end in himself, so now, for Moritz, art should be enjoyed as an end in itself, worthy of our enjoyment, not just use.[9]

Woodmansee's claim of historical influence ("In its origins the theory of art's autonomy is clearly a displaced theology" [AAM, p. 20]) seems correct. Too often the enjoyment of literature has been viewed as spiritual compensation for the mechanization of the Industrial Revolution and a modern loss of faith. This compensatory character should concern those who read literature to explore the freedom of individual consciousness. But that doesn't mean we should or could eradicate aesthetics' theological roots. It simply means that aesthetics should not substitute for theology, and here a bad theology, as it seems to do in Moritz's formulation, and also in early Hartman.[10] The question about theology should not be whether it can be isolated from other disciplines—it cannot—but whether it is adequate to them. I would claim that the direction theology can give for aesthetics, as for economics, sociology, and the like, is one of the practical measures of its worth.

Woodmansee's work in the New Economic Criticism places her in the second camp named in the introduction to this essay, the group that doesn't want to further our understanding of consciousness so much as to improve our politics. While economic literary criticism could be found in the earlier work of individual authors, New Economic Criticism developed an institutional history through a 1994 conference at which Woodmansee, fellow editor Mark Osteen, and economist Deirdre McCloskey brought together forty economists and sixty literary scholars. The notice for that conference anticipated two topics: "how the disciplines of economics and literary studies understand such notions as value, circulation, exchange, property, and so on" and "the situation of Marxist and neo-Marxist thought after the fall of the Soviet Union."[11] If Schiller is a reasonable starting point for thinking about literary study that hopes to further the understanding of human consciousness, Marx is the logical counterpoint for literary study that seeks to improve politics. One need not be Marxist, of course, to seek such improvements, just as one needn't be committed to disinterestedness in order to take the understanding of human consciousness as the goal of literary study. One could also be libertarian, like Noam Chomsky, and still try to place literary discourse within the broader spectrum of social discourse.[12]

In his comparative study of Chomsky and Marc Angenot, Robert Barsky gives a helpful catalogue of interests that the politically interested student of literature will pursue. He or she will be interested in all that influences the production and reception of literature—the publishing business, the government, the academy that teaches the work, and so forth. Literature will then be placed alongside or within "the broader compendium of social discourse." It might be studied for the ways it reflects contradictions within society, or increases what is sayable, or forms attitudes, or challenges at the same time as it proliferates social discourse, or deblocks our perceptions and understanding of society. Literature might reveal the constraining systems otherwise hidden to an indoctrinated society. It might help one extricate oneself from such systems of thought control.[13]

As one can hear by the end of that catalogue, those students of creative writing who develop a politically and economically interested criticism can end up focusing on individual consciousness as much as those whose stated goal is to learn how consciousness works. One asserts a more private, one a more public, means, but in both cases the freedom of individual consciousness remains the highest goal. This can be a lonely freedom, however, because what comes with it is distance. This is most clear in political and economic criticism, which often functions like the higher criticism of nineteenth-century theology, scrutinizing literature's contexts and means of production at the expense of the pull of the text and attentiveness to its subject. That is to say, those who object most to the social dangers of commodification can repeat that depersonalizing movement in their very attempt to expose its symptoms in literary texts. Home economics too often loses out to Apollonian critique.

While Woodmansee helps us see the weaknesses in a study of literature whose focus is the further understanding of human consciousness, recent work in the history of reading exposes the narrowness of much politically and economically invested study of literature. Let me take Ivan Illich's *In the Vineyard of the Text: A Commentary to Hugh's Didascalicon* as an example.[14] In Illich's commentary, as well as in other recent books on the history of reading,[15] we see the purposes of reading change according to time and place, technology and ethos. Though Illich locates himself within the (possibly ending) epoch of the bookish or scholastic text, he values some of the elements of the monastic text and of meditative reading, and hopes they might give more choices than our present givens. Illich argues that in this earlier tradition, writing and reading are two almost indistinguishable sides of the same *studium* (*IVT*, p. 9). Though Christ and wisdom were thought to be the supreme *remedium*, remedy is also the purpose of learning and reading (*IVT*, p. 11). Though remedial, reading is also pleasurable. Hugh's reader harvests the text as if it were a vineyard or garden, picking, bundling, and collecting what is needed (*IVT*, pp. 57–58). Virtues are needed for and developed by such reading (*IVT*, p. 15), and reading is therefore "a moral rather than a technical activity" (*IVT*, p. 75). The aim of *studium*, for example, is friendship (*amicitia*), its classical value reinterpreted as "a union in the arms of a delightful God" (*IVT*, p. 28). As if Woodmansee's account were in the background, Illich writes that "Hugh's meditation is an intensive reading activity and not some passive quietist plunge into feelings" (*IVT*, p. 54). The studies and habits of reading are connected through memory to a way of living (*IVT*, p. 37). Thus, reading is tied to both a historical and a social order, with the historical order the more important of the two. For it to become meaningful, the reader must insert what he or she reads at the point where it belongs between Genesis and the Second Coming (*IVT*, pp. 32–33). Finally, the book of Hugh's time pointed to nature, according to Illich, more than to mind: "'All nature is pregnant with sense,' Hugh wrote, 'and nothing in all of the universe is sterile'" (*IVT*, p. 123). These elements of meditative reading, though superseded in our epoch by the bookish or scholastic text, help us think about the choices made and not made during our modern relationship to texts. We might group them under these three headings: (1) Reading is a matter of home economics, affecting and affected by choice, memory, virtues, a way of living; (2) Reading shapes and corrects desire; through our interaction with the text (the images are agricultural), it provides both remedy and pleasure; (3) Reading fits a larger order—of desire, of society, of history, of nature, with the historical and natural orders given even more weight than the social and psychological ones.

While I agree with Woodmansee that we should view with suspicion the separation of aesthetics and rhetoric in the late eighteenth and early nineteenth centuries, the relatively new subdisciplines of the history of the book and history of reading suggest that her political and economic focus is too narrow. For example, while remedy is still an essential part of what Woodmansee reads for, she may not connect it enough to pleasure or memory, that is, to a home economics in which memory connects knowledge to action and pleasure lengthens the memory. All of us may read against the grain so much that the text is more a challenge, a mystery to be unlocked, an oyster to be cracked open, as Willie Loman says in *Death of a Salesman*, than it is a friend or, better, a neighbor.[16] Finally, we may have become so suspicious of conventions masquerading as "natural" that we ignore the second exchange of most writing, certainly creative writing—not only the exchange between creator/producer and receiver/creator but also the exchange between text and world. Tracking both, together, allows us to say with Alan Jacobs "that literature, carefully read, is an irreplaceable tool in the development of discernment or practical wisdom" (*TR*, p. 1).[17] The New Economic Criticism, by comparison, tends to be reductionistic, absolutizing one mode at the expense of others.

This critique of Woodmansee and the New Economic Criticism from the side of the history of reading suggests that they move both too far and not far enough from interest in the freedom of individual consciousness. They are certainly right to emphasize that we read within a particular social, linguistic, and institutional context, but their readings risk bouncing between freedom and determinism without recognizing the neighborliness of the text. While we find their instrumental readings an insufficient alternative to the emphasis on the freedom of individual consciousness, their emphasis on economics does invite us to reconsider the importance of exchange in literary transactions.

Resources in John Calvin for an Alternative Response

The importance of the neighbor is clear in John Calvin's theology and its economic images. Calvin, like Augustine, understood the world to be created by God, down to the details. Every aspect of creation had a double reference: to its limits apart from God and to its glory as ordained by God, in whom all things have their being. Calvin begins the *Institutes*, for example, with the now famous statement that the knowledge of God and the knowledge of self are two parts of the same wisdom.[18] He pictures the world as a theater, various and crowded and all participating in God's gift of life.[19] In that varied interaction of its parts the world points back to its created order and forward to a restored order that breaks through the obscuring, and sometimes crippling, force of sin. The term Calvin uses to describe such interaction is "exchange," an economic term with theological depth.

"God has created man," Calvin says, "so that man may be a creature of fellowship." Andre Bieler explicates the normative value of fellowship for economics as follows: "Companionship is completed in work and in the interplay of economic exchanges. Human fellowship is realized in relationships which flow from the division of labor wherein each person has been called by God to a particular and partial work which complements the work of others. The mutual exchange of goods and services is the concrete sign of the profound solidarity which unites humanity."[20] Bieler helps us see that Calvin values exchange for its role in human fellowship, or solidarity, and that he describes economic exchange within the context of a theological anthropology.[21] David Little describes Calvin's view of economics as "functional" rather than preferential or hierarchical: "The economic order is to be evaluated in terms of general usefulness—that is, of maximum production and just and equal distribution among the community of mankind. Furthermore, roles or vocations in this scheme are assigned fundamentally with reference to functional utility or 'eminent usefulness'" (*ROL*, p. 60). Little remarks that Calvin himself had written, "It is certain that a calling would never be approved by God that is not socially useful, and that does not redound to the profit of all" (*Corpus Reformatorum*, pp. 51, 639; quoted in *ROL*, p. 60).

In fact, the relationship between theology and economics is so close in Calvin that theological truths are often described in economic terms. In his commentary on the parable of the talents in Matthew 25, Calvin writes, "Those who employ usefully whatever God has committed to them are said to be engaged in trading. The life of the godly, is justly compared to trading, for they ought naturally to exchange and barter with each other, in order to maintain intercourse. . . . Now the gain which Christ mentions is general usefulness, which illustrates the glory of God." Little concludes from this and other passages that "[i]f we are rightly to understand what Calvin means by true order, we shall not be able to leave economic categories out of account." He quotes Bieler's summary: "The religious life and the material life of the believer are both subjected to the same order of God" (*ROL*, p. 64). Describing Calvin's emphasis on exchange in more anthropological terms, Little writes, "What man was created to be—a freely obedient being who responds gratefully to the gifts of God, ardently sharing them with all [his or her neighbors] and turning them to corporate use—is put by Calvin again and again in the language of economic action" (*ROL*, p. 66).

While Little gives more attention to Calvin's writings on the Gospels, Bieler and Ford Lewis Battles turn to Calvin's sermons on Deuteronomy. In his introduction to Benjamin Farley's translation of *John Calvin's Sermons on the Ten Commandments*, Battles writes, "The series of two hundred sermons on Deuteronomy [written between 1555 and 1556] . . . contains Calvin's critical study of the economic and social aspects of ancient Israel." Such social and economic analysis was not a happy accident but the legacy of Calvin's early training. Battles asks, "Could one expect any less from someone taught by the great Guillaume Bude', author of *De Asse*, a pioneer work of the Renaissance on the economic and social history of the ancient classical world?"[22] The work of Bieler, Little, and Battles helps us see the importance of exchange to Calvin's notions of a Christian anthropology. This concept of human nature and human needs provides a more suitable base for developing a rhetorical aesthetic than can be found through asserting the autonomy of human consciousness or through critiquing large economic and political forces from afar.

The problem with an abstract or distant critique of large economic forces is that it only widens the gap between economics as self-enrichment and economics as stewardship. The ancient Greeks used the terms *oikonomia* and *chrematistike* to describe economic activity. *Oikonomia* referred to the steward's task of managing an estate such that it "would continue to bear fruit and thus provide a living for everyone who lived and worked on it." *Chrematistike* "expressed the pursuit of self-enrichment, for ever greater monetary possessions, if need be at the expense of others." Contemporary economist Bob Goudzwaard, whose distinctions these are, writes that in Western civilization "the meaning of the word *economics* has increasingly become synonymous with *chrematistike*, while progressively it lost the meaning of *oikonomia*, the careful maintenance as steward on behalf of others of all that is entrusted to man."[23] In his later work, Goudzwaard, working out of a Dutch Calvinist tradition, challenges the narrower meaning of economics as *chrematistike* by defining economics as "the caring administration of what has been entrusted to us."[24] Defining economics this way requires us to consider not only objects of use but also objects of care, such as human health, the environment, and "natural resources poised for extraction" (*BPA*, pp. 53–54). Indeed, it helps us recall that everything in economic life is a surface with depth, referring beyond itself to its Creator in whom it finds its being. And it helps us remember that things and people don't find their being, their gift of life, alone but in relationship to the rest of created reality and the potentialities found within it.

But how does the concept of human nature rooted in exchange affect the purpose and study of writing? We will be able to answer this question better if we turn first to Augustine, the church father who influences Calvin most. Augustine has a view of human needs and human nature that prepares for Calvin's emphasis on exchange. Near the beginning of *On Christian Doctrine*, Augustine writes, "Therefore [Christ] binds His body, which has *many members performing diverse offices*, in a bond of unity and charity which is, as it were, its health."[25] This notion of diversity within unity, an interaction associated with health or justice, depends not only on the theology of the church but on the theology of the Trinity and its divine economy. In language, Augustine sees clearly, we humans often enough arrive at a false economy or contrived exchange.

The curtains hanging over the doors of the schools of literature, for example,

Augustine doesn't describe as marks of distinction but as coverings for error (*CD*, I.xiii.22). He refers to these schools' studies as "empty" instead of useful and to the knowledge proffered as "the river of human custom" or "the stream of custom" or even "this hellish river of custom" (*CD*, I.xvi.25–26). Teachers are "buyers and sellers" of literary knowledge or of words effective for persuasion. Students either perfect the habit of seeking their own will through speech or have it converted to a more healthful habit through crisis and healing (thus anticipating Hugh's "remedy" and echoing Socrates' description of justice as a kind of medicine). What stood in the way of such a conversion of habit or such a breaking of chains was the stunning humility of Scripture, its *sermo humilis*, which we know took Augustine the better part of a decade to take in.[26] Chains, curtains, buyers and sellers, a river of custom that threatens to overwhelm all those near it: these are the images of a false economy of words, a contrived exchange.

But there are also images of a true economy of words, a trustworthy exchange. They include food (good exchange being not only useful but hospitable), healing (as in Plato's *Gorgias*, exchange makes correction—and hence the beginning of healing—possible), and the triad of asking, seeking, and knocking with which the *Confessions* both begins and ends (exchange both depends upon and is the result of need or desire). This last triad of images, taken from Matthew 7:7–8, frames the thirteen books of the *Confessions*, with the final page ending with "So, so shall it be received, so shall it be found, so shall it be opened," with "opened" (*aperietur*) the final word of Augustine's text, marking a continuing rather than a completed exchange.

The difference between a true and a false exchange is shown in the two narratives we find, back-to-back, at the middle of Book 5, as well as in the images described above. The first narrative describes Augustine's much anticipated meeting with Faustus, the second his sneaking away from Monica.[27] Augustine had longed to meet Faustus because the other Manichees, who could not answer his questions, were sure Faustus could. Even after Augustine's disappointment with Faustus, he spends much time reading literature with (or more likely, to) him. Augustine writes that Faustus has some sense of his own limits and had a good intelligence and natural grace. What, then, was false about his exchange with Augustine? Two problems are clear: first, it was difficult to speak with Faustus "by talking to him as man to man with each of us speaking in turn" (C, V.vi.11), and, second, his words, when Augustine did get to question him, were eloquent but not useful. Augustine imagines his words as containers: "My thirst," he says, "could not be relieved by expensive drinking vessels and a well-dressed waiter" (C, V.vi.10). Faustus proffers speech without exchange.

This narrative of Augustine's break with Faustus is naturally compared to the Book 6 narrative about meeting Ambrose, which signals the end of his relationship to Manichaeism. But it is the corrective force of the Augustine-Monica narrative that occupies the middle of Book 5, hence of Books 1–9. This narrative echoes Virgil's account of Aeneas leaving Dido under cover of darkness,[28] and in doing so it images both a false economy and an alternative to that economy. In both Virgil's and Augustine's narratives, the male character leaves Carthage for Rome. Both narrators say the characters were goaded to do so in order to fulfill their destiny or their predestination. In both stories the male character is associated with rational choice and the female character with passion—first love and then the strongest of Stoic passions, distress.[29] In both stories, it is the male character who lies and the female character who is lied to. This is the second kind of false exchange: the deliberately constructed gap between character and self-presentation. The story of Monica, however, also revises the story of Dido, for Monica's frantic tears led to persistent prayer instead of suicide, and those prayers led to Augustine's new life. While Aeneas's deception receives his narrator's approval, Augustine's does not. His is not the image of the oak tree buffeted by winds but still standing upright, its roots sinking as far down into the rocky land as its branches reach up into the sky. Rather, he is like the medical patient being prepared through crisis for later cure.[30]

In this narrative, however, Augustine presents through Monica an alternative to the false exchanges that he, as well as Faustus, had managed. He rewrites the Virgil whom he had loved as a child and whom he cites as many as 108 times in his adult writings.[31] In Book 1, Augustine had written that he had won a civic contest for reciting the speech of Juno from the beginning of the *Aeneid*, the speech in which Juno decries her inability to keep Aeneas from sailing to Italy and founding Rome. Both the speech and the prize were set, the prize going to the schoolboy who "while preserving the dignity of the character he was representing, gave in his performance the best imitation of the passions of anger and grief and found the most appropriate words to express his meaning" (*C*, I.17). Though Augustine must have especially identified with the goddess who favored Carthage above all cities—as an adult he still wonders why the speech and contest meant so much to him—other North African schoolboys entered the same civic contest or others similar to it. Their earlier education taught them not only the requisite linguistic ability but also the cultural and psychological force to make such a recitation effective.

In Book 5, Augustine creates a new moral and emotional community of readers (or listeners). He revises but also rescues Virgil's account. Monica's discourse not only is humble but it is finally hopeful. It grows out of a converted passion, not the repressed passion Aeneas hides with a brave face from his men and, later, from Dido. The account of Monica's response to Augustine's deceit returns us, as it were, to the faithful response Dido had made to Sychaeus's death rather than the suicide she committed after Aeneas left.[32] This is one change Augustine rings. The other is reading Monica in light of the persistent widow of Luke's parable whom even an unjust judge must listen to—and, if an unjust judge, how much more God? Augustine is brought to new life by the tears and prayers of his mother. It is not Rome that is valorized but her North African prayers. Against Faustus, we can say that her earthenware dishes hold wholesome food. These two narratives, of Faustus and Augustine and of Monica and Augustine, suggest a strong ethical criterion for the most artful as well as for the simplest speech. In fact, it seems to me that Augustine's later ability to read the humble Scriptures coincides with his respect for his mother's humble speech.

Not only these two narratives at the midway point of the autobiographical books but also the framing and the varying modalities of the *Confessions* suggest the value of a true exchange. The framing of the book with the triadic activities of seeking, knocking, and opening portrays both the receptivity and the effort of exchange. The multiple modalities of narrative, analysis, and meditation engage author and reader in more than one kind of exchange with each other, with God, and with the world. It is easy to imagine the *Confessions'* close proximity in time to *On Christian Doctrine* (c. 396) and its instructions for the Christian teacher/preacher. Rather than pronouncing from on high, the Christian teacher Augustine instructs "must persuade laterally," temporarily teaching a text from the authority of God but living under the text as surely as his auditors do (*RRD*, 76), exchanging interpretations and life stories with them.

Augustine's theory of reference—that things themselves ask that we not take them in themselves but refer them to their Creator—finds its corollary in Calvin's theory of exchange. In this respect, the humanist Calvin shares less with the early modern than with the classical and early Christian world, which thought the parts of the world participated in a larger natural and social order. That order existed, pseudo-Dionysus wrote, as a concord of differences.[33] This makes it easier to imagine Calvin's anthropology based on exchange and fellowship. Though we live in a time that has seen the isolation and dominance of economics over education, politics, and most social relationships, economics could also serve the interplay of legitimate norms for social, aesthetic, and political life.[34] All of life comes equally under God's care and depends equally upon him for its being, according to the Augustinian tradition, or, in Calvin's terms, it exists as a theater of his glory.[35] Within this theater, exchange teaches us both our limits and our participation in each other's lives, what Calvin refers to as fellowship or social intercourse. Calvin's interpretation of the Ten Commandments shows us how imaginative and constructive an interpretive view based on an anthropology of fellowship or exchange might be. First I will give a general analysis of his treatment of the Ten Commandments and then use his interpretation of the sixth commandment for a particular case in point.

That Calvin gave so much attention to the Ten Commandments was not anything his contemporaries could have assumed, the Ten Commandments being less a focus of teaching or preaching then than now.[36] And yet, Calvin includes them in the 1536 *Institutes*, where his emphasis is on teaching through catechesis ("De lege" is the first of six sections), and in the longer 1539–60 editions, where his emphasis is more on doctrinal formulation and disputation. In the 1559 edition, used here, the Ten Commandments appear in the eighth chapter in the second of four volumes. While the first volume had been called "The Knowledge of God the Creator," this second volume is titled "The Knowledge of God the Redeemer in Christ, First Disclosed to the Fathers under the Law and Then to Us in the Gospel."[37] One hears in the title Calvin's effort to join law and gospel under the knowledge of Christ, that is, of God as Redeemer compared to God as Creator (Volume One). Before we turn to the eighth chapter of Volume Two, we should note that it is preceded by a section titled "The Law Was Given, Not to Restrain the Folk of the Old Covenant under Itself, but to Foster Hope of Salvation in Christ until His Coming." In this chapter title we again see Calvin's effort to link law and gospel. Perhaps this is Calvin's most radical move, that these commandments were not given to restrain lifestyle but to foster hope. This becomes especially important once Calvin states that form should be condemned as vanity if separated from its end.[38] Calvin describes three uses for the Ten Commandments in chapter eight, roughly, to prepare, to restrain, and to profit us.[39] While preparation and restraint fit modern expectations, it is the third category, our profit, that Calvin thinks primary. This "profit," of course, is not that generated by the alienated labor and surplus value of late capitalist societies. It is, rather, connected to the idea of an obedience that would allow our life to flourish in God. Quoting Augustine, Calvin calls the obedience revealed as God's will in the Ten Commandments "sometimes the guardian and mother of all virtues, sometimes their source" (*ICR*, p. 372).[40] The commandments, in this view, are like hedgerows that will guide us to life in God. Or, to put it in New Testament terms, they will help us become the branches of his vine. Calvin's discussion focuses on this primary use of profiting us. Any interpretation of the Ten Commandments that analyzes form without connecting it to this purpose misses the meaning of form. Such an interpretation would allow form to stand alone, as it were, outside of any reference to God or of God's meaningful exchange with us.

Calvin's writing on the profit of the law can help us think through several other critical questions about interpretation besides the question of form. First, while intention is usually part of Calvin's discussion of the individual commandments, it is more often the third or fourth than the first or second matter he discusses. When discussed, intention is discussed in terms of character (*ICR*, 415) rather than mental state (we know much more about the first than the second, when it comes to God, but this may also be true about each other). The question about intentionality is here not about psychological exchange so much as about social exchange based on consistency of character. It is according to God's character as lawgiver, for example, described in the introduction to the law as well as in the rest of Scripture, that the law is to be appraised (*ICR*, p. 372). Second, Calvin is sure that the commandments "always contain more than is expressed in words" (*ICR*, p. 374), and that the words themselves tell us so, especially through the figure of the synecdoche. "For we must always come back to this," Calvin writes, "one particular vice is singled out from various kinds as an example, and the rest are brought under the same category, the one chosen being an especially foul vice" (*ICR*, pp. 411–12).[41] Calvin writes, "[P]lainly, a sober interpretation of the law goes beyond the words." The justice of such a "going beyond," moreover, depends upon whether it recognizes or degrades the authority of the law and whether it "dashes [or encourages] the hopes of understanding it" (*ICR*, p. 374). Exchange is not limited to words. Exchange includes what words refer to, how words fit their speaker, and how words can be understood by their auditors, in this instance especially as encouragement. Third, we must interpret not only according to the purpose and substance (scope) of the commandment, but according to the implicit commandment or prohibition that is its other side.[42] These are regularly the first three steps in Calvin's interpretive process: purpose, substance, and "an argument from the other side." Since Calvin trusts that God's purpose in the Ten Commandments is to profit both believers and the public community, an interpretation that promotes refraining from vice is not complete until it also gives us "contrary duties and deeds" (*ICR*, p. 375). It is not restraint but effort, not abstinence but proper exchange, that the Ten Commandments require.

Let us take Calvin's interpretation of the sixth commandment, "You shall not kill," as our test for what is stated more generally, above. The sixth commandment receives Calvin's shortest treatment (II.viii.39—just over one page in the McNeill/Battles edition), which makes Calvin's interpretive moves clearer, and more dramatic. The basic three moves (statement of purpose, statement of substance, and the argument from the other side) take place in the opening three sentences:

> [1] The purpose of this commandment is: the Lord has bound mankind together by a certain unity; hence each man ought to concern himself with the safety of all. [2] To sum up, then, all violence, injury, and any harmful thing at all that may injure our neighbor's body are forbidden to us. [3] We are accordingly commanded, if we find anything of use to us in saving our neighbors' lives, faithfully to employ it; if there is anything that makes for their peace, to see to it; if anything harmful, to ward it off; if they are in any danger, to lend a helping hand.

After these three moves have been made, Calvin refers to God's intention. But God's intention, here as elsewhere, refers less to a mental state than to decipherable character: "If you recall that God is so speaking as Lawgiver, ponder at the same time that by this rule he wills to guide your soul."

The rest of the interpretation, roughly two-thirds of Calvin's brief commentary, is given over to the argument from the other side. Calvin explains, "Therefore this law also forbids murder of the heart, and enjoins the inner intent to save a brother's life." The negative command and the positive duty both stand upon the same grounds: "man is both the image of God, and our flesh." These grounds are articulated more fully in the two parallel statements that follow: "Now, if we do not wish to violate the image of God, we ought to hold our neighbor sacred. And if we do not wish to renounce all humanity, we ought to cherish his as our own flesh." Calvin reiterates the grounds for interpreting both the negative command and the implied positive duty: "to reverence [God's] image imprinted in man, and to embrace our own flesh in him." This time he calls them "those two things which are naturally in man," that is, as a matter of creational blessing.[43] Finally, Calvin indicates the scope of God's warning and the extent of the implied positive command (the argument from the other side): "If you perpetrate anything by deed, if you plot anything by attempt, if you wish or plan anything contrary to the safety of a neighbor, you are considered guilty of murder. Again, unless you endeavor to look out for his safety according to your ability and opportunity, you are violating the law with a like heinousness."

What can be generalized from Calvin's interpretation of the sixth commandment that might serve a rhetorical aesthetics? First, the question of intentionality is less mental and less private once slanted toward character. Second, words, like all else in creation, ought not to be taken in themselves but directed toward some larger order(s). They themselves tell us so. How far we can expand or explore their interpretation in that direction depends especially upon what it does to the character of the speaker of those words, but also upon what it does to those who hope to understand them. Third, we have the freedom, even the requirement, to develop the implicit "other side" to what is explicitly given, especially as that affects human practice.

Calvin's Hermeneutic and Ancient Rhetoric

Calvin's interpretive approach to the Ten Commandments is rooted in ancient and patristic rhetoric. In addition to picking up the ancient rhetorical question of status (see n. 38, above), Calvin emphasizes purpose in the interpretive enterprise much as Augustine had emphasized it as the leading guide for composition in *On Christian Doctrine* (see IV.17–18, e.g.). Recognition that purpose was more flexible than the fixed letter of the law had led, earlier, to the ancient rhetorical concern for equity, translated into patristic rhetoric as charity. Kathy Eden writes, "[C]*aritas* represents the Christianization of *aequitas*, or equity. Like equity, charity corrects the rigidity of the law" (*HRT*, p. 58). For the sixth commandment, this means that *already in the statement of purpose* Calvin interprets "from the other side" the prohibition of murder: "The Lord has bound mankind together by a certain unity; hence each man ought to concern himself with the safety of all." Finally, by tying intention to character, Calvin shows his greater interest in historical and textual context than in the sharing of a mental state. In this, he echoes Cicero's *De Inventione*:

> [B]ut it is not right to regard as ambiguous what becomes plain on consideration of the whole context *(ex omni considerata scriptura)*. In the next place, one ought to estimate what the writer meant from his other writings *(ex scriptis)*, acts *(factis)*, words *(dictis)*, disposition *(animo)*, and in fact his whole life *(vita)*, and to examine the whole document which contains the ambiguity in question in all its parts, to see if any thing is apposite to our interpretation or opposed to the sense in which our opponent understands it. For it is easy to estimate what it is likely that the writer intended from the complete context *(ex omni scriptura)* and from the character of the writer *(ex persona scriptoris)*, and from the qualities which are associated with certain characters. (2.40.117; quoted in *HRT*, p. 18)

In light of charity and context, including the character of God as lawgiver, the interpreter not only can but must interpret "from the other side" the negative prohibition or positive command found in each one of the commandments. Both the synecdochic nature of their language and the nature of equity or *caritas* give a range of responsibilities for one who hears the law aright, that is, as appropriate to the particularities of his or her life. What Eden writes about Augustine also seems true for Calvin's general reader: "Thus historically and textually contextualized, the words of Scripture . . . reveal the divine willingness to read us even as we have read" (*HRT*, p. 63). God's character as lawgiver is as much that of guide as of judge, and so we must infer an "interpretation from the other side" in order to be faithful to his intention.

Calvin's interpretation of the Ten Commandments has roots in two other ancient and patristic rhetorical concepts besides equity: society and economy. The two are related, with the first more often describing discourse, the second describing both discourse and its interpretation. Eden chooses Quintilian to show the link between discourse and society: "To discuss this special coherence of discourse as a unified multiplicity, Quintilian relies not only on the traditional metaphor of organic unity but, more important for our purposes, on that of the social unit, or *societas*, in which no member suffers estrangement but all are familiar, at home" (*HRT*, p. 29). She quotes the *Institutio Oratoria*: "Thus different facts will not seem like perfect strangers *(ignotae)* thrust into uncongenial company from distant places *(distantibus locis)*, but will be united with what precedes and follows by an intimate bond of union *(societate)*" (7.10.16–17; qtd. in *HRT*, p. 30). Such a notion of text as *societas* allows the parts of the whole to retain their productive differences at the same time as their speaker and interpreter seek to understand how they cooperate within the whole.

Among the patristic authors, Basil especially emphasizes economy as a principle of textual context. Known as the "Father of Economy," he wrote so pervasively about economy in interpretation that George Kustas could recently claim, "It would not be much of an exaggeration to claim that [*oikonomia*] or synonymous terminology appears on practically ever page of Basil's writings. The emphasis is testimony to how deeply ingrained in him is the social instinct, the thirst for context, on which the conception is essentially based."[44] Basil's emphasis on economy is rooted in the theological understanding of accommodation, God's making his will known to us through means we can understand. Eden writes that *oikonomia* has been "an operative principle in the Eastern Church since Basil's day" (*HRT*, p. 45). Still today, that church's understanding of *oikonomia* bears a family resemblance to Aristotle's notion of equity, as we see in this description of the Orthodox priest:

> The sympathy, philanthropy and condescension to be demonstrated by the steward of souls are not simply human affections but imitate Christ, and the resulting "economy" is not capricious or arbitrary but rather based on an objective assessment of the plight of the sinner and how to remedy his situation. The steward of souls . . . must take into account the total fabric of who and what the individual sinner is: his condition in life, his age, his marital status, etc. And even more than these "prelapsarian" factors, he must assess the sinner's zeal for amendment of life, the sincerity of his repentance, and above all, whether he

> has given up his sin.[45] (What admirable exchange! Humankind's Creator, taking on body and soul, in his kindness, is born from the Virgin: and, coming forth as man, yet not from man's seed, he has lavished on us his divinity.)[46]

In literary matters, the idea of economy helps Basil affirm the value of a pagan classical tradition for a Christian education. The principle of economy also pertains to individual texts, helping the interpreter "resist rigidity [*akribeia*] and partiality in favor of flexibility, generality, accommodation, and integrity or wholeness" (*HRT*, p. 45). Calvin's humanism leads him to follow Basil's principle of economy in relation to other traditions. In Calvin's Commentary on Titus, he points his detractors to Basil's counsel:

> From this passage [Titus 1:12] we may infer that those persons are superstitious, who do not venture to borrow anything from heathen authors. All truth is from God; and consequently, if wicked men have said anything that is true and just, we ought not to reject it; for it has come from God. Besides, all things are of God; and, therefore, why should it not be lawful to dedicate to his glory everything that can properly be employed for such a purpose? But on this subject the reader may consult Basil's discourse [to the young men on reading Greek literature].[47]

Calvin's Notion of Exchange and a Contemporary Rhetorical Aesthetic

Calvin's emphasis on God's call and our response—this idea of exchange, with roots in ancient rhetoric's emphasis on equity, *societas*, and *oikonomia*—is based on Calvin's understanding of the Trinity and the Incarnation as a divine economy. Pointed forward, this idea of exchange can help develop a rhetorical aesthetics that is content neither with formal analysis nor with diagnosis of public authority, though it may be concerned with both.[48] The purpose of such a rhetorical aesthetics would be a deepened exchange between author, reader, other readers, and world. We might almost say that the critic incurs a second indebtedness for moving beyond the response of everyday knowing toward critical analysis, for the purpose of such analysis must remain a deepened exchange. He or she would seek out the action of the text that makes certain obligations upon us, that calls forth an answerable response that the text both guides and depends upon.[49]

When discussing the two tables of the law, Calvin writes that the criteria for interpretation include reason and the Lord's authority (II.viii.12 & 27). But reason and God's authority are not separate resources. The first is a gift given by, and rightly exercised under, the second. Reason and what it reasons about and where and with whom—all fall under God's care and find their right place only when they acknowledge participation within that care.[50] Such participation can be intimated in unique ways by creative writing, but we curtail the power of such writing when we attend only to the means of intimation and not to the sophisticated exchange(s) it both enables and depends upon.

The exchange that literature enables can be about more than aesthetic appreciation or political critique. Literature can contribute to corporate worship (Donald Davie's championing of the eighteenth-century hymn), give counsel (Walter Benjamin), hold up a mirror for moral reflection (utopias and dystopias), make accepted instruction or history memorable (classical and medieval poetry manuals, contemporary panegyric), lead old forms to new uses (the conversion of the Petrarchan sonnet to seventeenth-century religious and political uses). In most of these ways, we see a double exchange, involving both world and reader(s). Where I live and work outside of Chicago, we see civic use of art that doesn't let consciousness separate itself from life interests, or politics from home economics. The city, for example, hosts an annual week-and-a-half event called the Chicago Humanities Fest, with sessions open for a nominal fee (three dollars) to any citizen; launched an initiative titled "Advancing the City's Civic Agenda through the Arts"; and recently released a preliminary statistical survey of arts organizations throughout Chicago. In part as response to the city's initiatives, one of the major area universities held a social work and public policy conference on the arts' role in constructing communities.[51] As elsewhere, various universities hold courses, primarily for alumni and others, on literature and doctoring, or lawyering, or doing business. Museums and libraries sponsor readings and lectures for the general citizenry as well as for special interest and age groups; and so forth. This is as it should be.[52] Our attention to aesthetics should serve the larger purpose and responsibility of an exchange that both images and prompts human solidarity.

A rhetorical aesthetics may also help its readers understand the difficulties or failures of exchange. Such difficulty or failure is exposed in most of Raymond Carver's short fiction and most of Studs Terkel's *Working* interviews. Both expose our society's skewed exchanges, characterized more by the pressures of commodification than by the goal of social intercourse.[53] The curt, stoical account given in the face of an overwhelming yet seemingly anonymous de-personalization of labor, the paring down of almost all connectives and the use of quick repetitions, the combination of boredom and dream, the gaps in discourse signaled by ellipses—all these elements of Terkel's interviews also characterize Carver's stories. Like Terkel's interviews, Carver's tales afforded late-twentieth-century workers a public forum. We hear in Carver's transcription-like stories the workers' concerns and language, their lifeworld. In fact, Carver's narrators give us more responsibility to help create sense out of their world than the workers gave to Terkel. Once Carver slips us into the role of auditor, we experience the demand to make sense of, not only to collect, a pivotal moment in another's life story. When that demand cannot be fulfilled, when the exchange fails, we are left to consider what stood in its way and under what conditions the narrator/character could have managed the linguistic exchange such that it could have led to change in his or her life. Of course, that we wonder how we could have helped them, or their shadows that walk through our everyday life, also points to the effective exchange Carver initiates with us, his readers/auditors.[54]

The purpose of these tales, like the purpose of Terkel's shaped interviews, is not only to chronicle but also to make a moral statement about the loss of value in a working life, usually but not always a blue-collar working life. We come to realize, though, that the tragedy of Carver's "low-rent tragedies" (the phrase comes from "One More Thing") is not, finally, the broken marriages or drunken violence we meet in his stories, but the characters' inability to go beyond their puzzlement over the significance of such events. They have neither the understanding nor the conditions for such speech. It remains an unrealized desire.

Just as *Working* gives us laborers who accepted Studs Terkel's invitation to enter a public sphere to sort out the meaning of work with him, so Carver's fiction gives us characters throwing out a narrative bridge to an auditor outside their personal sphere of influence who might help them understand the reasons for change in it. There are several characteristics that Carver's fictive narrators share with Terkel's workers in their attempts to enter or re-create a public sphere. First, they speak to an anonymous rather than a familiar auditor. This auditor is placed in the public position of judge or interpreter, as in Eudora Welty's "Why I Live at the P.O." But unlike Welty's narrator, who tries to draw us from our public position into her private sphere, Carver's narrators are more interested in self-understanding than in self-justification. Theirs is a chastened prose that insists upon our public standing and the discipline of giving a public account. Second, the concerns of these narrators include the public as well as private significance of marriage, work, family, death. These characters have difficulty articulating, but nonetheless feel on their pulses, the anonymous social forces that shape them beyond their understanding. Whatever else these stories are about, they are about the difficulty of creating a forum for understanding the public conditioning of private events. Third, these stories can be described as an uneasy explosion of speech from a usually stoical narrator, almost like a verbal flare that seeks contact before it burns itself out. The intensity, combined with the puzzlement, of the narrator suggests an almost desperate desire for contact. The narrator hopes against hope that together we can find the language necessary to move from event to significance.

Carver's compositional strategies lead the reader to experience firsthand the difficulty of establishing meaningful communication, of creating a discourse that navigates between personal experience and anonymous steering systems. His stories regularly situate the reader as silent partner to a narrator who tries (and usually fails) to establish a meaningful association with his or her auditor. That association seems a necessary precondition for understanding. The stories, increasingly told from a first-person point of view, are most often cast as tales, complete with teller, listener, and inferable situation. They set up expectations of counsel and interpretation. That is, they seem to implicate us, asking about our responsibility for the broken testimony, the socially impoverished lifeworld, revealed in the strange but not quite unreal discourse of the teller's tale. Even story titles such as "Put Yourself in My Shoes," "Will You Please Be Quiet, Please?" "Where I'm Calling From," or, especially, "What We Talk about When We Talk about Love" show the complicity between speaker and auditor.[55]

These elements are seen most clearly in the opening to "Sacks": "I want to pass along to you a story my father told me when I stopped over in Sacramento last year."[56] The son passes on his father's story and storytelling situation to us. In the son's telling of his father's story of adultery, we are given the same role by him that he had been given by his father: "'You're an educated man, Les,' his father had said. 'You'll be the one to figure it out'" (*WWT*, p. 39). His father's sexual betrayal was bad enough, to be sure. But the tragedy lies in not being able to figure out how things like this happen, how the life one had lived suddenly sustains one no longer. "'You see what I'm saying?' the father had said. 'A man can go along obeying all the rules and then it don't matter a damn anymore. His luck just goes, you know?'" (*WWT*, pp. 42–43). But the father wonders how such a transitory rush could have overcome him. That's what he had hoped talking to his son would help him figure out: What had happened to the beliefs, thoughts, structures he had lived by, that they could so easily be overthrown?

We can infer from the son's story that he hadn't recognized or hadn't admitted his father's request for help in interpreting these facts. He had wondered, instead, about the plot of the story—whether the husband of the Stanley Products woman had caught his father when he went crashing through their window. The son sees surfaces without seeing their depth, just as, earlier, he had seen only a sack and the candy it held rather than his father's attempt to give him a gift for his wife and children. The story ends with a comparable interpretive puzzle for the auditor. The son tells us that he had forgotten the sack on the bar at the airport. "Just as well," he tells his auditor. "Mary didn't need candy, Almond Roca or anything else." The story ends with the one-line paragraph, "That was last year. She needs it now even less" (*WWT*, p. 45). We may ask why the son is telling us this story he had shown every sign of not wanting to hear himself. Are we really supposed to confirm that his wife needs the sack with his father's gifts even less now than she did a year ago? Has the son followed in his father's footsteps—or perhaps preceded them? And what about us? Are we similarly unable to make the storyteller's offering effective? Do we also require the counsel this tale would try to construct? By cornering the reader in such a way, these low-rent tragedies bring into sharp relief the plight of middle-class or lower-middle-class narrators who have forgotten, if they once knew, how to exercise membership in a public sphere. The narrators try to reconstruct such a sphere for reflection with the auditor to whom they tell their tales. We assume that auditor's role as we read the stories and, stymied by story's end, we experience firsthand the difficulty of creating and sustaining a public sphere for rational discourse.

But Carver also situates us at the end of these tales in such a way that we have to interpret "from the other side" what might make such discourse possible. With the publication of *Cathedral* in 1982, a few of Carver's stories conclude more hopefully than the bleak or quizzical endings associated with his name. These hopeful endings are productive; social intercourse gets established in them. The narrator's initiative begins to issue into general usefulness, both in the action represented by the story and in the narrative proper. When these narrators negotiate the move from event to significance, we can see what Carver imagines the requirements for such negotiation to be. We can isolate in Carver's stories at least three positive requirements for negotiating the move from event to significance. First, such a move requires recognition or confession that one's own language or narration is insufficient to the task. Second, the effort to find a larger language and a larger meaning for experience requires a complementary, not a single, effort. Third, it often requires a new view of social enclosures. Speaking of the narrator in "Cathedral," Kirk Nesset writes, "the narrator begins to realize just how exhilarating confinement can be, once one sees beyond the narrow enclosure of self that larger, more expansive, enclosure of society."[57]

Labor without companionship figures importantly in Carver's stories of failed understanding, whether as symptom or as cause. And that seems to be as true for narrative labor as for labor in the marketplace. The narrative efforts of Carver's storytellers mirror, even as they try to overcome, their lack of meaningful exchange in the rest of their workaday world. Their labor, whether physical or narrative, leads to one of the goals of work, production, but not to the other, companionship; we, as auditors, are implicated in that failure. What Calvin wrote about labor also applies to the construction of speech. Social intercourse is the larger goal of both labor and language. It is only through social intercourse that we can achieve both individual initiative and general usefulness. For Calvin, those were the dual requirements one found in looking back to a creation order and in looking forward to a new order, the Kingdom of God. Indeed, Calvin's insistence on the importance of companionship and exchange is another example, besides its emphasis on vernacular translations and on literacy, of the Reformation's contribution to the development of a modern public sphere.[58] As more civic and academic groups have grown concerned about the diminishment of that public sphere in increasingly formal democracies, more programs like those I described for the city of Chicago have emerged; the ideal of the public intellectual has even reappeared. A rhetorical aesthetics can contribute to this renewing of a public sphere, both in the preparatory work of the classroom and in public discourse. Its attention to literature as a sophisticated social communication can give to literary criticism a middle ground between formal appreciation and social diagnosis.

NOTES

1. Noam Chomsky, *Language and Politics* (Montreal: Black Rose, 1988), p. 143.

2. David Lyle Jeffrey, *People of the Book: Christian Identity and Literary Culture* (Grand Rapids, MI: Eerdmans, 1996), p. 10.

3. See Roger Lundin, "Interpreting Orphans: Hermeneutics in the Cartesian Tradition," in *The Promise of Hermeneutics* (Grand Rapids, MI: Eerdmans, 1999), especially pp. 6–53.

4. Steven Mailloux has done groundbreaking work in American Studies on what he refers to as rhetorical hermeneutics, placing neopragmatism, the history of rhetoric, and philosophical hermeneutics in conversation with each other. I have done almost no work in American Studies and am more interested in reconstructing a tradition of Christian pragmatism. I am also less oriented toward reception history than Mailloux is, which is why I

use the term "rhetorical aesthetics." See Mailloux's *Rhetorical Power* (Ithaca, NY: Cornell University Press, 1989) and *Reception Histories: Rhetoric, Pragmatism, and American Cultural Politics* (Ithaca, NY: Cornell University Press, 1998). Kathy Eden persuasively demonstrates in *Hermeneutics and the Rhetorical Tradition* (New Haven, CT: Yale University Press, 1997) the intertwining of interpretive and rhetorical traditions (hereafter abbreviated as *HRT*; subsequent page numbers given in text). Don H. Compier, a student of Mailloux, applies similar strategies to theology in *What Is Rhetorical Theology? Textual Practice and Public Discourse* (Harrisburg, PA: Trinity Press International, 1999).

5. See Friedrich Schiller, *On the Aesthetic Education of Man, in a Series of Letters*, ed. and trans. Elizabeth M. Wilkinson and L. A. Willoughby (New York: Oxford University Press, 1967), esp. Appendix I: "The Text and its Story," pp. 334–37. Earlier letters Schiller had written in 1793 for Duke Friedrich Christian of Denmark were destroyed by fire, then rewritten and expanded between 1794 and 1795. There is considerable critical debate whether the final letters were of a more conservative cast than Schiller's earlier thought, due to the increasing violence of the French Revolution. See the introduction, esp. xv–xlii, for critical differences over the impact of the French Revolution on Schiller's aesthetics.

6. This is the argument of Harold Bloom, e.g., in *Dante's Divine Comedy: Modern Critical Interpretations*, ed. Bloom (New York: Chelsea House, 1987), pp. 2 and 5–6. But many critics have referred to Hamlet as the modern character in English literature.

7. *Beyond Formalism; Literary Essays 1958–1970* (New Haven, CT: Yale University Press, 1970; rpt. 1975), p. 55. Hereafter abbreviated as *BY*; subsequent page numbers will be given in the text.

8. David Lodge, *Consciousness and the Novel: Connected Essays* (London: Secker and Warburg; Cambridge, Mass.: Harvard University Press, 2002), p. 10. The second phrase comes from James Friel's review in *Cercles; Revue pluridisciplinaire du monde Anglophone* 8 (2003); updated June 28, 2003. Retrieved from http://www.cercles.com.

9. This contrasts with Augustine's distinction between use and enjoyment (*uti/frui*) in *On Christian Doctrine* (I.iii–v). Augustine, *On Christian Doctrine*, trans. D. W. Robertson (Indianapolis: Bobbs-Merrill, 1958). Hereafter abbreviated as *CD*; subsequent page numbers will be given in the text.

10. Hartman inherits Moritz's position but also challenges it, as we have seen, correctly marking its ahistorical character and its naïve optimism.

11. "SCE News and Notices" (Spring/Summer, 1992). The New Economic Criticism can be dated to a couple of "SCE News and Notices" entries in 1991 and 1992 for the Society for Critical Exchange and to a conference in 1994 that drew upon exchanges between forty economists and sixty literary scholars brought together by Deirdre McCloskey, Mark Osteen, and Martha Woodmansee. A collection based on those conference presentations came out by the end of the decade (*The New Economic Criticism: Studies at the Intersection of Literature and Economics* [New York: Routledge Press, 1999]). Essays from a 1998 international conference were published in the spring 2000 issue of *New Literary History* titled "Production, Consumption and Value." Projects since that time include work on gift exchange, on trust, and on "economies of writing" ("SCE News and Notices" 13 [1999–2000]).

12. See the *Boston Globe* review, "Crisis Theory: Academic All-Stars Debate War, Politics, and the Anxiety of Non-Influence" (April 20, 2003). The *New York Times* ran a review titled "The Latest Theory Is That Theory Doesn't Matter" (April 19, 2003).

13. Robert Barsky, "Literary Knowledge: Noam Chomsky and Marc Angenot" in *Di-*

alogism and Cultural Criticism, ed. Clive Thomson (London, Ontario: Mestengo Press, 1995), pp. 21–46.

14. Ivan Illich, *In the Vineyard of the Text: A Commentary to Hugh's Didascalicon*. Hereafter abbreviated as *IVT*; subsequent page numbers will be given in the text.

15. For a longer discussion of recent works on the history of reading, including Illich's, see my review essay, "What Is Reading For?" in *Christianity and Literature* 52:1 (Autumn 2002): 57–83.

16. See Alan Jacobs, *A Theology of Reading: The Hermeneutics of Love* (Boulder, CO: Westview Press, 2001), p. 13. Hereafter abbreviated as *TR*; subsequent page numbers are given in the text.

17. Jacobs is both summarizing and affirming Martha Nussbaum's use of literature in ethical studies. See *An Early Commentary on the Poetria Nova of Geoffrey of Vinsauf*, ed. Marjorie Curry Woods (New York: Garland, 1985), for an interesting counterexample to our ping-ponging between mechanical and organic images for writing. Geoffrey moves easily from the image of writing as building a house, for example, to the image of writing as following a path.

18. "Nearly all the wisdom we possess, that is to say, true and sound wisdom, consists of two parts: the knowledge of God and of ourselves. But, while joined by many bonds, which one precedes and brings forth the other is not easy to discern. In the first place, no one can look upon himself without immediately turning his thoughts to the contemplation of God, in whom he 'lives and moves' [Acts 17:28]. For quite clearly, the mighty gifts with which we are endowed are hardly from ourselves; indeed, our very being is nothing but subsistence in the one God. Then, by these benefits shed like dew from heaven upon us, we are led as by rivulets to the spring itself" (John Calvin, *Institutes of the Christian Religion*, trans. Ford Lewis Battles, ed. John T. McNeill [Philadelphia: Westminster Press, 1960], I.1, pp. 35–36. Hereafter abbreviated in the text as *ICR*). McNeill notes that "The French version of 1560 expresses even more strongly the association of the two aspects of sound knowledge: 'In knowing God, each of us also knows himself'" (36 n. 2). McNeill also compares Calvin's opening to the opening of Augustine's *Soliloquies* (I.ii.7): "I desire to know God and the soul."

19. See Susan Schreiner, *Theater of His Glory: Nature and the Natural Order in the Thought of John Calvin*, Studies in Historical Theology 3 (Durham, NC: Labyrinth Press, 1991).

20. Quoted in David Little, *Religion, Order, and Law: A Study in Pre-Revolutionary England* (New York: Harper and Row, 1969; rpt. University of Chicago Press, 1984), p. 60. Hereafter abbreviated as *ROL*; subsequent page numbers given in text.

21. This notion of economic exchange also leads to an interpretation of a legitimate usury. See Michael Wykes, "Devaluing the Scholastics: Calvin's Ethics of Usury" in the *Calvin Theological Journal* 38:1 (April 2003): 27–51. In addition, it leads to the Geneva consistory's concern for the responsibility of the prodigal husband toward wife and child. See *Registers of the Consistory of Geneva in the Time of Calvin*, vol. 1, 1542–1544, ed. Thomas A. Lambert and Isabella M. Watt, trans. M. Wallace McDonald (Grand Rapids, MI: Eerdmans, 2000), p. 184.

22. Ford Lewis Battles, "Introduction" in *John Calvin's Sermons on the Ten Commandments*, trans. Benjamin Farley, p. 9.

23. Bob Goudzwaard, *Capitalism and Progress: A Diagnosis of Western Society* (Grand Rapids, MI: Eerdmans, 1979), p. 212. See pp. 211–21.

24. Bob Goudzwaard, *Genoeg van te Veel, Genoig van te Weinig; Wissels Omzetten in*

de Economie, 3rd ed. (Baarn, the Netherlands: Ten Have, 1991); trans. *Beyond Poverty and Affluence: Toward an Economy of Care* (Grand Rapids, MI: Eerdmans, 1995), p. 42. Hereafter abbreviated as *BPA*; subsequent page numbers given in text.

25. *CD*, I.xvi.16; my emphasis.

26. *The Confessions of Saint Augustine*, trans. Rex Warner (New York: New American Library, 1963; rpt. 2001), III.5, pp. 43–44 (hereafter abbreviated as *C*; subsequent page numbers given in the text). On the influence of the Bible's humble style, see Erich Auerbach, "Sermo humilis," *Literary Language and Its Public in Late Latin Antiquity and in the Middle Ages*, trans. Ralph Manheim (New York: Bollingen/Random House, 1965), pp. 27–66.

27. If Robert McMahon is correct that the first nine books of the *Confessions* are written in ring structure, then these two narratives fall at the center of the central book of that ring structure and draw more attention to themselves by doing so (*Augustine's Prayerful Ascent: An Essay on the Literary Form of the Confessions* [Athens: University of Georgia Press, 1989]).

28. Other critics have noticed this parallel. For a discussion and interpretation see Sarah Spence, *Rhetorics of Reason and Desire: Vergil, Augustine, and the Troubadours* (Ithaca: Cornell University Press, 1988), pp. 57–59. Hereafter *RRD*; subsequent references given in text.

29. See *Cicero on the Emotions: Tusculan Disputations 3 and 4*, trans. and with commentary by Margaret Graver (University of Chicago Press, 2002): "For every emotion is a misery, but distress is a very torture-chamber. Desire scalds us; wild delight makes us giddy; fear degrades us; but the effects of distress are worse: gauntness, pain, depression, disfigurement. It eats away at the mind and, in a word, destroys it. This we must shed; this we must cast away, or else remain in misery" (III.27, p. 14; also see IV.82, p. 69).

30. Cf. *Aeneid*, trans. Robert Fitzgerald (Random House, 1980), IV.442–51, pp. 111–12, to *Confessions* VI.11, p. 98. In VI.9, Augustine writes of Alypius, "Nevertheless, this was already being stored up in his memory for his future healing" (*C*, p. 113). Other references to correction and healing can be found on pp. 81, 91, 92, 105, 107, 118, and 122.

31. Spence relates this claim by D. Bassi. Spence also refers to J. O'Meara's article on "Augustine the Artist and the *Aeneid*" (*Mélanges offerts à mademoiselle Christine Mohrmann* [Utrecht-Antwerp: Spectrum, 1963], pp. 252–61) as "by far the most insightful on the profound creative influence that Vergil had on Augustine" (*RRD*, p. 139 n. 2).

32. At the beginning of Book 4 of the *Aeneid*, we hear of Dido's vow not to marry again after the death of Sychaeus. Christine de Pizan, who treats Dido in *The Book of the City of Ladies* as an example of constancy, writes that "Elissa [Dido] was so distraught at his death that she nearly died of grief. For a long time, she gave herself over to weeping and wailing for the loss of her beloved lord, cursing her brute of a brother for having ordered his murder" before rescuing herself and a remnant of her people from the wicked king (I.46).

33. In *The Divine Names*, Pseudo-Dionysius writes that the "supreme Cause" precedes oneness as well as multiplicity (13.2, 128). Difference expresses God's beneficence in both word and action. Pseudo-Dionysius refers, for example, to "divine differentiations" (2.11, 66) or to God's "rejoicing in all things" (5.9, 102) or to the need, in describing God as Life, to find "words . . . drawn from all of life for [God] teems with every kind of life" (6.3, 104).

34. For the roots of these developments, see Bob Goudzwaard, *Capitalism and Progress: A Diagnosis of Western Society*, trans. Josina Van Nuis Zylstra (Grand Rapids, MI: Eerdmans, 1979), especially pp. 55–71.

35. See Susan Schreiner, note 19, above.

36. See Robert James Bast, *Honor Your Fathers: Catechisms and the Emergence of a Patriarchal Ideology in Germany 1400–1600* (Leiden: Brill, 1997); but also see McNeill, 367 n. 1.

37. Books 3 and 4 of Calvin's *Institutes* are titled "The Way in which We Receive the Grace of Christ: What Benefits Come to Us from It, and What Effects Follow" and "The External Means or Aids by which God Invites Us into the Society of Christ and Holds Us Therein," respectively.

38. At the beginning of Book 7, Calvin writes, "[I]f the forms of the law be separated from its end, one must condemn it as vanity" (*ICR*, p. 349). Near the end of Book 8, under "The Sum of the Law," Calvin returns to this claim: "It would, therefore, be a mistake for anyone to believe that the law teaches nothing but some rudiments and preliminaries of righteousness by which men begin their apprenticeship, and does not also guide them to the true goal" (*ICR*, p. 415).

39. Despite the section title ("Not to Restrain the Folk . . ."), restraint reenters the discussion, doing so as "a necessity for the public community of man" (*ICR*, p. 359). McNeill notes a similar use in Book 4 (xx.3) and in Melanchthon: "*publicae pacis causa*" (*Loci praecipui theologici*, ed. Hans Engelland, p. 322), in *Melanchthons Werke in Auswall*, ed. R. Stupperich II, i (Gütersloh: Berthelsmann, 1952).

40. The passage echoes *City of God*, xiv.12.

41. This emphasis on synecdoche is similar to the speech Dante gave Cacciaguida two hundred years earlier to justify his most dramatic examples of vice: "Therefore only the souls known of fame have been shown to you within these wheels [*Paradiso*], upon the mountain [*Purgatorio*], and in the woeful valley [*Inferno*]; for the mind of him who hears rests not nor confirms its faith by an example that has its roots unknown or hidden" (*Paradiso* 17.136–42; trans. C. S. Singleton [Princeton: Princeton University Press, 1975]).

42. Calvin's description of "substance" corresponds to Melanchthon's concept of "status." Kathy Eden writes: "this concept forms the very core of not only Melanchthon's rhetorical but also his hermeneutical theory. For both the reader and the writer must begin by locating the *status* of the discourse in question:

> No part of the art (of rhetoric) is more necessary than the precepts dealing with the status of the case (*de statibus*), in respect of which, this is first and foremost: in relation to every problem (*negocio*) or controversial question (*controversia*) we consider what the status is, that is, what is the chief subject of inquiry (*principalis quaestio*), the proposition that contains the gist of the matter (*summam negocii*) toward which all arguments are aimed, in other words, the main conclusion. No matter of debate can be comprehended, nothing can be explained, stated or grasped in an orderly fashion, except some proposition be formulated which includes the sum total of the case (*summam causae*). [A Critical Translation of Philip Melanchthon's *Elementorum Rhetorices Libri Duo*, trans. Sister Mary Joan La Fontaine (Ph.D. diss., University of Michigan, 1968), p. 115]

Status, then, is introduced as the proposition containing the *summa negocii* or *summa causae*, what we might call 'the heart of the matter'" (*HRT*, pp. 83–84).

43. See Daniel Ritchie, *Reconstructing Literature in an Ideological Age: A Biblical Poetics and Literary Studies from Milton to Burke* (Grand Rapids, MI: Eerdmans, 1996), esp. ch. 3, pp. 136–46, where Ritchie argues that "[t]he language of 'blessing' is . . . the most useful domain in which a biblical poetics may locate culture" (pp. 144–45). Ritchie de-

velops the implications for a biblical poetics of Claus Westermann's theological analysis in *Blessing in the Bible and the Life of the Church,* trans. Keith Crim (Philadelphia: Fortress Press, 1978).

44. "Saint Basil and the Rhetorical Tradition," *Basil of Caesarea, Christian, Humanist, Ascetic: A Sixteen-Hundredth Anniversary Symposium,* vol. 1, ed. Paul Jonathan Fedwick (Toronto: Pontifical Institute of Mediaeval Studies, 1981), p. 254; quoted in *HRT,* p. 48.

45. John H. Erickson, "*Oikonomia* in Byzantine Canon Law," in *Law, Church, and Society: Essays in Honor of Stephen Kuttner,* ed. K. Pennington and R. Somerville (Philadelphia: 1977), p. 228; quoted in *HRT,* pp. 45–46. Something of this sense is still found in the Western church, too, as in the antiphon at vespers, January 1, Feast of the Holy Mother of God:

> *O admirabile commercium!*
> *Creator generis humani,*
> *Animatum corpus sumens,*
> *de Virgine nasci dignatus est:*
> *et procedens homo sine semine,*
> *largitus est nobis suam deitatem.*

46. The passage is quoted as epigraph in Franz Jozef Van Beeck, *God Encountered; A Contemporary Catholic Systematic Theology,* vol. 2/1: "The Revelation of the Glory" (Collegeville, MN: Liturgical Press, 1993).

47. *Commentaries on the Epistles to Timothy, Titus, and Philemon,* trans. William Pringle (Grand Rapids, MI: Eerdmans, 1948), pp. 309–10; quoted in Daniel Ritchie, *Reconstructing Literature in an Ideological Age* (Grand Rapids, MI: Eerdmans, 1996), p. 144.

48. I have in mind Jürgen Habermas's phrase in *The Structural Transformation of the Public Sphere,* trans. Thomas Burger with the assistance of Frederick Lawrence (Cambridge, MA: MIT Press, 1993), especially p. 30.

49. A rhetorical aesthetics has much more to learn from the long history of rhetoric, from the most general, such as the distributive, occasional, and contested nature of meaning, to the categorical, such as the five parts of rhetoric (invention, arrangement, style, memory, and delivery) or the three kinds of speeches (forensic, deliberative, and epideictic). It also might learn from more specific matters such as the relationship of intentionality to invention and equity. (See *HRT,* pp. 15–16, especially.) A rhetorical aesthetic would need to reconsider both parts of the purpose of poetry that Horace summarized: to please and to instruct. The connection of pleasure to memory, and hence to instruction and persuasion, would require further study. (In *The Book of Memory: A Study of Memory in Medieval Culture* [New York: Cambridge University Press, 1990], for example, Mary Carruthers argues that memory was thought to be "the key linking term between knowledge and action, conceiving of good and doing it" [p. 64], i.e., the reader had to take responsibility for the ethical or constructive nature of memory.) The nature of the change brought about when "instruction" was altered to rectification of the feelings in Wordsworth's literary criticism would have to be carefully analyzed. (I have in mind especially the 1800 Preface to the second edition of *Lyrical Ballads.*) There will be specific historical lessons we can learn, such as George Herbert's comparison of the commerce between countries to the exchange between critics: "and that as one Country doth not bear all things, that there may be a Commerce; so neither hath God opened, or will open all to one, that there may be a traffic in knowledge between the servants of God, for the planting both of love, and humility." (See *George Herbert: The Country Parson, The Temple,* ed. John N. Wall Jr. [New York: Paulist Press, 1981],

ch. 4, p. 59.) Augustine's careful redefinition of style according to purpose (to persuade, to please, to instruct) and audience (to listen intelligently, willingly, obediently, IV.26) still bears further consideration. (See *CD*, p. 162.) These are some examples of the work that might contribute to a rhetorical aesthetics. The most important matters will require us to see aesthetics under the aegis of rhetoric and rhetoric under the heading of anthropology.

50. For the argument that the *for whom* and the *where* are as important as the *what* of education, see Brian Walsh and Steven Bouma-Prediger's recent article, "Education for Homelessness or Homemaking? The Christian College in a Postmodern Culture," in *Christian Scholar's Review* 23:3 (Spring 2003): 281–95.

51. *University of Chicago Chronicle* (April 11, 2002), pp. 1 & 3.

52. See Nicholas Wolterstorff's argument in *Art in Action: Toward a Christian Aesthetic* (Grand Rapids, MI: Eerdmans, 1980) and in *Works and Worlds of Art* (New York: Oxford University Press, 1980) for the multiple uses of the arts in addition to the use of aesthetic contemplation.

53. For an extended treatment, see my "Narrative Labour in Raymond Carver," in *Literature and the Renewal of the Public Sphere,* ed. Susan Van Zanten Gallagher and M. D. Walhout (New York: St. Martin's Press, 2000), pp. 105–21.

54. The discussion that follows in the next two pages was first published in my essay "Narrative Labor in Raymond Carver," in *Literature and the Renewal of the Public Sphere,* ed. Susan Van Zanten Gallagher and M. D. Walhout (New York: St. Martin's Press, 2000), pp. 108–10, 113, 115.

55. The latter three are also titles of story collections.

56. *What We Talk about When We Talk about Love* (New York: Alfred A. Knopf, 1981; rpt. Random House, 1982), p. 37. Hereafter abbreviated *WWT*; subsequent page numbers given in text.

57. Kirk Nesset, "Insularity and Self-Enlargement in Raymond Carver's *Cathedral,*" *Essays in Literature* 21 (1994): 127.

58. Habermas is strangely silent on this point.

PART 4

The Ethics of Interpretation: Improvisation, Participation, Authority

10

The Improvisation of Hermeneutics

Jazz Lessons for Interpreters

Bruce Ellis Benson

As if the myriad—or "conflict"—of interpretations were not enough, there is likewise a myriad of interpretation theories.[1] And each of these theories has a particular emphasis. For instance, whereas E. D. Hirsch claims that interpreters should seek to discern the *author's intention,*[2] Monroe Beardsley contends that one has access only to the *author's text.*[3] While Hans-Georg Gadamer likewise makes the *text* the locus of interpretation, he and Jacques Derrida emphasize that the *interaction of text and reader* never results in a simple "repetition" of the text. Gadamer explains this interaction by way of the metaphor of a "fusion of horizons" in which the horizon of the text and that of the interpreter intersect to produce a new meaning.[4] Derrida uses such terms as *différance* and *iterability* to emphasize the inevitable "difference" between the text and any interpretation of it.[5] Further, Gadamer and Derrida would both agree with Stanley Fish in at least one respect: that there are no "lone" interpreters but only interpreters embedded in *interpretive communities.*[6]

Given these respective emphases, it might seem that we simply have to choose one to the exclusion of another. Either we privilege the *author* and her intention, or we privilege the *text,* or we privilege the *interpreter* of the text, or we privilege some *interpretive community.* Yet is there any way of giving each of these aspects their "due"? Can we recognize, for instance, that authors' intentions are important while likewise recognizing that interpreters and interpretive communities play at least some sort of role in giving the text meaning? Derrida is no doubt right in reminding us (though not in regard to hermeneutics per se) that it is impossible to render justice adequately. In hermeneutics—as in everything else—there are too many "others" (both authors and interpreters) to whom one owes justice.[7] Yet, keeping that caveat in mind, is there a way to keep from *unduly* privileging any one member of a hermeneutical conversation?

Here I will argue that jazz improvisation provides a model of something at least *approximating* a "hermeneutical justice." In particular, I will attempt to demonstrate that jazz is a hermeneutical practice in which there is a balancing of authors' intentions, the tradition from which texts and performances arise, the continuing tradition (or "interpretive community") that preserves and nourishes those texts, and the role of particular interpreters. That claim, of course, needs some qualification in advance. I do not intend to suggest that the interpretive practices in jazz are simply identical to those in other disciplines. Reading Leviticus, say, is not exactly the same as playing a Gershwin tune.[8] To cite just two differences, it is immediately apparent that interpreting sacred texts usually involves different expectations of fidelity than interpreting a show tune and that reading words is not the same as playing musical notes. Yet, without minimizing differences, I think there are some essential features of jazz interpretation that are sufficiently analogous to interpretation of literary, legal, biblical, theatrical, and other sorts of musical texts. It is those features on which I intend to concentrate here.

To bring out those features, I will do the following: (1) define "improvisation" by comparing it to other sorts of "creation"; (2) consider the ways in which composers and authors "improvise"; (3) provide an account of the improvisational aspects of interpretation; and (4) discuss some similarities and dissimilarities between jazz improvisation and other improvisational activities. Along the way, I will make reference to various hermeneutical theories.

What Is "Improvisation?"

When bassist Calvin Hill says that he *used* to think of jazz as some kind of "magic," he sums up the way many listeners think about jazz improvisation: it's as if improvisers pull things out of thin air.[9] Even the OED describes improvisation as "the production or execution of anything offhand."[10] Such an account gives us a picture of improvisation almost ex nihilo, one that remarkably parallels our usual conception of musical composition.

Consider what Jerrold Levinson says regarding musical composition:

> There is probably no idea more central to thought about art than . . . that it is a godlike activity in which the artist brings into being what did not exist beforehand—much as a demiurge forms a world out of inchoate matter. . . . There is a special aura that envelops composers, as well as other artists, because we think of them as true creators[11]

We often *do* think this way not only about composers and improvisers but also about authors. Indeed, precisely this conception of composition and authorship is crucial to debates concerning authorial intention. Why? First, if we define composing or authorship following Levinson, then the author is privileged as "demiurge" or genius (in Kant's sense). Second, it naturally follows (as a corollary) that the act of performing or reading should be conceived *primarily* (even if not *exclusively*) as "repeating" what the demiurge has created. The composer/author has a "meaning" or intention; that meaning or intention is encapsulated in the score/text; that meaning or intention is reproduced aurally or in the mind of the reader. It is no coincidence, then, that the composer Paul Hindemith describes the performer's role as being to "duplicate the preëstablished values of the composer's creation" or that Aaron Copland insists that the performer "exists to serve the composer."[12] On this account, the goal of the performer or reader is merely to discern the composer's or author's intention and then translate that intention into sound or meaning.

Given this demand of extreme faithfulness to the composer/author (whether we construe this in terms of faithfulness to intentions or the text), it is not surprising that there were at least two distinct and opposite responses in the past half-century that were roughly contemporaneous. On the one hand, the early music movement was a logical outgrowth of the conception of *Werktreue* [faithfulness to the musical work] or *Texttrue* [faithfulness to the score]. The ideal of the composer as authoritative demiurge results in the conception of the performer as mere "transmission station" and the ideal of an "authentic" performance is one that attempts to bring the score to sound in such a way that listeners would hear music of the past "just as the composer intended."[13] On the other hand, in literary theory one finds a rebellion against this strong sense of authorship in the proclamation of the "death of the author." Although Roland Barthes's claim that "the birth of the reader must be at the cost of the death of the author" is clearly the best known of these proclamations (and probably the most strident), Barthes was certainly not alone.[14]

Yet one must situate *both* the early music movement and Barthes's demand for the author's death in light of the strong conception of author or composer as "demiurge." It is not surprising that such a conception results in the twin responses of obsequiousness and outright rebellion. Yet suppose that we had a different idea of what composers and authors do than that of acting as demiurge. What if we conceived of composers and authors as improvising—that is, improvising along with the rest of us? Then there would be no need for either the abject submission to the author's intentions or the violent reaction that calls for the author's death. Interpreters could then see themselves as working alongside the composer or author (and still—at least in cases where it would be appropriate—give the author a measure of privilege). Of course, we should be clear on at least one aspect: the composer and author *as demiurge* must die. But such a composer or author never really lived, except as a romantic conception. As it turns out—*pace* Levinson—*real* composers and authors are not demiurges and do not compose or write "out of nothing." Rather they more accurately—following one definition of "improvisation"—"fabricate out of what is conveniently on hand."[15] As we shall see in the following sections, composers and authors—as well as interpreters—operate within a context and follow sometimes quite strict rules of composition and interpretation. Thus, "improvisation" provides us a way of thinking not merely about *interpreting* texts but also about *composing* or *writing* those texts.

To see why improvisation is a helpful way of thinking about both interpretation and writing, we need to turn to how texts come into being and then consider how they are interpreted.

How Do Composers and Authors Improvise?

One way of explicating the claim that composers and authors improvise is in terms of Edmund Husserl's conception of "ideal objects." Husserl thinks that, for a musical or literary work, there is an *Erstmaligkeit*—an originary (temporal) moment at which the "work" first comes into existence.[16] Clearly, there is something like that in the creative process: one gets an idea. The question is really one of how *pure* that origin (*Ursprung*) really is. Such a theory of a "*reine Ursprung*," of course, fits reasonably well with Levinson's demiurge who creates out of inchoate matter.[17] Elsewhere, I have argued extensively that this pure origin of musical works is questionable even in "classical music," where one would most likely expect it to be the case.[18] But that kind of pure origin is even less evident in jazz. One could say that jazz is improvisatory "all the way down." Let me work out that claim in three different though related ways.

First, that improvisatory nature is found in the history of jazz itself, which has no founding or originary moment. Out of such diverse roots as European classical music, traditional folk musics of Britain, France, and Spain, gospel music of many denominations, and the blues, jazz has always been inscribed in the Heraclitean flux—which continues as jazz itself has mutated. So it's impossible to pinpoint an "origin" of jazz, even if we say that early-twentieth-century New Orleans marks an important moment in its evolution and probably the closest thing to an *Ursprung*.

Second, since jazz musicians have generally both performed and composed, their "compositions" have taken on shape in the flux of interpretation. Consider the composer/interpreter Duke Ellington: after coming up with a tune, he'd perform it with his band on the road, and over time that tune would be shaped by Ellington and by players in the band. The result was a tune that was molded by communal collaboration.

This leads us to a third—and particularly significant—point: the twin issues of composer and piece identity. The close connection between performance and improvisation in jazz has a twofold result. On the one hand, jazz pieces tend to grow out of performance, sometimes in the more literal sense in which improvisational riffs gradually become tunes themselves (and there are many such instances) or else in the sense that jazz composition is highly influenced by the melodic or harmonic "ideas" of particular members of the group, the rhythms that they (and other groups) develop, and simply the interchange that results when one plays in community. On the other hand, performance in turn affects the identity of those pieces that develop. Obviously, this occurs in varying degrees or ways, over shorter or longer periods of time. A particularly remarkable example is Thelonious Monk's "'Round Midnight," which he composed in 1944. When Cootie Williams recorded it a few months later, he embellished the melody—which was and is standard jazz practice. Then, when the sheet music version was published, it included Williams's embellishments. When Dizzy Gillespie recorded it in 1946, he kept those embellishments but also added an introduction and coda. By this time, Monk *himself* was playing the tune with Williams's and Gillespie's additions. And then in 1955, Miles Davis added three new measures to the end of the first chorus.[19] If you play "'Round Midnight" today, you normally play *all* of that—since those aspects are now part of the identity of the piece.

To sum up this last point, it is safe to say that in jazz the roles of composer and performer are so closely interwoven that a *clear* distinction between the two is significantly complicated—even though there is still a distinction. In this respect, jazz is remarkably similar to Baroque music.[20] So are there composers in jazz? Certainly. Even in the case of "'Round Midnight," Thelonious Monk is still listed as the composer. While one can argue that crediting Monk is certainly appropriate, such a case raises a host of questions regarding authorship, "rights" of an author (including copyright), and control. Is it *simply* Monk's tune? How do we acknowledge the role of Williams, Gillespie, and Davis? Shouldn't they get "credit" too? Probably so. Sometimes those who collaborate get credit; sometimes they don't.[21] In any case, composer identity is often much more problematic in jazz than classical music.[22] Likewise, since the tune and the performance are more closely connected, we have more complications with the identity of a jazz piece than, say, a symphony by Beethoven. Of course, it is important to note that these kinds of complications are not unique to jazz. One can find them, for instance, in the composition of biblical texts such as the four Gospels. Since the Gospels were written at some temporal distance from the actual time of Jesus' life (and Luke, for example, wasn't even an eyewitness to what he records), there is good reason to think that the authors were working with narratives that were known and had been passed down in the Christian community. Their authorship, then, comes in how they weave those narratives together, what they choose to include and exclude, and their respective emphases. There is, of course, the further complication that these texts are not simply the product of *human* authorship but also have the Holy Spirit as their author. So one cannot talk about the Gospel of Luke as being "simply" by Luke.[23]

Having briefly considered how authorship in jazz is often—to greater and lesser degrees—complicated by its improvisatory nature, we need to turn to the improvisation of interpretation.

How Do Performers Improvise?

While there are various aspects of jazz improvisation, here I'll consider five: (1) what we might call the "practice" of jazz; (2) the *interpretive* aspect of jazz performance; (3) the "structure" of jazz pieces; (4) the relation of text and author; and (5) the way in which jazz performance is "creative."[24]

First, an aspect that has served as a horizon in all that I've said so far is the "situatedness" of improvisers in a "tradition" (to speak with Gadamer) or "practice" (to use Alasdair MacIntyre's language that improvises on both Gadamer and Aristotle). Practices are social activities that are regulated by goals and standards.[25] There are rules as to how one puts melodies and chords together, as well as how one improvises upon those melodies and chords. Not only are there basic guidelines in jazz (the twelve-bar blues form would be one example), there also are specific rules for different types of jazz (such as what one can do in bebop versus what one can do in New Orleans jazz). So both composers and performers are limited by the conventions of a given genre's practice. And even the most "original" improvisers are still guided by those rules.[26] Of course, one can hardly complain about these limitations, since they are precisely what make jazz possible.[27] Note that even in what is today called "free jazz," one can't just do anything.[28] Still, even though practices and traditions have ways of governing themselves, the process of working within them cannot help but improvise upon those practices themselves. Jazz provides many examples of this improvisation upon the tradition itself. New Orleans jazz still exists, for example, but from it has developed such jazz traditions as bebop, cool jazz, and fusion. So "jazz" now encompasses all of these traditions (or "sub-practices").

To be situated in a performance practice such as jazz means one knows the scales and chords, understands the difference between a blues tune and a bop tune, has heard the standard ways in which tunes are played, and has listened to multiple solos (maybe hundreds or even thousands) by influential practitioners. But those are merely some of the *possibility conditions* for jazz improvisation. How does one actually improvise? Pianist Tommy Flanagan puts it nicely when he says that "soloists elaborate upon what the structure of the piece has to say."[29] Flanagan's comment raises three further aspects of jazz improvisation—the "elaboration" involved in improvisation, the "structure of the piece," and what that piece "has to say."

Regarding elaboration, improvisation is always based *on* something, a point that has been surprisingly overlooked in some writing on improvisation. Most jazz is based on "pieces"—whether standards or something written by someone in one's band. In other words, jazz improvisation is usually hermeneutical in the sense of interpreting a preexisting schema.[30] And that hermeneutical dimension can be worked out in other ways: not only is most improvisation on a particular tune, but also it interprets the ways in which that tune has been played before, and even the performance tradition itself. "Blue in Green" is indeed by Miles Davis. But not only does the performance practice of playing that tune clearly influence how it is played, but also one's playing is in effect a "commentary" or interpretation of that performance practice. So improvisation is hermeneutical in multiple senses.

As to the "structure of the piece," jazz "pieces" are considerably "*under*determined" by the charts that one finds in a fake book or even sheet music. Usually, that underdetermination is actually the *intent* of the composer. So improvisation is always necessary. The questions are, though: (1) how much improvisation is needed? and (2) how much improvisation is allowed? The answers to those questions depend upon the genre of jazz (and, as we shall see later, the genre of other sorts of interpretation). Whereas early News Orleans jazz had relatively little space for improvisation, the history of jazz is—generally speaking—a history of widening space and thus fewer constraints.[31]

The last issue raised by Flanagan's comment is what "the structure of the piece *has to say*." I think it's very hard to separate this "saying" of the piece from the author—at least in any strict sense. Thus, I affirm E. D. Hirsch's emphasis on "authorial intention"—in at least one important way. Clearly composers (or authors) have intentions, or else they wouldn't come up with pieces (or theories or stories or poems) that they try to embody in charts, scores, and texts. Nor do I think that, once having come up with, say, "A Foggy Day," George Gershwin is simply out of the picture. Derrida himself provides what I take to be a telling example of the connection between author and text. Derrida translates Husserl's use of *Bedeutung* (meaning) as "*vouloir dire*"—wanting to say.[32] I take it that George Gershwin or any writer "wants to say something" (a phrase that certainly could be worked out in multiple ways). Even though Derrida is certainly right that a text can *mean* without the presence of the author,[33] we usually don't *simply* disconnect the two.[34] Note that Derrida himself *doesn't* simply disconnect them: in responding to John Searle, Derrida (rightly) accuses him of having "avoided reading *me*."[35] So Derrida sees a connection between himself and his text. In any case, I see no need to resurrect the author, simply because I think authors are always connected to texts, in varying ways and degrees.[36] Their death—as Mark Twain would put it—has been greatly exaggerated.

Practically, though, when I read a chart from a jazz fake book, I have the chart in front of me, and usually *not* the composer or author telling me what she meant.[37] Given that reality, it is understandable that theorists such as Beardsley and Gadamer make the text the locus of interpretation.[38] I assume, of course, that the chart was written by someone and that she had some intentions regarding how that chart ought to be played. Indeed, jazz improvisers routinely speak of what composers are "trying to say," and generally care about allowing that to come through in their improvising.[39] But, like most interpretation, jazz improvisation centers on whatever intentions of the author "made it" into the text or chart. Those intentions, of course, are interpreted in light of both current and past performance practice. Jazz, though, often has a third source of guidance or resource for interpretation—the way the "composers" play it themselves.[40] Of course, recordings made by the jazz composer are never taken as authoritative models to be *duplicated*, especially since multiple renditions (live or recorded) by a given composer of a particular piece will undoubtedly differ, and often substantially.[41]

The fifth aspect of jazz performance significantly overshadows the previous ones. If we were to speak in Derridean terms, we might put it as follows. The chart—along with performance practice—provides the "guardrail" that keeps an interpretation of "All the Things You Are" from turning into, say, "All the Things" or just "any old thing." It is what establishes the "boundaries" of a tune and what gives it ontological (as well as legal) identity. Yet the point of jazz isn't what Derrida terms a "doubling commentary" (i.e., the attempt to interpret a text as "literally" as possible).[42] In fact, "doubling" is what jazz musicians work so hard to avoid. One may start out by copying other improvisers, but that's not at all where one wants to end up. The goal is not "repetition," at least not in a literal or doubling sense. Although one can still be said to "play the piece," there is something *added* to it that transforms it.

Toward an Improvisational Hermeneutic

How might these features of jazz improvisation be applied to hermeneutics in general? As I said earlier, my proposal is that interpretation is inherently "improvisatory" in nature. That means we *might* substitute the term "improvisation" for "interpretation." In speaking that way, we would be acknowledging that interpretation is always a kind of "fabricating" out of that on hand. And we would likewise be pointing out that interpretation is never *simply* repetition, even though it is *always* that too. But, of course, there is a danger in simply substituting the term "improvisation" for "interpretation." Normally, we use the term "improvisation" to refer to particular sorts of musical or theatrical practices. Expanding the term "improvisation" to cover interpretational practices in general runs the risk of minimizing the particularity of these practices and losing a term that specifically designates them. So my goal here is *not* to replace the term "interpretation" with "improvisation." Rather, it is to show how interpretive practices have improvisational qualities.

In order to demonstrate the improvisational aspects of interpretation, I first will consider both points of analogy and ways in which jazz improvisation may be dissimilar to other types of interpretive activities. Second, I will turn to the ontological implications for the identity of the structure of either a piece of music or a literary text if both creative and interpretive activities have an improvisatory quality to them. Finally, I'll raise and briefly consider the question of whether there is a need for a special hermeneutic regarding biblical texts and their interpretation.

That jazz improvisers are situated within a practice is nothing unique. Anyone involved in a creative or an interpretive activity—indeed any activity—is always situated within such a practice, and usually multiple practices. It shouldn't be difficult to see that authors and composers improvise their texts from within such practices, as a few examples should make clear. One could point to Mozart's *Così fan tutte* as an "improvisation" on the opera buffa form that both stays remarkably close to the form (even imitating an aria from another opera) and yet shows Mozart (to quote John Platoff) "altering, subverting or transcending" its conventions.[43] Both the composition and the performance history of Shakespeare's plays provide layers of improvisation—in terms of the blurring of lines between "author" and "performer" and evolving identities over the centuries due to significantly different ways of performing them.[44] Biblical texts also provide multiple examples of such authorial improvisation. For instance, consider how Paul builds upon and expands Deuteronomy 6:4 ("Hear, O Israel: The Lord is our God, the Lord alone") and the early Christian hymn that he himself cites in Philippians 2:6–11 (especially verse 11, which reads "and every tongue should confess that Jesus Christ is Lord, to the glory of God the Father") in 1 Corinthians 8:6. There he says: "yet for us there is one God, the Father, from whom all things and for whom are all things through whom we exist." Paul "improvises" upon this Old Testament passage and early Christian hymn in such a way that inscribes a new reading within an old one, affirming both but transforming the old so that it can no longer be read in the same way. We could describe this improvisation in terms of Derrida's "iterability."[45] What Paul does is *both* repeat and alter, cite and transform.[46] Clearly, Christians would point out that Paul is not acting alone in this improvisation, but is guided by the Holy Spirit. Yet Paul is no less improvising for that.

To be sure, not all examples of writing are "improvisational" in these obvious senses. Often the way in which composers and writers "improvise" is much more subtle and noticeable only if one is familiar with the tradition in which the author is situated. And, of course, it may be that the more an author is "innovative," the less an author can be seen as "improvising" (though the exact correlation of "innovation" and "improvisation" is, I think, open to question). A further question, though, is the extent to which interpretive activity in general can rightly be called "improvisational." If we continue with a musical comparison, we can see that jazz performance practice differs considerably from the performance practice of classical music. The distinction between composer and performer is comparatively strong in classical music—not merely in terms of theory but also in terms of practice. What is allowed in jazz performance—such as the altering of the melody, the enrichment or substitution of chords, the repetition or deletion of particular parts of the piece—is generally not allowed in classical music. As a result, performers of classical music are far less important in establishing the identity of a particular piece of music. Thus the score—along with the guidelines of performance practice—is the primary determinant of the piece. Similarly, the author/reader distinction is much more akin to that of classical music than that of jazz, the result being that texts are much more like the "works" of classical composers than like the pieces found in jazz.

These dissimilarities, though, involve two basic aspects that need further qualification, and perhaps some rethinking. First, is the difference between the practice of jazz and that of classical music merely *quantitative*, or is it *qualitative*? Answering that question is not so easy. Underdetermination is likewise to be found in pieces of classical music, so performers are still involved in shaping those pieces—albeit to a much less significant degree. Further, how those notes are *played* explains why an interpretation by von Karajan or Stokowski not only *sounds* so different from one, say, by Hogwood or Harnoncourt, but may well have a different *effect* on us—and that effect may well cause us to favor one over the other. A particular rendition can mean something *different* to us than another, and may well affect us differently. So, even today, classical musicians are required to determine indeterminacies of the score in ways that have significant effects. Moreover, they are also able—again, within some limits—to choose which instructions of the composer they wish to follow or how to follow them. In performances of Beethoven symphonies, for example, his metronome markings are routinely ignored. Why? The answer is: that's just part of performance practice in classical music.[47] So even the score as notated is not necessarily *fully* authoritative. And there is a further complication in regard to classical music: although performance practice of classical music *today* is relatively rigid in its restrictions, even just a century ago those constraints were considerably less constraining than they are today. The result was that alterations to notes, elimination of movements, or significant changes in orchestration were comparatively common.[48] Indeed, the further one goes back in the performance practice of classical music, the fewer restrictions there are, with the result that the performer becomes an increasing contributor to the final result of the piece.[49] Contemporary performance practice of classical music is—in relation to the musical tradition out of which it grows—comparatively rigid.

But there is a second—and more significant—problem with these dissimilarities. For what we've discussed so far has to do only with the notes that are played (and, correspondingly, words on the page), rather than the *meanings* of either. Once we move to the level of meaning, the improvisational role of the interpreter becomes much more evident. For attempting to determine what "the piece has to say" or "the text has to say" is not merely a matter of playing the "right" notes or reading the words. Assuming that we really *do* care about authors and their intentions and thus consult their texts with care and with all the critical tools at our disposal, can the "performer" or reader *simply* repeat what the author has said? Earlier we mentioned Derrida's conception of a "doubling commentary" that acts as a "guardrail" for the text. While Derrida clearly thinks such a commentary is important, he also thinks that this "doubling" is possible only to a limited extent. For even in doubling there is already an improvisatory moment. Why? At least one reason is due to the underdetermination of texts that requires interpreters to "supply" aspects of the meaning (aspects that form what we usually term "context"). But, interestingly enough, that doubling (worthy as it is) is actually problematized precisely by the very theorist who insists that "*an unlimited number of different intentional acts can intend the same verbal meaning*"[50]—Hirsch himself. Consider what Hirsch says:

> Determinacy does not mean definiteness or precision. Undoubtedly, most verbal meanings are imprecise and ambiguous, and to call them such is to acknowledge their determinacy: they are what they are—namely ambiguous and imprecise—and they are not univocal and precise.[51]

The result of textual underdetermination coupled with "imprecise and ambiguous" meanings would seem to be that performers and readers are *always* "improvising." That is, for there to be an interpretation, performers and readers are required to fabricate out of what is on hand simply to "make" sense of what the text (or author) says. If one is serious about the author's intentions as expressed in the text, then that fabrication will be guided by the text. Moreover, that fabrication will surely differ culturally and historically—whether we are talking about "the Christian community" or "the jazz community" (assuming there are even such neatly defined communities). I need not provide a survey of the history of biblical exegesis, nor the history of interpretations of, say, Milton, nor the differences of performance practice of, for example, Bach's *St. Matthew Passion* to make that clear.

While my suggestion that interpretation is always improvisational—in varying degrees and senses—might seem "new" or "innovative," one finds it already in the classical rhetorician Quintilian, who writes the following:

> It is generally easier to make some advance than to repeat what has been done by others, since there is nothing harder than to produce an exact likeness, and nature herself has so far failed in this endeavour that there is always some difference [*différance*?] which enables us to distinguish even the things which seem most like and most equal to one another.[52]

Even when we try to be mere "imitators" or provide "literal" translations of texts, those imitations and translations invariably go beyond the text. What I am describing as "improvisation" is similar to what classical rhetoricians have described as "*inventione*," essentially the ability to improvise on the basis of an accumulated knowledge of rhetorical principles and examples. Here it is helpful to make a distinction between "rhetorical improvisation" and "Romantic improvisation." Gerald L. Bruns works out that distinction as follows:

> Rhetorical improvisation is related to embellishment and ornamentation or adornment; it is an art of doing something to what has already been done. In music or poetry it is a way of exceeding what is written by working between the lines or in the margin. . . . Romantic improvisation begins with a blank sheet of paper.[53]

I have already argued against the conception of Romantic improvisation by showing that it does not reflect actual practice. But one could likewise criticize it for being unduly individualistic and promoting a conception of artistic creation that neglects the significance of the community.

But, if interpreters are really "improvisers" (in the sense of "rhetorical improvisation," the sense for which I've argued in this essay), then what is the relation between improvisation and "the structure of the piece of music" or the "text"? Here we come to an important ontological question, and at least three possibilities suggest themselves.

The first ontological possibility is that *within* the very structure of the piece there are multiple meanings or profiles, so that the history of performance/interpretive practice is simply the history of *revealing* the possibilities that were always there. Improvisation, then, is not really a matter of making or fabricating anything "new" but simply bringing something to light. It is *merely* discovery. A second possible explanation would be that the "piece itself" or "text itself" is merely a bare schema, with the result that improvisational changes do not affect that piece or text. They are, instead, mere additions. On either of these construals—the first being what I'd characterize as the "thick" version of the piece or text, the second being a comparatively "thin" version—the piece or text remains essentially unchanged. A third possibility is that performance practice actually affects the very identity of the piece, not in the weak sense of bringing out possibilities but in the strong sense of actually "creating" (or, rather, improvising) them. But this complicates the identity of the piece. For, if such is the case, then the piece becomes in effect a historical entity that is affected by subsequent interpretations. On this account, the identity of the piece may subtly *change* over time, even though its identity would still be *continuous*. In such a case, its identity would be similar to many other historical entities, such as human persons, who retain their identity despite mental and physical changes. We might say that such a musical entity is situated *between* authorial and performer/reader improvisation, an *Ergon* [work] that finds its place within the musical *Energeia* [activity]. Gadamer's description of this situation is that such an entity "experiences, as it were, *an increase in being*," since the relationship is not merely "*one-sided*."[54] "'Round Midnight" provides a particularly dramatic example of performance practice affecting the identity of the piece, but far less dramatic examples abound in jazz. For instance, as I mentioned earlier, in jazz performance practice the "official" chords are often supplanted by other chords, which become the ones that everyone plays. Effectively, the piece *as played* redefines the identity of the piece.

But, of course, the issue here is whether performance/interpretive practice really has such a crucial effect on the piece as notated or the text as written.[55] I'm not sure that any argument could establish this question one way or the other. My own view is that pieces and texts are not quite so "ideal" as Husserl would have them and thus they are actually affected by history *ontologically*. Husserl believes that ideal objects are in no way affected either by their textual inscriptions or by their subsequent existence (as interpreted), a position with which Hirsch agrees. Yet it seems difficult to think that either pieces or texts are quite so "ideal" as that. In any case, even if they are ideal in this sense, our knowledge of them or access to them is clearly affected by the ways in which they are performed or read. So there may be no *ontological* effect, but there is clearly an *epistemological* effect. Still, as I say, I suspect that the adherents of each of these respective positions are unlikely to be persuaded to think otherwise, nor do I think there are any arguments that are sufficiently compelling.

In any case, the result of arguing for an improvisatory view of interpretive (and also creative) activity is that interpreters are not important merely in bringing the meaning of the text to life or to light but also become important in shaping that meaning—in either the weak epistemological sense or the strong metaphysical sense. But is this or *should* this be the case for the interpretation of scriptural texts? In other words, do we need a "special" hermeneutics for biblical texts (not in the sense of "helping us to interpret them" but in the sense of "explaining what interpreters do")? Actually, it seems to me that biblical hermeneutics has tended to serve as the pervasive model for interpretation in general. Nowhere is this more evident than in classical music, in which scores of composers are often treated much like holy writ. Yet it's not at all clear *why* the scores of composers should be treated this way, nor is it clear that a relatively narrow conception of interpretation is appropriate for the interpretation of, say, Dante or Carl Sandberg.

Yet the question still remains whether the improvisatory view is "fitting" for biblical interpretation. I think it is, though with two important caveats. First, to say that interpretation is improvisatory is to emphasize the role of interpreters in "fleshing out" the meaning of the text. Given that texts never "mean" by themselves and so must be "resuscitated" each time they are read (or performed) by interpretation, the role of the interpreter (or performer) is crucial. As I've argued, even the interpreter who is fully committed to the goal of respecting the text and the author's intentions is never simply "repeating" the text (or score). If texts and scores are "underdetermined," then the reading that results from an interpretation is *always* improvisatory. Second, having said that, there are clearly varying confines as to the "improvisation" that takes place—whether in performing jazz, classical music, or Shakespeare, or in reading the Old Testament. The limits on improvisation in bebop are not the same as those in New Orleans jazz. Nor is a pastor allowed to "improvise" on 1 Corinthians for a sermon in the same way that Paul was "allowed" to improvise on Old Testament and early Christian texts in composing 1 Corinthians. There are ways in which an improvisation can be deemed "faithful" to a text and ways in which it can be deemed "unfaithful." But the constraints on improvisation in interpretation are always dependent upon a given "discourse" or "practice," and cannot be easily codified into something like an "improvisational manual." So hermeneutical practices vary, and that variance seems perfectly appropriate. Moreover, there are variations even within, say, a practice such as Old Testament scholarship. Some Old Testament interpreters see themselves as working within relatively narrow boundaries, while others allow for considerably more interpretational "space."[56]

Conclusion

I began this paper by asking whether we could give justice to authors' intentions, the tradition from which texts and performances arise, the continuing tradition (or interpretive community) that preserves and nourishes those texts, and the role of interpreters. My concern here is a deeply ethical one. If the author should not die so that the reader may live, then neither should the reader have to die so that the author may live. As much as I want to honor authors and their texts, I likewise want to honor traditions and even individual interpreters. As interpreters, we owe much to authors and their texts. But authors and texts are—if not *equally*—at least *clearly* dependent upon interpreters and interpretive communities. Without interpreters, there can be no interpretation. And, without interpretation, there is no reason for an author to write or a text to exist. While authors' intentions are worthy of great respect, their intentions are not the only intentions to be respected.

So how might we both conceive and practice the "justice" of hermeneutics? Here I think jazz improvisation provides a helpful model. We have seen that jazz improvisers "elaborate" upon what Flanagan calls the "structure of the piece." The typical way in which jazz pieces are performed is that the "head" or melody is stated, then succeeding choruses improvise upon it, and then the performance concludes with a restatement of that melody. The goal of those choruses in between is to allow something to develop that is both linked to the "structure of the piece" and yet goes beyond it. The further one can go—and still remain in touch with the piece's structure—the better the improviser one is. Yet these choruses are framed by the head, within which improvisation takes place. Jazz improvisation, then, is situated within Derrida's "doubling commentary." While the first and last choruses are attempts to "get it right," those in between attempt to open a space for developing ideas, allowing different voices to emerge and considering alternative possibilities.

Such a model may not provide "true hermeneutical justice," but at least it takes us in that direction.

NOTES

1. Here I am referring to Paul Ricoeur's *The Conflict of Interpretations: Essays in Hermeneutics*, trans. Don Ihde (Evanston, IL: Northwestern University Press, 1974).

2. E. D. Hirsch, *Validity in Interpretation* (New Haven, CT: Yale University Press, 1967).

3. Monroe Beardsley, "The Authority of the Text," in *Intention and Interpretation*, ed. Gary Iseminger (Philadelphia: Temple University Press, 1992), pp. 24–40. The classic statement of Beardsley's position is found in William K. Wimsatt Jr. and Monroe C. Beardsley, "The Intentional Fallacy," in William K. Wimsatt Jr., *The Verbal Icon: Studies in the Meaning of Poetry* (Lexington: University Press of Kentucky, 1954), pp. 3–18.

4. Hans-Georg Gadamer, *Truth and Method*, 2nd rev. ed., trans. Joel Weinsheimer and Donald G. Marshall (New York: Continuum, 1989), pp. 306–307.

5. *Différance* is an aspect found (explicitly or implicitly) in most of Derrida's texts, though the essay "*Différance*," in *Margins of Philosophy*, trans. Alan Bass (Chicago: University of Chicago Press, 1982), pp. 3–27, provides the most extended discussion of it. For *iterability*, see Derrida's essay "Signature Event Context" in *Margins of Philosophy* (pp. 309–30) and his *Limited Inc* (Evanston, IL: Northwestern University Press, 1988). I will have more to say about both of these notions later.

6. Stanley Fish, *Is There a Text in This Class? The Authority of Textual Communities* (Cambridge, MA: Harvard University Press, 1980).

7. See Jacques Derrida, "Force of Law: The 'Mystical Foundation of Authority,'" in Jacques Derrida, *Acts of Religion*, ed. Gil Anidjar (New York: Routledge, 2002), pp. 230–98.

8. And yet the two are not as different as we might think. Interestingly enough, upon reading one of my early articles on jazz improvisation, an Old Testament scholar remarked: "Did you by any chance have Old Testament interpretation in mind when you wrote this? Because what you say about jazz describes what we do in interpreting the Old Testament. We take the text and improvise upon it." The article to which he referred is "Ingarden and

the Problem of Jazz," *Tijdschrift voor Filosofie* 55:4 (December 1993): 677–93. Although I had interpretation of other sorts of texts in mind (including biblical texts) while writing that article, this essay is my first attempt at working out that connection.

9. Quoted in Paul Berliner, *Thinking in Jazz* (Chicago: University of Chicago Press, 1994), p. 1.

10. *The Oxford English Dictionary*, 2nd ed., s.v. "improvisation."

11. Jerrold Levinson, "What a Musical Work Is," in *Music, Art, and Metaphysics: Essays in Philosophical Aesthetics* (Ithaca: Cornell University Press, 1990), pp. 66–67.

12. Paul Hindemith, *A Composer's World: Horizons and Limitations* (Garden City, NY: Anchor, 1961), p. 153; and Aaron Copland, *What to Listen for in Music* (New York: McGraw-Hill, 1957), p. 258.

13. Hindemith actually uses the metaphor of "transmission station" to describe the performer.

14. Roland Barthes, "The Death of the Author," in *Image, Music, Text*, trans. Stephen Heath (New York: Hill Wang, 1977), p. 148. Barthes wrote this essay in 1968, right at the time that the early music movement was gaining momentum.

15. *Merriam-Webster's Collegiate Dictionary*, 11th ed. (Springfield, Mass.: Merriam-Webster, 2003), s.v. "improvise." *This* definition—as I will show—much better reflects actual improvisational practice.

16. Edmund Husserl, *Formal and Transcendental Logic*, trans. Dorion Cairns (The Hague: Martinus Nijhoff, 1978), p. 81; and Jacques Derrida, *Edmund Husserl's* Origin of Geometry: *An Introduction*, trans. John P. Leavy (Stony Brook, NY: Nicolas Hays, 1978), p. 48.

17. Mozart is probably the quintessential example of such a conception. But our view of Mozart is largely predicated on a forged letter by the music critic Friedrich Rochlitz. As an adherent of Kant's theory of genius and a great supporter of Mozart, Rochlitz actually went so far as to forge a letter supposedly by Mozart, in which Mozart describes his creative process in precisely the way Kant speaks of the genius coming up with ideas out of nowhere. See Maynard Solomon, "Beethoven's Creative Process: A Two-Part Invention," in Maynard Solomon, *Beethoven Essays* (Cambridge, MA: Harvard University Press, 1988), pp. 128–29.

18. See Bruce Ellis Benson, *The Improvisation of Musical Dialogue: A Phenomenology of Music* (Cambridge: Cambridge University Press, 2003), ch. 2.

19. *Thinking in Jazz*, p. 88.

20. David Fuller, "The Performer as Composer," in *Performance Practice*, vol. 2, ed. Howard Mayer Brown and Stanley Sadie (Houndsmills, U.K.: Macmillan, 1989), pp. 117–46.

21. Note that Mel Torme gets partial credit for reworking the "The Christmas Song," which he found on the piano of his friend Robert Wells, who'd written the song in a particularly hot July in order to get his mind off the heat and was out in the pool when Torme arrived at his house.

22. Perhaps the issue of proper "credit" regarding "'Round Midnight" might well be more important to the Monk estate—for obvious financial reasons—than to either players or those chronicling the history of jazz.

23. A further—and fascinating—example of multiple authorship is that of film scripts. It is common practice for a studio to buy the rights to a script from a screenwriter (or screenwriters) and then have that script reworked by as many as a dozen people. Because this multiple authorship makes the notion of credit difficult to establish, there is actually an

official review board that makes decisions as to who exactly gets credited with having written the script. Oddly enough, given the formulas by which the review board establishes who counts as the writers, the "original" screenwriter (from whom the studio bought the rights) is often not even mentioned as one of the screenwriters in the film credits.

24. While it is true that *both* performers and listeners are improvisers, pursuing the implications of the "improvisation" of listening is beyond the scope of this paper.

25. See Alasdair MacIntyre, *After Virtue*, 2nd ed. (Notre Dame, IN: University of Notre Dame Press, 1981), p. 190. While MacIntyre gives us a relatively "benign" conception of communal activities in the notion of a "practice," Michel Foucault reminds us that such activities (or, to use his term, "discourses") always have a dimension of power at work in them. See, for instance, "The Discourse on Language," in Michel Foucault, *The Archaeology of Knowledge*, trans. A. M. Sheridan Smith (New York: Pantheon, 1972), pp. 215–37. Also see Nicholas Wolterstorff's "The Work of Making a Work of Music," in Philip Alperson, *What Is Music? An Introduction to the Philosophy of Music* (University Park: Pennsylvania State University Press, 1994). Here Wolterstorff presents an account of the composition of classical music in terms of MacIntyre's conception of a practice.

26. While Kant may be partially right in claiming that "if an author owes a product to his genius, he himself does not know how he came by the idea for it," the "inspiration" that we might find in authors, composers, readers, and performers is always situated within the context of a practice. See Immanuel Kant, *Critique of Judgment*, trans. Werner Pluhar (Indianapolis: Hackett, 1987), §46.

27. Gadamer, for instance, emphasizes that rules make play possible. See *Truth and Method*, p. 107.

28. Some of the constraints of free jazz arise from playing in a group (which means that one needs to listen to what others are playing and "play along"—whatever form that takes). But other constraints are there simply because one is playing "jazz" (however far-out and experimental) rather than "rap" or "bluegrass."

29. *Thinking in Jazz*, p. 170.

30. While this claim may seem obvious, note that Philip Alperson says "interpretation, a prime feature of conventional musical performance, may be safely said to be absent from an improvisation: it makes no sense to characterize an improvisation as an interpretation or to praise it as a good interpretation of a previously existing work since no such work exists." See Philip Alperson, "On Musical Improvisation," *Journal of Aesthetics and Art Criticism* 63 (1984): 26.

31. As with any generalizations, this one certainly has exceptions. Just one exception would be the big band arrangements of Stan Kenton, which were designed to be played more or less "as is."

32. Jacques Derrida, *Speech and Phenomena*, trans. David B. Allison (Evanston, IL: Northwestern University Press, 1973), p. 32.

33. If, as Derrida argues, "my death is structurally necessary to the pronouncing of the I" (*Speech and Phenomena*, p. 96), then my death is certainly structurally necessary to the writing of a text.

34. Similarly, I agree with P. D. Juhl that when we appeal to the text in favor of a particular interpretation (and this could be musical or otherwise), we are usually—or at least often—appealing indirectly to something like the author's intention. See P. D. Juhl, *Interpretation: An Essay in the Philosophy of Literary Criticism* (Princeton: Princeton University Press, 1980), p. 149.

35. *Limited Inc*, p. 113 (my italics).

36. One way of thinking of the presence of the author in a text is in terms of the trace, a notion that Derrida picks up from Levinas. See Emmanuel Levinas, "La Trace de l'autre," *Tijdschrift voor Filosophie* 25:3 (September 1963): 605–23.

37. Or else I've learned the tune from listening to someone else play it, either live or from a recording.

38. Thus Beardsley claims that "literary works are self-sufficient entities" in his essay "The Authority of the Text," p. 24. While Beardsley is right to move the locus of interpretation from mental divination of the author's intentions to the intentions of the author as embodied in the text, his account fails to ground the text in the tradition, or what we might call the "reading practice," of interpretive communities. In contrast, Gadamer accomplishes both moves in *Truth and Method.*

39. The pianist Marian McPartland makes an even stronger claim when she says that she finds it helpful to know the lyrics of the tune in order to play it (an interesting claim, since the lyrics are often written by someone else and often at a later—or earlier—date).

40. Such may be the case whenever the composer and performer are contemporaries, for jazz musicians tend to know one another, listen to each other's playing, and often play together. Even in the case of dead composers, their own renditions have often been recorded. In this regard, jazz is different from, say, the interpretation of New Testament texts, for there is no possibility of that sort of contemporaneity.

41. An interesting—if somewhat odd—example of the attempt to duplicate the performances of a composer is by Jean-Yves Thibaudet (who, not surprisingly, is a classical musician). His CD "Conversations with Bill Evans" (London 455 512–2) contains transcriptions of Evans playing his own tunes and those of others. Of course, Thibaudet may play the same notes, but he makes no pretensions of playing them the same way. So the attempt at duplication is only partial.

42. Jacques Derrida, *Of Grammatology*, corrected ed., trans. Gayatri Chakravorty Spivak (Baltimore: Johns Hopkins University Press, 1998), p. 158.

43. John Platoff, "How Original Was Mozart? Evidence from *opera buffa*," *Early Music* 20 (1992): 105–106.

44. See Stephen Orgel, "The Authentic Shakespeare," *Representations* 21 (1988): 1–25.

45. Derrida describes iterability as "alterability of this same idealized in the singularity of the event, for instance, in this or that speech act. It entails the necessity of thinking *at once* both the rule and the event, concept and singularity." See *Limited Inc*, p. 119. Although Jacques Derrida explicitly works out the notion of "iterability" in "Signature Event Context" and *Limited Inc*, the idea is already present in his discussions of Husserl, particularly *Edmund Husserl's* Origin of Geometry: *An Introduction* and *Speech and Phenomena.* Certainly, it is connected to the notion of *différance* (and Derrida explicitly connects them in "Signature Context Event"). So we might say that the concept of iterability is an example of iterability.

46. Note that Derrida says that "everything begins with reproduction" in "Freud and the Scene of Writing," in *Writing and Difference*, trans. Alan Bass (Chicago: University of Chicago Press, 1978), p. 211, and likewise that "everything, 'begins', then, with citation" in "WriTing, EncaSing, ScreeNing," in *Dissemination*, trans. Barbara Johnson (Chicago: University of Chicago Press, 1981), p. 316.

47. For anyone who has heard those symphonies performed at full tilt, it's clear that the difference is dramatic (rather than merely "negligible").

48. Although Gustav Mahler (conductor of the New York Philharmonic from 1909

to 1911) was criticized by some regarding his free alterations to Beethoven's orchestration, Otto Klemperer claimed that Mahler remarked (regarding his own Eighth Symphony) that anyone could make changes to it "with an easy conscience." See Lawrence W. Levine, *Highbrow/Lowbrow: The Emergence of Cultural Hierarchy in America* (Cambridge, MA: Harvard University Press, 1988), pp. 138–39.

49. Of course, on the other hand, perhaps the freedom to change melodies and harmonies that one finds in jazz can become so great that the difference becomes *qualitative* in nature. In jazz improvisation, one can wander so far from the piece as written that the result is something that sounds remarkably different from the piece played "straight." I suspect that the only way to decide either way would be to examine different styles of jazz and individual cases of improvising. Even then, I'm not sure that the "quantitative/qualitative" question would be truly decidable.

50. *Validity in Interpretation*, p. 38.

51. Ibid., p. 44.

52. Quintilian, *Institutio Oratia*, vol. 4, trans. H. E. Butler (Cambridge, MA: Harvard University Press, 1922), 10.2.10. This quotation from Quintilian—and the connection to classical rhetoric—was brought to my attention only *after* I had written an earlier draft of this paper.

53. Gerald L. Bruns, *Inventions: Writing, Textuality, and Understanding in Literary History* (New Haven: Yale University Press, 1982), p. 147.

54. *Truth and Method*, p. 140.

55. Here I will avoid the issue of non-notated music.

56. Of course, this raises the possibility of a difference between what people *actually do* and what they *think they are doing*.

11

Ethical Hermeneutics and the Theater

Shakespeare's *Merchant of Venice*

Ben Faber

In his magisterial lectures on Shakespearean tragedy published in 1904, A. C. Bradley speaks of Shakespeare's characters as though they are real, as though outside the play they have an existence in which they behave in a manner consistent with their behavior on the stage.[1] Bradley could speak about Shakespeare's characters in this way because he believed that each character has an "essence" that is greater than the sum of the parts that the character plays on the stage. An actor's performance of the character may vary in interesting ways from other actors' performances of the same character, but it must always be a true representation of the character's essence. The work of most twentieth-century critics, such as Catherine Belsey, Terry Eagleton, and Jonathan Dollimore, is deliberately anti-essentialist in its critique of the notion of the autonomous, stable human subject of liberal humanism.[2] Writing as heirs of Nietzsche, Marx, Sartre, Wittgenstein, and other existential materialists, academic critics in the latter half of the twentieth century seek to demonstrate that the universalist notions of personality, character, and essence are merely illusions.

The anti-essentialism of Shakespeare criticism is reflected in the anti-illusionism of many productions of Shakespeare on the stage. To reveal the fictiveness of an essentially coherent world on stage, anti-illusionist productions are often visually minimal, with an emphasis on *hearing* over seeing, *sound* over sight, even *voice* over body.[3] While realistic stage settings perpetuate the illusion of an orderly world by presenting such a world ready-made, anti-illusionist productions force the audience to construct the world of the stage and the reality of its characters. Bertolt Brecht and George Bernard Shaw, and later Samuel Beckett and Eugene Ionesco, deliberately alienated their audiences in order to shatter the illusion of essence and coherence that the theater as an institution continued to promote. Since anti-illusionism shatters the aesthetic completeness of the play, the audience struggles to compose its fragments into a coherent whole; the wholeness/coherence of the play (plot as well as character) is not objective and actual, but subjective and constructed. Shakespeare was himself interested in the role of the audience in the problem of theatrical representation. In *A Midsummer Night's Dream,* Shakespeare uses a company of amateur actors to perform a play-within-the-play that highlights the nature of theatrical representation. The aristocratic audience, for whom the play-within-the-play is performed, comment on the bad acting of the amateur performers:

> HIPPOLYTA: This is the silliest stuff that ever I heard.
> THESEUS: The best in this kind are but shadows; and the worst are no worse, if imagination amend them.
> HIPPOLYTA: It must be your imagination then, and not theirs.
> (5.1.209–211)[4]

For these characters, the transformative power of the imagination "amends" the "shadows" or illusions to allow the audience to see a coherence in a world that is presented as fundamentally incoherent. Thus, in post-structuralist productions of Shakespeare's plays, one further illusion needs to be dispelled: the myth of a unified audience. The cultural diversity of the postmodern condition suggests that, rather than a single entity ("the audience") constructing meaning from the representation of reality on the stage, individual spectators generate meaning—the hermeneutic experience in the theater becomes private, individual, heterogeneous. The anti-illusionist theater shatters a double hegemony: that of an authoritarian (directorial) imposition of coherence from the stage and that of a totalizing interpretation by a homogeneous audience.

The Bradleyesque conception of character in criticism and the traditional, realistic representation of character in the theater have been irreparably damaged by post-structuralist criticism and anti-illusionist production of Shakespeare. The deliberately politicized, theory-driven practices in many productions of Shakespeare's plays have the effect of alienating audiences who long for a nostalgic return to the Shakespeare of their imagining. Post-structuralist theory and practice have been too successful in alienating the audience, to the point where Shakespeare has become inaccessible and almost meaningless. The question is: Can productions of Shakespeare's plays be relevant, pertinent, vital, and effective without reverting to either the naïve naturalism or the aesthetic formalism that preceded the anti-illusionist phase? Can the theater function as a site of meaningful exchange without invoking premodern myths of reality, even "myths" of character, time, representation, and the unified subject? Can the debate at the "crossroads" of hermeneutics help ease the crisis of representation in the theater? This paper will modestly propose that reading and staging Shakespeare's plays with an "ethical hermeneutics" can liberate, energize, even redeem post-structuralist criticism and production. Drawing on the work of Hans-Georg Gadamer and Paul Ricoeur on the ontological status of art, I will then turn to Emmanuel Levinas for an ethical philosophy that will result in a hermeneutical practice that seeks to understand and respond to the face and voice of the Other in the act of reading. The "text" that is read by the audience in the theater is the performance event as it unfolds in time, in which the audience encounters the Other in a real and embodied, rather than an imaginary or abstract, person of the character. Such an encounter with the Other in the theater requires an ethical hermeneutics, a reflection upon the obligation that one owes to the representation of the other, as a brief discussion of the character Shylock in Shakespeare's *The Merchant of Venice* will demonstrate. Our very unease about this allegedly antisemitic play can be productive of justice and charity when one sees it as an encounter with the other in the hermeneutical experience of the world of the play while we exist with it.

Ethical Hermeneutics and the Ontological Status of Art

Gadamer's Fourth Wall

The first part of Gadamer's *Truth and Method* addresses "the question of truth as it emerges in the experience of art" in order to establish the aesthetic basis of the hermeneutic theory that unfolds in *Truth and Method*.[5] Gadamer begins his work on hermeneutics with aesthetic theory, rather than ontology or some other branch of metaphysics, in order to address the prevailing Romantic model of interpretation. Specifically, Gadamer begins with a critical engagement of Kantian aesthetic theory in order to revise the subjective conception of hermeneutics in the Romantics. In the subjectification of aesthetic truth by Kant and the Romantics, the subject is differentiated from the object of art: truth (destabilized and relative in such a perspectivalist approach) is in the "I" of the beholder, not in the art-object. The hermeneutical question (where is meaning located?) is thus a variation of the aesthetic question: where does truth lie?[6] Gadamer answers this question by shifting the discussion of aesthetics to the ontology of the work of art. The experience of art is ontological (not merely aesthetic) for reasons that are central to his hermeneutic; the status of art and the beholder's participation in its existence are the ground of Gadamer's hermeneutic. Rather than a separation of subject and object, the two are joined in the hermeneutical experience.

The work of art does not "exist for-itself" or "in-itself," but for the beholder who completes it. The "fourth wall" of art—that is, the beholder, audience, spectator, reader—is not separate from the performance of art but is necessary for its existence: "the play itself is the whole, comprising players and spectators" (109). It is the presence, not the absence, of a fourth wall that defines art. Rather than the aesthetic differentiation of the aesthetic consciousness—when the spectator retains self-consciousness as "spectator"—Gadamer makes the beholder a participant of the thing that is "art": "The spectator does not hold himself at the distance characteristic of an aesthetic consciousness enjoying the art with which something is represented, but rather participates in the communion of being present" (132). The being of the spectator is not a *subjective* but an *objective* reality of the existence and essence of the play (124–25): the spectator is "being-there-present" (in participation, involvement, unity) rather than "being-attentive-to-the-thing" (in difference, distance, alienation). The temporal dimension of aesthetic experience is thus not a projection of the present into the past of the art (a "making-it-contemporary"), but a contemporaneous existence (*gleichzeitig*) in the "essence of being present" (127) that is the aesthetic experience. "[T]he spectator belongs essentially to the playing of the play" (130), transcending the subject/object distinction in the temporal aspect of art, and in the location of its truth. "The player, sculptor, or viewer is never simply swept away into a strange world of magic, of intoxication, of dream; rather, it is always his own world, and he comes to belong to it more fully by recognizing himself more profoundly in it. There remains a continuity of meaning which links the work of art with the existing world and from which even the most alienated consciousness of a cultured society never quite detaches itself" (133–34).

What Gadamer proposes for the reading of art is particularly apropos for hermeneutics in the theater. The members of the audience are not subjects, merely observing an object at a distance from them: instead, we have a special relationship as we coexist with the world on the stage and share the same air as the characters. With the general demise of the proscenium-arch stage—which saw its rise in the aesthetic phase of theater production, when the action of the play was framed like a picture—the distinction between playing area (stage) and audience is even further elided. Rather than objectively beholding the action of a play, Gadamer's ontological hermeneutics has us "being-present" with the subjects in the world of the stage. The analogy with the game that Gadamer develops in this portion of *Truth and Method* has further relevance for the play; the audience willingly suspends its disbelief, allowing itself into delusion for the duration of the "play" (*lusus*). Furthermore, the continuity of meaning between the work of art and the existing world that Gadamer argues is central to the hermeneutical experience of art is particularly felt in the audience's participation in a play. Unlike a static painting or the repeatable viewing of film or the *déjà-ecrit* (already written) nature of a novel, which may have the illusion of contemporaneity, the world of the play is literally and really happening before the audience. The "text" is performed by the actors, in collaboration with the script, the set, and the director, whose meaning is understood by the audience as it emerges over the course of the play. Meaning, which is the goal of the hermeneutical undertaking, exists in the dynamic "becoming" of the play as it is performed, often with the subtle contribution of the audience and the context of the performance. The ontological oneness with the work of art that the audience experiences makes the act of understanding a play less an aesthetic and more an ethical one, when one considers that the "text" consists of persons, not things, whose faces the audience sees and whose voices the audience hears. The audience is the silent participant in the events, nonspeaking witnesses of the words and actions on the stage, with whom the characters coexist for the duration of the play.

Ricoeur's Participatory Belonging

Ricoeur adds to Gadamer's notion of the reader's ontological oneness with the work the idea that this belonging also implies a surrender to the world of the text. If "fusion" is a word that one associates with Gadamer, then "mediation" is a word one could associate with Paul Ricoeur.[7] Ricoeur refers sympathetically to at least three dichotomies or paradoxes that Gadamer resolves: temporal, hermeneutical, and ontological. First, there is the problem of immediacy and critical differentiation: what Ricoeur calls "a paradox of otherness, a tension between proximity and distance" (61) that Gadamer resolves in the "fusion of historical horizons." The problem of temporal estrangement is solved, in Ricoeur's terms, when the reader receives the world opened to her/him by the text. Second, Ricoeur describes Gadamer's project as deciding the debate between "alienating distanciation" of the scientific approach to *explanation*, and the "experience of belonging" of the humanities approach to *understanding* (60). Ricoeur negotiates a similar resolution to the tension between these two attitudes or purposes of reading with his "hermeneutical arc":

> If . . . we regard structural analysis as a stage—and a necessary one—between a naïve and a critical interpretation, between a surface and a depth interpretation, then it seems possible to situate explanation and interpretation along a unique *hermeneutical arc* and to integrate the opposed attitudes of explanation and understanding within an overall conception of reading as the recovery of meaning. (161)

Rather than opposing poles—the distanciation of anti-historicist *explanation* (*erklaren*, sense) and the participation in the world of the text in *understanding* (*verstahen*, meaning)—the two collaborate in an overall conception of reading. A third problem remains to be addressed—the ontological dichotomy of subject and object.

As we saw earlier, Gadamer describes an ontological fusion that includes artist, art-object, and beholder in the performance of play: "Neither the being that the creating artist is for himself—call it his biography—nor that of whoever is performing the work, nor that of the spectator watching the play, has any legitimacy of its own in the face of the being of the artwork itself" (Gadamer, 128). Ricoeur often sounds remarkably Gadamerian, as in the phrase "co-belonging with the text," but also in his reference to an existence within the text: "to understand a text, we shall say, is not to find a lifeless sense which is contained therein, but to unfold the possibility of being indicated by the text" (56). Without a reader to unfold the possibility of being in the text, such being remains consigned to eternal potentiality. Not only do readers realize the possibility of the being in the text, "the possible modes of being" in the text are "possible symbolic dimensions of our being-in-the-world" (177). But further to a symbolic reflection of our situation of being (*Umwelt*), Ricoeur holds to a "participatory belonging" (131) to the world opened by the text in the experience of "appropriation," by which Ricoeur means the following:

> that the interpretation of a text culminates in the better self-interpretation of a subject who thenceforth understands himself better, understands himself differently, or simply begins to understand himself. (158)

Ricoeur's essay entitled "Appropriation" springs off from Gadamer's meditation on the aesthetic sphere, specifically the section on the ontological status of the artwork and the idea of art as "play." Ricoeur appropriates Gadamer's reflections on the subjective experience of art in order to describe "the way in which a text is *addressed to* someone" (182). The objectification of meaning may be a necessary step between the writer and the reader, but is only en route to the appropriation of meaning by the reader: *Aneignen*, or "'to make one's own' what was initially alien" (185). "Appropriation is the concept which is suitable for the actualisation of meaning as addressed to someone" (185). As in Gadamer's notion of "play," for Ricoeur, the reader forgets his subjectivity in playing: "we hand ourselves over, we abandon ourselves to the space of meaning which holds sway over the reader" (187), we experience a metamorphosis from "cognition" to "recognition"—from seeing an object to seeing ourselves: "it is always a question of entering into an alien work, of divesting oneself of the earlier 'me' in order to receive, as in play, the self conferred by the work itself" (190). Paradoxically, therefore, "appropriation" is simultaneously active and passive, "making one's own what is alien" and letting go, relinquishing, divesting, receiving: "appropriation ceases to appear as a kind of possession, as a way of taking hold of. . . . It implies instead a moment of dispossession of the narcissistic *ego*" (192). Ultimately, for Ricoeur, the "theme of appropriation" is subordinated to the "theme of manifestation" (193): "To understand is not to project oneself into the text; it is to receive an enlarged self from the apprehension of proposed worlds which are the genuine object of interpretation" (182–83).

Ricoeur's "participatory belonging" to the world opened to the reader by the text is similar to Gadamer's coexisting with the text in that it places the audience in a dynamic relationship with the text of the play. Not quite the same as the fusion of horizons in Gadamer, the mediation between the reader and the text in Ricoeur is a process of recovery, not only of the historical distance between the reader and the world of the text, but of the reader's sense of self. The sort of hermeneutics that Ricoeur proposes has particular relevance to the question of reading Shakespeare. Being a participant as a member of the audience in a production of *Julius Caesar*, for instance, involves the mediation of a number of historical and conceptual fields: with a play set in ancient Rome, spoken in Elizabethan English, and produced in the twenty-first century, the audience have to make sense of this performance of *Julius Caesar and* recover the meaning of the play for themselves. It is as though Ricoeur takes Gadamer's concepts of the ontological oneness and the dynamic performance of meaning one step further to reflect upon the reader's self. Co-belonging to the world of *Julius Caesar* brings one to self-interpretation and self-understanding.

Producing an Ethical Hermeneutics

If we take literally Ricoeur's metaphorical "audience," and if we redefine his "text" as discourse animated in speech and action on the stage (rather than "discourse fixed by writing" [145]), the implications of Gadamer's meditation on the aesthetic sphere are provocative for considering the theater: the hermeneutical experience of the audience as participants in the play involves a losing of oneself in the world of the performance. Without negating our own historical situatedness, as members of the audience we become participants in the "real time" of the performance: the duration of the action of the play is simultaneous with our temporality. Our individual and collective "horizons" are fused temporally and ontologically with the characters and the world on the stage. Our existence for the duration of the performance is coterminous with the existence of the characters and world in the play; we share our existence for the time being. We are not beholding (attending) a play, but are participating in its very existence. Despite their emphasis on one's relationship with the world of the text, even with the "otherness" encountered in the text, neither Gadamer nor Ricoeur develops fully the *ethical* dimension of the relationship with the world opened by the text. Ricoeur may gesture at the historical "otherness" of the text, to which we open ourselves, but we need to consider more fully the reader's obligation or responsibility toward the other. The hermeneutical experience for Gadamer and Ricoeur is ultimately more about the self than the other—an enlarged, enriched, deepened self, but a "self" nonetheless. As John Caputo has written: "Gadamerian hermeneutics needs to be pushed beyond itself, pushed in a direction it says it wants to go but about which it drags its feet, enticed to welcome an other for which its anticipatory forestructures cannot prepare or be prepared. That results in a more radical rendering of hermeneutics by deconstruction, one that holds the feet of hermeneutics more mercilessly to the fires of facticity and alterity."[8] How, then, do we construe our encounter with the other in the experience of the theater? What is our obligation toward the other in the shared existence of the play?

In order to understand our relationship with the characters with whom we participate in the shared experience of art, we must first consider the nature of a character's existence on the stage. Although Aristotle deals with "ethos" as "character" in *Poetics* 15, the use of the word "character" to describe the traits or personality of a fictional person is relatively recent.[9] Before the idea of character in the current sense, "character" was a typographical term referring to a sign or letter that was consistent and recognizable. Further in the history of "character," the term came to refer to stereotypes of personalities such as the braggart, the hypocrite, the gourmand, the puritan, the merchant, and so on. Here "character" functions as an emblem, referring to a set of features or characteristics common to the type of person it describes. Medieval morality plays rely heavily on the ready identification of such stock characters on the stage for the audience, and Shakespeare is among the first to develop realistic characterization. Characters in the plays of the mature Shakespeare do not simply conform to type, but are more complex, with psychological depth and conflicted motives. These characters are not types but persons, presented by actors who appear in their stead—just as a press secretary stands in the place of the person she/he represents, so the actor speaks in the voice and persona of the character.[10] Thomas Hobbes, writing on authority and agency in *Leviathan* (I.xvi), remarks:

> a *person* is the same that an *actor* is, both on the stage and in common conversation; and to *personate* is to *act* or *represent* himself or another; and he that acts another is said to bear his person, or act in his name. . . . And then the person is the *actor*, and he that owns his words and actions is the AUTHOR, in which case the actor acts by authority.[11]

The audience encounters not a mere literary creation, but a person who "personates" the character of the play; we do not encounter "some*thing*" but "some*one*." The difference, then, between a character in a novel (even a character in a film) and a character in a play on the stage is the person.[12] When John Marston publishes *The Malcontent* in 1604, he apologizes in the epistle to the reader that "Scenes invented, meerely to be spoken, should be inforcively published to be reade." He then adds:

> my inforced absence must much relye upon the Printers discretion: but I shal intreat, slight errors in orthography may bee as slightly or'e-passed; and that the unhandsome shape which this trifle in reading presents, may bee pardoned, for the pleasure it once afforded you, when it was presented with the soule of lively action.[13]

One is tempted to conflate the two absences in the publication into one image of the removal "acting by authority" that Hobbes described in relation to "personation": not only is Marston physically absent from the printing of *The Malcontent*, but "the soule of lively action" on the stage is absent from the play in print form. All that remains of the life that was animated by action on the stage is the "unhandsome shape" of the book and the lifeless traces on the page. The other direction, that from text to performance, involves the incarnation of person in the body:

> The movement from script to performance liberates the play from its exclusively linguistic embodiment: language becomes speech, directions become *mise-en-scene*, implied presence becomes performance reality. Production realizes the play as something outside the printed text, and as such it stands on its own, shaped only invisibly by the text it seeks to embody.[14]

Thomas Heywood, in *An Apologie for Actors* (1612), expresses positively what Marston complains of in the lifeless printed play:

> Oratory is a kind of speaking picture. . . . Painting likewise, is a dumb oratory. . . . A Description is only a shadow received by the eare but not perceived by the eye: so lively portraiture is meerely a forme seene by the eye, but can neither shew action, passion, motion, or any other gesture, to moove the spirits of the beholder to admiration: but to see a souldier shap'd like a souldier, walke, speake, act like a souldier . . . as if the Personater were the man Personated.[15]

If the stage is about embodiment and actual presence, rather than abstraction and absence of person, then the hermeneutical experience in the theater takes on special ethical importance. The sort of hermeneutical question that one asks in experiencing a play, as Gerald Bruns suggests regarding tragedy, is not "What is it to understand *King Lear*?" but "What is it to *be* King Lear?"[16] Stanley Cavell observes: "After Paul Scofield's performance in *King Lear*, we know who King Lear is, we have seen him in the flesh."[17] The fleshliness of the character on the stage is, then, not merely a figurative incarnation of character but a real incarnation of person. Unlike our relationship with literary fictional characters, which Peter van Inwagen has described as being "theoretical entities," we meet dramatic characters in the theater as actual entities. Referring to a colorful character in Dickens, van Inwagen writes: "Mrs. Gamp is a theoretical entity of criticism, and we could no more touch her than we could touch a plot or a sonnet."[18] The relationship that the reader has with a character in a novel is different from the relationship the audience has with a character on the stage; the difference is not only in the degree of illusion necessary to make the character believable, but also in the kind of illusion involved. I am arguing here that the theatrical character has a different ontological status precisely because we *can* touch him or her, even though the character ceases to be when the curtain drops and the actor reemerges from the character she or he has played. Without returning to Bradley's essentialist view of character with which this paper began, and without referring to mystical notions of "aura" in artistic representation, we can yet imbue the character in the theater with personhood and the substance that it entails. This has obvious ethical implications: How then do I receive the person I encounter in the theater? What is my obligation to him/her? If, following the ontological argument of Gadamer and Ricoeur, I "belong to" and "participate in" the world of the text, how am I received by the person on the stage?

Ethical Hermeneutics on Stage

Levinas: Seeing the Face, Hearing the Voice

For Emmanuel Levinas, the ethical encounter with the "other" is not focused exclusively on the face, but is also attentive to the voice. Given our participation in the ontological space and time of the world on the stage, the audience (not "spectators") hear the otherness of characters in the spoken word. In his essay on the French poet Michel Leiris, Levinas writes of a "presence" in the living or spoken word that transcends the merely symbolic or iconic function of the written sign; Levinas contrasts "the living word, which is destined to be heard" and "the word that is an image and already a picturesque sign":

> Words are disfigured or "frozen," when language is transformed into documents and vestiges. The living word struggles against this transfer of thought into vestige, it struggles with the letter that appears when there is no-one there to hear. . . . To speak is to interrupt my existence as a subject and a master, but without offering myself up as a spectacle. I am simultaneously a subject and an object.[19]

Elsewhere, Levinas depicts the ethical encounter as the "situation of the face-to-face."[20] Although the spoken word realizes the presence of the other in a way that the image of the face does not, Levinas can be read as holding "a theory of meaning based on literal envisaging," in the words of George Steiner:

> this is to say of the vision we have of the face, of the expressive "thereness" of the other human person. The "open impenetrability" of that visage, its alien yet confirmatory mirroring of our own, enact the intellectual and ethical challenge of the relations of man to man and of man to that which Levinas terms "infinity" (the potentialities of relationship are always inexhaustible).[21]

Whether one emphasizes the voice or the face, the word or the image, in his aesthetics, Levinas ultimately cannot accept the notion of art as merely the representation of "other"; such a mimetic conception of art is essentially idolatrous.[22] The theater is the place of the word spoken and of the face presented.

Hath Not a Jew Eyes? Shylock's Challenge of Ethical Engagement

Let us imagine a late-twentieth-century American production of Shakespeare's *The Merchant of Venice* with a primarily non-Jewish cast and audience. If we were not aware of the controversy about the play's alleged antisemitism before we took our seats in the theater, the director's notes in the program undoubtedly will allude to her or his handling of the sensitive subject of racism. We may be vaguely aware of the history of antisemitism in Europe in the early-modern period; we may have heard about the medieval laws that officially banned Jews from England; we may even be aware of the hypocrisy of economic practices in Elizabethan England that relied on the wealth of Jews to bankroll colonization. Perhaps we can imagine living in the 1590s in London, a city bustling with prosperity, under a Protestant monarch in a nation that saw itself as the crown jewel of Christendom, where Jews were not ubiquitous but also not uncommon, and going to the Globe Theater to see *The Merchant of Venice*. Then, as we read further in the program notes, the director refers to antisemitism in the nineteenth and twentieth centuries, to the use of *Merchant of Venice* for propagandist purposes in Nazi Germany, to the Holocaust. Perhaps the director will refer to more recent examples of racism in our own community—swastikas painted on the doors of the local synagogue, desecration in the Jewish cemetery. With the brief history of antisemitism, the director justifies the Edwardian costumes and setting used in this performance. Before we can think through the implications of the vexing and complex issue of antisemitism, as well as our complicity in history, the houselights in the theater grow dim and the play begins.

Admittedly, in Shakespeare's text, Shylock does not play a prominent role: he appears in only five scenes. Nevertheless, Shylock plays a central role in the single most emotionally charged scene of the play: the court scene. But Shylock's heightened significance in our imagined performance comes not from the text of Shakespeare's play. Shylock's importance in the play comes from the history of antisemitism of the past four hundred years, especially of the twentieth century. For the duration of the play in the theater, several historical horizons converge: Shakespeare's England (especially through the language, but also its sociopolitical context), the play's setting in sixteenth-century Venice, the setting for this production in England of the 1920s, and the historical facticity of North America in the year of the performance. Shylock's importance in the play is not the product merely of Shakespeare's intention, nor simply the historical reality of the Venice that Shakespeare represents, nor exclusively the atrocities of the Holocaust, nor predominantly the events in our community, but all of these. We are not in a suspension of historicity in the theater—we are present in an omni-temporality, a fusion of all those horizons.[23]

Shylock is not an attractive character in the play. He makes no secret of his deep hatred for Antonio and his fellow Christian merchants; he drives a hard bargain, is Machiavellian in his practices, and takes pleasure in the prospect of Antonio's demise. He is a harsh father to Jessica, an intolerable master to Lancelot. What is the source of Shylock's animus against Antonio and the merchants of Venice? Listen to Shylock's response to Salerio, who asks him what good a pound of Antonio's flesh will be:

> If it will feed nothing else, it will feed my revenge. He hath disgrac'd me and hind'red me half a million; laugh'd at my losses, mock'd at my gains, scorned my nation, thwarted my bargains, cooled my friends, heated mine enemies. And what's his reason? I am a Jew. Hath not a Jew eyes? Hath not a Jew hands, organs, dimensions, senses, affections, passions, fed with the same food, hurt with the same weapons, subject to the same diseases, healed by the same means, warmed and cooled by the same winter and summer, as a Christian is? If you prick us, do we not bleed? If you tickle us, do we not laugh? If you poison us, do we not die? And if you wrong us, shall we not revenge? If we are like you in the rest, we will resemble you in that. If a Jew wrong a Christian, what is his humility? Revenge. If a Christian wrong a Jew, what should his sufferance be by Christian example? Why, revenge. (*The Merchant of Venice*, 3.1.47–68)

These words have an ethical dimension because they are spoken by someone, present with us, in the flesh, with a face we must look into. Shylock asks these questions of us, and demands a response of us, by virtue of his real existence, in the flesh through the surrogacy of the actor.

Shakespeare's contemporaries would have identified with Antonio and friends—they are the similar, the familiar, while Shylock is the "other." The question is not whether Shakespeare saw "the other" with sympathy, or whether Shakespeare's original audience would have seen "the other" with sympathy; or whether later audiences responded with sympathy to Shylock. The question is how we—not some abstract notion of "the audience"—receive the otherness of Shylock. How do we stand indicted in Shylock's plight, and how complicit are we in orchestrating his plight?[24]

Traditional readings of *Merchant* often impose a thematic higher meaning to the play in order to justify its content, or to argue for Shakespeare's ironic intention—that Shylock is so nasty, that Shakespeare is actually offering an argument against the injustice of racial stereotyping. Some argue that the play enacts the triumph of Christian soteriology of grace over a Jewish value-system of the law (as Neville Coghill did [1949]). Such elaborate attempts to justify Shakespeare or to save appearances privilege the literary theme over and above the ontological and ethical experience of the "text" that is the performance. Yet, after Levinas, one cannot reduce Shylock as the emblem of the ethnic and religious "other," for such a reduction is the limitation of the absolute "other" to a static, mute image. Such a reduction would amount to the abrogation of our ethical responsibility to the otherness of Shylock. With Shylock's "do we not bleed?" speech and in his humiliation in the court scene, the audience's response is an ethical one, not because Shylock is the underdog or because he is in the minority or because of his liminal status in Venetian society, but because he is my neighbor. If, with Gadamer's description of the aesthetic event, I participate "in the communion of being present" for the duration of the play,[25] then Shylock and I occupy the same ontological space and time. Shylock is not "l'autre" in an abstract sense, but in an actual reality of the living voice and the face-to-face situation. The member of the audience is placed in the position of the self-justifying Pharisee to whom Christ told the parable of the Good Samaritan (Luke 10:30–37). The selfless gift of charity from the anonymous Samaritan is an indictment: Shylock is my neighbor.

Ultimately, I am arguing for a type of essentialism different from that of Bradley, even to the point where "essentialism" begins to lose its essence in its traditional sense. Bradley infers that the character of Lady Macbeth, for example, has a consistent essence on the page—an essence created by the illusion of language, not substantially different from a fictional character in a novel. An ethical hermeneutic such as has been argued here is based not on the abstract essence of a literary character, but on the embodiment of character in performance—what John Marston in 1604 called "the soule of lively action." Neither does such an approach deny the contribution of anti-illusionist practices in the theater and the academy, particularly as it shifts the focus from the illusion of reality on the stage to the ethical response of the audience. In fact, post-structuralist approaches in postcolonial, feminist, and new-historicist readings of the plays have already made the ethical turn, with careful attention given to the body, the voice, and silence in Shakespeare. The humility and charity of Gadamer, Ricoeur, and Levinas should ensure that the ethical orientation will not "subsume," "colonize," or "disempower" such post-structuralist interpretations of Shakespeare. In fact, the ethical response required by this sort of hermeneutic would ensure that political readings of Shakespeare would be particular, real, and effective.

NOTES

1. A. C. Bradley, *Shakespearean Tragedy* (London: Macmillan, 1974).

2. Catherine Belsey, *The Subject of Tragedy: Identity and Difference in Renaissance Drama* (New York: Methuen, 1985); Jonathan Dollimore, *Radical Tragedy: Religion, Ideology and Power in the Drama of Shakespeare and his Contemporaries* (Brighton: Harvester, 1984); Terry Eagleton, *William Shakespeare* (Oxford: Basil Blackwell, 1986).

3. A number of recent studies of the Shakespearean stage have placed listening at the center of inquiry. See Bruce R. Smith, *The Acoustic World of Early Modern England: Attending to the O-Factor* (Chicago: University of Chicago Press, 1999); Wes Folkerth, *The Sound of Shakespeare* (London: Routledge, 2002); Christina Luckyj, *'A moving Rhetoricke': Gender and Silence in Early Modern England* (Manchester: Manchester University Press, 2002).

4. G. Blakemore Evans, ed., *The Riverside Shakespeare,* 2nd ed. (Boston: Houghton Mifflin, 1997). All quotations from Shakespeare are taken from this edition.

5. Hans-Georg Gadamer, *Truth and Method,* 2nd rev. ed., trans. Joel Weinsheimer and Donald Marshall (New York: Continuum, 1998).

6. One thinks here of the enigmatic conclusion of John Keats's "Ode on a Grecian Urn" (1819): "Beauty is truth, and truth beauty."

7. Paul Ricoeur, *Hermeneutics and the Human Sciences,* ed. and trans. John B. Thompson (Cambridge: Cambridge University Press, 1981).

8. John D. Caputo, *More Radical Hermeneutics: On Not Knowing Who We Are* (Bloomington: Indiana University Press, 2000), p. 43.

9. See Edward Burns, *Character: Acting and Being on the Pre-Modern Stage* (New York: St. Martin's Press, 1990); Bruce R. Smith, *Shakespeare and Masculinity* (Oxford: Oxford University Press, 2000), ch. 1; Jonathan Goldberg, *Voice Terminal Echo: Postmodernism and English Renaissance Texts* (New York: Methuen, 1986), pp. 86–90; and Stephen Orgel, *Authentic Shakespeare and Other Problems of the Early Modern Stage* (New York: Routledge, 2002), ch. 2: "What Is a Character?"

10. I am reminded here of Gadamer's image of the lawyer "standing in" (*ver-stehen*) for his client as an analogy of the act of interpretation in *Dialogue and Deconstruction,* ed. Diane P. Michelfelder and Richard E. Palmer (Albany: SUNY, 1989), p. 118. The actor both interprets and presents character—standing in for the textual configuration (character) of person (character) in the script.

11. Thomas Hobbes, *Leviathan* (Indianapolis: Bobbs-Merrill, 1958), pp. 132–33.

12. Ricoeur's notion of "oneself as another" may have further implications of the encounter of self and other in the theater; see *Oneself as Another,* trans. Kathleen Blamey (Chicago: University of Chicago Press, 1992).

13. John Marston, *The Malcontent* (London, 1604): "To the Reader."

14. Stanton B. Garner, *The Absent Voice: Narrative Comprehension in the Theater* (Chicago: University of Illinois Press, 1989), p. xiv.

15. Thomas Heywood, *An Apology for Actors* (London, 1612), B3v–B4r.

16. *Hermeneutics Ancient and Modern* (New Haven: Yale, 1992), p. 227.

17. *The World Viewed: Reflections on the Ontology of Film* (1971), p. 28. On the other hand, Bert O. States, in *Great Reckonings in Little Rooms: On the Phenomenology of Theater* (Berkeley: University of California Press, 1985) and *Hamlet and the Concept of Character* (Baltimore: Johns Hopkins University Press, 1992), argues that "character," like actions, remains an illusion on the stage, regardless of how more convincing the illusion may be than that of character in a novel.

18. Peter van Inwagen, "Creatures of Fiction," in *Ontology, Identity, and Modality: Essays in Metaphysics* (Cambridge: Cambridge University Press, 2001), p. 51.

19. Emmanuel Levinas, "The Transcendence of Words" (1949), in *The Levinas Reader*, ed. Sean Hand (Oxford: Blackwell, 1989), pp. 148–49.

20. *Time and the Other*, in *The Levinas Reader*, p. 45.

21. George Steiner, *Real Presences* (Chicago: University of Chicago Press, 1989), pp. 146–47.

22. Peter Schmiedgen, "Art and Idolatry: Aesthetics and Alterity in Levinas," *Contretemps* 3 (July 2002): 148: "Levinas' ethics as a whole is an ethics of iconoclasm, . . . which posits as its highest goal engagement with the other and not our representations of the other." See also Brian Schroeder, "The Listening Eye: Nietzsche and Levinas," *Research in Phenomenology* 31 (2001): 188–202.

23. For an application of Levinas to modern fiction, see Norman Ravin, "Have You Reread Levinas Lately? Transformations of the Face in Post-Holocaust Fiction," in *The Ethics in Literature*, ed. Andrew Hadfield, Dominic Rainsford, and Tim Woods (New York: St. Martin's, 1999), pp. 52–69. For an extended consideration of the opportunities for an ethical hermeneutics based on Levinas, see Robert Eaglestone, *Ethical Criticism: Reading after Levinas* (Edinburgh: Edinburgh University Press, 1996). As for modern theater, see Jon Erickson, "The Face and the Possibility of an Ethics of Performance," *Journal of Dramatic Theory and Criticism* 13:2 (Spring 1999): 5–21.

24. The question that a Jewish member of the audience asks in relation to Shylock may be different, but it is nonetheless an ethical one.

25. *Truth and Method*, p. 132.

12

(Revelation, Interpretation) Authority

Kierkegaard's *Book on Adler*

Norman Lillegard

The topic of Kierkegaard's *Book on Adler* is authority. The concepts of revelation and interpretation are treated in that work as functions of the concept of authority, as the form of the title of this essay is meant to suggest.

"The calamity of the age," Kierkegaard claimed, is "not doubt about the truth of the religious but insubordination to the authority of the religious."[1] This calamity is partly the result of conceptual malaise. The *concept* of authority, Kierkegaard avers, has "been entirely forgotten" in his age (*BA*, p. 4). On his view the forgetfulness is not innocent. It is due to lack of character and to insubordination. The kind of conceptual clarity that is required is a mark of *moral* respect for qualitative distinctions (*BA*, pp. 84, 89). The age, and Adler, lack that respect, he claims (*BA*, p. 127).

That forgetfulness is also part of a general "leveling process" that includes as a crucial component the invasion of the ethical/religious domain by "disinterested knowing." By it he means the "offense" that occurs in the situation of contemporaneity is avoided (*BA*, pp. 39–41). Readers familiar with Kierkegaard's other writings, particularly the *Philosophical Fragments*, will understand how central the concept of contemporaneity becomes for him. And of course "disinterested knowing," particularly the speculative sort popular in his own Hegelianized age, is the butt of jokes and the target of his polemic throughout his writings.

Prima facie the basic claims of *The Book on Adler* are nonetheless rather surprising. How could a concept that is still used and that Kierkegaard writes about in an illuminating way, with the intention that it be read by others, be "completely forgotten?" How could conceptual confusion or amnesia be due to lack of character? Does Kierkegaard really want to claim that *all* people who reject "religious authority" are insubordinate, disobedient, rather than plagued by doubts or convinced by contrary reasonings? And how does Kierkegaard's characteristic stress on "contemporaneity" fit into his account? I will try in the following remarks to explain and defend these surprising claims.

The Concept of Authority

Kierkegaard has a great deal to say about authority in *The Book on Adler* and rather little to say directly about revelation. He does say that the concept of revelation has become "confused" (rather than forgotten). Revelation as construed by Kierkegaard is internally connected to divine authority, however. An inquiry into revelation "comes to the same thing" as an inquiry into divine authority (*BA*, p. 4). The person who claims authority does so by virtue of the revelation fact (*BA*, pp. 33, 32). By speaking of the revelation *fact* Kierkegaard de-emphasizes its content. "It does not depend, as is taught in the confused philosophy of our age, upon the content of the teaching, but the revelation fact and the divine authority that follows from it are what is decisive" (*BA*, p. 32). For example, the issue is not *what* Jesus commanded or asserted but rather *that* Jesus commanded or asserted (*BA*, pp. 62, 183–84).

Now it belongs to the concept of authority that where there are commands, promises, and claims issued with authority, there will be *interested* knowing on the part of those addressed, *interested* reactions generally, in the sense that what is commanded, or asserted, must be dealt with. The hearer must come to terms with what is commanded, for instance. To contemplate a command, to parse it grammatically and historically, in the situation of contemporaneity, that is, in the situation where it is issued, would be comical and absurd, or a deliberate insult. The absurdity is conceptual. It belongs to the concept of authority that where it applies, indifference and disinterested curiosity are logically amiss.[2]

Where these points are kept in mind it becomes clearer why Kierkegaard connects conceptual malaise with matters of character, and why contemporaneity is an important category in this work. To be in the situation of contemporaneity is to be in a position where one is actually confronted, here and now, with commands, claims, and promises, and thus feels the "sting" of the existence of the other (*BA*, p. 41). That immediate confrontation produces a tension that compels a person to not leave their response undecided. They must either reject, be offended, or obey and believe (*BA*, p. 42). The situation of contemporaneity can profitably be compared with the situation of hearers or readers in relation to the theater, the newspapers, and "at-a-distance" communications. In such cases people can comfortably adopt opinions, or comfortably have uncomfortable feelings aroused, or comfortably refrain from doing anything whatsoever. It is quite different when something actually happens *to* a person confronted with the other, so that they must come to grips with the event. In the case of Christ it is clear that a claim to authority is being made, which must be either dismissed as unfounded or responded to with obedience or rebellion. In effect he says, "all power has been given to me in heaven and on earth," so, whether I speak a parable or narrate a history or deputize someone else to do the same, the essential relation must be obedience or rebellion (*BA*, p. 185). More generally it is *people* whom we believe or disbelieve, obey or disobey.

I claim that authority is the first preoccupation of *The Book on Adler* even though the immediate occasion was a Danish pastor's claim to a private *revelation.* Kierkegaard thinks of revelation as coming to individuals, apostles, and prophets, who are then able to speak with authority. I will comment later on Kierkegaard's seeming deference to the office of the ministry, which, he frequently implies, may confer authority, even though pastors are not recipients of revelation in the ways either apostles or prophets might be. What needs to be emphasized immediately is that even though the occasion of this book was a Danish pastor's claim to having received a revelation, what the Danish pastor actually said was that the Spirit of Jesus *spoke* to him. In fact it is quite clear that what the *Book on Adler* is concerned with is divine discourse, which should be distinguished from revelation in ways some of which I will discuss in the section "Interpretation, Authorial Discourse, and Authority." What matters is that God *spoke.* There is *no* discussion in this work of the content of what God purportedly said to Adler. The attempt to treat discourse as revelation easily assimilates to a kind of romanticism in which the normativity of discourse disappears. That is something Kierkegaard clearly wanted to avoid.[3] Normativity is discussed further below.

The points already made can be reinforced by canvassing Kierkegaard's notion of qualitative dialectic. His examples indicate that he means by that a procedure in which what is peculiar to a concept is brought out by contrasting it with related concepts, or by contrasting different uses of the same term in order to show how they "negate" one another. Thus the concept "authority" applied to a police officer is importantly different from the concept applied to an expert. The authority of the former is a function of position, of the latter a function of genius or exceptional grasp of some matter. The criteria of application in each case are logically distinct, and the term as applied to the police involves a "negation" of the term as applied to a genius. The authority of the police is *not* a function of genius, and that is a conceptual or logical or grammatical fact, not some kind of misfortune. One aim of qualitative dialectic is thus conceptual clarity.

Qualitative dialectic can also be thought of as an assembling of reminders. Kierkegaard's reminders come sometimes in the form of judgments against the age. People are curious about religious claims and injunctions; they wish to inquire into their philosophical or historical credentials or genealogy, while sidelining the question whether or not to submit to them. Or they may be impressed by a depth or beauty that some of those claims seem to have. All that is insubordination or even blasphemy, Kierkegaard claims. His descriptions seem apropos when considered in the light of examples from the domain of immanence. It would be considered at the least an impertinence to endlessly discuss the philosophical status of a royal edict or police regulation, or to admire the manner of their expression. The thing is to obey, or disobey.

The analysis offered does in fact bring together the ethical and the logical, broadly understood. We can draw upon Austin's distinctions between locutionary, illocutionary, and perlocutionary acts in order to get these points in sharper focus.[4] A crucial conceptual point is that certain conditions must obtain in order for the illocutionary act of commanding to even exist. For example, the one who commands must be in a relevant position, such as the position of an elected or appointed person who is by contract in a position to issue commands. Commanding requires something like constitutive rules, rules specifying what counts as what in certain circumstances.[5] The rules include a specification of who has authority and when. Where those rules and conditions do not apply or obtain, no amount of shouting, no amount of eloquence or brilliance, will turn a locution into a command. Otherwise put, it must be a mistake to look for psychological, scientific, philosophical, or aesthetic qualities in a locution or generally to seek an *interpretation* of someone's locutionary acts in order to determine whether they contain anything authoritative. For that purpose the mere determination of illocutionary stance and the position of the speaker suffice. So much is conceptual or grammatical truth, the denial of which is merely risible. By being reminded of such facts, people who have forgotten the concept of divine authority might be reminded of at least one of its features. Thus Kierkegaard mocks Adler for appealing to philosophical and aesthetic criteria in the attempt to warrant his claim to having had a revelation, and thus to having authority. If he has had one, he should appeal to the revelation itself, confront people with it, and show that he himself understands that the concept of a religious revelation is internally connected to the idea of religious authority, to which people may submit or which they may resist, but which in any case they may not admire or analyze.

The most important qualitative distinction with respect to the concept "authority" for Kierkegaard is the distinction between immanent and divine authority. The authority of the king, the police, the parent over the child, all belong to the domain of immanence. On Kierkegaard's account, that entails that however else they may differ, they have this in common: the authority of each is transitory and can be revoked. Though some kings might disagree, the basis for this claim is in our common life and shared agreements. There will be disagreements about the extent of immanent types of authority, about what grounds them (social contracts, divine rights, and so forth), about the point of revocability. There may be some who actually try to divinize immanent authority. But even Socrates, who in the Crito refuses to countenance any abridgement of the community's laws, thus acknowledging their authority, disregarded positive state enactments when he disobeyed the oligarchy of the thirty. And despite frequent claims to the contrary I do not believe that Hegel directly divinizes institutionalized mores. However, it is certain that neither Socrates nor Hegel so much as toyed with the idea of putting "the state itself *in suspenso*" (*BA*, p. 146).[6] Some people in Kierkegaard's day had done just that, and he implies that they had done so because they had *no* notion of there being anything binding in the law, no notion of any authority vested in any agent or any institution or any practice. Thus they ipso facto had no concept of authority at all, immanent or transcendent. They had "completely forgotten" the concept.

Kierkegaard surely exaggerates when he claims that the people of his age (all of them?) are complete amnesiacs, but he was, I believe, tracking an actual loss of clarity respecting even immanent authority. At any rate, considering some of the outcroppings of enlightenment autonomy in his day, and still in ours, the idea seems not far-fetched. It is, however, divine authority, or what usually comes to the same thing, the authority of those commanded or deputized to speak in the name of the divine or whose words are appropriated by the divine speaker (prophets, apostles), that concerns him most directly.

There are issues in regard to divine authority that I cannot explore here but that deserve mention. Some theologians and philosophers have held that God has authority over all rational beings. Given that there *is* a God, that has seemed obvious to some, in fact. The following has been offered as a general account of what it is for A to be an authority over B: if A is an authority over B then A must be in a position to command B to X (to X is to perform some action, including refraining from some action), and *that* A has so commanded must itself be a constitutive reason for B to X, and it must be a decisive reason. This general account of authority excludes the commands of a genius qua genius as authoritative, since such commands could only when effective cause a recognition of reasons that already (prior to the command) exist for B to X.[7] Now this account does not amount to an *analysis* of authority. It claims that A's being a (practical) authority provides reasons for certain types of actions, and that is true. But the analysis of authority needs to proceed with reference to the conditions for speech acts.[8]

In any case, if divine authority exists where necessarily A's command to B to X provides a constitutive and decisive reason to X, then divine authority is entailed by normative divine command ethics. But there is a strain in Kierkegaard that runs counter to normative divine command ethics and that is particularly evident where there is a stress on the importance of submitting oneself to divine authority. On the account just given, to submit to any authority is to acquire *new* reasons for acting. If submitting is essential to being under divine authority, then it is not the case that God has authority over all rational beings. I believe Kierkegaard does not endorse normative divine command ethics and that he does not hold that all rational beings are ipso facto under divine authority. If he did, the analysis of authority and divine discourse presented in *Adler* would, I think, fall apart. But this matter requires more treatment than can be given here.

Recognitional Criteria for Legitimate Authority

Since there are always competing claims to divine authority, the need for a way to distinguish the legitimate from the bogus can seem exigent. Are there criteria for authority and thus for bearers of a genuine revelation? Kierkegaard in fact attempts to extract criteria by employing qualitative dialectic. There is a qualitative distinction between divine authority and any other kind, which consists in part in the fact that divine authority is not revocable or transitory. How does he know that? It seems that he must have ab initio criteria for divine authority, and his procedure indicates that he thinks he does. But where did he get those criteria? Not from the theology of the Olympians. Some of the Greeks seemed to think that a mark or criterion for divine inspiration and revelation was a kind of madness, brilliance unaccompanied by many normal discursive abilities.[9] Kierkegaard relies upon the fact that his readers are not Greek polytheists but rather are able to relate his remarks to their own Christian, or at least monotheistic, background, in which apostles or prophets are not, or are not regarded as, for the most part, ravers, nor as brilliant artists or geniuses momentarily possessed by flashy truths. It looks then as though his claim that people have completely forgotten the concept of (divine) authority depends upon some agreements about the divine, and the communication of the divine, of a sort that suggest that the concept, in its Christian version, has *not* been completely forgotten.

But nothing said so far is sufficient to enable us to choose between Adler and Paul, or David Koresh and Joseph Smith. Kierkegaard suggests three criteria for distinguishing authentic from bogus authorities in the religious domain. The first has already been mentioned. The individual who speaks with authority in the religious domain must appeal to the *fact* of having been commanded by God. To do otherwise is to be confused, at the least. The revelation, for the religious community, is something like the royal edict for the polis. The proclaimer of the edict would insist that it is indeed a royal edict. Trying to prove it by noting its profundity would be almost comical.

However, it surely seems possible that someone might pass this criterial test and yet be mad. So it does not appear that this criterion provides a sufficient condition for someone's having religious authority. It also seems at first glance that someone might fail this test and yet make claims that are in fact reports of the divine will, or intentions. A second glance will, I think, lead us to question that possibility, however, *provided that* we are already standing within a more or less Christian (or monotheistic) tradition. Does it make sense to suppose that Paul might have uttered divine truths and at the same time appealed to their philosophical profundity or aesthetic qualities as grounds for accepting them? In fact "Paul" denotes an individual who fulfills a certain complex definite description, and that description is integral to the claims respecting what *counts as* a divine revelation and authority within Christianity. To suppose that Paul might have acted as Adler did is to suppose a different *concept* of revelation, one that is at least not internally connected to authority in the ways discussed above. Paul's behavior belongs to a package that is itself criterial, that is, determines what counts as a revelation (I am not claiming that it sufficient for that determination). And from that it follows that it does not make sense to suppose he might have behaved as Adler did even while bearing a divine revelation. Thus this criterion does give us a necessary condition for a person's being a bearer of divine revelation.

A second criterion proffered by Kierkegaard could be called the "anti-worldliness" criterion. The bearer of a genuine revelation will not use "worldly" means to bring about acceptance of the revelation. The use of force, manipulation, or "worldly" prestige to leverage the revelation is ruled out for the genuine apostle (*BA*, p. 186). Worldly prestige is the sort of thing proper to the politically powerful or the illustrious or the wealthy or those otherwise adorned with aesthetic splendors such as garner quick recognition and provide an individual with an edge in worldly dealings. This criterion, it seems to me, is even more obviously dependent upon Christian conceptions. It will have criterial force for those already initiated into a Christian ethos and pathos. It is internally related to the first criterion in obvious ways. Once again it seems at first sight that a madman might pass this criterion. A person could, it seems, eschew all worldly support while uttering nonsense. But once again I think it is not the case that someone who *did* rely on such worldly means could be counted as a genuine apostle. If someone relied on such means (which Paul clearly did not) that would not merely be evidence that he was not a genuine bearer of revelation. Rather he could not *count as* one.

The third criterion depends even more explicitly upon Christian categories. Kierkegaard claims that the divine authority's mark is the possibility of offense (*BA*, p. 33), where the kind of offense in question is ethical, not aesthetic. Paul is again a very pertinent example, for he explicitly presents Christianity as an offense, primarily in the sense that it offends ethical consciousness, the sense of righteousness. I cannot see that any such notion plays a role in the revelational claims of Mohammed, or Joseph Smith, or David Koresh. In claiming this as a criterion, therefore, Kierkegaard is already moving within explicitly Christian categories. I have already mentioned the central Kierkegaardian theme operative here. The paradoxical character of the "God-man" is taken in the *Fragments* to be the safeguard against idealism, and idealism can stand for every immanental religion or religio-ethical posture whether articulated philosophically or not. Kierkegaard presents the God/man paradox as an explicitly Christian idea, as rudimentary and fundamental as anything in the catechism. It thus has nothing to do with generic avatars. It is uniquely offensive to reason and to ethical norms, though not to ethics per se when broadly conceived.[10]

Given that Kierkegaard's criteria for distinguishing genuine from spurious claims to revelation/authority give us necessary conditions only, and largely depend for their force upon Christian categories, one might well wonder what use they could be to anyone not already situated at least to some extent within a Christian life view. This matter deserves some exploration.

First, Kierkegaard's claim that the age has completely *forgotten* the concept of authority suggests that what is required is not some *new* claim, or a beginning *de novo* for "the age," but reminders. Though he will later attack it, Christendom evidently plays a positive role as background to his procedures, his particular qualitative dialectic. If from a position purportedly outside any religious view we are puzzled by the variety of persons who claim to have had revelations, and wonder how to sort out the genuine from the bogus, we get no help from Kierkegaard. We can on his view distinguish Christian authorities from non-Christian, or confused quasi-Christian, by these criteria, but it does not immediately appear that there is any way to show the *inferiority* of a non-Christian claim, or the superiority or rational preferability of Christian claims. It is natural in these circumstances to think of an analogous situation in general epistemology, as Evans does. Evans summarizes the views of Chisholm in the following way:

> The proper way to proceed in epistemology is to begin with examples of what we actually know and then to reflect on these examples so as to see if criteria can be developed to account for what we know. The criteria, obviously, are dependent on our willingness to commit ourselves to certain items of knowledge.[11]

In like manner, perhaps we should think of the religious believer as one who begins with certain faith commitments or "things she believes," and manages by reflecting on those commitments to extract criteria for genuine candidates for religious authority.

However, there is something fundamentally unclear about what "committing ourselves" amounts to in this discussion. Most people simply find themselves believing certain things, or they claim to know certain things. Where does "committing" come into the picture? Some cases might be like this: One can imagine Augustine, say, reaching a point where he ventures "hazards" himself. Evans insists that that would hardly be a case of a blind leap or "criterionless choice" however. For Augustine must consider whether he dares or is able to begin to make sense of himself from within this new point of departure, and that requires a grasp of the criteria. But how does that whole package become a live option for Augustine? It would be useful here to explore in more detail the very notion of making a commitment. I will offer only a few sketchy remarks.

If a person submits herself to a religious claim, she will need to have some idea of what she is submitting to in order for it to be submission to *that.* Criteria are operative, not everything goes. Suppose they are Christian criteria. The few remarks above about general epistemology may lessen any sense that it is only in religion that we are limited, when our beliefs are formed, by our participation in particular traditions of life and thought. Nonetheless there is still a worry here, particularly respecting beliefs as peculiar as religious beliefs often appear to be. Perhaps a few reflections on the distinctiveness of the religious domain, particularly the Christian version, may help to defuse the thought that getting in the grip of religious criteria involves some arbitrary leap or choice or simply a tendency to thoughtless compliance.

It appears that in many domains we find ourselves with givens in the form of criteria of various sorts that show us what counts as what. These givens can be challenged, but not from some purportedly neutral standpoint. An episode in the history of science made famous by Kuhn illustrates the point. There was, at the end of the eighteenth century, no appeal to standards of proof, procedure, or evidence, existing entirely independently of the tradition of phlogiston chemistry, on the one hand, and the "new point of departure" afforded by oxygen chemistry, on the other. The former simply gradually collapsed, for all but a few who were securely in the grip of the phlogiston mode.[12] Now religious ways of thinking can also collapse. However, the way in which religion grips people is quite different from the way in which phlogiston chemistry might have gripped Priestly. Religious preoccupations are by nature pervasive. Ways of thinking, acting, perceiving, weighing alternatives, and determining what counts as what may run through a whole life—may regulate, at a certain level, *all* that is done. Priestly qua chemist had to decide what counted as what in his experiments, but qua human he had to have some way of deciding whether or not the very activity to which he devoted himself could count as something worthy. It is to such pervasive considerations that ethics, and more deeply religion, are addressed.

It is I think peculiar to religion, and also ethics understood as Kierkegaard understands it,[13] precisely that they can get a grip on people because, or to the extent that, people appreciate the pervasiveness of religio/ethical concerns. I must *live* somehow. I must decide how to live. It is unavoidable. Religion and ethics are precisely the names given for ways of doing that. Such deciding is not like deciding what job to take. I can postpone that without violating the very notion of "taking a job." I cannot postpone how I live, since I will be living while "postponing." More interestingly and in a different way, in the Christian case it is not like deciding whether or not to obey a royal edict. I can understand "immanently" how a royal edict arises. It will reflect interests that arise with human life naturally. That is why it is essentially "vanishing." But the most distinctive feature of divine edicts on the Christian view is that they do not arise within human life, cannot be absorbed into general explanations of life, cannot, in important senses, be understood. The mark of divine authority is, as already mentioned, the paradox, the very idea of which could not have arisen in the human heart. Kierkegaard has explored how the particular Christian/paradoxical claim upon people meets certain deep and pervasive human demands, even though it does not arise from human ideas of how to meet them. He argues, for instance, that passionate reason wills its own downfall, and that the paradox "fills the bill" in that respect.[14] I can only note this point, and gesture toward the rest of the authorship for further materials on the ways in which religious address is able to evoke a response and get a grip on thought and life. I will not attempt here any further analysis of the "immanent conditions" under which religious authority (claiming to speak for God, with all that entails) might win acknowledgment. The point that needs to be grasped here is that such conditions provide the settings for coming to see what counts as what, what constitutes what, in the religious domain. It would be a confusion to suppose that something or someone can become authoritative for a person only because that person has neurotic needs for authority. Rather the notion of authority and other normative notions are built into language.

The actual phenomenology of belief acquisition and change is no doubt complex. In some cases what commands assent and governs conduct cannot be something that is quickly put on or shuffled off. If we recur to the case of Priestly and Lavoisier, we can see how gradually, under specific kinds of pressures, whole ways of thinking, talking, interacting with equipment, and the like, gradually collapse, "go dead." In the religious domain an analogous collapse would have pervasive consequences, due to the pervasive nature of religious concerns.

Kierkegaard reads his own age as one in which Christian concepts have begun to "go dead." In such a situation one must effect a revival by assembling reminders or face the fact that a new revelation or some other new point of departure may be needed. (Marx was in fact just around the corner.) Adler certainly does none of this. He presents himself as on a par, say, with Paul, but then immediately confuses matters, shows that he understands neither himself, Paul, nor what authority or revelation are. For example, his claims to having had a revelation bring with them no claim to a new point of departure, and ultimately, no claim even to authority!

In effect Kierkegaard supposes that the recognition that speech engenders responsibilities and rights has waned. Talk generally is not taken seriously. Genuine discourse has been replaced by a kind of feuilleton journalism. Significant, responsibility-forming speech has degenerated into chatter. Suppose that even in its immanent versions authority and perhaps much else (promising, forgiving) have been drained of force. That is how Kierkegaard reads his age. His complaints here are not the bleatings of an unhappy conservative in the new liberal age of Orla Lehman and the impending revolutions of 1848. Rather he claims to detect a kind of deep confusion and a lack of moral regard for distinctions in terms of which authority can be understood. That lack of regard may ramify, lead to a general corruption of speech and thought and action, to what Kierkegaard calls "leveling." It is that which Kierkegaard may have in mind when he says that the age has completely forgotten the concept of authority. If so, there is much to be said in support of his claim.

Interpretation, Authorial Discourse, and Authority

Most of what Kierkegaard has to say about interpretation, which in this case means the activity of scriptural hermeneutics and exegesis, is just insulting (*BA*, p. 34). Much of what is offered as interpretation, he claims, amounts to insubordination, or it is blasphemous distraction or comical confusion, or a mixture of these.

These ad hominem assertions are, however, supported by a challenging analysis of authority and revelation. One thing that stands out in Kierkegaard's discussion is his emphasis upon individual persons. He seems not to know the word "text." It is Paul, or James, an apostle or prophet, who receives a revelation, and can speak with authority. Kierkegaard explicitly mocks any approach to Scripture that ends up treating it as having been written by "anonymities" (*BA*, p. 35). The bearings of this fact upon the notion of interpretation are perhaps by now becoming evident. It is worth noting that Kierkegaard was quite familiar with the "higher criticism" even in its most radical forms. His emphasis on authorship is not the result of ignorance respecting critical discussions of authorship or of anything else in Scripture.

It seems to me that Kierkegaard is very close to anticipating a view like Wolterstorff's, in which a distinction is made between speaking and revelation.[15] Speaking is not identical with revealing, even though a perlocutionary effect of some of God's illocutionary acts may well be that someone comes to see or understand what was hidden. Kierkegaard's focus on individuals, on apostles and others who speak to us and who have been called and sent by a God who does things like calling and sending, fits that idea of speaking and divine discourse.

Kierkegaard was revolted by the biblical scholarship that was gathering steam in his own day, the kind that has been called "excavative."[16] The term is apropos since it suggests archeological curiosity, the very sort of thing that on Kierkegaard's view is so out of place in relation to Scripture. One should rather treat these "texts" in their own terms, as what they (and indeed many texts) largely are—as commands, promises, warnings, assertions, offers, and the like. The text should be understood as a medium through which we are *addressed.* Treated in that way it has a chance of escaping the infinite approximations of scholarship, within which texts become objects of our scrutiny, rather than addresses that might force us to scrutinize ourselves, acknowledge various responsibilities, or recognize certain rights such as the rights of one to whom a promise has been made. Kierkegaard wants to show how to take up the Scriptures in such a way that attention is directed to what illocutionary acts are being performed with or through them.

Learning to do that contrasts with much of what has come to be regarded as interpretation in several ways. It requires, for instance, that the interpreter try to realize what the speaker intended, in the sense of what illocutionary acts they intended. It requires that we go outside of the text in various ways, and thus abjure the notion of the "sense of the text" (Ricoeur). I will discuss here briefly one of the ways in which Kierkegaard's discussion conflicts with the hermeneutical endeavors of Ricoeur.

Ricoeur makes a sharp distinction between text and discourse. The distinguishing feature of the former is distanciation. The author of the text is not available (of course that is not always the case) and thus cannot be directly questioned about her intentions. We are forced to rely upon the text itself and leave out of consideration anything that cannot be ascertained from the text itself. The text cannot be the voice of someone present. Hermeneutics begins where dialogue ends. On Ricoeur's view, no one can be in a situation of "contemporaneity," as Kierkegaard would put it, with a text in the way one can be with a speaker by whom one is addressed here and now.[17] I believe that on Kierkegaard's view Ricoeur's way of thinking about the biblical text is just the way to open the door to "scribblers" and to a host of moral confusions that are tragic in a way but also pretty funny:

> What is needed above all is to get the huge libraries and scribblings and the eighteen hundred years out of the way in order to gain the view. . . . I would regard it as altogether the most exquisite comedy that could ever be written in the world:

> to have all the modern exegesis and dogmatics go through their courses—in the situation of contemporaneity. All those deceptive psychological devices, all that "to a certain degree" and then again to a certain degree, all that bravura of profundity, and then above all the showy mediation that explains—all that, since what is explained occurred eighteen hundred years ago, would make a splendid showing in contemporaneity with what was reinterpreted. It is altogether certain that one single Aristophanean comedy in that style would clear up the confusion of modern Christian scholarship much better than all scholarly combat. (*BA*, pp. 44–45)

Doesn't Kierkegaard have a point here? Even with respect to some secular literature serious distortions and losses may result from scholarly exegesis. One does not need to denigrate the value of a "lower criticism" that unearths the meanings of obsolete terms or clarifies a designative content, or the value of having one's attention called to various genres, to textual connections, and the like. But the idea of putting a Shakespeare scholar right there by the stage to explain things as the play proceeds strikes me as absurd. I'm reminded of a portion of *Looking for Richard.* That film included cuts to a Harvard Shakespeare scholar who mumbled a great deal precisely in the manner of what Kierkegaard calls infinite approximation. The actors consulted him as they tried to understand the play in a way that would enable them to enact it, that is, act it. At one point one of the actors strongly challenges the relevance of consulting that scholar. What does *he* know? They are the ones who have to put it on, to find the life in it. They have to position themselves in relation to the text as actual participants in the dialogue it presents. Kierkegaard would claim that in relation to Scripture something similar is a fortiori the case. The challenge is not of course to one's ability to act, to render a script for an audience. But the religious texts require to be entered by the reader or hearer as one who is commanded, encouraged, judged, and doing that requires the "view," by which he means an ethical stance, ethical seriousness as exhibited in responsibility, earnestness, fear and trembling. The reader must encounter the discourse that the text is.

It seems to me that the idea of authorial discourse interpretation is explicative of Kierkegaard's polemic, since that interpretative approach turns upon the idea that God speaks, now, through apostles and prophets and other delegated speakers, so that the interpretative task begins, as in a conversation, with trying to establish the noematic content of illocutionary acts. (I might also mention here, but cannot develop, the relevance of canon criticism [*pace* Brevard Childs, Hans Frei, and the Yale School] as an illuminating framework for considering Kierkegaard's account of scriptural authority, interpretation, and application. Canon criticism provides a way of preserving authority and in a sense apostleship, and where the idea of authority is intact, application should follow. These ways of thinking about interpretation and Kierkegaard's way of appealing to apostleship can be brought together to provide a positive side to Kierkegaard's largely negative polemic.)

Here I want to return to Kierkegaard's own discussion of the forgotten concept of authority in order to strengthen the connections I claim to exist between that discussion and authorial discourse interpretation. His qualitative dialectic shows us what divine authority *is* precisely by stressing something like this idea that God speaks or performs illocutionary acts.

In saying what authority is, Kierkegaard employs the following example: "When someone who has the authority to say it says 'Go' and when someone who does not have the authority says 'Go' the utterance (Go!) and its content are indeed identical . . . but the authority makes the difference. . . . If the authority is not the other (*to heteron*) . . . then there simply is no authority" (*BA*, p. 179). That is a case of qualitative dialectic, and it is also a perfect illustration of the idea that the illocutions open to any individual depend upon his situation, and cannot be identified with his locutions. In order to issue commands one must have certain rights and be in a position to impose obligations. It is this sort of thing Wolterstorff refers to when he speaks of the normativity of discourse. Even at the level of immanence there could not be such a thing as authority without that kind of normativity.

Now in speaking of Paul in the same treatise, Kierkegaard says that Paul

> must appeal to his divine authority. . . . [H]e would surely say to the individual, "Whether the image is beautiful or it is threadbare and obsolete makes no difference; you must consider that what I say has been entrusted to me by a revelation; so it is God himself or the Lord Jesus Christ who is *speaking*. . . . I cannot, I dare not compel you to obey, but through the relationship of your conscience to God, I make you eternally responsible for your relationship to this doctrine by my having proclaimed it as revealed to me and therefore by having proclaimed it with divine authority." (*BA*, p. 177; my emphasis)

God is *speaking* through Paul. What matters, so far as the authority of what is said goes, is that it is God who speaks, since God, among all possible discoursers, is preeminently in a position to command and perform various other pertinent illocutions, and thus to stand in the sorts of relationships to the addressees as are required for there to *be* authoritative commands, which can only be obeyed or disobeyed—real promises, which establish obligations and legitimize expectations and effect confidence in the future, and so forth. In the passage just cited Kierkegaard has imagined how Paul would respond to a challenge to his claim to speak for God, or, what comes to the same thing, his apostolic status. That Paul would in fact respond to a challenge to his status in that way is verified by his actual procedure as described in Galatians 4. Adler on the other hand responded to the challenge to his claims by trying to show how profound he was and how moved he was. Whether or not he was profound or moved is irrelevant. His response shows that he does not understand what authority is, what revelation is, what being an apostle is, what he himself is. It is as though he had completely forgotten the concept of authority.

It is evident that the notion of "author" and the notion of "authority" are related. Authorial discourse interpretation is interpretation that takes account of the normativity of discourse, thus explicating that relation. All discourse has normativeness, but it is particularly obvious how the issuing of commands requires it.

This sort of interpretation of course raises many issues that I have not even mentioned. But I hope to have said enough to show how we might better understand the relations of authority to revelation and interpretation, in Kierkegaard's account, by reference to the notion that through the personal speaking of apostles and prophets God *speaks*.

There is one matter that still requires discussion. Kierkegaard frequently insists that his own discourses are not sermons, since they were not produced by one who is ordained, and for that reason they are "without authority." The ramifications of this expression of Kierkegaard's are still far from clear to me, but if my discussion so far is at all on track it may provide some guidance. The ordained person has been sent in the name of God to proclaim with the authority of an apostle. It is, I suppose, his relation to the apostles, his being delegated to speak for, or in the name of, another, rather than in his own name, which positions him properly, so that his words will count as divine commands, requests, pronouncements of mercy, and the like. It is his position that makes it possible for him to speak with authority, not his profundity or aesthetic qualifications. His position in relation to the apostles is analogous to the apostle's position in relation to God. Or it is analogous to the position of an ambassador deputized to speak for the president. Because of her position in a normative network what the ambassador says *counts as* the very word of the president, and thus carries whatever authority he has, even when she uses her own words.[18]

The Book on Adler is not an attempt to do everything. Kierkegaard certainly knows that the Scriptures contain a great variety—poetry, fictional narrative, historical narrative, even new forms such as "gospels." He does not take up the task of showing how authorial discourse interpretation might work in all of that variety. Nor does he address "wax nose" anxieties directly, though his stress on criteria shows the way out, since grasping them amounts to "knowing God," and *that* is the way out.[19] His concern is with what he considers to be a disastrous intellectual, moral, and religious failing. The age has forgotten the concept of authority. That is due to an intellectual failing, a logical lapse, in a broad sense of "logic." It is also an ethical failing, since it requires that the age ignore, or become confused about, various conditions of discourse, conditions under which one becomes obligated, acquires rights, or becomes entitled in other ways. To be ignorant or confused in that way *is* to lose or suffer a deterioration in one's relation to commanding and obeying, promising and honoring promises, forgiving, and most of whatever else constitutes ethical life. Put briefly, it is to lose the ethical. And if there can be *divine* discourse, then for the same kinds of reasons that forgetting would also be a religious failure.

NOTES

1. Søren Kierkegaard, *The Book on Adler*, ed. and trans. Howard Hong and Edna Hong (Princeton: Princeton University Press, 1998), p. 5. Hereafter referred to as *BA*, with page numbers, in text.

2. The connections between authority and interested knowing are already operative in the composition of *Either/Or*. See the notes assembled by Hong from the Journals in *BA*, p. 213.

3. Cf. Nicholas Wolterstorff, *Divine Discourse* (Cambridge: Cambridge University Press, 1995), p. 35.

4. Austin, *How To Do Things With Words* (New York: Oxford University Press, 1965), passim.

5. The authority of a parent might not appear to be a function of constitutive rules. We must either take the notion of a "rule" to cover a wide spectrum of kinds of agreements and standards, or downplay the place of constitutive rules. Wolterstorff takes the latter path (*Divine Discourse*, pp. 80–82). I find the notion still useful.

6. Alistair Hannay's comments on a Journal entry from 1834 are pertinent here (Alastair Hannay, *Kierkegaard: A Biography* [Cambridge: Cambridge University Press, 2001], p. 59). The entry concerns the "master thief" who does not contest the idea of the state as such but only the abuse of the state's own standards, as evidenced in his trial. Several Kierkegaardian preoccupations are at work here, including an interest in humor and the absurd, exhibited in this case in the incommensurability between the (state's) ideal and its practice. Humor requires that something be taken seriously, otherwise the absurdity cannot emerge. Kierkegaard takes the state and positive law seriously by not making them "dialectical."

7. Cf. Mark Murphy, *An Essay on Divine Authority* (Ithaca: Cornell University Press, 2002), ch. 1.

8. The fact that this account, which derives from Joseph Raz, does not provide an *analysis* of the concept of divine authority was pointed out to me by Nicholas Wolterstorff.

9. Cf. Plato's *Ion*.

10. Søren Kierkegaard, *Philosophical Fragments*, trans. Howard Hong and Edna Hong (Princeton: Princeton University Press, 1985), passim.

11. Stephen Evans, "Kierkegaard on Religious Authority: The Problem of the Criterion," *Faith and Philosophy* 17:1 (2000): 64.

12. Thomas Kuhn, *The Structure of Scientific Revolutions* (Chicago: University of Chicago Press, 1962), chs. 6–8.

13. It is very clear that Kierkegaard understands ethics in terms of pervasive concerns rather than, say, as a set of problems or quandaries to be solved by the application of principles. Cf. Norman Lillegard, "Passion and Reason: Aristotelian Strategies in Kierkegaard's Ethics," *Journal of Religious Ethics* 30:2 (Summer 2002): 251–73, p. 252 and passim.

14. *Fear and Trembling / Repetition*, trans. Howard V. and Edna H. Hong (Princeton: Princeton University Press, 1983), chs. 3–4.

15. *Divine Discourse*, ch. 2.

16. Ibid., p. 16.

17. Cf. *Divine Discourse* for a summary, and critical discussion, of Ricoeur's hermeneutics. My few remarks here follow his summary.

18. The notion of deputation figures importantly in Wolterstorff's account of divine discourse (*Divine Discourse*, pp. 38–51 and passim). Kierkegaard employs analogies that make exactly the same point. For instance, he compares Paul to one who delivers a letter, or is an envoy to a foreign court (*BA*, pp. 186–87). By such means someone (God) can perform an illocutionary act without actually speaking or writing, or inspiring any thoughts or utterances, or revealing something hitherto hidden. In speaking for the one who sends him, the envoy speaks with the authority of the sender, even if he disagrees with the content, or does not fully grasp it. Moreover, Kierkegaard stresses that Paul is an "apostle." The word itself, he points out, refers to deputation, to being sent (*BA*, p. 176).

19. *Divine Discourse*, p. 239.

Contributors

Bruce Ellis Benson is Associate Professor of Philosophy at Wheaton College. He is author of *Graven Ideologies: Nietzsche; Derrida and Marion on Modern Idolatry;* and *The Improvisation of Musical Dialogue: A Phenomenology of Music;* and coeditor of *The Phenomenology of Prayer.*

Christina Bieber Lake is Assistant Professor of English at Wheaton College. She is author of *The Incarnational Art of Flannery O'Connor.*

John D. Caputo is the Thomas J. Watson Professor of Religion and Humanities at Syracuse University. He is also David R. Cook Professor Emeritus of Philosophy at Villanova University, where he taught from 1968 until 2004. His most recent publications include *The Weakness of God: A Theology of the Event; More Radical Hermeneutics: On Not Knowing Who We Are;* and *The Prayers and Tears of Jacques Derrida: Religion without Religion.*

Eduardo J. Echeverria is Associate Professor of Philosophy at Sacred Heart Major Seminary in Detroit, Michigan. He has published articles in professional journals including *The Thomist, Logos, Philosophia Reformata, The Journal of Markets and Morality,* and *Revista Portuguesa de Filosofia.*

Ben Faber is Associate Professor of English and Theatre at Redeemer University College in Ancaster, Ontario. His chapter here is part of a larger project on Shakespeare and ontology.

Norman Lillegard is Professor of Philosophy and Coordinator of Philosophy and Religious Studies at the University of Tennessee, Martin. He is author of *On Epicurus,* and his essays have appeared in *Philosophy and Theology, The Journal of Religious Ethics, Znak,* and *Kulturos Barai.*

Roger Lundin is the Blanchard Professor of English at Wheaton College. He is author of *Emily Dickinson and the Art of Belief* and *The Culture of Interpretation: Christian Faith and the Postmodern World.*

Brian McCrea is Professor of English at the University of Florida, where he has served as Director of the William and Grace Dial Center for Written and Oral Communication. His publications include *Henry Fielding and the Politics of Mid-Eighteenth-Century England; Addison and Steele Are Dead: The English Department, Its Canon, and the Professionalization of Literary Criticism;* and *Impotent Fathers: Patriarchy and Demographic Crisis in the 18th Century Novel.*

James K. A. Smith is Associate Professor of Philosophy and Director of Seminars in Christian Scholarship at Calvin College. He is editor and author of *The Fall of Interpretation; Speech and Theology: Language and the Logic of Incarnation; Introducing Radical Orthodoxy: Mapping a Post-Secular Theology;* and *Jacques Derrida: Live Theory.*

Michael VanderWeele is Professor of English at Trinity Christian College. His articles on Augustine, Dante, Gerbert, Wordsworth, Charlotte Brontë, and Raymond Carver have appeared in *Religion and Literature, Renascence, Nineteenth-Century Literature, Christianity and Literature,* and the *Denver Quarterly.*

Kevin J. Vanhoozer is Research Professor of Systematic Theology at Trinity Evangelical Divinity School. He is author of *Is There a Meaning in This Text? The Bible, the Reader, and the Morality of Literary Knowledge; First Theology: Essays on God, Scripture, and Hermeneutics;* and *The Drama of Doctrine: A Canonical-Linguistic Approach to Theology.* He has edited *The Cambridge Companion to Postmodern Theology* and *Dictionary for Theological Interpretation of Scripture.*

Nicholas Wolterstorff is Noah Porter Professor Emeritus of Philosophical Theology and Fellow of Berkeley College at Yale University. He is author of *Divine Discourse; John Locke and the Ethics of Belief; Thomas Reid and the Story of Epistemology; Educating for Life;* and *Educating for Shalom: Essays on Christian Higher Education.*

Index

à venir, 102
Absalom, Absalom (Faulkner), xvi, 133–134, 137–138, 139, 140, 147n19
absence, 115, 117, 120–121, 123–124; for Derrida, 127n33
aesthetic theory, 213
aesthetics, 165, 166–167, 169, 180; Kantian subjectification of, 146n14; rhetorical, 177, 179, 180, 183, 188n49
alterity, 73, 83–84
anti-illusionism, 211–212
aporia, 44
appropriation, 18, 216
arrivant, 102
art, xvii, 213–214; as it pertains to Gadamer's philosophical project, 91n6
assertion(s), 63–64
audience, 215, 219; as participants, 217
Augustine, St., 171–174; Augustine's theory of reference, 174
author(s), 12–13, 14, 32n62, 46, 123, 125, 193, 205, 237; death of, 195. *See also* intention, authorial; discourse, authorial
authorial otherness, 12
authority, xvii–xviii, 68, 112–113, 225–229, 234, 236–237, 238n2; divine, 228–230, 233; religious, 228, 232
authorship, 112
autre. See *l'autre*

Barth, Karl, 6, 8, 9–13, 16, 25–26, 28, 30n16, 144, 148n25. *See also Römerbrief*
Barthes, Roland, 195; Barthes's "The Death of the Author," 35
Beardsley, Monroe, 38, 44, 193, 209n38
being, mystery of, 86–87, 88–89
being-in-itself, 69
Bible, 5, 17, 33n77
Book on Adler (Kierkegaard), xvii–xviii, 225–226, 227, 238

Calvin, John, xvi–xvii, 165, 169, 170–171, 174–177, 183; his anthropology, 174; theory of exchange, 174; Calvin's view of economics, 170. *See also* exchange
Carver, Raymond, 180–183
character, 217–219, 224n17
chrematistike, 171
Christ event, 155
Christian, 104; anthropology, 171; concepts, 234; contextualization of Christian faith, 95, 107; perspective, 150, 151, 161, 162n20
Christianity, 102; for Derrida, 110n15
Christology, 16
commitment, 232
communication, 116–117, 122, 123–124; risk of, 124
communities, 122; interpretive, 193, 205
community, 122, 164; of the Church, 124; moral and emotional, 164; role of, 120
Concluding Unscientific Postscript (Kierkegaard), 135
consciousness, 165–166; effective historical consciousness, 25; individual, 164, 167, 168, 169
contemporaneity, 225–226, 235; illusion of, 214
context, 116, 118, 119–123
conversation, 22, 139; openness of, 61
coram deo. *See* God

death, 99, 103
deconstruction, xiii, 107, 110n8
deconstructionists, 38, 44, 46, 114. *See also* Derrida, Jacques
decontextualizability, 120
decontextualization, 119, 123
Defoe, Daniel, xiv, 151–153, 155–158, 160, 161. *See also Robinson Crusoe*
deliverance, 151, 159
democracy, 107

Derrida, Jacques, xiii, xv, 36, 43, 47, 99, 106, 113–124, 125n7, 126n18, 128nn34,35,37, 193; on hermeneutics, 110n8
Descartes, René, xiv, 28, 30n12. *See also* *Discourse on Method*
dialogue, 84–85
différance, xv, 102, 193, 206n5
Discourse on Method (Descartes), 6–8, 13–14
discourse, 14, 17, 20–21, 27, 29n6, 178, 205, 235, 237; authorial, 11–12, 20–21; corporeal, 24; incorporeal, 23; normativity of, 237; as revelation, 227
distance, 68–69, 71, 82, 156, 168, 214; divine, 227; historical, 136; original, 159–160, 161
Divine Discourse (Wolterstorff), xiv, 35, 38, 46, 50n9
dogmatism, 84
doubling commentary, xvii, 200, 202, 205

Eberhard, Philippe, 14, 15, 17, 26
ecclesiology, 125
economic(s), 169, 170–171; economic criticism, 168; criticism of economic forces, 164; dominance of, 174; home economics, 168–169; economic individualism, 152, 153
economy, xvii, 178–179
enlightenment, for Gadamer, 28
epistemology, 232
essence, 211
essentialism, 222
eternity, 99, 103
ethical: dimension, xiv, 217, 221; encounter, 219–220; failing, 238; hermeneutics (*see* hermeneutics, ethical)
ethics, xiv, 233; Kierkegaard's understanding of, 239n13
excess, 100
exchange, 165, 169, 170–174, 175, 179–180, 183; economic, 185n21
experience, 141–142

faith, 26; condition of, 161
fallenness, 29
fallibilism, 59–60, 64; Gadamer's fallibilism, 65
Faulkner, William, 133–134, 137, 139, 142–145; treatment of human understanding, 137. *See also Absalom, Absalom*
finitude, 29, 61 82, 87, 143; Gadamer's philosophy of human finitude, 90n1; historical, 56; human, 52, 141

formalism, 166; aesthetic, 212
Frederiksen, Paula, 156
freedom, 164; of human consciousness, 165, 168
Frege. *See* Gadamer, Hans-Georg, *Gedanke*

Gadamer, Hans-Georg, xiii, xiv, xv, xvi, 3, 4, 6, 8, 13–17, 19–21, 22–27, 28, 34n83, 37, 38, 51–53, 55–57, 60–66, 76, 82, 137–139, 141–145, 193; on art and aesthetics, 213–214, 215, 217; on discourse, 29n6; on the epistemological problem, 66–70; exposition of relationship between tragedy and interpretation, 140; Gadamer's hermeneutics, xiv, 52; *Gedanke*, 39–40, 41, 42, 70; on ontology of the text, 70–76; on recognizing otherness, 83–84; and a theological dimension, xiii; on the theological question, 32n60; on thinking and openness to questions, 84–85; on understanding as communion through language, 85–87. *See also Truth and Method*
God, 99, 103; for Barth, 8; (equality) before God, 96–98, 109; God's speaking, 124
Gospel(s), xvi, 156, 160, 197
grace, 24, 27
Grondin, John, xi–xv, 57–60

hauntological, 107–108
hauntology, 95, 103, 105
hermeneutic(s), xiii, 19, 68, 83, 89, 125n1, 134, 194, 235; biblical, 204–205; of the Christ-event, 155; ethical, xvii, 213, 222; hermeneutic experience becoming private, 212; general, 5, 12; hauntological, xv, 99–100, 102, 107–108 (*see also* hauntology); hermeneutic orthodoxy, xiv, 38; ontological, 214; performance hermeneutics, 213; pneumatological, 125; hermeneutics of the question, xv; radicalization of, xiii; of scripture, 125; special, 5, 125, 125n1, 204; subjective conception of, 213; of witnessing, 151
hermeneutical: arc, 215; anarchy, 56; distance, xvii; experience, 213, 219; justice, xvii, 194, 206; practice, 194
Hirsch, E. D., 52, 55, 57, 77n9, 193
historicism, 74–75, 144
historicity, 138, 142; of experience, 144
history, 102, hating history, 136
Holy Ghost, 103, 108
Holy Spirit, 28, 197
horizon(s): of communication, 115; fusion

of, 15, 26, 34n83, 83, 85, 193; fusion of historical, 215
Huizinga, Johan, 138
human: fellowship, 170; nature, 171; needs, 171

idealism, 231
illocutionary act(s), 41–42, 47, 48, 63, 228, 235, 236, 239n18
imagination, for Denise Levertov, 91n26, 92n27
improvisation, xvii, 194–196, 198, 200–201, 203, 205
incarnation, xvii, 22–23, 26, 113, 124, 125; as divine economy, 179
intention, 48; authorial, xv, 21, 31n35, 112–113, 114, 122–123, 175, 195, 199; authority intention, 124; author's intention, 124, 125, 193, 202, 205, 208n34; concept of, 122; God's intention, 176
intentionality, 111n20, 115, 175, 177
interpretation, xiii, xvii, 32n64, 36, 61–62, 69, 85, 101, 140, 143, 159, 161, 175, 194, 200, 202–203, 225, 234–236; authorial discourse interpretation, 47, 72, 113–114, 236, 237; biblical, 205; Christian, 150, 161; criteria for, 179; Derrida's account of, 124; descriptive and normative approaches to interpretation, 4; dialogic view of, 147n17; goal of, 36–38; improvisation of, 197; locus of, 199, 209n38; performance interpretation, 33n65, 46; text interpretation, 71; textual-sense interpretation, 38, 41–44, 46; theories, 193
interpreter(s), 9, 15, 177, 193, 195, 205; Christian, xiii
inventione, 203
iterability, xv, 113, 115, 118, 119, 122, 127n19, 193, 201, 209n45. *See also* Derrida, Jacques

Job, book of, xv, 82

Kierkegaard, Søren, xv, xviii, 96–98, 225–233, 239nn6,18; on absolute equality, 109n7; his understanding of ethics, 239n13. *See also Book on Adler*; *Concluding Unscientific Postscript*; *Philosophical Fragments*; *Works of Love*

l'autre, xiv, xvii. *See also* Other, the
language, 15, 22–23, 31n46, 76, 85, 116; Derrida's analysis/account of, 114, 129n46; features of, 119; truth-stating function of, 71–72, 76
Lessing, Gotthold Ephraim, xvi, 135
Levertov, Denise, xv, 83, 86–90, 91n19; "Primary Wonder" (Levertov), xv, 86
Levinas, Emmanuel, 213, 219–220
literary theory, 150
literature, 164–165, 167–168, 169, 179–180
locutionary act, 63

Marx, Karl, 151–152
meaning(s), 33n66, 202, 214
mediation, 215, 216; historical, 135
Merchant of Venice (Shakespeare), xvii, 220–222
Messiah, 101–103, 110nn15,16
messianic, 102, 103–107, 110n15; desire, 110n13; pure, 105
messianisms, xv; concrete, 103–107
metaphysics, 66–67; for Gadamer, 31n49
Mitte, 14–15

Nachdenken, 11
New Economic Criticism, 167, 169
Nietzsche, Friedrich, 136
nihilism, 53

objective, 121
objectivism, 54, 58. *See also* realism
objectivity, 58–59
oikonomia, 171, 178
ontological, 165; explanation, 137–138; identity, 200; oneness, 214–215
ontology, 5, 13, 22, 25, 27, 43, 87, 213; of meaning, 41; of the text, 70–71
origin, prior to interpretation, 158
Other, the, xvii, 213, 217, 219, 221–222
Otherness, paradox of, 215

past, the, 137
perlocutionary act, 63
perspectivism, 57, 78n27
Philosophical Fragments (Kierkegaard), 125
play, 137–138, 142–143, 208n27, 216; Kantian subjectification of, 146n14
poetry, 83, 86, 89–90
post-structuralism, 150
post-structuralist: theory, 212; approaches, 222
practice, xvii, 198, 200, 204, 205, 208n25
prejudice(s), 65–69, 82–83, 142
presence, 43, 102, 114, 115, 121, 123–124
Protestant, 135–136
purpose, 176, 177

qualitative dialectic, 227, 237
question(s), 62–63, 83–88, 143–144
Quintilian, 178

rationality, 56, 58
reading, 168–169, 195; history of, 168–169
realism, 53–54, 60–61; perspectival, 69
reason, 67–68, 179; for Descartes, 28
relativism, xiv, 51, 52, 53–55, 57–60, 74–76, 77n11, 144
religion, 110n13, 233; without religion, 101
repeatability, 118
revelation, 10, 17, 124, 144, 225, 226, 227, 230–231, 234, 235; divine, 231; religious, 228
Richetti, John J., 153–155, 157–158, 159, 160
Ricoeur, Paul, xiii, xiv, xvi, xviii, 4, 17–18, 19–21, 40–42, 155–156, 161, 215–216, 217, 235
Robinson Crusoe (Defoe), xvi, 151, 155
Römerbrief (Barth), 9
Rorty, Richard, 78n38

Sache, 4–5, 8–17, 18, 22–24, 25–27, 31n46, 33n71; of the Bible, 9, 28; of scripture, 9
Schleiermacher, Friedrich, 9, 37
Scripture, 9, 17, 28, 112, 125, 236; approach to, 234; for Gadamer, 144
Searle, John, xiii, xv, 114–116; his position on language, 127n21
secret, 99–101, 103, 104, 108
secularity, 24
sin, 143; original, 115, 152–153
society, 178
The Sound and the Fury (Faulkner), 134–135
spectator, xvii, 213–214
speech, 40
speech act theory, xiii, xiv, 41, 63
subject, Gadamer's rejection of the turn to the, 66

Ten Commandments, 174–178
text(s), 18, 32n62, 36–37, 40, 193, 199, 205, 213, 214, 235; as discourse, 217; as underdetermined, 205
thing-in-itself, 69–70
trace, 209n36
tradition, xvii, 5, 14, 65, 67–69, 198, 205; Anglo-American, xiii; Christian, xiii; flaws of hermeneutical tradition, 36; for Gadamer, 144
tragedy, 140, 143
Trinity: as divine economy, 179; theology of, 171
truth, 60–61, 213; absolute, 58, 78n18; Christian, 145; Descartes's criteria for, 7; propositional, 71
Truth and Method (Gadamer), xvi, 36, 213

undecidability, 101, 102, 104, 108, 120
undeconstructible, undeconstructibility, 102
underdetermination, 201; textual, 202
understanding, 4–5, 7, 13, 15–17, 22, 26–27, 62, 83, 85, 87, 90, 137, 139; active agent of, 18; for Barth, 10–11; God's word, 11; human understanding, 143, 144; intention of, 61; miracle of, 9, 19, 22–23, 24, 26, 27–29; understanding scripture, 17

Vanhoozer, Kevin J., 36, 47–48, 114
virtue(s), 168

wisdom, 90
witnessing, xvi, 150–151, 155, 160, 161n1
Wolterstorff, Nicholas, 113, 239n18. *See also Divine Discourse*
Woodmansee, Martha, xvii, 166–167, 169
word: external, 23; of God, 10–11, 17, 110; inner, 23, 84; the Word, 124
Works of Love (Kierkegaard), xv, 97